The Encyclopedia of Container Plants

The
Encyclopedia
of
Container
Plants

More than 500
Outstanding Choices
For Gardeners

▫ ▫ ▫

Ray Rogers

Photography by
Rob Cardillo

Timber Press
Portland ▫ London

Photographs copyright © 2010 by Rob Cardillo.

Frontispiece: Design by Shari Edelson, Scott Arboretum,
Swarthmore, Pennsylvania.

Published in 2010 by Timber Press, Inc.

The Haseltine Building
133 S.W. Second Avenue, Suite 450
Portland, Oregon 97204-3527
www.timberpress.com

2 The Quadrant
135 Salusbury Road
London NW6 6RJ
www.timberpress.co.uk

Printed in China

Library of Congress Cataloging-in-Publication Data

Rogers, Ray (Raymond Joseph)
    The encyclopedia of container plants : more than 500
outstanding choices for gardeners / Ray Rogers ; photography
by Rob Cardillo. — 1st ed.
       p. cm.
    Includes index.
    ISBN 978-0-88192-962-1
    1. Container gardening—Encyclopedias. 2. Plants, Potted—
Encyclopedias. I. Cardillo, Rob. II. Title.
    SB418.R638 2010
    635.9′8603—dc22
                                                2009053693

Catalog records for this book are available from the Library of
Congress and the British Library.

To Ken Selody II, owner of Atlock Farm in Somerset, New Jersey,
a unique specialty nursery where I've been generously allowed
to pursue container gardening for twenty years.
—RR

To the inspired staff and gardeners of Chanticleer in Wayne,
Pennsylvania, where poems are written with plants.
—RC

Contents

Introduction

"Ray could hold a trowel before he could walk." Or so my mother often said. Since I can't remember a time when I didn't dig in the soil or plant a few seeds or admire a flower, I have no reason to doubt Mom. After all, the same could probably be said about her, three of her sisters, both of their parents, and who knows how many members of the generations before them. Our extended family experienced gardening together, tending perennial and vegetable beds, starting seeds, planting, weeding, staking, harvesting, and savoring the rewards of having a little dirt under our fingernails, the scents of flowers in our nostrils, and the flavors of fruits and vegetables on our tongues.

However, I'm the only one of that green-gened crowd that turned gardening into a career, working in public gardening and book publishing before realizing my current incarnation as author and speaker. When I'm not writing or yakking about gardening, chances are very good that I'm gardening somewhere or thinking about it. I am, therefore I garden.

Why has working in the soil (or potting mix, to link to the topic of this book) and raising plants sustained me all this time? It's not simply because I enjoy the yearly rituals and results of gardening; I like eating, but I didn't become a chef. No, it's much more than that: it provides an outlet for my creative and competitive urges at flower shows. It pays the bills (fortunately for me!). It brings me together with like-minded green-thumbers. It takes my mind off other stuff for a while, conjuring up images of and associations with the world around me. Most of all, it stirs up memories of plants, pots, and the people who have left their mark on me and who inspired me to share my passion at Atlock Farm, the nursery where I play in the state of New Jersey, where I may have finally rooted.

This book is essentially a volume containing a whole lot of useful information on 180 genera of plants suitable for growing in pots. Its pages include many aspects of container gardening that I hope you will find interesting and relevant to your own container-gardening activities. I've directed a plethora of questions, observations, and suggestions at you, my readers, to get you thinking. But more than doing that, I sincerely hope that my words and Rob Cardillo's magnificent photographs will conjure up your own opinions, preferences, and sensory experiences.

A brief exploration of container gardening

Simply put, growing plants in pots employs the same gardening techniques as raising them in the open ground, with a few modifications that address the unique situation that a container presents. No matter where they grow, potted plants require a location that provides a suitable medium (often soil or a potting mix, but not always) in a container, along with plant-specific amounts of light, heat, water, and nutrients. Attentive care that includes pruning and training, providing support, and offering protection from weather hazards and troubles (pests, diseases, and physical and physiological maladies) keeps them happy and looking good.

What are those modifications? Here's a speed course on container gardening.

Medium (or soil, dirt, potting mix, potting soil, or whatever you call it). Suit the medium to the plant, not the other way around, please. Many plants grow beautifully for a single season in any number of media widely available, assuming you know the plants' needs and can make adjustments when necessary (such as for succulents or aquatics). For starters, I recommend using a bark- and coir- (coconut fiber) based mix for almost anything: it holds water and nutrients for a growing season (sometimes longer), which for many container plants is most of their life. Many succulents will do surprisingly well in this medium, assuming you're very careful with the watering (and don't leave your plants outside during a wet summer), and so do aquatics, provided you contain the mix in some way to prevent it from floating away. Plants that you intend to keep for more than one season can be repotted into fresh medium each spring, or you can add a little real garden soil to the mix, which will help keep the medium in good shape (open and well drained) for at least one more growing season.

The container. The pot holds the medium, creating what is a very limited world for a plant. You are in charge of figuring out the size, material, weight, and color, and it's also up to you to site the container where the plants receive enough of what they need (more on that to come). However, the pot en-

Opposite: Pick a pot you (and the plants seem to) like.

Get your hands dirty with a suitable medium.

ables you to exercise a container-gardener's advantage over in-ground gardeners: you can move pot and all if you determine that one or more of the needs isn't being met (or you decide you'd like a nice planting over there instead of here). Obviously, the smaller the pot, the easier it is to move, but even large pots will move readily if fitted with rollers or placed on a wheeled base (or you can muster a strong back or two to help you move the pot).

Light. You need to figure out how much direct sunlight or deep shade is best for a given plant, so do some research in this book and other print publications, online and via other electronic media, with your gardening friends, and wherever else you seek information. *But* keep in mind plants don't read books (not even this one), and if a plant is unhappy with its light situation, it will tell you in subtle or not so subtle ways. If a plant seems to be telling you that the light situation isn't working, move it (pot and all, usually). Happily, many plants will tolerate a wider light range than one specified in a book, so keep your eyes open and make note of any envelope-pushing (with light conditions as well as with heat, water, and nutrients). That's useful to know.

Heat. Some plants blacken even in the absence of frost,

Let the sun shine in . . . or not. It depends on the plants.

Cold can kill plants, and expanding ice can lead to cracked pots.

All plants heed the need to feed, but appetites (and meals) vary.

Watering can mean the difference between satisfaction and disappointment.

others need a substantial cold period to return the next season, and others thrive in the cool temperatures of spring or the hot, steamy conditions of summer. Many tolerate an amazingly wide temperature range but do their best within a more limited one. Learn (in information media) and watch, just like for their light needs.

Water. An open medium in a pot exposed to the hot sun and drying wind (and often jam-packed with roots) usually dries out more quickly than a comparable volume of soil in the open ground. Containers in shade can dry out quickly, too, so keep an eye on those as well. Hanging baskets and windowboxes are especially prone to drying out, hanging out the way they do up in the often-moving air and against walls that can retain (and then release) drying heat. I've discovered that many plants in containers tolerate an inch or so of standing water at the base of the pot (except shallow containers, especially when the pots hold succulents and other plants prone to root rot). A saucer, then, might save you quite a few watering sessions over the course of a season. Learn and watch.

Nutrients/fertility. That limited volume of medium in the pot often cannot provide enough of the nutrients a plant needs to grow well over an entire season, so keep the fertilizer handy. Many long-season tropicals, annuals, and aquatics have huge, seemingly insatiable appetites, while many perennials and hardy woody plants have more modest needs. You need to figure out (by learning and watching) what works best for you (organic v. inorganic? water-soluble, granular, or pelleted?), but I want to point out that for many years I have used nothing but water-soluble fertilizers on virtually all my con-

tainer plants, whether single-season annuals or prize-win-
ning specimen succulents.

Pruning and training. Many single-season container
plants never (or almost never) require any pruning or training, but certainly many will benefit from the removal of wayward shoots, dead flowers, or growth tips to encourage more
shoots and/or flowers, and hardy trees and shrubs will in
time need some attention. Do you like standard topiaries? Get
a good pair of pruning shears (to assist your fingers). Climbers
can be allowed to cascade from containers (you aren't required to make them climb), or you can create tour de force
specimens of the same climbers by training them onto forms.

Support. Sure, you can grow a 5-ft. anything in a pot, but
do you really want to look at a floppy plant? Keep on hand
some thin but sturdy stakes and some sort of string or other
ties, and don't forget that the weak can be allowed to lean on
(or grow through) the strong.

Weather hazards. Siting containers in protected spots
will lessen the damaging effects of wind (and hail; it takes
only one good-sized pellet to ruin a slow-growing, perfect succulent, and a good-sized storm will shred just about every
plant in its way). Hot spots will benefit heat-loving tropicals
and usher in a premature demise for cool-season growers. If
the pots aren't too heavy (and you don't have an army of them),

Make no mistake: stakes aren't the only visible means of
support.

Climbing plants can reach impressive heights of artistry.

Homely, yes, but it's prepared to take on the slings and arrows
of colder weather.

Not all insects represent demon hordes bent on destroying your garden.

it shouldn't be a major task to take them to temporary safety. Do I need to point out that many plants are not winter hardy and so need to be overwintered somewhere?

Troubles. Bugs and wilts and other stuff happens to container plants, too, but there's a good chance you will notice them more quickly on elevated plants in pots than on plants in the open ground (and you're already keeping a keener eye out for their needs, anyway). Learn about what might be lurking out there and watch for them. Please don't automatically annihilate every creature that appears on or among your plants, though. Many are harmless or even beneficial, and some are as attractive and interesting as the plants.

Two terms you need to know. I use the terms "monopot" and "combopot" throughout this book. A monopot contains a single specimen of a plant or any number of the same kind, such as a single-stemmed standard topiary or a big

Monopots all (and Cleo the cat): from the left, gorgeous containers hold *Asparagus densiflorus* 'Myersii' (foxtail fern), *Solenostemon scutellarioides* 'Compact Red' (a trailing, flowering coleus), and *Furcraea foetida* var. *mediopicta* (striped agave).

Combopots contain two or more different kinds of plant and can offer a great deal of interest. They might also provide the inspiration for fascinating garden tableaus and for extended dissertations on garden design.

pot holding a dozen plants of one specific petunia selection. A combopot includes two or more different kinds of plant, often drawn from different genera, in any possible combination of numbers.

How to read the A-to-Z entries

Important note: Much of the culture and design information that opens each entry applies broadly to an entire genus. Notable exceptions within a genus are pointed out, either on the spot or in the genus essays that follow.

Genus. A genus (the plural is "genera," not "genuses") is one of the basic groups into which plants are classified. You'll see the capitalized genus name at the beginning of a scientific plant name (along with a specific epithet and/or other word or words that make up a plant's "official" name). Only a few genera are not universally agreed upon. For example, *Chrysanthemum* (with its fellow travelers *Argyranthemum* and *Leucanthemum*, among others) has been broken into other genera (*Dendranthema, Melampodium*) and rearranged over the past few decades. Whatever.

Common name. I've included at least one common name for every genus (or specific plants in the genus). These are usually familiar, often evocative words, and gardeners use

them all the time. However, common names can vary widely from one part of the world (or country, or state, or room) to another; for example, how many plants can you think of called "lily"? Most of them aren't true lilies in the genus *Lilium*, but we commonly call them lilies. That's why we use scientific names to make sure we all know exactly what we're talking about (or at least appear to).

Family. A family is the next organizational level up from genus in plant taxonomy, the system of classifying plants. All family names end in -aceae. Some families contain many genera (such as the grass family, Poaceae), while others contain just one. I care about families because I like to see how plants relate to each other, and it's fun to drop family names when in conversation with other gardeners. Also, knowing a plant's family can often give a general idea about how the flowers might look or how the plant might want to be grown.

Cultural group. I've attempted to assign at least one cultural group for all the plants in this book, but some plants can't neatly be pigeonholed, and plenty of genera contain examples of more than one group. Also, a cultural group can depend on how a given plant is usually grown; many plants that are shrubs or perennials in their native habitat (especially the tropics) are grown in as single-season annuals. Here are my categories:

- **Annuals** are the plants we grow for one growing season and then discard (that's the plan, anyway). Some are "true" annuals (growing, flowering, setting seed, and dying in a single season, such as zinnias). Many others are capable of living for two or more seasons, but we usually don't let them (such as petunias: surprise!). Many so-called annuals can be overwintered to return for at least one more season.

- **Aquatics** are plants that live in the water or at least a very, very wet medium of some kind. Obviously, their watering needs are often demanding. Here are the plants that want to grow in containers that lack drainage holes or drain very slowly. Some aquatics, such as members of the genus *Equisetum*, can be grown under less saturated conditions. Experiment to find out exactly what pleases them.

- **Bulbs** include "true" bulbs (tulips, daffodils) as well as plants that grow from corms, rhizomes, tubers, and other structures that plants use to survive challenging conditions (such as drought or cold winters), store starches and other nutrients, and do other things they need to do. Many of them go dormant, with the top growth dying back to leave only the bulb or other structure. You need to know the hows and whens of a given plant's dormancy behavior if you want to enjoy your bulbous plants for at least two growing seasons.

- **Climbers and trailers** (or vines, if you wish) are a widely varied lot; the one thing they have in common is their propensity to grow and twist around things (climbers) or grow along the ground or hang down (trailers). They can be grown as annuals or over two or more growing seasons, and many of the ones we grow are tropical in origin.

- **Perennials** (which I should call "hardy herbaceous perennials," but "perennials" is quicker) die back to a crown or other overwintering structure to survive the cold and other adversities of winter, or they are evergreen. Of course a plant that is hardy in Virginia might not be hardy in Minnesota, so you need to know the hardiness zones that a given plant is known to survive in as well as the zone you live in). This book gives hardiness zones as a suggestion: they're not engraved in stone, and I have seen many a plant survive well beyond its "official" hardiness zone.

- **Succulents** include cacti and a great many other plants that really know how to survive in the face of drought. However, some cacti and other succulents are native to rather wet climates, or they can withstand (or even thrive under) surprisingly wet cultural conditions. Please do not treat all cacti and other succulents as a monolithic mass of plants that can grow in sand, unless you want to watch most of them die.

- **Tropicals** are native to the tropics or subtropical areas. About the only other trait they have in common is that they don't grow actively during cold temperatures. Some can be easily overwintered in an above-freezing structure, while others give up the ghost when the mercury drops into the 40s. Many of them grow like gangbusters during hot, humid summers and are treated as large annuals, and quite a few of them have seemingly insatiable appetites for water and fertilizer.

- **Woody shrubs and trees**, as with herbaceous perennials, should be preceded by the word "hardy," so please see the information above relating to perennials. Unlike perennials, woody shrubs and trees don't die back to the ground for winter. In time, most of them require pruning and other long-term care.

Height. I've provided my best take on how much a plant might grow in a single season (this also applies to width), but this can vary from place to place, season to season, and gardener to gardener. Many entries state a height "in time," meaning after at least two growing seasons. Think of height as "reach" for some plants, since some might grow only a few inches high but spread, trail, or climb for a few feet or more.

Width. As for height, approximates are given; your plant could end up much skinnier or broader. With climbers and trailers, their final dimensions depend on the number of plants in the pot and how they are trained; one stem of English ivy might measure a few inches wide, but several stems trained together on a form would be much broader.

Light. I've given general recommendations for the amount of sunlight a plant needs to grow well, but remember that light is just one factor among several that interact with a plant. Also, the intensity of sunlight varies with your geographic location; it's generally more potent the further south you live in the Northern Hemisphere and the higher your elevation above sea level. I encourage you to observe your plants and experiment with them; you'll be surprised at how tolerant many plants are of wide-ranging cultural conditions. Please use my recommendations as guidelines only.

Temperature. "Cool," "warm," and "hot" are of course relative terms, but let's think of cool as 45–70°F, warm as 70–85°F, and hot as 85°F and up. Give or take. Often, your plants will tell you if the temperatures don't suit them by doing something easily observable, such as no longer blooming, dropping their leaves, sitting there without seeming to grow at all, or turning any number of unattractive colors. Or dying.

Overwintering. If you wish to grow your plants during the next and perhaps succeeding growing seasons, you'll need to try to overwinter them. I've given tips for overwintering many plants, but success depends greatly upon you and your attentiveness. Don't throw a leafless, dormant plant in the basement or garage and expect it to survive without checking on it every now and then, and keep in mind that some plants can be kept in active growth all winter if their needs are met.

Moisture. "On dry side" means "Take it easy, already."

"Moderate" means "Don't spend your life watering this plant, but keep an eye on it." "Ample" means "Somebody will probably need to water this plant at least once every day when it's growing actively." "Constant" means "Keep the water level near the top of the barrel or pool" or "Always keep water in the saucer."

Drainage of medium. Well-drained potting media let water run out of the drainage hole while retaining some moisture and air, and most plants benefit from that. "Tolerates standing water" means you can keep an inch or so of water in the saucer (and so can turn your attention to others things besides watering your plants), while "requires standing water" means the plant better be swimming or nearly so.

Fertility. Some plants, such as many annuals and succulents, will grow amazingly well with little or no fertilizer added to the medium … for a while. Most other container-grown plants will require regular applications of fertilizer to do their best. "Low" means you'll need to apply fertilizer once or twice during active growth, "average" about twice monthly, and "high" indicates that your plants could probably be fertilized every week. Feeeed meeee!

Ease/speed of growth. Some people make difficult plants look easy, while others … well, it's all relative. Most gardeners of any experience level should expect success from the plants I describe as "easy" (assuming some effort is made on the gardener's part), while "moderate" implies more attention and savvy might be required. "Challenging" plants require more experience, attention, and sometimes luck to keep them going. Of course I included some in his book; don't you like to push yourself every now and then? Speed of growth is *very* dependent on the nature of the plant and on your care: even a sprint-capable morning glory will limp along if it doesn't receive what it needs. "Slow" refers to plants that sometimes seem to sit still for long periods of time; "moderate" describes plants that look bigger when you look at them once a week, and "fast" is reserved for those that almost seem to grow as you watch them.

Propagation. Every gardener at some point wants more of a given plant. The easiest propagation method is to buy more, but of course plants may be increased by division, seeds, cuttings, grafting, and other methods. This book does not go into detail with propagation, but I hope the methods listed will point you in the right direction.

Problems. I list the ones that have tormented me in my own gardening or strike me as likely miscreants. You might never see a spider mite on your English ivy (may I touch you?), or something totally unexpected might come along and make your gardenia disappear. Keep your eyes peeled, and consult other references when you need to.

Principal interest. This refers to a plant's most attractive attributes (according to me, with some input from others),

whether flowers, foliage, fruit, form, and/or fragrance. Flowers and foliage are almost always the star players, but please don't overlook fruit, form, and fragrance. A few might even catch your eye with their attractive stems and bark.

Length of seasonal interest. Some plants are shooting stars, while others keep shining like the sun over the Sahara. "Brief" refers to an attribute remaining attractive for a couple of weeks, while "moderate" implies that you should get two or maybe three months of interest from a plant. "Long" tells you to expect a nice long ride. "All year" generally applies to actively overwintered tropicals and hardy evergreen plants.

Design attributes. Put on your artistic hat here, please, because many of the photo captions in this book deal exclusively with a plant's design attributes, or elements, without saying a word about its precise identity or how to grow it. Thinking about design takes your gardening to another level and will result in plenty of satisfaction as well as some mental stimulation. I promise. *Very* briefly (books have delved into this, including my own *Pots in the Garden: Expert Design and Planting Techniques* from Timber Press), here are some things to consider about the Big Five:

▣ **Color** is often the first attribute noticed in a plant (or piece of clothing or furniture, or painting, or many other things that catch our eyes). To many gardeners, it represents the make-or-break aspect of how it looks or combines with other plants. I don't pretend to be an expert in color (and some of my terminology in this book might not be in the lexicon used by those who speak color fluently), but I have made an informal study of it, and some of my experiences and preferences appear in this book. For an easy crash course in color I recommend you find a color wheel. You can find plenty of online versions (and sites that explain color theory in far more detail than I can here), but don't overlook the old-fashioned ones you can hold and spin and easily take outside. On the wheel you will see the primary colors (red, blue, and yellow), the secondaries (purple, green, and orange), and the six tertiary colors that lie between a primary and a secondary (for example, yellow-green sits between yellow and green). The wheel will also show how colors relate to each other according to their distance from each other as complements and analogous combinations (among other aspects, including what happens when you mix them with other colors or add white or black).

While color beautifies our lives, excites our eyes, suggests emotional states, and seduces us (ever see a car commercial?), I'd like to invite you to put on your black-and-white-vision glasses after you've had a chance to admire the colors in this book's photographs. Doing so will (I hope) give you an appreciation for the other four design attributes, which can all make valuable contributions to a container planting.

⊡ **Line** implies movement, taking your eye from one place to another (and maybe your feet, depending on how powerful the lines are). Simple, straight or curved lines are usually the ones taken in first, with more complicated ones (such as zigzagged or looped ones) taking a little more time to digest. Placing one sort of line next to another one sets up a contrast that might strike you as pleasing or perhaps discordant, while a great deal of the same kind of line suggests unity and stability (or maybe monotony). As with all design attributes, the perception of line is very subjective, so I encourage you to play with line and decide what you like (or dislike). Note: every plant offers some sort of linear interest, but sometimes it can take a long time to see it. Others almost seem to wave it in your face.

⊡ **Form**, or shape, can be easily described (for example, the precise cones and rectangles of clipped topiary or the instantly recognizable roundness of waterlily leaves), but often it requires more inspection to figure out and define the shape you see. Shrubby plants can often come across as lumpy, while many others suggest the forms of familiar things, such as pillows, chains, mops, animals, fountains, clouds, or whatever you happen to see in them. Form can also subliminally suggest emotions and sensuality, depending on how your brain processes what your eyes are seeing. An assortment of shapes within a container planting adds visual interest and will make the planting more

Several spokes of the color wheel interact in this masterful planting: look for primary yellow and red, the (here) predominant secondaries green, purple, and orange, and tertiary red-violet and yellow-orange. Also note how the quietly but richly colored pot allows the foliage and flower colors to stand out while still playing a role in the overall combination.

This photo superbly illustrates the irresistible power that line has over your eyes. Can you stop looking from top to bottom (or vice versa) long enough to watch the explosions? Assuming you can, you might want to check out the energy in the spiral topiary to the right and then finally note the many lines that make up the building.

engaging, but too many can make it look like a dorm room after a keg party.

□ **Space** is the most abstract of the five design attributes, since in a way it isn't there. But it often helps define a plant's form, either when contained within the plant (such as the abundant spaces between the leaves of an agave or banana plant) or existing around it (such as that around precisely defined shapes). The easiest way to appreciate how space works is to give plants some space between them … or not. In the former situation, you'll be able to recognize the individual plants more easily, while in the latter, everything might look like a solid mass of stuff (which looks pleasing in a hedge but might bring yawns in a container planting). Space might be the final frontier for you as a student of container-planting design, but I encourage you to boldly go where you might not have gone before.

□ **Texture** here refers to the visual perception of delicacy

Above: The most immediately discernible "geometric" form (all forms have their own geometry, but we tend to associate the word with spheres, cubes, and other simple, precise shapes) in this photo is the cube-shaped base, but once you start looking at the plants you'll discover flower-like rosettes and chains and maybe even a feather headdress. Do you think the container is circular or oval? Would it matter?

Below: There's not a whole lot of visible space contained within the plants in this pot (some appears within the cut foliage of the coleus in the upper left), but can't you feel the spaciousness of the setting (and how it defines the outline of the plants and pot)? Of course removing some of the foliage would increase the appearance of space, but that would be a funny thing to do. Sometimes you might not choose to include or imply space, and that's perfectly fine.

Texture doesn't get any more obvious than this: the abundant, skinny leaves and almost misty flowers of the fine-textured grass contrast sharply with the far fewer, broad leaves of the coarse hosta. The colors here are pleasing, but can you see how color plays a secondary role in the overall impact of this combination?

and airiness (as in fine texture) or sturdiness and massiveness (as in coarse texture), not of tactile qualities such as roughness or smoothness. Many ferns and grasses epitomize fine texture; hostas and cannas sit on the coarse end of the range. Quite a few plants reside in the much less obvious middle. Space interacts closely with texture: generally, an abundance of little spaces in between and within plant parts creates fine texture, while fewer, larger spaces implies coarseness. Color fits in here, too; light-colored and variegated leaves and flowers often look finer than their solidly colored counterparts. As with the other design attributes, widely different textures placed next to each other create energetic, eye-catching contrasts, while similar ones grouped together engage the eye less. Not that there's anything wrong with that; uniformity can be very soothing and restful.

I encourage you to think about all five design attributes as you look at the photos in this book. Many of the captions will ask questions to get you thinking about them. Feel free to disagree with my preferences (or what you might perceive as mine). It's your garden.

One final note. Remember, we're not working with only plants in *container* gardening. A well-chosen pot brings a lot to the party. While not as ever-changing as most plants, their color, line, form, space, and texture can play major parts in a container planting. In the photo captions, you'll be asked to think about them as well. Don't forget the pot!

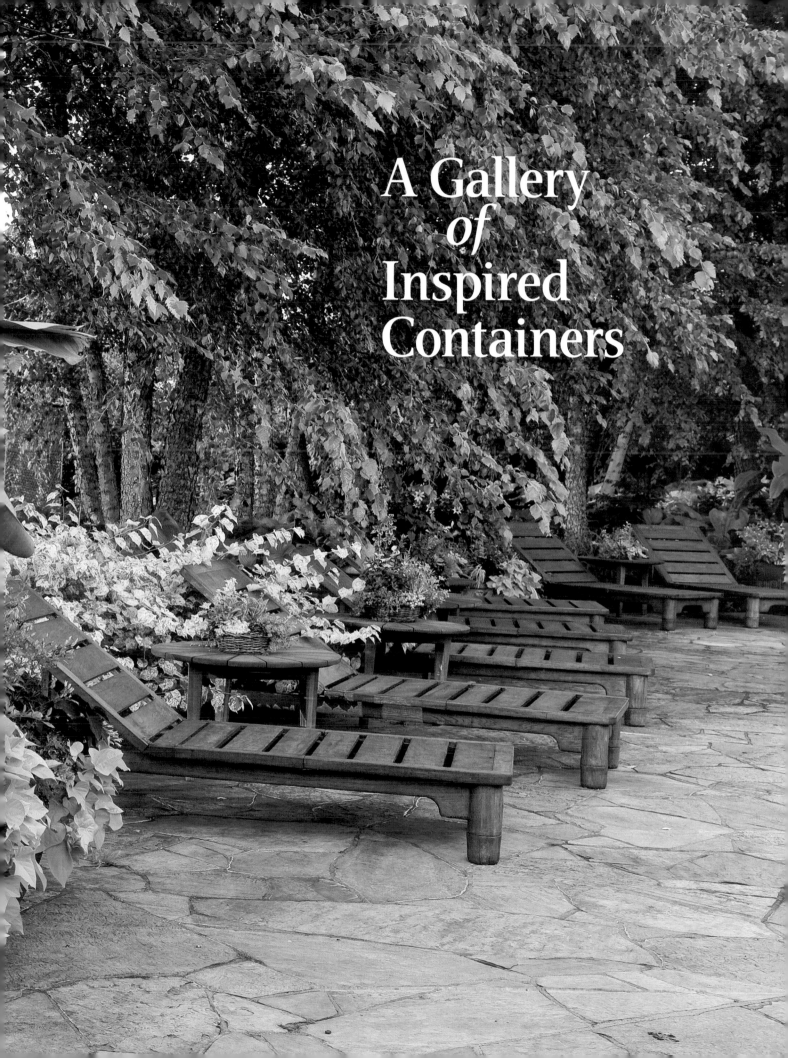

A Gallery
of
Inspired
Containers

1 *Pentas lanceolata* cultivar
2 *Hedera helix* cultivar
3 *Verbena* ×*hybrida* cultivar
4 *Asparagus densiflorus* 'Myersii'
5 *Salvia guaranitica*

A chubby, dark blue pot contains plants that offer three strong, saturated colors (blue-purple, orange-red, and purple)—so why doesn't this feel like a chromatic battle scene? Notice how the strong colors appear as dabs instead of masses within an expanse of green in various shades. Many expressions of green can serve as useful peacemakers in a container combination, but keep an eye on yellow-green (seen as a few spikes at the top and in the trailing ivy): some people see it more as a combatant than a diplomat. I view (and use) it in both roles.
Design by Danielle Odhner, Bryn Athyn Cathedral, Bryn Athyn, Pennsylvania.

1 *Rhapis excelsa*
2 *Chamaerops humilis*
3 *Butia capitata*

While the color green can bring a feeling of peace and harmony to a planting, too much of it might appear to put a container combination to sleep. However, taking full advantage of one or more of the other Big Five design elements (line, form, space, and texture) will bring some exciting diversity. Here, the powerful linearity and almost explosive forms of the three palms add pizzazz. So do the elegant, strongly lined pots and the colorful plants in the carpet bed in the foreground. Cover the pots and/or the bed to see what happens.
Design by Seibert & Rice/Landcraft Environments, Mattituck, New York.

1 *Kalanchoe thyrsiflora*
2 *Sempervivum arachnoideum*
3 *Agave americana* 'Mediopicta'
4 *Sedum* cultivar
5 *Echeveria* cultivars
6 *Graptopetalum paraguayense*

If you think succulents are boring little things best reserved for office desks and windowsills, think again. Can you almost feel the energy pulsating from this group? While basically a combination of complementary red and green, other colors play memorable parts as well (look for white and yellow). What also catch my eye are the plant forms that seem to clap and erupt and spin, and the potent textural contrasts of the fine little leaves and fuzzy rosettes with the much coarser clusters of fat pads. The sweeping lines of the central pot aren't shy, either.
Design by Thomas Hobbs, Vancouver, British Columbia.

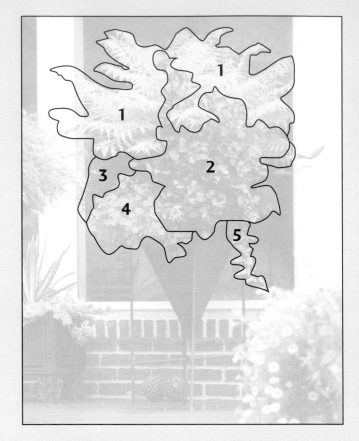

1 *Rhus typhina* Tiger Eyes (= 'Bailtiger')
2 *Iresine herbstii* cultivar
3 *Alternanthera* cultivar
4 *Calibrachoa* cultivar
5 *Solanum laxum* 'Variegatum'

Somebody's not afraid to combine three very strong colors! Yellow-green, shocking pink, and yellow-orange duke it out in a darkly toned but emphatically shaped container. Try to imagine what this composition would look like in a more mundane terracotta pot (picture both its color and form). I think the colors wouldn't play with each other nearly as well, and they would seem to be screaming for freedom from their plain confines. How would this masterpiece look in front of an expanse of white? How about gray? Or yellow? Or brick red?
Design by Inta Krombolz, West Chester, Pennsylvania.

1 *Furcraea foetida* var. *mediopicta*
2 *Salvia* ×*sylvestris* cultivar
3 *Carex oshimensis* 'Evergold'

Much as a chef might deconstruct a complex dish into its separate ingredients to create an out-of-the-ordinary culinary experience, so too can a container artist draw attention to the plants that might normally be grown together in a single pot. Separating each plant into its own pot—and using eye-catching containers, such as these sections of debarked tree stumps—makes for an intriguing and satisfying creation. While the colors don't jump out, the forms certainly do, and do you see the strong presence of line in the plants and "pots"?
Design by Terrain at Styers, Glen Mills, Pennsylvania.

1 *Solenostemon scutellarioides* cultivar
2 *Hosta sieboldiana* var. *elegans*
3 *Pachysandra terminalis*
4 *Solenostemon scutellarioides* 'Saturn'
5 *Ipomoea batatas* 'Margarita'
6 *Lamium maculatum* 'Beacon Silver'
7 *Scaevola aemula* cultivar

Container gardening doesn't occur in a uniformly colored and otherwise constructed vacuum: there are plants in garden beds, and trees, and balconies, and all sorts of other elements in the real world out there. Think about where a container would look its best, and then see if it in fact works there. Just for fun, cover up the blue hosta foliage and decide if you'd want to move this container elsewhere, or maybe you'd want to place it in front of a solid swath of the all-green pachysandra. Or maybe a gray wall behind it would do the trick? Design by Gale Nurseries, Gwynedd, Pennsylvania.

1 *Clematis* cultivar
2 *Serissa foetida* 'Variegata'
3 *Sarracenia* cultivar
4 *Syzygium paniculatum*
5 *Solenostemon scutellarioides* cultivar
6 *Solenostemon scutellarioides* 'Sedona'
7 *Verbena* ×*hybrida* cultivar

A happy mélange of plants, pots, and accessories eloquently expresses the appeal of gardening in containers. All five design elements play their parts in this snapshot of a given time, but try to imagine how this scene might have looked yesterday or will look tomorrow. Plants will grow larger, bloom, and fade, while some containers and accessories might come and go as well. The overriding theme in container gardening (and in gardening in general, as well as in life) can be: if you don't like something now, it can be better next year.
Design by Andrew Hartnagle, Bucks County, Pennsylvania.

A-to-Z Plant Directory

ABUTILON

flowering maple, parlor maple, Chinese lantern bush, Indian mallow

Family: Malvaceae

Cultural group: annuals

Height: 1–4 ft., 10 ft. in time

Width: 1–4 ft.

Light: sun to limited partial shade

Temperature: warm to hot

Overwintering: min. 45–50°F, water occasionally, bright light; generally hardy in Z(8)9–11

Moisture: moderate to ample—they don't like to dry out and will wilt quickly

Drainage of medium: well drained

Fertility: average to high

Ease/speed of growth: easy/moderate to fast

Propagation: cuttings

Problems: whitefly, aphids, spider mites, leaf spots

Principal interest: flowers, foliage

Length of seasonal interest: long

When you look up and into the open flowers of an abutilon, you might be tempted to add "bell bush" to the list of common names. But the buds (and the red calyces) certainly suggest Chinese lanterns, don't they? No matter what you see, the forms stand out, holding their own against the colors.

Design attributes

Color: flowers in white, red, pink, orange, and yellow; calyces sometimes red and quite showy; foliage medium to dark green, sometimes variegated with white or yellow

Line: long, straight or hanging stems

Form: shrubby

Space: variable but often open

Texture: medium to coarse

Sometimes common names perfectly suit the plant. From a medium distance, most members of the genus *Abutilon* look just like some sort of maple (*Acer*): their lobed leaves are ringers for those of red maples and others. But then you spot the beguiling flowers, little lanterns or hoopskirts dangling among the foliage, and are forced to rethink your identification. The Internet site The Garden Helper describes the flowers as a cross between a hibiscus and a hollyhock, which fits most of them.

While flowering maples may not be the most buttoned-down plants in the stable, their maplelike foliage and ready willingness to bloom (year-round if kept warm, moist, and sunny) keep me going back to them for container combinations and as specimens. Whether grown as open shrubs among other plants or trained up on a bare stem as a loose standard (don't expect a perfect ball on a stick), they will grab attention.

I have no direct experience with the so-called hardy flowering maples, such as *Aa.* ×*suntense* and *vitifolium*, which can become large shrubs in Z8 and warmer, especially in Great Britain and similar climates. By all means try them in suitable areas; gardeners in colder areas might want to experiment with them as overwintered die-back shrubs.

References and catalogs sometimes offer abutilons by color and not cultivar name. But since I've never seen an ugly cultivar, I recommend trying them all.

'Boule de Neige' means "snowball," a fitting description for the flowers.

'Huntington Pink' offers cotton-candy pink blooms.

'Kentish Belle' bears flowers with orange-yellow petals and purplish stamens that emerge from red calyces. The stems are darker than many. Gorgeous.

'Linda Vista Peach' has smallish flowers, but their delicious color compensates for that shortcoming.

A. megapotamicum and its selections, including 'Ines' (light yellow, probably a hybrid), 'Pink Charm' (light to medium pink), and 'Orange Hot Lava' (orange with red veining), are shorter, broader-spreading, and spindlier than most flowering maples.

'Moonchimes' dangles large, almost spooky yellow lanterns from its stems.

A. pictum 'Thompsonii' flaunts its yellow-splashed leaves

on long, outreaching stems, but the smallish orange flowers add a certain something, too.

'Souvenir de Bonn' and 'Savitzii' are quite similar, with cream- to white-edged leaves that remind me of the excitingly variegated foliage of *Acer platanoides* 'Drummondii' (yet another connection to the "regular" maples of *Acer*). The red-veined orange flowers of 'Souvenir de Bonn' either add interest or detract from the foliage display, depending on your personal preferences.

'Thomas Hobbs' is another apricot-orange beauty.

'Victor Reiter' easily exceeds the general dimensions given earlier, and the broad orange flowers are the biggest I've seen of the bunch. Almost steroidal.

I've never laid eyes on these, but their descriptions sound promising: 'Dame Vanessa' (clear yellow to yellow-orange flowers), 'Melon Sorbet' (cantaloupe sorbet but with red veining in it), and 'Voodoo' (rich, some say blood, red).

Cultural tips: Heavy nitrogen doses push growth but inhibit blooming. Chop them back as needed ("pinch" is inadequate here) to contain them and to promote bloom. You can also grow them unpinched to produce a large, open plant or to encourage growth in relatively flat "planes" (especially *A. megapotamicum*). Keep a plant or two in a warm sunny spot in winter to enjoy the blooms year-round.

A striking variegation pattern adds excitement to the cut-out, maplelike leaves of *Abutilon* 'Souvenir de Bonn'. Do you honestly care what the flowers look like, with all the color and form (and sense of movement) being expressed by the foliage?

Abutilon megapotamicum 'Variegatum' brings a different look to the genus, with pinch-waisted flowers and yellow-splashed foliage on near-black stems. Note the gray container: many other colors would compete with or obscure the details of the flowers and foliage.

The buds and open flower on this *Abutilon* 'Thomas Hobbs' remind me of a photo sequence showing a butterfly emerging from its chrysalis. These and other images are out there if you look for them and let the plants and other objects suggest them to you.

ACALYPHA

chenille plant, red-hot cat's tail (*A. hispida*);
Joseph's coat, Jacob's coat, copperleaf, beefsteak
plant, match-me-if-you-can, fire dragon
(*A. wilkesiana*); dwarf chenille plant (*A. pendula*)

Family: Euphorbiaceae
Cultural group: annuals
Height: 2–3 ft.
Width: 2–3 ft.
Light: sun to (limited) partial shade
Temperature: warm to hot
Overwintering: min. 55°F (although leaves may drop off),
    water occasionally, bright light; hardy in Z(9)10–11
Moisture: moderate to ample; let surface dry
Drainage of medium: well drained
Fertility: average to high
Ease/speed of growth: easy to moderate/slow

Propagation: cuttings, air layering
Problems: spider mites, scale insects, mealybugs, rots and
    spots
Principal interest: flowers (*Aa. hispida* and *pendula*;
    A. hispida is dioecious—the females are the showy
    ones), foliage (*A. wilkesiana*)
Length of seasonal interest: long

Design attributes

Color: pink-red flowers (*Aa. hispida* and *pendula*); foliage in
    green and earthy/sunset shades of red, orange, yellow,
    and purple-red (*A. wilkesiana*)
Line: long, hanging "caterpillar" inflorescences (*Aa. hispida*
    and *pendula*)
Form: rounded masses; some taller than wide
Space: somewhat open (*A. hispida*), dense (*Aa. wilkesiana*
    and *pendula*)
Texture: mostly coarse; a few medium to fine *A. wilkesiana*
    selections

I can almost feel heat radiating from the foliage of this *Acalypha wilkesiana* selection. These colors would combine quite well with other hot ones (and yellow-green, as shown in the younger foliage), but how do you think they look with a pink companion, such as the one at the bottom of the photo?

No, the fuzzy red things aren't caterpillars eating the leaves; instead, you are looking at the inflorescences (flower clusters) of *Acalypha hispida*. Their linearity adds a very strong suggestion of movement, which is what lines do best in a design. Try to picture this same plant with fuzzy balls.

Look to this genus for two very widely different expressions of plant personality: *Aa. hispida* and *pendula* for striking and memorable flowers (if you can call red caterpillars "flowers") and *A. wilkesiana* for infinitely variable foliage.

I'll admit it: my first interaction with *A. hispida* as a little kid was not entirely positive: I was convinced the dangly catkins were in fact caterpillars or worms, especially the one being dangled down my neck [insert yelling and gesticulations here]. But I've long since gotten over my childhood scoleciphobia, and to anyone out there who won't grow chenille plant because of worm-, insect-related, or other icky associations, I say: get over it. The masses and sometimes curtains of red "caterpillars" (or pink to off-white catkins in *A. hispida* 'Alba') are simply irresistible, from both a visual and tactile standpoint. If you like them abundant and long, grow *A. hispida*; those of you who are still a bit hesitant to embrace the whole idea can start your therapy with the less numerous and shorter catkins of *A. pendula*. Nothing looks like a chenille plant, and both species offer lots of interest for container plantings, whether as specimens in pots or hanging baskets or as members of combopots. Fascinating, and begging to be played with.

Copperleafs (*A. wilkesiana*) are a whole 'nother animal, if you will. Their foliage seems to reveal their wild, exuberant, constantly changing personalities, expressed through widely different leaf shapes and coloration. In fact, I challenge you to find two identical leaves on any one plant. The combination of darker and brighter shades of several colors suggests (to me) fire and passion, and copperleafs shake up a potent, hot-blooded combination with other brightly colored foliage and flowers. Does anyone hear Carlos Santana playing his guitar? By the way, if you look closely at a mature copperleaf, you'll find smaller, far less assertive versions of the "caterpillars" flaunted by its relatives. Cultivars include 'Haleakala', 'Macafeeana', 'Serrata', and 'Tricolor', all offering variations on the wild theme. Some other selections of or hybrids involving *A. wilkesiana*:

'Ceylon' has twisted, rounded leaves (reminding me of potato chips or similar snacks) in bronzy red with lighter, scalloped margins.

'Cypress Elf' and 'Godseffiana' offer dark red to medium green, elongated leaves with erratic markings.

'Macrophylla' bears large leaves (as its cultivar name suggests) with plenty of variable variegation.

'Sizzle Scissors' can have quite a bit of green in its cutleaf foliage, especially if given more than normal shade.

Cultural tips: Acalyphas grow slowly but steadily, so a small plant will not begin to reach its full potential until at least its second year. Buy larger plants if you're impatient, or overwinter your first-year plant for future enjoyment. Don't combine smaller specimens with much faster-growing plants in the same pot, or the bruisers may overwhelm them. Once established, they can be cut back hard to keep them manageable. Most copperleafs reach their full leaf-color potential in full sun, but you might also enjoy the different expressions brought out by some shade.

The snipped and slashed leaves of *Acalypha* 'Sizzle Scissors' take the meaning of "cutleaf" to a new level. Whoever thought up the name for this plant deserves some sort of award. Besides color, can you see how line and form add to the overall visual punch?

ACER
Japanese maple (*A. palmatum*)

Family: Aceraceae
Cultural group: woody shrubs and trees
Height: 2–4 ft., maybe more
Width: 1–3 ft., maybe more
Light: sun to partial shade
Temperature: cool to warm to hot
Overwintering: keep totally dormant at just above freezing, very little to no water, light not necessary, potted in their growing medium; hardy in Z6–8, a few to Z5 with protection

Moisture: moderate to ample
Drainage of medium: well drained
Fertility: average
Ease/speed of growth: moderate/slow to moderate
Propagation: grafting, seeds (but not to perpetuate cultivars)
Problems: spider mites, rots and spots
Principal interest: foliage, form (tied with foliage in many cases), sometimes bark (you won't see this mentioned very often in this book)
Length of seasonal interest: all year (even after leaf drop)

Design attributes

Color: foliage green, often marked or tinted with white, red, yellow, and purple (fall color in shades of red, orange, and yellow); bark usually dark red, a few forms red-orange ('Sango-kaku')
Line: from trunk, stems, petioles, leaf veining, elongated leaf lobes
Form: shrubby to treelike, upright, spreading, or cascading
Space: from limited to abundant; can be increased through selective pruning
Texture: fine to medium

No, I'm not suggesting you grow a big ol' red maple or sugar maple in a pot. I am, however, hoping you'll think about including a Japanese or other (for a while) smaller maple in your container gardening. Of course, Japanese maples can in time attain impressive size in a pot, certainly more than most people can accommodate with their space, budget, and personal strength limitations. However, while they're still relatively small and manageable, they will impress you with their embarrassment of design riches.

When I think of Japanese maples (*A. palmatum*), both color and form immediately spring to mind. Not only do they offer a vast range of foliage colors over the growing season, but most of them also take on vivid coloration in fall. Some, such as 'Chishio', create the impression of October in April as their new leaves emerge. Their flowers and fruits (samaras, or "keys" or "helicopters") often take on red shades. Plus, the twigs offer rich shades of red-purple in winter. Put those colors on upright, spreading, or weeping plant forms (and keep in mind the lobed to finely cut foliage), and already you have more design interest than most plants can offer. Line? Check out a Japanese maple in winter if you want to appreciate the beauty and subtlety of line in the landscape. Space? Most Japanese maples display it literally among the leaves and branches or suggest it with cloudlike or even misty shapes. Also, you can increase the space by selectively thinning out shoots in summer (not spring, because the sap may bleed copiously). Texture? Take a gander at the cutleaf forms for starters. Very few

container plants have as many check marks in the "Yes" column as do Japanese maples.

While younger, smaller maples will play nicely with other plants in the same pot, in time they will need all the root space they can get, so be prepared to grow them as specimens. Remember, you can place them among other pots to create combinations, too.

Choosing a single Japanese maple from the myriad offerings in a specialty reference or catalog can be daunting at best. Here's a general guide:

Cutleaf forms range from those having leaves with long, pointy lobes to intricately cut (yes, "lacy" definitely applies here) foliage. Look for cultivars with "Dissectum" in their name as well as specific cultivars, including 'Filigree', 'Garnet', 'Linearilobum', and 'Red Pygmy', among many others, often with beautiful transliterated Japanese names. Quite a few (the form *atropurpureum* and the cultivars 'Bloodgood' and

A colorful pot and neutral topdressing turn this *Acer palmatum* 'Shaina' into a container planting worthy of featuring as a focal point on a patio or other high-traffic area. Do you think the pot would be as eye-catching if it held plants with foliage and flowers in several different colors?

'Crimson Queen' are just three of many) offer dark red foliage over much of the season. 'Shaina' combines both attributes.

Looking for variegated foliage? 'Butterfly' is arguably the most well known and sought after, with white- and pink-splashed, irregularly lobed foliage. An examination of Vertrees and Gregory's *Japanese Maples* (Timber Press) will introduce you to many more. Some Japanese maples weep gracefully, even when young, such as 'Dissectum Atropurpureum' (and it's a cutleaf form with dark red foliage, to boot) and 'Waterfall'. Naturally dwarf forms, readily adopted by bonsai enthusiasts, are suitable for pots, but keep in mind that these are often expensive and slow growing.

If I were forced to select one Japanese maple to grow in a pot, I would unhesitatingly choose 'Sango-kaku' (sometimes seen as 'Senkaki'), the coralbark maple. The common name refers to its fiery red-orange bark, which shows off dramatically in winter (especially against snow). The foliage is very attractively cut, and it turns clear yellow in fall, contrasting with the red petioles. Give me a loaf of bread, a jug of wine, and a nice-sized 'Sango-kaku'.

Other maples you might try include *A. griseum* (paperbark maple), *A. japonicum* (full-moon maple, Japanese maple), and the snake-bark types (such as *Aa. davidii* and *tegmentosum*). With proper care, all maples will grow considerably larger than most container plants. When they get too big, plant them out in your garden or give them to someone who can accommodate them. In the meantime, you will have enjoyed a very satisfying and evocative genus, and your gardening friends will be impressed with your sophistication.

Cultural tips: Provide a roomy pot, and don't let them dry out. If you suspect your maple isn't hardy in your area, provide an extra measure of winter protection. Check out the offerings at a specialty nursery or botanic garden to help you choose your favorite.

Acer palmatum 'Shaina' brings the vivid colors of fall foliage to spring and summer. Plenty of sunlight keeps the colors bright. From a distance you won't be able to admire the individual form of the deeply cut leaves, but you certainly can close up, which will also reveal the wide variety of colors.

ACHIMENES
hot water plant, magic plant, cupid's bower, nut orchid, widow's tears, orchid pansy

Family: Gesneriaceae
Cultural group: bulbs
Height: 1–2 ft.
Width: depends on the number of plants and their cascading tendencies
Light: sun to partial shade to shade
Temperature: warm to hot
Overwintering: keep dormant rhizomes dry and at min. 55°F (60°F better) in the potting mix
Moisture: constant
Drainage of medium: well drained
Fertility: low to average
Ease/speed of growth: moderate/moderate
Propagation: division (of the pinecone-like rhizomes), cuttings, seeds
Problems: drought, whitefly, aphids, thrips, leaf spots, root rot
Principal interest: flowers, foliage
Length of seasonal interest: long

Design attributes
Color: flowers white, red, pink, blue, red-violet, and purple (rarely yellow and orange); foliage medium to dark green, sometimes shiny
Line: upright to semi-trailing
Form: shrubby
Space: not immediately apparent
Texture: fine to medium

One of the catalog offerings that seduced me into parting with my allowance as a kid was a cheerful little pink-flowered representative of this genus. Some years later I became enamored with the whole family to which *Achimenes* (that's a-kim'-a-knees) belongs. Besides the predictable *Saintpaulia* (African violets), *Episcia* (flame violets), and *Sinningia* (gloxinias and others), other gesneriophiles recommended a few achimenes to me, and they were sensational. Plenty of water and high-phosphorus fertilizer, warmth, and the benign illumination of an indoor-light setup allowed them to thrive. A few placed outdoors in pots did almost as well. But the major reason for their splendid success? I pinched out the growing points a couple of times and then let them grow out and bloom.

"Hot water plant?", you ask. While you don't need to heed the Victorian-age advice to pour hot water on the surface of the potting mix after you plant them, it does pay to keep these plants warm and *almost* wet while in growth. Allowing them to dry out during active growth usually sends them into dormancy before you have a chance to enjoy charming flowers among the perky foliage.

Achimenes 'Snow Princess' might look like a petunia, but it isn't. It won't tolerate dry soil like a petunia does, either, but the cheerful flowers that appear over a long season make this under-appreciated, old-fashioned plant worth a try. Note how the form of the flower makes an impression before its color.

Catalogs still seduce kids and older gardeners with a number of cultivars. Buy the colors that appeal to you. I think 'Peach Blossom' is the one that first caught my eye, and I suspect 'Snow Princess' has been around for a while, too. 'Ambroise Verschaffelt' bears white flowers with purple tracery. And by all means seek out ×*Achimenantha* 'Inferno', a hybrid relative, for its ardent red-orange blooms, all the more glowing seen against its dark foliage.

Cultural tips: Because of their need for constant moisture, I suggest growing these as monopots. Pinch out those growing tips, which will encourage the plants to become bushy or gently cascading. Keep them warm and moist (but not wet) in a sharply drained medium. Feed them regularly. Reduce water at the end of the season to induce dormancy. Build up colonies of rhizomes in pots over a couple of years for an impressive display. Give some to your kids or grandkids.

ACORUS
sweet flag (*A. calamus*); grassy-leaved sweet flag (*A. gramineus*)

Family: Araceae/Acoraceae
Cultural group: perennials
Height: 3–10 in. (*A. gramineus*), 3–4 ft. (*A. calamus*)
Width: 6 in. or more in time (*A. gramineus*), 1–3 ft. or more (*A. calamus*)
Light: sun to partial shade
Temperature: cool to warm
Overwintering: min. 50°F, water occasionally, bright light; hardy in Z4–11 (*A. calamus*), Z10–11 (*A. gramineus*)
Moisture: ample
Drainage of medium: tolerates standing water
Fertility: low to average
Ease/speed of growth: easy to moderate/moderate
Propagation: division
Problems: root rot (especially when overwintered too wet)
Principal interest: foliage
Length of seasonal interest: long

Design attributes
Color: foliage green or variegated with white or yellow
Line: upright-linear
Form: strappy masses (*A. calamus*), low "carpets" (*A. gramineus*)
Space: dense
Texture: fine to medium

It seems easy enough to explain the "sweet" part of the common names: apparently it refers to the pleasant scent of the leaves and dried rhizome (much like that of orris root, *Iris florentina*) used in herbal pursuits. The "flag" part has me

Even low-growing, grasslike sweet flags look like a bunch of lines in constant motion. *Acorus gramineus* 'Hakuro-nishiki' offers even more interest with its chartreuse foliage, set off here by the pale blue gray of the simple pot.

Sweet flags of many kinds bring visually irresistible, upright-arching linear interest to container plantings, especially variegated selections, such as *Acorus calamus* 'Argenteostriatus'. Whoosh! The taller-than-wide pot accentuates the upright momentum; a more shallow one would slow it down. Cover the bottom two-thirds of the pot to see what I mean.

conflicted, though; some sources maintain that it refers to the wavy and waving (flaglike) leaves of *A. calamus*, but the long-time iris enthusiast in me believes the "flag" refers to the strong resemblance of the leaves to those of our native blue flags (*Iris virginica* and others). Whichever the origin, these flags make sweet additions to imaginative container plantings.

You have two extremes to choose from, mostly, namely the tall (*A. calamus*) and the small (*A. gramineus*). Both species include intriguing variegated cultivars that add more punch. The big ones add exclamation points to plantings, while the little ones impersonate grass or spiky hair. I like to feature the little ones in monopots and place them where their color and mass of lines can be noticed and enjoyed. All contribute assertive lines to any planting.

All-green *A. calamus* is interesting enough, but 'Argenteostriatus' (aka 'Variegatus') offers much more with its white and cream striping, making an eye-catching monopot, especially when included among strongly contrasting plants and pots.

A. gramineus and its cultivars, while all shorties, pack a disproportionate amount of punch. Whether all green and maybe 1 ft. tall (the species), striped green and cream and maybe 10 in. tall ('Ogon' and 'Variegatus'), lively chartreuse and maybe 6 in. tall ('Hakuro-nishiki'), or dark green and less than 6 in. tall ('Pusillus'), they all mesmerize, especially when viewed close up and contained in complementary (but not competing) pots. Sweet.

Cultural tips: The clumps can be torn apart and immediately replanted (preferably in spring) for gratifyingly quick increase. *A. gramineus* and its cultivars remain in active growth if kept at about 50°F or higher and provided some sun.

ADIANTUM
maidenhair fern

Family: Pteridaceae
Cultural group: perennials, tropicals
Height: up to 2 ft.
Width: up to 2 ft.
Light: partial shade to shade
Temperature: cool to warm

Overwintering: min. 50°F, water occasionally, bright light;
    variously hardy in Z3–10
Moisture: moderate to ample
Drainage of medium: well drained
Fertility: low to average
Ease/speed of growth: easy to moderate/moderate
Propagation: division, spores
Problems: scale insects, sensitivity to some pesticides
Principal interest: foliage
Length of seasonal interest: long

Design attributes

Color: fresh-looking green foliage; new fronds often red,
    yellow, or sometimes almost white
Line: energetic upright to arching stems; branching fronds
Form: shrubby masses of circles or triangles
Space: variable; strongly suggest spaciousness
Texture: fine, sometimes extremely so

So many of us know the common name for these beautiful ferns: maidenhair fern, of course, derived from their resemblance to some styles of feminine coiffure. But how many of us are aware that the name *Adiantum* means "not wetting"? When watered from above, plants seem to transform water droplets into beads of mercury. I remember staring transfixed at a clump of maidenhairs at Atlock Farm during a summer drizzle, watching drops of water form and then slide off the fronds, gently animating the entire planting as they fell to the ground.

To paraphrase Will Rogers (no relation), "I never met a maidenhair fern I didn't like." All take beautifully to container gardening, whether hardy or tender for you. A monopot or ten of them sets a mood of lushness combined with extreme delicacy, of visual activity with repose. Many have black or dark purple stalks, and the pinnules (think of them as leaflets) of many start out red or even yellow or white before taking on colors suggesting emerald or jade or other coveted bits of mineral.

My personal jewelbox includes, of the hardier sorts, *A. aleuticum*, with energetic, rounded hairstyles on a remarkably hardy plant (Z3–8); *A. pedatum*, similar in appearance and hardiness to *A. aleuticum* but shorter; and *A. venustum*, more triangular-looking than the previous two and less hardy, to Z5–8. More tender ones include *A. capillus-veneris*, another triangular-looking one; *A. caudatum*, with a rounder look (and often bearing little plants at the ends of the fronds) and needing temperatures above 50°F; *A. raddianum* and its cut- and tiny-pinnuled forms, which will withstand temperatures to 45°F or so, and *A. tenerum*, another variable one with large, almost chunky or sometimes cut pinnules, hardy in Z9–10. There are many more species and forms; all are worth growing.

Overly enthusiastic pot-scrubbers take note: look how the color of the fronds of this adiantum echoes the bright green of the algae on the terracotta pot. Can you see the far more subtle repetition of the fern's dark stems in the plant behind them?

Three maidenhair ferns on a plant stand suggest an overhead shot of a large crowd at a Green Party event. Color plays an important role here, but I would be remiss if I failed to point out the role of texture. These are ferns, and "ferny" is often used as a synonym for fine texture.

Cultural tips: Try your best to keep water on the fronds. Like many ferns, maidenhairs resent a dry potting mix as well as dry air and hot sun, so place them in spots where you can satisfy their wet and shady desires for moisture and humidity. If scale insects find them and multiply freely (they probably will), about the only thing to do is to cut the plants back severely, apply a spray for scale insects (I suggest you start with an insecticidal soap), and then wait patiently for new fronds to emerge. Ferns are notoriously sensitive to potent and not-so-potent pesticides, their new and often older fronds being severely damaged by exposure to them.

AECHMEA
vase plant, urn plant

Family: Bromeliaceae
Cultural group: tropicals
Height: 1–3 ft.
Width: 1–3 ft.
Light: partial shade to sun

Temperature: warm to hot
Overwintering: min. 50°F, water occasionally, bright light; some hardy in Z9–11
Moisture: moderate to ample, and don't forget to water the "vase" every now and then
Drainage of medium: well drained
Fertility: average (doesn't need much, if any, nitrogen from fertilizers)
Ease/speed of growth: easy to moderate/slow to moderate
Propagation: division, offsets, seeds
Problems: scale insects, mealybugs, root rot, rots and spots
Principal interest: form, foliage, flowers
Length of seasonal interest: all year (form and foliage); moderate to long (flowers)

Design attributes
Color: foliage green, sometimes marked with red, yellow, purple, and silver-gray; flowers (and bracts) in red, pink, yellow, blue, and purple

Cover the modest pot and the immodest (and arguably distracting) inflorescence of this impressive *Aechmea nudicaulis* var. *flavomarginata* to appreciate the powerful linear activity of the foliage. Then uncover the pot and be amazed by its (relatively) teeny size. Many bromeliads require next to no (or no) medium at their base.

Line: immediately noticeable from strappy leaves, flower stems, pointed bracts

Form: open rosettes, vases with fanciful brushes coming out of them

Space: usually abundant between leaves and around flowers

Texture: medium to coarse

Honestly, I don't have much experience with this genus beyond admiring its representatives in many greenhouses and shopping malls (especially the gray and pink *A. fasciata*) and a few tropical gardens. But I didn't want to omit them from this book, because they're worth a try, whether to enjoy their exuberance for a single season or to keep them going for a much longer time. Like other bromeliads (members of the family Bromeliaceae), their strappy, sometimes boldly marked leaves almost always form rosettes (or vases, if you will) that collect water as it falls from the sky, watering can, or hose. From those vases emerge fantastically shaped and colored flower spikes that Carmen Miranda might have used as brushes (you imagine the kind) or maracas in an energetic Busby Berkeley dance number.

Grow aechmeas as a single, flashy rosette to feature as a focal point, or build them up into masses. Being epiphytes, many can grow without a pot or potting medium, so feel free to insert a rosette or two in a combination pot that needs some spiky, colorful action.

Start with *A. fasciata* (silver vase plant) if you're an *Aechmea* newbie. You've probably seen this one in retail or business concourses, reaching outward from upper-level planters and/or at the base of escalators in oversized pots. Don't hate this one because it's ubiquitous. Love it for its striking combination of mostly gray foliage, pink bracts, and blue flowers. Where else can you get that combination?

Cultural tips: Aechmeas like high humidity and freely moving air. Splash water on them occasionally, especially in summer, and keep the vases filled. Use a low-nitrogen fertilizer every now and then. If you feel compelled to put them into a potting mix, make sure it's very open, such as coarse bark chips or tree-fern chunks.

AEONIUM
dinner plate, saucer plant, rose tree, pinwheel plant

Family: Crassulaceae
Cultural group: succulents
Height: a few inches to 2–3 ft.
Width: 1–3 ft.
Light: partial shade
Temperature: cool to warm; often nearly dormant in high heat

Overwintering: min. 50°F, water regularly but not excessively, bright light or sun; many grow actively in winter

Moisture: on dry side to moderate

Drainage of medium: well drained

Fertility: low to average

Ease/speed of growth: easy to moderate/moderate to fast

Propagation: cuttings

Problems: aphids (in bloom), mealybugs, root rot, toppling over

Principal interest: foliage, form

Length of seasonal interest: all year

Design attributes

Color: foliage green to purple-black (sometimes with cream or pink), shiny or matte

Line: stems often bare and attractively branched

Form: eye-catching leaf rosettes, individualistic plant form, pinwheels

Space: little (rosette types) to a great deal (treelike types)

Texture: coarse

The coarse leaves of this selection (probably of *Aeonium arboreum*) contrast pleasantly with the airy necklaces of angel vine (*Muehlenbeckia complexa*). Note how the spaces between the individual leaves of the rosette make it look more active than more closely arranged, solid-colored ones (but not as lively as the variegated *A.* 'Sunburst').

Why is this genus (which contains all five major vowels, please take note) not more commonly known as pinwheel plant? The thick leaves of most species emerge from a central point and appear to be moving around, so it doesn't take much of a leap to imagine them eliciting glee from kids or scaring crows away from the vegetable garden. As for me, I can get lost in the precisely mathematical Fibonacci pattern of the leaf arrangement of certain species (type "Fibonacci" and "aeonium" into your search engine and see what comes up).

If you hesitate to jump into the succulent pool ("Why?", I ask, but not facetiously, my reader), I suggest you start with one of these beauties. They grow relatively quickly, don't require full sun, and become increasingly more characterful if you overwinter them. Plus, they grow more actively in winter than in summer, so you can almost forget them during the gardening merry-go-round of the warmer months and lavish your attention and admiration on them when the ride stops (or at least slows down). (Yes, some succulents, including members of the popular genera *Aloe*, *Gasteria*, and *Haworthia*,

grow more actively in winter than in summer—surprise!) These eye-catchers are equally at home in monopots and combopots, but be sure to combine them with other winter growers in combopots. They'll all thank you for it.

A. arboreum and its all-green and red tinged selections

One energetic, flowerlike rosette of *Aeonium* 'Sunburst' in a simple pot makes an unforgettable focal point, chiefly from the linear variegation pattern that draws the eye into the center (or outward, depending on the eye). The gray wall sets it off like nobody's business, too.

The variously sized rosettes popping up along the floppy stem of this *Aeonium arboreum* selection offer plenty of interest of line and form . . . and there's not a flower among them.

Too much shade = green for many dark succulents, so be sure to give *Aeonium* 'Zwartkop' plenty of sun if you want to continue enjoying the dark, shiny appeal of its fast-moving rosettes.

remind me of pinwheel trees. All are naturally sparsely branched (abstemiously so, if you lean toward anthropomorphism) but respond well to pinching out the centers of the rosettes in active growth. That may strike you as ultraseriously painful to do, but you'll appreciate the results later.

'Sunburst', a probable hybrid of *Aa. decorum* and *arboreum*, is arguably the most desirable of the entire genus. Its grotesquely animated crested form looks like a batch of ribbon candy gone terribly wrong. Note: do not routinely water this and other crested succulents from above or let rainwater accumulate among their ripples and folds, unless you want to watch your curiosity melt (rot) away.

A. tabuliforme must have inspired the common name of dinner plate: a well-grown specimen can reach a foot or more wide and seem as flat as a plate. Water carefully; providing too much and at the wrong time can result in edema, nasty-looking patches of bumps on the leaf surfaces.

A. undulatum holds its big, strappy pinwheels on a sparsely branched framework ("armature" could apply here; look that up in your Funk and Wagnalls). It might be considered the sequoia of aeoniums.

Everyone wants a piece of 'Zwartkop', a hybrid whose shiny blackness deepens with increasing sun or very strong indoor light.

Cultural tips: Push their growth in winter with moderate amounts of water-soluble fertilizer. If a big plant falls over and breaks up (or branches fall off), root the individual rosettes and start some new specimens.

AGAPANTHUS
lily of the Nile, African lily

Family: Alliaceae/Liliaceae
Cultural group: perennials
Height: 1–5 ft. (in flower)
Width: 1–3 ft., more in time
Light: sun to partial shade
Temperature: cool to warm to hot
Overwintering: min. 40°F, water occasionally, bright light;
    Headbourne hybrids and some others are hardy if given
    some protection in Z6; the rest are hardy in Z7–10

Happy 4th of July (or Bastille Day, or Chinese New Year)! Pots of agapanthus inevitably evoke associations with fireworks. So would even just one blue head.

Moisture: moderate to ample
Drainage of medium: well drained
Fertility: average to high
Ease/speed of growth: moderate/slow to moderate
Propagation: division, seeds
Problems: slugs and snails, root rot
Principal interest: flowers, foliage
Length of seasonal interest: moderate; flowers might
 repeat but not as abundantly

Design attributes

Color: blue and white flowers; foliage medium to dark
 green, marked with white or cream in a few selections
Line: long flower stems; long, upright to arching leaves
Form: mounds of straps; flowers add "balls on sticks"
Space: very noticeable in bloom
Texture: medium to coarse

I could describe these plants as "blue or white balls on sticks over a bunch of strappy leaves," and many would agree. But anyone who has seen an established pot of any agapanthus in full glory knows that they more than transcend that prosaic description. There's something about them that defies analysis. Is it simply the rich color of the blue forms or the purity of the white ones? Perhaps it's the contrast in form between the flowers and the leaves, or maybe the way the flowers seem to rise and float magically above the foliage. Some people associate agapanthus with pleasant times briefly spent in milder climates, and those memories elevate these plants to a special status. Others might observe a single pot or patio filled with bloom and instantly connect with their *je ne sais quoi.*

One pot makes an irresistible focal point that draws everyone's eyes to The Spot, while two or more add an air of exotic luxury to any garden. Gild your (lily or swimming) pool with them. A single (or double, but have smelling salts handy) row of agapanthus cries out for a red carpet and a big party among the stars.

Although you might start with a single division, in time that little piece will become a great mass. Be happy as you watch your investment literally grow. They can remain in the same pot for a few to several years, but be prepared for some heavy-duty effort after they become obviously potbound, which is the time to divide them. After the flowers fade, remove the flower stems (otherwise, they'll get in the way and smack you in the face, believe me), wrest the clump from its pot, then insert two digging forks back to back in the center of the clump. Pull the forks outward and downward—don't cringe when you hear the roots snapping, crackling, and popping—and repeat until you have a number of intact, sturdy-looking divisions. Repot as soon as possible and repeat again

in a few years. By the way, this technique works very well for daylilies (*Hemerocallis*) and other densely rooted perennials.

Because they seem to flower more heavily and predictably as they become progressively potbound (within reason), I suggest you grow agapanthus as monopots and increase the pot size every few years. Alternatively, their linear leaves might please you as a feature in a combopot.

The many tempting cultivars offered by references and catalogs are in the main selections or hybrids of *Aa. africanus*, *campanulatus*, and *praecox* subsp. *orientalis*. I can recommend 'Blue Giant' (4 ft. or so in bloom); 'Storm Cloud' (3–4 ft.); and the variously blue to blue-purple Headbourne hydrids, which are touted to survive in the open ground during a moderate Z6 winter if mulched lightly but thickly. Container gardeners, of course, can increase their survival chances by overwintering the pots. The relatively newer 'Blue Heaven' and 'White Heaven' may also be hardy to Z6 and are reported to reach 2–3 ft. in bloom. Also try blue-flowered 'Peter Pan', 1.5 ft. tall in bloom, and the handsomely variegated *A. campanulatus* 'Albovittatus' with (sometimes less than abundant) blue flowers, 2–3 ft. tall. Otherwise, I suggest you beg a piece from a friend's plant, named or not, and offer to bring a suitably sized digging fork when it's time to split the clump. Bring a dining fork, too, and make a party out of it.

Cultural tips: Wait patiently for the clumps to enlarge and put on a show. Recently acquired divisions often take at least a year to begin blooming. Plenty of bloom-boosting fertilizer should increase your chances of abundant flowering.

AGASTACHE
giant or wild hyssop

Family: Menthaceae
Cultural group: annuals (culturally), perennials (over a wide
 area, so try overwintering)
Height: 2–5 ft.
Width: 1–3 ft.
Light: sun
Temperature: warm to hot
Overwintering: variously hardy in Z4–11; many can be kept
 at min. 40°F indoors, water occasionally, bright light
Moisture: moderate
Drainage of medium: well drained
Fertility: low to average
Ease/speed of growth: easy/moderate to fast
Propagation: cuttings, seeds
Problems: mildew (if too dry)
Principal interest: flowers, foliage, fragrance; attracts
 wildlife
Length of seasonal interest: moderate to long (especially
 foliage and fragrance)

Design attributes

Color: flowers in many colors; foliage often gray-green
  (yellow-green in *A. foeniculum* 'Golden Jubilee')
Line: upright to outward-leaning stems
Form: shrubby; some open-floppy
Space: plenty around flower spikes
Texture: medium

Whether pronounced ag-a-stack'-ee or a-gas'-tuh-kee or ag-a-stash', here are a bunch of plants that appeal to me on multiple fronts: they all smell spicy-minty-flowery when you rub their leaves; they produce colorful flowers (but not profligately); and bees, butterflies, and hummingbirds seem to like them even more than I do. They are easy to grow, easy to root from cuttings or grow from seed, and associate beautifully with other plants. But please don't think these are going to be the stars of your show; they could best be described as part of the general cast. That's not a bad thing: any well-considered garden (or combopot or group of monopots) features both standouts and less noticeable elements, with top billing changing with time and the gardener's inclina-tions. So enjoy this genus for all its virtues, but don't expect them to bring down the house.

If you have a problem with insects in general (indicator #1: you refer to them all as "bugs"), I strongly recommend you think twice about growing hyssops. Bees, butterflies, syrphids (flower flies), wasps, and other creatures visit the flowers constantly and abundantly. Do you hang a hummingbird feeder in your garden? A pot of agastaches will take its place and not require routine changing of the sugar solution (which, if it remains too long in the bottle, might harbor bacterial populations that could harm the hummers). In these days of bee colony collapse disorder and dwindling butterfly populations, offering some agastaches to your garden visitors strikes me as a very good thing.

Every agastache I've had contact with is worth a try. Honestly. Your friends with an herbal predilection will probably be able to list quite a few more of their favorites beyond this list:

A. aurantiaca 'Apricot Sunrise' bears light orange flowers with purple shadings on the calyces and stems, especially if provided enough sun. Z7–10.

A. cana produces red-violet flowers, mostly, and leaves scented of camphor and bubblegum. It reaches to 3 ft. or so unless pinched back. Z5–10.

'Firebird' appropriately offers orange flowers and can reach 6 ft. tall. Z6–10.

A. foeniculum (anise hyssop) is indeed anise scented. Blue flowers arise from purple calyces on plants to about 4 ft. if you are good to them. If you treat them well, expect self-sown progeny the following year. Z6–10.

A. foeniculum 'Golden Jubilee', without question, would be the one agastache I'd grow if I were forced to choose. Yellow-green foliage (mostly green if in too much shade) and plenty of blue-violet flowers (and all those critters visiting it): what more could I (or you) want from one of these guys? Reaches maybe 3 ft., hardy to Z7. Try it.

'Tutti-Frutti' has bright red flowers and gray-green foliage on a plant to 6 ft. tall.

Cultural tips: A pinch or two early in the season usually produces denser plants and more flowers, if that's what you're looking for. Otherwise, let them grow as they will. If you find a particularly attractive form, take some cuttings of it and share them with your friends.

Too bad you can't smell the anise-scented foliage of this *Agastache foeniculum* 'Golden Jubilee', but you *can* appreciate the eye-catching tertiary color contrast between the flowers and leaves. Do you see any triangles?

AGAVE
century plant

Family: Agavaceae/Liliaceae

Cultural group: succulents

Height: 1–2 ft. (some 6 in. to 6 ft.)

Width: 1–2 ft. (some 6 in. to 6 ft.)

Light: sun

Temperature: warm to hot; some tolerate light frost

Overwintering: to 40–50°F, water occasionally, bright light or sun; a few withstand temperatures around 32°F

Moisture: moderate

Drainage of medium: well drained

Fertility: low to average

Ease/speed of growth: moderate/slow

Propagation: division, offsets

Problems: not many for them (maybe for their careless handlers), but watch out for hail and root rot

Principal interest: foliage, form

Length of seasonal interest: all year

Like kids, most *Agave americana* selections grow up quickly, assuming a grand size in a less-than-grand length of time. These teenagers will require careful attention, especially if you get too close to them (they can bite)!

Design attributes

Color: green foliage, sometimes with white and yellow variegation

Line: linear foliage, often with large spines at tips and on margins; spines and variegation increase linear look

Form: distinctive plant outlines; many in rosettes (*A. americana* twisty-floppy in time)

Space: a great deal between leaves, often suggesting triangles

Texture: mostly coarse, a few surprisingly fine (*A. geminiflora*)

I'm enamored of this genus. Not only does it offer a wide range of sizes and foliage attributes among its startling rosettes (as well as tequila, the potent potable distilled from *A. tequilana*), but most agaves will bite. You see, I grow several of the rare and choice smaller ones for competition, and there's always someone in the admiring crowd who wants to find out if the plants are real. After one startling and inevitably painful tango with an agave spine, most victims decide to leave them alone. Call me cranky, but I learned a long time ago to keep my mitts off things that don't belong to me unless the nice lady (or man, or signage) says it's OK to touch, and I expect that civilized behavior of others, thank you very much.

Their tendency to bite makes agaves logical candidates for safe confinement within the rims of monopots, but they can be accommodated within larger combopots. No matter the association, an agave will command attention (and respect, after the first bloodletting). If you fear someone could get dangerously close to the 2-in. spines of the bigger ones, decide from among the following: 1) move the plants out of reach, 2) cut off the spines, 3) stick wine corks on the spines, or 4) give the plant(s) to someone who can deal with them. Option 3 will make garden visitors laugh and think you're an artist or some other creative thinker. Or a nut.

Most widely encountered are *A. americana* and its gorgeous variegated cultivars. The species is a big bluish spiny thing, even when young, and requires careful placement. 'Marginata' offers yellow-edged foliage; the more dramatic 'Mediopicta' struts clean white down the middle of its leaves. All three quickly assume flailing, melted-looking Dr. Seussian forms that want to reach out and impale someone.

A. geminiflora might start small, but in a few years it will be pushing 2 ft. high and wide. Don't let the thin green leaves fool you: they will at least nibble you if not bite hard.

I like the mid-sized hybrid 'Joe Hoak' for its linear variegation and upward-outward look of the rosette. Joe likes to eventually surround himself with his offspring, but you might choose to remove them before they spoil Dad's symmetry.

But it's the small agaves I embrace and most frequently and heartily recommend. Start with the compact form of *A. victoriae-reginae*, and treasure it as a single rosette or dense

Opposite: A bird's-eye view makes it easy to appreciate the diversity found in the genus *Agave*. Barely yellow-edged *A*. 'Joe Hoak' at the bottom mingles with the coleus, as does a small, distinctively white-striped *A. americana* 'Mediopicta' above it. The burst of long, skinny leaves belongs to *A. geminiflora*. Big Blue at the top is a small (!) specimen of *A. americana*. I cannot identify the smaller blue one, but it's still pretty, isn't it?

cluster that suggests Queen Victoria (for whom this species is named) and her numerous offspring. The spectacular yellow- and white-variegated forms of *A. victoriae-reginae* become full-sized versions of the species after several years, but you won't mind that they've grown up. Similarly, *Aa. parryi* (and its var. *patonii*) and *potatorum* are small-growing (or grow slowly into midsize models); their variegated forms inspire much covetousness.

Cultural tips: Don't keep agaves totally dry in winter, but don't go crazy with the water, either. Their leaves will pucker if kept too dry. Carefully remove a smaller specimen from its pot and use a pair of sharp scissors to remove the dead and dying lower leaves. Approach the Big Spiny Things with much more caution and heavier artillery. *Do not* use oil-based sprays on the bluish forms; the oil will destroy the beautiful glaucous coating and it won't grow back. Keep aloe and bandages handy.

Note: If the center of the rosette appears to be rising up and above the rest of the plant, be prepared to enjoy the unusual act of a potted agave in bloom, but also brace yourself for the plant's inevitable demise: agaves are monocarpic, meaning they bloom once and die. However, most will send out offsets ("pups") at some point before blooming, so remove the pups after they develop several leaves and grow them on.

In contrast to 'Mediopicta', the striping on *Agave americana* 'Marginata' decorates the margins of the foliage, not the centers. Choose between the two or enjoy them both. Note too how the square and circular outlines of the containers (all blue, but not agave blue) add to the linear composition of this photograph.

AGERATUM
floss flower, blue fleece flower

Family: Asteraceae
Cultural group: annuals
Height: 6–12 in. (*A. houstonianum* 'Blue Horizon' to 2 ft.)
Width: 6–12 in.
Light: sun to partial shade
Temperature: warm to hot
Overwintering: rarely done; *A. houstonianum* 'Blue Horizon' min. 55–60°F with regular, careful watering in high light, maybe
Moisture: moderate to ample
Drainage of medium: well drained
Fertility: low to average
Ease/speed of growth: easy/fast
Propagation: seeds, cuttings (sometimes, for *A. houstonianum* 'Blue Horizon')
Problems: root rot, leaf blight; powdery mildew in dry conditions
Principal interest: flowers
Length of seasonal interest: moderate to long

No lumpy plant mounds here: *Ageratum houstonianum* 'Blue Horizon' lifts its flossy flowers well above the ground on sturdily leaved stems. The argument could be made that the flower clusters are lumpy, but at least there's plenty of space around them, making them seem less heavy and plodding than those of many of their relatives.

Design attributes

Color: blue or white (rarely pink) flowers
Line: nearly absent, except in *A. houstonianum* 'Blue Horizon'
Form: mounded, except the upright-shrubby to sometimes floppy *A. houstonianum* 'Blue Horizon'
Space: nearly none, except in the much more open *A. houstonianum* 'Blue Horizon'
Texture: fine to medium overall; fuzzy flowers can seem very fine

I didn't learn these plants as floss flower or fleece flower; they were ageratums from the beginning. For Decoration Day (as my family called Memorial Day back in the 1950s), we always planted the low-growing blue one, with bright red geraniums, and for a long while I didn't realize there were white and even pinkish lilac selections. But all were lumps: neat little blobs that bloomed for months, in decorated cemeteries and elsewhere, gradually becoming taller, more open, and a bit less glob-like.

I still like the lumpy ones. Planted closely they can create a sumptuous-looking fuzzy carpet in a container or in the open ground. But my current preference is *A. houstonianum* 'Blue Horizon', a taller, more natural-looking plant that—while it doesn't offer a mass of color—does carry the same beautiful blue flower clusters. It associates attractively with many other plants, often gently leaning on or almost flopping through its companions, which can include red geraniums if you like.

Cultural tips: The unlumpy ones make useful cut flowers. Try to buy and plant *A. houstonianum* 'Blue Horizon' before it reaches 1 ft. tall and its roots completely fill the cell pack or other nursery container. Pinch back for a denser plant.

AGLAONEMA
Chinese evergreen, drop-tongue

Family: Araceae
Cultural group: tropicals
Height: to 2 ft. (unless allowed to grow long and spindly)
Width: to 2 ft.
Light: partial shade to shade; amazingly tolerant of low light
Temperature: warm to hot
Overwintering: min. 60°F, water occasionally but sparingly, bright light
Moisture: moderate
Drainage of medium: well drained
Fertility: low to average
Ease/speed of growth: easy/moderate
Propagation: cuttings
Problems: stem and root rot, mealybugs, scale insects
Principal interest: foliage
Length of seasonal interest: all year

Chinese evergreens shouldn't be confined to dark offices and malls. Their colors and patterns bring plenty of interest to outdoor containers; they can then either be (easily) overwintered or (heartlessly) allowed to perish in fall and bought anew each spring.

Design attributes

Color: green foliage, often variegated with white or silver
Line: mostly from petioles; snaky bare stems on older plants
Form: dense and shrubby to loose, floppy, and trailing
Space: nearly absent in younger plants; much more in older ones
Texture: coarse

Along with their very similar-looking relatives in the genus *Dieffenbachia*, Chinese evergreens don't exactly knock people off their feet. We've all seen them used as houseplants, usually relegated to dark and out-of-the-way corners or under escalators in shopping malls. Yes, you can heap neglect and almost abuse on aglaonemas, and they'll keep hanging in there, perhaps to remind you that some plants don't need to be even remotely coddled. But a little attention is well repaid with sturdy, leafy growth and maybe a little calla-like flower every now and then. They will perform quite nicely over a single season and can go from strength to strength if over-

Now this is a satisfying and relaxing composition: the rich greens and silver of an aglaonema combine subtly with a beige container and brownish gray gravel. Very mellow. Notice that I mentioned the gravel: sometimes the area underneath a container can play an important role instead of simply being there.

wintered and given some occasional attention. Got (heavy) shade? Try some of these. Their variations on a theme of green and silver harmonize with other flowers and foliage and, of course, with each other.

References list a fair number of species and cultivars (especially of *A. commutatum*). They're all rather similar and equally stalwart, so I suggest you visit a florist, nursery, box store, or other general retailer to see what's being offered. Choose whichever ones appeal to you, and grow them as monopots or in combopots with other shade denizens. Whether you allow them to grow ever longer and snakier is up to you.

Cultural tips: You can forget these for a while with no ill effect, but don't go too far. A little fertilizer every now and then will pay benefits. Chop off taller shoots and reroot them (easily in water or potting mix) to keep them shorter and looking like someone cares.

ALLAMANDA
golden trumpet(s), yellow bell(s), buttercup flower (*A. cathartica*)

Family: Apocynaceae
Cultural group: tropicals, climbers and trailers
Height: easily 2–3 ft., to 50 ft. in time
Width: depends on training
Light: sun to limited partial shade
Temperature: warm to hot
Overwintering: min. 60°F to prevent leaf drop, water occasionally, bright light
Moisture: moderate to ample
Drainage of medium: well drained

Whether (res)trained onto a form or grown as a big, sprawling mass of stems, be sure to give *Allamanda cathartica* a big pot, and be prepared to pay attention to it. It will pay you back with flowers the color of sunshine and a shape that won't be ignored.

Fertility: average to high
Ease/speed of growth: easy to moderate/moderate to fast
Propagation: cuttings
Problems: spider mites, whitefly, aggressive growth that bullies most companions
Principal interest: flowers, form (if trained)
Length of seasonal interest: moderate to long

Design attributes
Color: sunny yellow flowers
Line: very linear or not noticeable, depending on age and training
Form: upright shrubby to formal to messy, depending on training
Space: minimal, unless trained thinly on an open trellis
Texture: medium to coarse

This boisterous climber is definitely not a candidate for a combopot, unless you have a mighty capacious container: he (or she, depending on your viewpoint, of course) merits the title of Big Plant. But Big Plants offer Big Possibilities, and a single specimen of an allamanda will make a Big Statement about your green thumb and designer's eye. Go for it.

By far the most dramatic way to grow an allamanda in a container is as an oversized topiary, such as the one in the photograph, taken at Longwood Gardens (a garden in the Philadelphia area that thinks big). Train a small plant up a very sturdy stake, preferably a metal one securely anchored in the pot. When the shoot reaches the top, pinch it out, and then repeatedly pinch the sideshoots to produce a dense head. After the first couple of years of training, shorten the previous year's shoots back to three or four nodes (growth points) in spring before growth resumes, and then await the floral extravaganza in summer and fall. Older plants will benefit from removal of the oldest, thickest stems in spring as well. You might also want to try covering a beefy tuteur (think three-dimensional trellis) with an allamanda; this approach will require more effort to direct the stems up and around the structure and to keep the plant cut back and thinned out.

I've often admired *A. cathartica* and its cultivar 'Hendersonii' (aka 'Brown Bud'), which has brown-tinged buds, in northern gardens, but those of you out West and down South (and in other warm climes) may have enjoyed other members of the genus. I look forward to joining your ranks.

From the Department of It's Sometimes Useful to Know What Inspired the Specific Epithet: the milky sap of *A. cathartica*, which can irritate your skin if exposed to it, also acts as a purgative (and not in the emotionally cleansing sense). Don't even think about eating this plant or allow or encourage anyone else to do so!

Cultural tips: Giving plenty of heat, sun, water, and fertilizer pays big dividends. You can reduce any or all of those factors if you must, but overall vigor—and flowering, the *raison d'etre* for growing golden trumpets—will be reduced, especially if light is insufficient.

ALOCASIA
elephant ear

Family: Araceae
Cultural group: tropicals
Height: 2–6 ft., a few even larger
Width: 2–6 ft., a few even larger
Light: partial shade to shade
Temperature: warm to hot
Overwintering: min. 50–55°F, water occasionally but sparingly, bright light; try a darker site to force dry, leafless dormancy
Moisture: moderate to ample
Drainage of medium: tolerates standing water
Fertility: average to high
Ease/speed of growth: easy to moderate/moderate to fast

Propagation: division
Problems: root rot (in cold, wet, heavy medium), spider mites, leaf rots
Principal interest: foliage, form
Length of seasonal interest: long

Design attributes

Color: foliage in many shades of green (including purple-green), sometimes marked with silver, sometimes with purple-green undersides
Line: dramatic upward- or downward-pointing petioles and foliage
Form: triangular leaves, overall emphatic outline
Space: abundant, very open
Texture: unabashedly coarse

Elephant ear. *Elephant* ear? Does that sound like something that belongs in a garden? Trust me, gardeners everywhere are taking to them, well, like elephants take to peanuts. The

The striking leaf pattern of *Alocasia* ×*amazonica* 'Polly' reminds me of fish bones (and the skeleton costume I once wore for Halloween). Note how the alocasia stands out against the warm terracotta bookends of the pot and 'Sedona' coleus.

past decade or so has witnessed an explosion in the availability and popularity of alocasias, linked (I think) to the surging interest in container gardening as well as to the ever-increasing use of tissue culture to rapidly produce otherwise poky plants. But first, I must point out that *Alocasia* does not possess exclusive rights to the common name of elephant ear; other now-hot genera (*Colocasia*, *Xanthosoma*, and even *Caladium*) also travel under that moniker.

So, why are alocasias hot? While not every one is big or even massive (don't be surprised if some of the elephant ears dominating your patio in summer turn out to resemble horse ears or dog ears or something much less imposing), all have presence. Their shield-shaped leaf blades and long petioles definitely command attention, as does their arching, usually broad-shouldered form. Most are at least semi-glossy, and a few look constantly wet or appear forged from some kind of biometal. Once they hit their stride (usually when hot weather arrives to stay), they seem to expand or inflate, not merely grow. Give them plenty of water, fertilizer, heat, and light (careful with the direct sun, though), and they'll soon give you every reason to show them off.

Many alocasias produce running rhizomes in addition to big tubers, the better to make a bigger and more imposing display if allowed to remain as a clump. Don't be timid with elephant ears. Here is a sampling of the herd:

A. ×*amazonica* produces dark green shields (leaf blades) 1–2 ft. long, bearing a very sharply drawn, silver "spider." 'Polly' is the cultivar to look for.

'Calidora' dwarfs most plants encountered in container gardening, easily reaching 6 ft. tall with leaf blades 2 ft. wide.

A. cuprea brings giant, wet trilobites to my mind. This so-called giant caladium (common name confusion is spreading!) offers silvery leaves 1–2 ft. long with dark green "spiders" and dark purple undersides; the specific epithet is a reference to the coppery patches on the upper leaf surfaces.

'Frydek' (also 'Freydek') sports foot-long dark green leaf blades with a distinctively drawn white "spider," although in this case "fishbone" might be more evocative.

That towering mass of green elephant ears (in this case, *Alocasia* 'Calidora') really is growing in a pot. A quite big pot, in fact, which sits atop an upside-down pot to make the plant look even more imposing. Who says you can't enjoy a little theater (and perhaps a suggestion of the triumphal procession from *Aida*) in your garden?

Smaller than many in the genus, the alluring *Alocasia* 'Hilo Beauty' still makes a marvelous display. As the distance between you and the foliage increases, the light markings will merge into the darker green, lightening the appearance of the "ears" in the process.

Remember Al Pacino's famous line in *Scent of a Woman*, "I'm just gettin' warmed up"? So were these *Alocasia macrorrhiza* 'Lutea', photographed in May. At any size, the "ears" make an impression. Also note the color difference in the two big leaves on the right: one appears yellow-green, while the other seems bluer and less noticeably veined. Light passing through (as in the former) or falling on (as in the latter) translucent things will do that.

Look at these leaves and tell me you don't picture yourself on the dry side of a giant aquarium. Oddball shapes, such as these on *Alocasia* 'Stingray', almost speak the words "Use me as a conversation piece or short-distance focal point."

'Hilo Beauty' is the little guy of this group, with leaf blades barely a 1 ft. long on a 2-ft. plant.

'Jurassic Dark' (love the name) makes dark purple, wet-looking leaves with blades 1–2 ft. long on plants to 6 ft. tall.

A. macrorrhiza (giant taro) can reach 15 ft. high with leaves to 8 ft., their length pretty much equally divided between blade and petiole. The selection 'Lutea' makes chartreuse leaves, as its name suggests.

'Stingray', with leaf blades 1–2 ft. wide, depending on how attentive you are with the fertilizer, is most appropriately named: a few leaves of it immediately bring to mind a small school of the eponymous sea creatures.

Cultural tips: Provide plenty of what they want, and alocasias will reward you. It might take a couple of years to produce big specimens, though. Watch out for spider mites (especially on indoor plants) and dispatch them with extreme prejudice. Try growing them with constant moisture or even standing water during the height of the growing season.

Note: Like many in the arum family (Araceae), alocasias contain oxalic acid, which if ingested can produce a swollen tongue and/or a swollen throat, which in severe cases can lead to asphyxia and death. Please keep them safely away from pets and children.

ALOE
burn plant (*A. vera*); partridge breast (*A. variegata*)

Family: Aloaceae/Liliaceae
Cultural group: succulents
Height: 3 in. to 2–3 ft., some 6–20 ft. in time
Width: 3 in. to 2 ft., except for the big ones
Light: sun to partial shade (especially for variegated forms)
Temperature: warm to hot
Overwintering: min. 50°F, water regularly but not excessively, bright light or sun

Moisture: on dry side to moderate
Drainage of medium: well drained
Fertility: low to average
Ease/speed of growth: easy to moderate/slow to moderate
Propagation: cuttings, offsets, seeds (if you're patient)
Problems: leaf, stem, and root rots, scale insects, mealybugs
Principal interest: foliage, form, sometimes flowers
Length of seasonal interest: foliage all year; flowers in season or sporadically

Design attributes

Color: foliage green (sometimes variegated); hot-colored flowers
Line: linear leaves move out from center of rosettes; upright flower spikes
Form: active-looking single or massed rosettes (mostly), or shrubby to treelike, or unusual (such as the fanlike leaf arrangement of *A. plicatilis*)

Space: in between leaves, sometimes; treelike forms contain quite a bit of space
Texture: fine to medium to coarse

*A*loe counts among its members 300 species and quite a few hybrids. Probably every one of them can be grown in containers, and I invite you to try some. Hummingbirds go mad for the flowers, as I discovered one spring at the Arizona-Sonora Desert Museum outside of Tucson. Those of you who can grow aloes outdoors all year can enjoy the hummers' whizzing and chirping as they probe the aloes' tubular flowers. The rest of us can imagine those avian jewels visiting the flowers as they bloom indoors in winter and late spring. Yes, many aloes grow more actively in winter than in summer, so be sure to monitor the rainfall and other water that might get into the potting mix. Whether you allow the pups to remain on the parent plant to make a big clump, or you remove the pups and pot them up separately, is entirely up to you. Just remember that a big clump of mom and pups might become top-heavy

The flattened growth pattern of *Aloe plicatilis* sets it apart from many of its kin; aloes usually appear as rounded rosettes. This specimen breaks the mold further by being allowed to grow at a jaunty angle. Nice touch.

Big aloes cannot be forever contained in small pots and will in time either topple over or (in this case) appear to be walking away from their confines.

(or just plain heavy). Of course you'll need to overwinter them indoors in areas that go below freezing. It's worth it.

Most aloes are brittle, so keep them out of high-traffic areas and away from large dogs' tails and soccer balls. At the very least the leaf tips will break off, making the plants look a little frowzy. At worst, the entire plant could turn almost instantaneously to gooey, slimy green mush. That jelly-like material in the leaves does indeed soothe minor burns and rashes, whether from the medicinal aloe, *A. vera*, or others. New beauties (big and small) are increasingly turning up these days. Of the many commonly available aloes, I've grown and/or admired the following:

A. brevifolia makes a tight, precise rosette about 1 ft. wide and (eventually) high. Please don't break a leaf off its fabulous variegated selection for mere medicinal purposes!

A. ferox (as in "feral") is a savage-looking thing, but it grows quite agreeably in a pot. Figure 2 ft. wide and high as a container plant.

A. parvula is a little guy (less than 1 ft. tall and wide, even as a clump), but its appealing blue-gray foliage, readily clumping habit, and red-orange flowers more than make up for its size (assuming size is a problem for you).

A. plicatilis, with foliage in flat fanlike clusters, will reach 2 ft. in a pot.

A. polyphylla is the Holy Grail of aloes. In time the rosette forms a very distinct Fibonacci-like spiral, some individuals appearing to turn clockwise while others go counterclockwise. Fascinating. A mature specimen will reach about 2 ft. across and maybe 1.5 ft. high. Reference books tell me it bears pale red flowers. That's nice, but it would never need to bloom for me.

A. variegata (partridge breast) makes a spiky, triangular-feeling rosette of beautifully white-marked, dark green, very thick leaves. Foot-tall spikes of red or pink flowers add to the drama.

A. vera, the one to grow for your first-aid needs, will easily and quickly produce beefy rosettes, nearly 2 ft. tall and wide, and showy red flowers in big, bold, branched spikes.

Cultural tips: Remember, too much water—such as that emitting from lawn sprinklers that go off every other day, no matter what—will lead to root rot unless the plants are growing in Barad mix (see page 280) or other very well-drained medium. Growing aloes in an unglazed clay pot will promote good air and water passage through the pot, too.

ALPINIA
shell ginger, ginger lily

Family: Zingiberaceae
Cultural group: tropicals
Height: 2–4 ft. or more
Width: 2–4 ft. or more
Light: partial shade to shade; protect *A. zerumbet* 'Variegata' from hot afternoon sun
Temperature: warm to hot
Overwintering: min. 45–55°F, water occasionally, bright light (or cut back, put in a dark place, and hope they survive)
Moisture: moderate to ample
Drainage of medium: well drained
Fertility: low to average
Ease/speed of growth: easy to moderate/moderate
Propagation: division
Problems: spider mites if too dry, leaf spots, root rot
Principal interest: foliage, sometimes flowers
Length of seasonal interest: long

Design attributes
Color: foliage green, sometimes variegated (particularly *A. zerumbet* 'Variegata')

Alpinia zerumbet 'Variegata' (variegated shell ginger) emerges from its nearly obscured pot in a rush of elongated leaves marked with yellow lines that add to the energetic impression. The tumbling *Ipomoea batatas* 'Margarita' in the foreground and spouting grass behind contribute their own energetic forms.

Line: strongly upright-linear stems and outward-reaching
 foliage
Form: dense, shrubby
Space: some at outer edges of plant (between leaves)
Texture: coarse

I've barely begun to explore the genus *Alpinia* for its con-
tainer- gardening potential. About 200 species (and numerous cultivars) are counted among its ranks, but so far I've met
just one: the variegated shell ginger, *A. zerumbet* 'Variegata'.
Good start, I think. Although it can become quite large—you
should see it in warmer gardens where it's hardy, its leafy
masses easily pushing 6 ft. high and at least that wide—it will
grow fairly slowly at first in a container and can be kept
manageable through occasional (elbow-greased) division and
severe chopping back. It tolerates drought, which can occur
daily for a rootbound plant, and it performs well in many
degrees of shade. Although older specimens inevitably show
age spots (brown markings on the foliage), they rarely detract

A closer look reveals the unique nature of the individual leaves
on variegated shell ginger. It also makes me wonder if its yellow-
gold markings coordinate or compete with the bright chartreuse
of its sweet potato companion.

much from the overall impression of tropical exuberance.
With some luck a container-grown plant should produce
spikes of fragrant, white and pale pink, molluscan (seashell-
like) flowers. I've never seen them but hope to some day here
in New Jersey.

But of course the principal reason for growing many a
plant is for its looks, and here's where variegated shell ginger
delivers. Big, boisterous, animated, colorful, lush . . . and a perfect subject for a Hawaiian shirt. I'm waiting for one to appear
on the store racks, but in the meantime I'll admire the plants
themselves.

Cultural tips: Look the other way if you notice brown spots
on the leaves. If they bother you, grow a specimen as a monopot in a large pot, and be prepared to provide plenty of water.
Regularly. You can grow a big plant in a surprisingly small
container.

ALTERNANTHERA
Joseph's coat, parrot leaf, calico plant

Family: Amaranthaceae
Cultural group: annuals
Height: 2–12 in.
Width: 2 in. to indefinite
Light: sun to partial shade
Temperature: warm to hot
Overwintering: min. 45–50°F, water occasionally,
 bright light
Moisture: moderate to ample
Drainage of medium: well drained
Fertility: low to average
Ease/speed of growth: easy/moderate to fast
Propagation: cuttings
Problems: spider mites, root rot
Principal interest: foliage, form
Length of seasonal interest: long

Design attributes
Color: foliage in many bright and darker colors
Line: some a mass of little foliage lines; others have
 trailing stems
Form: carpets, little shrubs, or gentle cascades
Space: little in the dwarf, compact forms; plenty in
 the trailers
Texture: fine (the dwarf and compact ones), medium
 in trailers

I'm intrigued by the diversity of foliage colors and textures of
alternantheras, as others have been in the past. Within this
genus are perfect plants for appealing to your inner Victorian
gardener (or member of the landed gentry commanding a big,

impressive staff of gardeners). The little-leafed ones can be composed into intricate patterns and tightly sheared into colorful carpets, while the larger-leafed selections may be used to fill large beds contained within hedges and gravel paths.

Right. Most of us don't have the means or mindset for such a grandiose garden production, but we can enjoy a much-reduced reminder of Victoriana in a container. For the informally inclined, alternantheras can of course also be grown unclipped and unfettered, and the effect will be more or less the same as Compost Court or Manure Manor—except much smaller and far more reality based. They make excellent choices for both monopots (an arrangement of monopots of several different selections makes a colorful and stylish display) and combopots (in which they can serve as a "carpet" for many other plants, such as coleus, abutilons, and other Victorian favorites).

The nomenclature within this genus is a little loose, so I suggest you acquire the alternantheras that catch your fancy, make a note of the name on the label, and take photos of your plants. That way you'll have both written and visual backup with you on your nursery visit, by which time the names might well have changed. With that caveat in mind, savor these examples:

A. dentata 'Royal Tapestry' trails attractively and appears much more spacious than the selections of *A. ficoidea*. Its metallic red-purple combines beautifully with many other colors.

A. ficoidea 'Gold Thread' (which might be the same as 'Yellow Fine Leaf'), 'Green 'n' Gold', 'Purple Thread', and 'Red Threads' are all colorful variations on the theme of low and threadlike. All make loose to tight little mounds, depending

The yellow and green shreds of *Alternanthera ficoidea* 'Yellow Fine Leaf' stand out sharply against the neutral background. Don't expect this or any threadleaf selection to grow more than 1 ft. tall.

The rich dark greens and purples of this sumptuous threadleaf alternanthera pop against the bright egg-yolk yellow of the pot. However, the yellow does just the opposite for the leaves of the geranium, whose yellow-green edges seem wan in comparison.

Not many alternantheras offer much interest from their stems, but the branching, dark purple stems of *Alternanthera dentata* 'Royal Tapestry' certainly catch the eye. Note how the tiny flowers (another seldom-noticed attribute) at the nodes (stem junctions) "punctuate" the overall look.

A simple terracotta pot wears a frizzy maroon wig of *Alternanthera ficoidea* 'Red Threads'. Can you picture the wig over a gray or light green pot? How about white? Consider too the shape of the plant and whether it would be as eye-catching if it were combined with more angular and upright forms.

on how heavy-handed you are with the shears or your thumb and forefinger.

'Grenadine' looks and behaves much like *Iresine herbstii* (beefsteak plant). A pinch or two early on makes this hybrid denser and more upright, at least for a while.

'Partytime' flaunts pink-splashed foliage on another iresine-like plant form. As with many variegated plants, the amount of "paint" color changes from leaf to leaf (or disappears on shoots that have reverted to solid green).

Cultural tips: Ensure good drainage, or the roots will rot quickly. Don't be afraid to cut any of them back, sometimes severely. If you find an attractive sported shoot or two, try to root it before the weather becomes too cool.

Not all alternantheras produce skinny foliage. Many offer broader leaves, the better to show off splotchy or tree-like patterns. *Alternanthera* 'Grenadine' takes the arboreal approach. The curved leaf edges suggest motion, but of a less frenzied sort than the seething mass of movement apparent in thread-leaf selections.

Alternanthera 'Partytime' lives up to its name with an unpredictable mingling of neon pink and green. Take care with its companions: the neon pink splashes might not play well with other colors (imagine this with bright orange . . . yikes!)

AMORPHOPHALLUS
devil's tongue, umbrella arum, corpse flower,
voodoo lily, snake palm

Family: Araceae
Cultural group: bulbs
Height: 2–4 ft.
Width: 2–3 ft.
Light: partial shade to shade
Temperature: warm to hot
Overwintering: keep totally dormant at 50–60°F, very little
    to no water, light not necessary; can be kept potted in
    their growing medium
Moisture: moderate to ample
Drainage of medium: well drained
Fertility: low to average
Ease/speed of growth: moderate/moderate to fast
Propagation: division (of corms)
Problems: rot
Principal interest: foliage
Length of seasonal interest: long

Design attributes
Color: foliage mostly dark green with intriguingly spotted
    "stems" (actually petioles)
Line: dramatic upright "stems" and outwardly moving leaf
    blades
Form: like slashed umbrellas or upward-reaching hands
    (especially when emerging from the medium)
Space: plenty under and within the leaf blades
Texture: medium to coarse

Yes, the genus name means "misshapen phallus." If you take one look at what is inside a fully expanded inflorescence, you'll understand. Seeing one of the bigger species in bloom definitely amplifies the feeling of a dark-hooded presence suggested by the string of common names, especially *A. titanum*, the one that is the focus of live Web-cam transmissions from botanic gardens when producing its massive and smelly inflorescences. Maybe I'll start hybridizing and eventually introduce 'Darth Vader' to the gardening world (after checking with George Lucas, of course).

Darkness (and bizarro flowers) aside, you've got to love these plants for their intricately constructed, sometimes reptilian foliage, which persists in the garden far longer than those flash-in-the-pan flowers (assuming they appear in the first place). Few other plants look like amorphophalli, so you and your garden visitors will marvel at them, guaranteed. Their unique architecture and delicate root system lend them to monopot culture, but you could combine these with other plants that die down and go dormant at the same time

(such as small begonias and cannas). You might temporarily but carefully insert them into a combopot made for a special event. The clumping species (such as *A. konjac*) will in time thank you for their own private quarters of a monopot, however.

If you have the space, physical strength, and inclination, try growing *A. titanum*, if you can find it. But I suggest you start with these two species, both of which are easy to grow:

The foliage of *A. atroviridis* resembles that of many *Arisaema* species, to which genus it is related. Unlike the jacks in the pulpits, however, the foliage won't die down before the heat of summer. A younger plant is about 2 ft. tall, but older ones could reach 3 ft. or more.

A. konjac (aka *Aa. rivieri* and *rivieri* 'Konjac') makes a nice clump of variously sized plants in a short time. They'll eventually reach 3 ft. or so. The fascinatingly marked stems of this species may have inspired one of the generic common names, snake palm.

Cultural tips: Wait patiently for snake palms to emerge in spring or even summer after a totally leafless, bone-dry but

A miniature forest of *Amorphophallus konjac* offers plenty of interest, especially when featured as a monopot. The simple, dark pot sets things off even more. Looking at the foliage, you'd probably never guess that the inflorescence looks like a gigantic, liver-colored calla lily.

warm dormancy. They'll wake up when they're ready. Separate clumps carefully in late winter, pot into a dry potting mix, and keep them dry until new shoots emerge.

ANETHUM
dill, dillweed (*A. graveolens*)

Family: Apiaceae
Cultural group: annuals
Height: 1–3 ft., maybe more
Width: 1 ft., unless the plant flops around
Light: sun to partial shade
Temperature: warm to hot
Overwintering: no
Moisture: moderate to ample
Drainage of medium: well drained
Fertility: low to average
Ease/speed of growth: easy/fast
Propagation: seeds
Problems: black swallowtail caterpillars (only if you find gorgeously marked caterpillars and butterflies a problem)
Principal interest: foliage, flowers, fragrance
Length of seasonal interest: moderate to long (if successively sown)

Design attributes
Color: fresh green foliage; bright yellow flowers
Line: nothing but lines except for the "dot" flowers in the circular heads
Form: a cloud with lines going through it and umbrellas on top
Space: feels very spacious
Texture: fine (few plants are finer than *A. graveolens*)

I like dill. The fragrance is sharp-spicy-musty (to my nose), and the very strokable foliage and plant as a whole remind me of the mist that rises from the bottom of a waterfall. The flowers have that dynamic carrot-family fireworks structure to them (and they smell nice), and dill is *easy* to grow from seed. Throw a few seeds into a monopot or combopot in spring (the older they get, the less kindly they take to being transplanted—like people) and be prepared to have a multisensory experience.

Another important part of the dill experience (for me) is living with the creatures that also like this herb: bees, syrphids (flower flies), predatory wasps, and butterflies excitedly work the flowers for the goodies they provide. I've frequently grown some dill in the hopes of attracting black swallowtails to lay their eggs on them and then having the pleasure of watching their beautiful yellow and black-spotted green cater-

A single leaf of *Amorphophallus atroviridis* offers a detailed lesson in the nature and interactions of the five design elements. I want to see this in a light to medium gray pot, don't you?

Often described as snakelike, the branching and spotted stems (petioles here, actually, because we're looking at leaves) of *Amorphophallus konjac* offer as much visual interest as many flowers.

Can't you almost smell and taste the misty foliage and lively chartreuse flowers of this dill (*Anethum graveolens*)? Not all dill plants branch as erratically as this one—some are even more crooked! Note the sharp textural contrast between the ultra-fine foliage and the thick, much coarser stems.

Dill flowers reward close inspection, particularly by insects, who flock to and scramble over the nectar-rich individual flowers of every umbellule. Obviously, this photograph was taken during a break between feedings.

pillars grow up on the plants. Unfortunately, more often than not, yellow jackets and other predatory hymenopterans (and almost certainly birds, whether for their growing families or for themselves) carry them off before they have a chance to pupate. Even more discouraging is when "helpful" garden visitors smoosh the "icky bugs" eating my plants. At least that sort of disaster can become a teaching moment about the web of life and co-existing with other "lesser" creatures.

Sometimes dill will grow tall and fall over, so keep thin stakes handy if you want upright plants; however, the twisting stems of flopping dill can add some interesting curvy lines to your container plantings. Any old dill will do, I think, but some prefer the heirloom cultivar 'Mammoth'. They all add an extremely fine textural presence to container plantings.

Now I'd like to enjoy a pickle … preferably a fried dill at a county fair.

Cultural tips: Sow a few seeds every week or so for a continuous display of fresh new foliage. Full sun encourages sturdier growth. Older plants, with their long taproots, often transplant poorly, so move them when small and more resilient.

ANGELONIA
summer snapdragon

Family: Scrophulariaceae
Cultural group: annuals
Height: to 18 in. unless they fall over
Width: 12 in.
Light: sun to partial shade
Temperature: warm to hot
Overwintering: no, unless you want a challenge or have a vividly green thumb
Moisture: moderate (ample moisture can lead to root rot)
Drainage of medium: well drained
Fertility: low to average

Ease/speed of growth: easy/moderate

Propagation: cuttings, seeds

Problems: root rot, drought, transplant disturbance (larger plants)

Principal interest: flowers

Length of seasonal interest: long

Design attributes

Color: flowers in white, pink, blue, and purple

Line: upright-linear stems and outward-linear foliage

Form: narrowly upright-shrubby to gently falling over

Space: not readily apparent unless unpinched and grown individually

Texture: fine to medium

One summer at Atlock Farm I planted an intimate little garden almost entirely with *Angelonia* cultivars, and the results remained beautiful for months. The odd thing was that the hundreds of plants put into the "girly garden" (as it was known, for its color scheme) represented unwanted nurs-ery stock remaining after the big sales rush of May and June. The big nurseries have been pushing angelonias—hard—and the gardening media sing their praises. It's a puzzlement why the folks around here haven't discovered them, so I might routinely plant the girly garden with them until they catch on. The praying mantises that I routinely relocate to the garden (from inside the greenhouses, where their fate is uncertain) will thank me.

Summer snapdragons (are the traditional ones, namely *Antirrhinum*, now considered "spring snapdragons"?) do quite well in containers, especially when associating with sturdier plants that can prop them up in combopots. Even if they do (attractively) slouch a bit, they still keep blooming profusely and over a long time—colorful flower spikes carried over pretty, elongated leaves. While I've not heard or read of others noting their scent, my nose always picks up a fragrance that reminds me of grapes with another undefinable note thrown in.

I'm most familiar with members of the AngelMist, Angelface, or Carita series, selections of or hybrids involving *A. angustifolia*. All are beautiful and capable of adding delicate

Angelonias offer flowers in candy (or perhaps ice-cream) colors on tall spikes. These summer snapdragons are the permanently jaws-wide-open sort, not the fun ones (belonging to the genus *Antirrhinum*) you can open and close by pinching their "cheeks."

Summer snapdragons (such as this *Angelonia* Angelface Pink) can look a bit lonely as a monopot. Companions (or a thin, obscured stake or two) will help them stay upright and help make them look a little less forlorn.

Broadly white-edged *Angelonia angustifolia* AngelMist Striped brings additional color-pattern variation to the world of summer snapdragons. From a distance, the flowers appear pale purple, thanks to the lightening effect of the white on the dark purple. Up close, the purple markings look like chubby, upside-down little people with really tall hair . . . to me.

abundance to your plantings. Buy, plant, and enjoy them so that more of their kind don't end up relegated to the girly garden.

Cultural tips: Pinching them back when young (less than 1 ft. tall) encourages branching, a denser, more sturdy constitution, and more flowers. If flowering slows down in midsummer, cut back most of the flowering stems to renew them. Good drainage is crucial to prevent sudden root rot, which exhibits the same symptom as drought (to which they are also prone), namely sudden and dramatic wilting. Grow them in a well-drained mix and keep the watering can handy.

ARCTOTIS
African daisy, monarch of the veldt

Family: Asteraceae
Cultural group: annuals (usually)
Height: to 2 ft., but many newer cultivars reach about 1 ft.
Width: about 1 ft.
Light: sun
Temperature: cool to warm
Overwintering: min. 45–50°F, water occasionally, bright light
Moisture: moderate
Drainage of medium: well drained
Fertility: low to average
Ease/speed of growth: easy to moderate/moderate
Propagation: seeds, cuttings (of attractive forms)
Problems: leaf miners, leaf spots, lack of bloom (some stop blooming in high heat)
Principal interest: flowers, foliage
Length of seasonal interest: moderate

Design attributes
Color: flowers (often multicolored or intriguingly banded) in white, pink, red, yellow, and orange, with black, blue, and purple discs; some have grayish foliage
Line: linear flower stems
Form: mounded to almost shrubby
Space: only around flower stems
Texture: medium

Kudos to plant breeders, who have successfully tamed some of this genus's burly, gray-leafy, wide-spreading, flower-stingy ways and produced some very satisfactory free-flowering selections. Some African daisies still bloom reluctantly during periods of hot, sultry, "dog days" weather (especially at night), and their flowers for the most part shyly remain closed on cloudy days. But when they are open, they offer plenty of eye candy, and their admirable drought tolerance suits them for semi-neglectful container growing, which many of us practice. Admit it. It's healthy and not a moral failure.

A Web search for *Arctotis* (aka *Venidium* or ×*Venidioarctotis*) and visits to local garden centers and public gardens will present lots of named and unnamed cultivars. I like the looks of 'Bumblebee' (bright yellow), the aptly named 'Flamingo', 'Pumpkin Pie' and 'Sunspot' (warm orange), 'Torch Purple' (bad-boy magenta), and the older *A. fastuosa* var. *alba* 'Zulu Prince' (white with assertive orange and purple bands around the central disc). You might also want to try *A. venusta*, with blue-centered white flowerheads.

Cultural tips: Throw plenty of sun at them, and make sure the potting mix is well drained. A bloom-boosting fertilizer

Enjoy the cheerful, open faces of African daisies on sunny days; cloudy days (and approaching nightfall) cause them to close. Note how the gray-green of the foliage cools down the heat of the orange and yellow (and black!) flowerheads.

You'd need a big pot to enjoy the impact of this many African daisies. To amplify the color impact of these, which are growing in the open ground, you could place a noticeably taller pot of the same *Arctotis* selection in the bed.

should pay dividends. Take basal cuttings of your favorites in late summer and overwinter the plants in a cool greenhouse.

ARGYRANTHEMUM
marguerite, summer daisy

Family: Asteraceae
Cultural group: annuals (usually)
Height: 1–3 ft., perhaps a bit more if trained into topiary
Width: 1–3 ft.
Light: sun
Temperature: cool to warm
Overwintering: min. 50°F, water occasionally, bright light; hardy in Z10–11
Moisture: moderate to ample
Drainage of medium: well drained
Fertility: average
Ease/speed of growth: easy to moderate/moderate
Propagation: cuttings
Problems: leaf miner, decrepitude (old specimens)
Principal interest: flowers, foliage
Length of seasonal interest: long

Design attributes
Color: white, pink, yellow flowers; green or gray-green foliage
Line: mostly from flower stems; *A. gracile* has threadlike foliage
Form: shrubby
Space: mostly around flower stems
Texture: medium (fine in *A. gracile*)

Do you enjoy the happy look of a daisy? Would you like to grow a plant that seems to flower forever in the midst of fleeting favorites? And would you like to try your hand at making a blooming standard topiary without too much effort and agita? If your answer to each of these questions is yes, then I strongly commend marguerite daisies to you. Easy, fast, free-blooming, and forgiving of a severe haircut, they will quickly become members of your gardening Pantheon. Picture flowers up to 2.5 in. across, in clean white or happy, sherbet-y shades of yellow and pink. Some take on the classic daisy form; others mimic anemones with a tuffet of florets in their centers. Then picture extensively cut foliage on robust-looking plants, and you'll have an idea of the appeal of marguerite daisies. Truly these deserve your attention.

Most marguerites travel solely under cultivar names. That's fine; whether they are selections of *A. gracile* or *A. frutescens* or hybrids with them matters little here. They will all reward you when given the same basic culture. Do try making a standard topiary with one of these, provided you have a suit-

Marguerite daisies, such as this petite 'Sassy White', usually bloom for several months, especially if you diligently remove the faded flowerheads. Would you notice the deeply cut, fine foliage if this plant were seen against a green background?

'Nelia Yellow' is early to bloom and compact. Wouldn't you like to see its cool yellow combined with maroon, light blue, or dark purple? How would it appear alongside hot colors, such as scarlet or bright orange?

able place to overwinter your creation. Specimens with at least a year under their belt produce impressive floral displays, especially if their handlers aren't afraid to cut them back hard in late winter.

'Cornish Gold' and 'Jamaica Primrose' bear single daisies in shades of yellow.

A. gracile 'Chelsea Girl' has an almost diaphanous appearance, its foliage reduced to long, wispy threads. It might not bloom as heavily as the others, but no big whoop. I'd take advantage of its texture in a combopot even if it never bloomed.

'Mary Wootton' and 'Vancouver' are both anemone-flowered types in sugary expressions of pink.

'Sassy White' and 'Snowstorm' (aka 'Jamaican Snowstorm') bear flowers in a basic color. You can figure it out from their names, I'm certain.

Also worth trying are 'Butterfly' (warm yellow), 'Nelia' (cool yellow), 'Sunlight' (bright yellow), and 'Vanilla Butterfly' (creamy). Plenty more await you out there.

Cultural tips: Periodically cut them back to keep the flowers coming. Use a bloom-boosting fertilizer. They root easily from cuttings, which you will then try to grow into standard topiaries. Go ahead; give it a try.

ARISTOLOCHIA
Dutchman's pipe

Family: Aristolochiaceae
Cultural group: climbers and trailers
Height: at least 3 ft., some much more
Width: depends on training
Light: sun to partial shade
Temperature: warm to hot
Overwintering: min. 50°F, water occasionally, bright light; variously hardy in Z5–9
Moisture: moderate to ample
Drainage of medium: well drained
Fertility: average to high
Ease/speed of growth: easy/moderate to fast
Propagation: cuttings, division, seeds
Problems: leaf spots and rots
Principal interest: flowers, foliage, form
Length of seasonal interest: moderate to long

Design attributes

Color: flowers in patterns of brown, yellow, and purple; green foliage
Line: depends on the reach of the stems and method of training
Form: almost shapeless to distinctive, depending on training
Space: depends on training
Texture: coarse

I can think of two major reasons for noticing or growing any aristolochia: the foliage brings some sort of Type-A adjective to mind (big, lush, vigorous, pretty, jungly), and the flowers bring, um, well, Dutchman's pipes or perhaps something anatomical—human or otherwise—to mind. So, see in these plants what you will—they all make potent statements in container plantings. Most are too vigorous to mix politely with companions in a combopot, so grow the relatively shorter and/or manageable ones as monopots and be prepared to provide a sturdy stake teepee, trellis, tuteur, or other support structure. You could also grow them in hanging baskets, although the vines will want to grow up the hanger instead of trail downward unless you use a firm hand.

Many Americans can picture a porch covered on at least one side in summer with a big-leafed, almost scary vine, which would in many cases be *A. macrophylla* (aka *A. durior*). Unless you have a very large pot and a similarly large structure for it to engulf, I suggest you grow this one in the ground, and let it devour your porch and make your younger relatives wonder if the plant might eat them. At the other extreme is *A.*

clematitis (birthwort), which barely reaches 3 ft., but its little yellow pipes are great fun to look at.

Although potentially a big boy, *A. littoralis* (aka *A. elegans*) submits to severe cutting back in late winter; it will send out shoots to at least 10 ft. in the next season. Brown flowers are followed by ridged fruits, which upon maturity open into parachute-like little collectibles suitable for a Victorian-era-inspired cabinet of curiosities.

And there are others. The Web contains many fascinating images of the seacreature-evoking *A. fimbriata*, the open-mouthed choirs of *A. cathcartii* (the flowers remind me of Hop Low, the little mushroom in Disney's *Fantasia*), and the impossibly formed, fuzz-crowned pipes of *A. chapada*, to name a tiny fraction. No matter which of these (or any plant) might entice you, conduct a little research on the plant (mostly within the categories relating to dimensions, attributes, and cultural needs) before diving headlong into the metaphorical pool.

Cultural tips: Keep the pruning shears and/or loppers handy. Don't provide a spindly support, except for the smallest among them. Aristolochias grow quickly and reach out with their twining stems for any support, so keep them away from plants that might be overwhelmed.

Note: Dutchman's pipes are host plants for the caterpillars of the gorgeous pipevine swallowtail (*Battus philenor*). If you plant a pipevine, the swallowtails might come.

ARTEMISIA
wormwood, dusty miller, mugwort, sagebrush

Family: Asteraceae
Cultural group: perennials, annuals
Height: 6 in. to 4 ft.
Width: 12 in. to indefinite
Light: sun
Temperature: warm to hot
Overwintering: variously hardy in Z3–9
Moisture: on dry side to moderate
Drainage of medium: well drained
Fertility: low to average
Ease/speed of growth: easy/moderate to fast
Propagation: division, cuttings
Problems: root rot, leaf spots
Principal interest: foliage, fragrance
Length of seasonal interest: long

Design attributes
Color: gray to green foliage, green/cream in Oriental Limelight
Line: mostly in leaves as they spring out from the stems (some foliage almost threadlike)
Form: mounded/subshrubby; some carpeting

Aristolochia littoralis (and other Dutchman's pipes) bear evocative flowers among their lush foliage. Yes, that weird brown thing is a flower, and the puffy mass underneath it is a bud waiting to add to the odd.

Space: not much, except in the threadlike ones
Texture: fine to medium

Every plant, even so-called thugs, can be put to some sort of garden use. Sometimes it requires a bit more creativity, coupled with maximum-security conditions provided by a container (just what this book is all about) and overseen by a diligent warden (that's you). Oddly, the genus *Artemisia* contains both shrinking violets (the most notorious being the glorious but short-lived *A. schmidtiana* 'Nana') and thugs: *A. ludoviciana* is reviled for its invasiveness (I prefer to think of it as pluck and stick-to-it-iveness). But almost all artemisias produce some of the most notably, almost radiantly silvery foliage you can employ in container plantings—and they offer fragrances that you *must* savor and enjoy. The five covered here cut a wide swath across the genus.

A. annua (sweet Annie) grows like a weed (admittedly, some swear at it and persecute as a demon) and easily reaches 4 ft. tall in a pot. The foliage is lacy and emits a characteristic

The fine, gray foliage of *Artemisia* 'Powis Castle' makes a strong textural and color contrast with the vriesea above it and the heavy, dark urn that contains them, showing why the adjectives "lacy," "misty," and "cloudlike" often accompany this plant's name. It's fitting.

sweet fragrance with the slightest touch. Even in death, it smells so good that some crafters weave the stems into wreaths and include the dried leaves in potpourri and sachets.

A. dracunculus (tarragon) looks like a weed, but all's forgiven when bits of it turn up in Béarnaise sauce or chicken pot pie. Grow the so-called French or European form, which is superior in several ways to the Russian form. Monopot culture is strongly suggested. Z3–7.

'Powis Castle', once the darling of every cutting-edge gardener, is still a mighty fine plant, provided it receives a severe haircut in spring and is allowed to grow as it will. As with many things gray or silvery, its foliage mixes well with many other colors. Z6–9.

A. schmidtiana 'Nana' might not live very long, but it makes a stunning monopot to use as a contrast for many colors, forms, and textures. And have you ever stroked a well-grown specimen of silvermound? I recommend it for that experience alone. Z5–8.

A. vulgaris Oriental Limelight (= 'Janlim') thumbs its nose at the Anti-Thug League with its very toothsome spring foliage in shades of green and yellow. Yes, it's a selection of the truly noisome mugwort, which is near impossible to eradicate in the open ground, but Oriental Limelight is easily contained in a … container. If/when the foliage reverts to plain green (as the season wears on or the plant produces the inevitable all-green shoots), remove the pot to an out-of-the-way spot or discard it (in the trash—no ordinary compost pile can contain mugwort). Z1–11, no doubt.

Cultural tips: Nearly starve, dehydrate, and sunburn them, except for tarragon. Their silvery-ness is greatly reduced if their diet is too rich and their quarters too shady, and the roots will rot in too-moist soil. Tarragon takes well to more "food" and can handle some shade.

ARUNDO
giant reed (*A. donax*)

Family: Poaceae
Cultural group: perennials
Height: 6 ft. (yes, it's much taller in the open ground)
Width: 3–5 ft. or more, depending on container and age
Light: sun to limited partial shade
Temperature: warm to hot
Overwintering: cut back and provide min. 40°F, keep dark and almost dry; hardy in Z6–10, var. *versicolor* to Z7
Moisture: moderate to ample
Drainage of medium: well drained
Fertility: low to average to high, depending on how gigantic you want it to be
Ease/speed of growth: easy/fast
Propagation: division, cuttings (in water)

Obviously, this giant clump of *Arundo donax* isn't growing in the pot in the foreground. A few-stemmed clump could, however, and it would bring drama to any location that might accommodate it.

Usually not as tall as the type, the less exuberant *Arundo donax* var. *versicolor* lends itself nicely to pot culture. A half-barrel works well as a pot. Note how the quietly colorful banding echoes the striped foliage. Very clever and stylish.

Problems: potential to deliver nasty paper cuts
Principal interest: foliage (and relaxing whooshing sound as the wind blows through large specimens)
Length of seasonal interest: long

Design attributes

Color: blue-green foliage, var. *versicolor* striped creamy white
Line: extreme linear expression from long stems (whether straight, curved, or floppy) and long, strappy foliage
Form: big bundle of leafy sticks
Space: quite a bit, especially when looking up into it
Texture: medium, despite its size

So you're beginning to read this short entry, already having gaped at the photo of the stand of *A. donax* topping out at 15 ft. in flower, and you're thinking I might be a little crazy, recommending giant reed as a container plant. Well, while not attaining the gargantuan stature of the straight species, *A. donax* var. *versicolor* (aka 'Variegata' or confused with the broader-leaved but shorter-growing 'Variegata Superba') also makes a mighty fine container plant. See the photo. Enough said!

Cultural tips: Keep a few very sturdy stakes handy if you decide to give giant reed a whirl, but resist the urge to keep the stems bolt upright. That might look forced. Rather, stake the stems at a gentle angle. Maximum sunlight keeps *A. donax* stockier but will burn the variegated selections. Be very careful when siting and interacting with any giant reed; the edges of the foliage are sharp and can give nasty lacerations akin to paper cuts. How fortunate are garden writers, who are potentially exposed to the same dermal assault indoors and out?

ASCLEPIAS
blood flower, swallow wort, Curacao milkweed,
annual milkweed, Indian root (*A. curassavica*)

Family: Asclepiadaceae
Cultural group: annuals, aquatics
Height: 3 ft.
Width: 1 ft., maybe
Light: sun
Temperature: warm to hot
Overwintering: no
Moisture: moderate to ample
Drainage of medium: well drained but tolerates standing
    water
Fertility: low to average
Ease/speed of growth: easy/moderate
Propagation: seeds
Problems: spider mites, aphids (but they add more orange
    and feed ladybugs)
Principal interest: flowers
Length of seasonal interest: long

Design attributes
Color: precisely carved red and orange flowers (rarely
    yellow)
Line: upright stems and outward-reaching foliage
Form: skinny shrubs (at best); skinnier unbranched
    sentinels (if not pinched)
Space: between leaves
Texture: medium

Plenty of species in this genus are tempting enough to include in the open garden, including moisture-loving *A. incarnata* (swamp milkweed), the admittedly weedy *A. syriaca* (plain old milkweed, generous provider of monarch caterpillar food), and the fiery *A. tuberosa* (butterfly weed). All produce intricately chiseled flowers (check one out sometime) and offer sustenance to butterflies in both their larval and adult stages. None of these North American perennials, however, are sufficiently tempting (to me) to include them in container plantings, either because of their weediness or resistance to being transplanted. But *A. curassavica*, a South American member usually grown as an annual, makes a fine container plant, and it too can provide for our sometimes beleaguered winged co-inhabitants of the planet while pleasing our eyes and minds.

Called by any or all of its common names, *A. curassavica* (named after the island of Curaçao, of orange liqueur fame) requires some introduction before being grown successfully. Likes its aforementioned kin, it sulks if transplanted beyond its youth, so try to incorporate plants into your containers be-

fore they are 1 ft. tall, at most. They grow tall and lanky if not cut back when young, don't bloom heavily, attract brilliant orange aphids, and go to seed easily. If you're looking for something in the league of flower-smothered petunias and marigolds, read no further.

For those of you still with me, here's why I grow *A. curassavica*: it's different. It adds variety. The hotly colored flowers are fascinating. I like the little fruit and the remarkably fish-scale-like arrangement of the seeds within, and I like watching these dance in the breeze as they emerge from their pods on their silky parachutes. I find satisfaction in knowing that the plants harbor those abundant but basically harmless orange aphids that feed ladybugs and little insectivorous birds who dart back and forth from the plants to their perches. But most of all, I'm thrilled when I find any white-, black-, and yellow-striped monarch caterpillars munching on their foliage. Ever since childhood, I've loved to watch those eating machines grow large, pupate (upside down), and emerge as regal orange and black butterflies. Even now, I'll put a few caterpil-

This photo doesn't show blood flower's gangly, open habit, or the orange aphids that often cluster abundantly on the stems, or the monarch butterfly larvae that can munch its foliage. Grow *Asclepias curassavica* and see for yourself. The bugs won't hurt the plants or you, and you might feel a little greener.

lars and leafy stems in a large covered jar (with holes punched in the lid) and safely raise a few to adulthood. I hope they've all made it to their southern wintering grounds, far away from here, and then returned north to start another generation.

Cultural tips: Transplant when small. Pinch plants back before they reach 1 ft. Expect the aphids to appear, and please consider leaving them be.

ASPARAGUS

asparagus fern; foxtail fern (*A. densiflorus* 'Myersii'); emerald feather, feather fern, emerald fern (*A. densiflorus* 'Sprengeri'); climbing asparagus fern (*A. setaceus*)

Family: Asparagaceae/Liliaceae
Cultural group: perennials, climbers and trailers
  (*A. setaceus*)
Height: 1–3 ft.; *A. setaceus*, indefinite
Width: 1–3 ft.; *A. setaceus*, depends on training
Light: partial shade
Temperature: warm
Overwintering: min. 45°F, water occasionally, bright light
  (*A. densiflorus*); hardy in Z10–11 (*A. setaceus*)
Moisture: moderate
Drainage of medium: well drained
Fertility: low to average
Ease/speed of growth: easy to moderate/slow to moderate
Propagation: division
Problems: rare in my experience, though books list a
  plethora
Principal interest: foliage, form
Length of seasonal interest: all year

Design attributes

Color: rich, lively shades of green
Line: upward-arching in *A. densiflorus* 'Myersii'; less obvious
  in *A. densiflorus* 'Sprengeri'; long, graceful lines
  (*A. setaceus*)
Form: explosive (*A. densiflorus* 'Myersii'); shrubby (*A. densi-
  florus* 'Sprengeri'); depends on training (*A. setaceus*)
Space: between the tails and feathers (*A. densiflorus*
  types); everywhere, if trained loosely (*A. setaceus*)
Texture: fine to medium (*A. densiflorus* types); stupefyingly
  fine (*A. setaceus*)

I didn't like asparagus as a kid, but of course I learned to like it as my taste buds became more educated. The same might be said about the way many gardeners acquire a taste for less flashy but truly useful foliage plants (such as asparagus ferns, conveniently for this entry) after they cut their horticultural teeth on more colorful, flower-laden temptations.

What's so satisfying about the genus *Asparagus*? Let's go through our five design elements, shall we? Yes, they are green, but their soothing shades combine beautifully with just about any color. All seem to be almost nothing but lines gathered together into very appealing arching, clumping, and climbing forms, and all incorporate interesting spaces within them to varying degrees. Texturally they are all quite fine, bringing to mind feathers and clouds and mist. But on a more sensory/sensual level, asparagus ferns strike me as just plain soft and fuzzy and warm, going beyond the visual realm and entering the world of association and memory and limbic connections to the past. Perhaps asparagus ferns do nothing like this for you, but I bet there are other plants that make you think about other places and times as you interact with them.

While the tail-like and cloudy (respectively 'Myersii' and 'Sprengeri') selections of *A. densiflorus* look best when grown as monopots, *A. setaceus* goes both ways, gracefully weaving frost patterns among other plants in combopots or covering its monopot support frame with a smoky haze.

The climbing foliage of *Asparagus setaceus* is made up of impossibly fine, extremely divided bits. Small plants cast a green mist over their companions, while a large specimen plant suggests an earthbound, emerald cloud. Kept too dry, it will suggest famine and death.

No, you're not looking at a true fern, but *Asparagus densiflorus* 'Myersii' certainly looks "ferny." Asparagus ferns thrive in containers, often attaining impressive size and age, and they look especially attractive in subtly colorful pots, such as this one.

A softly colored pot and some equally quiet, gray Spanish moss makes a suitable "frame" for this *Aspidistra elatior* 'Milky Way'. Look for splashed and lined selections, too, all of which will develop their full beauty in partially shaded spots.

Obsessive collector alert: there's a variant of *A. densiflorus* 'Myersii' that produces all-white "tails" among the usual green ones. If you see one, grab it. If the white turns brown (usually from too much sun), move the plant to a shadier spot.

Cultural tips: *A. densiflorus* selections store water in nifty structures that look like little white sweet potatoes and so can tolerate quite a bit of drought. On the other hand, *A. setaceus* shows less tolerance and will drop a torrent of its little green "hairs" if allowed to get too dry.

ASPIDISTRA
cast-iron plant (*A. elatior*)

Family: Convallariaceae/Liliaceae
Cultural group: perennials
Height: 2–3 ft.
Width: 1 ft. to indefinite (used as groundcovers where hardy)
Light: shade
Temperature: cool to warm to hot

Overwintering: min. 45°F, water occasionally, bright light; hardy in Z7–10
Moisture: moderate
Drainage of medium: well drained
Fertility: low to average
Ease/speed of growth: easy/slow to moderate
Propagation: division
Problems: tip burn, maybe mealybugs and spider mites, owners expiring before they do
Principal interest: foliage
Length of seasonal interest: all year

Design attributes
Color: leaves dark green, some with attractive cream or white variegation
Line: pronounced, from petioles to blades; even more so in those with linear variegation
Form: dense and active to downright agitated
Space: not much except for younger plants
Texture: medium

Without a doubt, these plants deserve the common name of cast-iron plant. They look nothing like a big piece of metal, but they do have cast-iron constitutions, able to tolerate dark, cold, sometimes fume-laden Victorian parlors as well as more modern but equally challenging settings. They will slowly but surely grow into a congested mass in the same pot for years until the roots break a clay pot or weirdly malform a plastic one. The darkest spot won't deter them, nor will periods of cold into the 30s. Too-dry potting mix will lead to brown leaf tips, but they can be trimmed off with no damage to the leaves. Do keep them out of strong sun, which is to a cast-iron plant what sunlight is to a vampire. While they look most impressive as a dense (eventually claustrophobic-looking) monopot, a smaller piece excised from a large clump lends a strong linear presence to a combopot.

Cultural tips: The variegated selections (most of which, often bearing poetic Japanese names, are not easy to track down, except for *A. elatior* 'Milky Way') appreciate a bit more light than the all-green species, but be on the lookout for those brown leaf tips if given too much light. Give them a break and divide congested clumps periodically (about every five years or so). Any slugs you see might be pollinating the soil-level flowers.

ASPLENIUM
bird's-nest fern (*Aa. antiquum* and *nidus*);
mother fern (*A. bulbiferum*); hart's-tongue fern
(*A. scolopendrium*)

Family: Aspleniaceae
Cultural group: tropicals, perennials (*A. scolopendrium*)
Height: 6 in. to 3 ft., maybe more
Width: 1–3 ft.
Light: partial shade to shade
Temperature: cool to warm
Overwintering: tropicals min. 50°F, water occasionally, bright light; hardy in Z6–8 (*A. scolopendrium*)
Moisture: moderate to ample
Drainage of medium: well drained
Fertility: low to average
Ease/speed of growth: easy to moderate/moderate to fast
Propagation: division, spores
Problems: scale insects, mealybugs, high birth rate per capita (*A. bulbiferum*)
Principal interest: foliage
Length of seasonal interest: all year

Design attributes
Color: shades of green
Line: immediately obvious in all but *A. bulbiferum*
Form: vase-shaped (*Aa. antiquum* and *nidus*); arching-shrubby (*A. bulbiferum*); like a bunch of knife blades (*A. scolopendrium*)
Space: plenty, especially in the center of the foliage (*Aa. antiquum* and *nidus*); random (*A. bulbiferum*); at edges of clump (*A. scolopendrium*)
Texture: medium to coarse (*Aa. antiquum* and *nidus*); fine (*A. bulbiferum*); medium (*A. scolopendrium*)

You can't pigeonhole members of the genus *Asplenium*. Some hail from the tropics, so they dependably turn black at the first hint of frost and grow quite large (or barely reach 1 ft. in height). Others survive underground through Z3 winters (which can see the mercury fall to -40°F) and maybe reach 2 ft. or so. Also, some of them don't look any more like a bird's nest than you or I do (I'm assuming certain things here).

Let's deal with the hardy ones first. Grow them in containers if you please, but don't expect any birds to be compelled to take up immediate residence in them. Diminutive *A. ceterach* (rustyback fern, Z5–8), compact *A. platyneuron* (ebony spleenwort, Z3–9), and elfin *A. trichomanes* (maidenhair spleenwort, Z5–8) all have the classic "ferny" look with lots of little bits (pinnae) arranged along a central stalk (rachis), while the relatively towering, 2-ft. *A. scolopendrium* (hart's-tongue fern, Z6–8) bears elongated, uncomplicated fronds that certainly resemble a tongue, hart's or otherwise. Give them all the same treatment you would any hardy herbaceous perennial in a monopot or carefully considered combopot.

I believe the tropical and subtropical ones offer the most potential for container gardeners, however. Mother fern (*A. bulbiferum*, Z8–11), aka mother spleenwort (which sounds like an epithet for an evil fairy-tale character to me) and hen-and-chicks fern, looks "ferny" and lush, but the fun begins when you realize it bears little plants on the fronds. They provide fascination for kids (of all ages) and readily drop into their

A simple pot lets the architectural beauty of a bird's-nest fern (such as this *Asplenium antiquum* 'Victoria') shine forth. These ferns can also play starring roles in combopots, stealing the scene from less eye-catching plants. Do you see a flying bird instead of its nest here?

own or neighboring pots to make plenty of new mothers. The babies reach at least 2 ft. in a fairly short time.

But it's the bird's-nest types that attract the most attention. The photograph shows the typical form, which in time adds a stalk that lifts the nest up into even more prominence. Feature any of them as a monopot or accompanied by a simple ground-cover or more elaborate set of companions in a combopot. Even better, group several monopots of different kinds together for an energetic tableau. *A. nidus*, by far the most familiar of the group, makes large nests (eventually at least 3 ft. tall), the fronds plain and flat to wildly rippled or slashed. Also worth a try are *A. australasicum*, a mansion of a bird's nest, and *A. antiquum*, which looks more like a nice little bird bungalow, at least for a while. Ferns and people being what they are, you can find plenty of other species and selections with a little effort. They're all worth a good home (or nest, if you will).

Cultural tips: Provide plenty of moisture; some of the more tender ones can be grown epiphytically without any potting mix (or pot, for that matter) if kept sufficiently wet and humid. As with many other ferns, most pesticides damage them. If you see scale insects or other critters taking up residence, try carefully scraping them off before testing a mild insecticidal soap on a small area of the plant.

AUCUBA
Japanese laurel, spotted laurel, gold-dust plant

Family: Aucubaceae
Cultural group: woody shrubs and trees
Height: 2–4 ft.
Width: 2–4 ft.
Light: sun (fully green forms) to partial shade to shade (heavily variegated forms)
Temperature: cool to warm to hot
Overwintering: min. 50°F, water occasionally, bright light; hardy in Z6–10
Moisture: moderate to ample but tolerates some drought
Drainage of medium: well drained
Fertility: low to average
Ease/speed of growth: easy/moderate
Propagation: cuttings
Problems: root rot, leaf spots
Principal interest: foliage, fruit (on female plants)
Length of seasonal interest: all year

Design attributes
Color: shiny green leaves, many variegated yellow
Line: not much; some linear presence in elongated leaves
Form: shrubby, neatly rounded mounds or more irregular
Space: not much
Texture: medium to coarse

Yes, Japanese laurels are shrubs, and they can grow to 10 ft. or so in the open ground: I remember my first look at a berry-bearing, variegated *A. japonica* selection sugared with snow at the Morris Arboretum in Philadelphia. But I've observed smaller plants in nursery containers at Atlock Farm over the past couple of years, and they've tolerated all sorts of conditions, including drought and winter cold. A specimen grown in a reasonably large monopot has the potential to make an attractive mass of foliage, especially the excitedly yellow-splashed ones. They'll tolerate a low plant decorating their feet, but I would caution against doing *Aucuba* in a combopot unless said pot is *quite* roomy.

As with hollies (*Ilex*), most aucubas bear either male or female flowers, and females have a good chance of bearing red fruit in fall if males are nearby and in bloom at the same time (and pollinators are available and willing to bring the potential parents together). Both male and female selections are either all-green or variegated, and some offer variations on the basic roughly oval leaf shape.

Shrubby gold-dust plants, whether plain green (therefore lacking the dust) or any of the many variegated selections, make solid additions to container plantings. Make sure you give them roomy containers and are prepared to protect them over winter (where necessary) if you want to watch a small plant grow impressively large.

'Crotonifolia', a female with yellow-splashed foliage, is one of the more widely seen selections. 'Gold Dust' and 'Variegata', also female, resemble it.

'Lance Leaf' (male) and 'Salicifolia' (female) produce elongated, unmarked foliage.

'Picturata', a female, stands out from the crowd by virtue of the large yellow marks in the center of her leaves.

Cultural tips: Provide extra winter protection in Z6, where plants are often marginally hardy in the ground, much less in a pot. Remove reverted (all-green or atypical) shoots on variegated selections before they outgrow the rest of the plant.

BACOPA
water hyssop

Family: Scrophulariaceae
Cultural group: annuals, climbers and trailers
Height: 3–4 in.
Width: depends on training
Light: sun to partial shade
Temperature: warm to hot
Overwintering: not usually; hardy in Z9–10
Moisture: moderate to ample
Drainage of medium: well drained
Fertility: average
Ease/speed of growth: easy/moderate
Propagation: cuttings, seeds
Problems: none in my experience
Principal interest: flowers, form (if trained)
Length of seasonal interest: long

A hanging basket of a white-flowered bacopa reminds me of constellations of stars against a green night sky. Even a small plant can evoke stellar images. The pink-, blue-, and lavender-flowered selections require a bit more effort to see stars, however.

Design attributes
Color: white (or pink, blue, or lavender) flowers against fresh green foliage
Line: pronounced if allowed to hang or trail
Form: method of growth determines final shape
Space: suggested by flowers against the green background
Texture: medium

These plants have been traveling under both *Bacopa* and *Sutera* for a while now. *Sutera* may well win out, but since I've seen them more frequently as *Bacopa* (*B. monnieri*, a traditional Ayurvedic herb used to boost memory, learning, and concentration, is all over the Web) and that genus name often does double duty as a common name, I'm sticking with *Bacopa*.

Feature bacopas in a big, lush hanging basket, or include them with one to several other plants in a roomy basket or earthbound container. I'm most familiar with *B. cordata* 'Snowflake', but I see there's a new and improved selection called 'Snowstorm', reportedly producing bigger flowers on a more vigorous plant. Look for it (I will). If a pink snowstorm sounds appealing to you, give 'Scopia Great Pink Ring' a try. The large (I don't know about "great") flowers are quite pink and seem even pinker when grown alongside the white bacopas. Bacopas with lavender, blue, and purple flowers are popping up, too, and look promising.

Cultural tips: Try them as groundcovers instead of hangers or cascaders. Promote heavier bloom by using a "bloom-booster" fertilizer.

BEGONIA
begonia, often accompanied by an adjective according to type: angel-wing, rex, rhizomatous, cane-stemmed, tuberous, shrublike, fibrous-rooted (aka wax, bedding, and semperflorens), species

Family: Begoniaceae
Cultural group: annuals, bulbs, tropicals
Height: 6 in. to 5 ft.
Width: 6 in. to 4 ft.
Light: sun to partial shade to shade
Temperature: warm to hot
Overwintering: min. 50°F, water occasionally (allow the surface of the medium to dry), bright light; tuberous begonias can be kept totally dormant at 50–60°F, very little to no water, light not necessary, potted in their growing medium
Moisture: moderate to ample, but allow the surface of the medium to dry slightly
Drainage of medium: well drained

Fertility: low to average (to high, if you want to produce
    showstopping specimens)
Ease/speed of growth: easy to challenging/slow to fast
Propagation: division (of tubers), cuttings, seeds
Problems: leaf, stem, and root rots, overwatering,
    mealybugs, thrips, mildew
Principal interest: foliage, flowers, form
Length of seasonal interest: long to all year

Design attributes

Color: flowers in white, red, pink, orange, and yellow; foli-
    age (often metallic) in endless shades and patterns of
    green, red, yellow, dark purple, brown, pink, and white
Line: almost absent (fibrous-rooted) to powerfully appar-
    ent (cane-stemmed); upright, arching, and cascading
    from stems, petioles, and pedicels; many rounded to
    spiraling and animated (rhizomatous)
Form: mounded-shrubby (many) to upright-massive to
fountainlike to stratified to weeping to totally individu-
    alistic (foliage often starlike, winglike, or spiraling)
Space: not their strongest suit; some spatial interest along
    stems or within foliage and flowers, or in more open-
    growing cane-stemmed, shrublike, and species begonias
Texture: medium to coarse

How do I love begonias? Shall I recount the ways? The sight
of them conjures up images of the tropics and Roberto
Burle Marx's fantastic gardens in Brazil. The range of colors
offered by their foliage and flowers is enormous; blue wasn't
invited, but just about everyone else was (I'll let the photographs here do a lot of the advocating). It's true that most begonia flowers are a bit plainly formed, but the clusters often
embody *abbondanza*, and some individual flowers rival the
voluptuousness of roses and camellias. A few are even fragrant, believe it or not ('Tea Rose', for proof). Their wide variety
of cultural preferences and challenges holds my interest (as
well as plenty of other people's; witness the large membership

The big, angular leaves of *Begonia* 'Guy Savard' and other angel-
wing begonias bring active movement to container plantings.
Those markings are silver, by the way, not white: shiny, metallic
silver is a rare color, valuable for "lighting up" shady spots. Does
this make you think of a mass of young trout at a hatchery
feeding frenzy?

Begonia 'Lotusland' offers a study in contrast between its big,
bold, coarse foliage and little, shy, fine-textured bursts of
flowers. Enjoy the flowers while you can: this and many other
rhizomatous begonias bloom only once a year, but you can
appreciate the foliage year-round if you overwinter the plants.

of the American Begonia Society). Finally, they remind me that even "uncool" members of a genus offer certain charms when used creatively. Have you ever seen a wall covered with old-fashioned fibrous-rooted begonias?

Start with these, in fact: they are plain but forgiving. Then graduate to the splendid 'Dragon Wings' selections, essentially fibrous-rooted begonias times ten. Then try your hand at the cane-stemmed sorts, which grow tall and lush—resembling bamboo—and tolerate a severe chopping back if the stems get too tall and bare at the base. Some make flower clusters as big as a baby's head. After you've killed your share of them but also savored some success (that's good gardening in a nutshell, after all), take the plunge into the tantalizing world of the rhizomatous begonias, where diversity (and challenge) rules supreme. Solomon in all his glory was never arrayed like many of these. Finally, see how many of the species, shrubby, and tuberous beauties you can handle before stating, "My name is _____ , and I collect begonias."

In my youthful innocence, I began with tuberous begonias—you know, the zaftig, full-petaled, rose-like confections in non-gourmet jelly bean colors. I was fascinated by the vaguely hairy brown tubers (they looked to me like weird, flat potatoes); I barely covered them with some sort of bagged potting mix in a roomy clay pot and placed it in the shady part of our backyard. Pink protostems erupted from the mix, turned green, and made big leaves but no flower buds—and then the plants rotted off at the soil line and toppled over. I had committed the Big Mistake of begonia culture: keeping the potting mix too wet. Learn from my childhood experience: err on the dry side with begonias. They are not one of them bog plants.

Monopot or combopot? Try both. Experiment. Fail. Succeed. Be a gardener.

Cultural tips: *Don't overwater them.* Begonias tolerate considerable cold while being overwintered—sometimes to 50°F—if kept on the dry side. Most do very well in a few hours of early morning sun, although the fibrous-rooted stalwarts will thrive in full sun if kept moist enough (there's a tightrope

You can grow a pot this size of *Begonia* 'Dragon Wings Pink' from seed in a single growing season if you start the seeds early enough. Believe me, I did, and it bloomed like this one for months. Three plants in at least a 12-in. pot (and plenty of water and fertilizer) should do the trick.

The voluptuous, mouthwateringly colored blooms of tuberous begonias (*Begonia* ×*tuberhybrida*) are worth all the effort. Grow them by themselves as monopots and scatter them around wherever you'd like to stimulate appetites or envy.

Above: Metallic-looking *Begonia* 'Benitochiba' stands out against green ferns. I'd like to see this specimen in a dark blue or dark green pot, where its coloration wouldn't compete with the feisty oranges of the terracotta.

to walk!). Most take all the high humidity thrown at them in summer (especially the rhizomatous types), but damp, still air at other times can lead to mildew and other afflictions. Use an open, organic potting mix, and keep the fertilizer analyses relatively low (except for those fibrous-rooted begonias again; they can grow in clay soil and feed heavily). Let tuberous begonias, including the magnificent 'Bonfire', go totally dry and stem/leafless and remain that way until spring. They'll show you when it's time to resume the game.

BERGENIA
pigsqueak, elephant ear (another one!), leather cabbages, picnic plates

Family: Saxifragaceae
Cultural group: perennials
Height: 8 in. (foliage) to 2 ft. (in flower)
Width: 8–18 in.
Light: sun to partial shade
Temperature: cool to warm

Whether a breeze is blowing or not, the elongated, curved flowers and foliage of *Begonia* 'Bonfire' appear to be in constant motion, and that fiery color carries across a garden. Even small plants with just one stem bring tongues of fire to a combopot. A specimen can bring to mind, well, a bonfire.

A line of bergenias makes an out-of-the-ordinary windowbox composition. Be sure a bergenia or any plant is normally hardy to at least one zone colder than your area if you plan on exposing it to winter conditions outdoors. The roots are often less able to handle the cold than the tops.

Overwintering: variously hardy in Z3–8
Moisture: moderate
Drainage of medium: well drained
Fertility: low to average
Ease/speed of growth: easy/slow to moderate
Propagation: division
Problems: leaf spots, slugs and snails
Principal interest: foliage, flowers
Length of seasonal interest: all year (foliage, except in hard winters, when it might die back); brief (flowers)

Design attributes

Color: foliage in rich green, red, and purple (often glossy); flowers white, pink, red, and red-violet
Line: strong line from flower stems
Form: irregularly mounded to amorphous inflorescences subtly echo foliage shape
Space: around flower stems
Texture: coarse

Winter container gardening is all the rage here in the greater Delaware Valley area. We embrace zonal denial, shake our fists in the face of Old Man Winter, and plant our pots up with deciduous hollies, osmanthus, conifers, hellebores, sedges, bulbs, and other plants that offer winter interest. Along with the rise of interest in winter container gardening, so has my interest in the genus *Bergenia* risen—from approaching zero to going up, if not meteorically then at least steadily. I remember when the genus was the darling of the gardening literati and cognoscenti, but I never joined the ranks of the bandwagoni. Bergenia's habit was too open and coarse for my taste; the plants looked like a drove of pigs might have lost their way and stomped over them, and I pigheadedly refused to see the virtues of their "lipstick on a pig" flowers.

But that was then. Now I'm happy to write that pigsqueaks have caught my eye. Perhaps I've grown to embrace anything that looks alive—often shiny and very colorfully attired in shades of red, bronze, and purple, even—in the middle of winter (the spring blooms, while pretty, seem like a bit player compared to the abundant foliage). Or maybe I've given them another chance to win me over. By all means give pigsqueaks a thought if you practice winter container gardening.

Why "pigsqueak"? If you rub a leaf just right with your slightly wet thumb and forefinger, you might coax a little squeal from both the leaf and anyone else who happens to be near you.

Which ones to grow? I suggest you start with 'Solar Flare' with yellow-variegated green foliage (pink-edged in winter) and bright red-violet flowers. Those with Bressingham in their cultivar name will probably prove satisfactory (Blooms of Bressingham has given us many good plants), as will any with German-sounding names, such as 'Abendglut' (Evening Glow), 'Glockenturm' (Bell Tower), 'Morgenröte' (Morning Red), 'Purpurkönigin' (Purple Queen), 'Rotblum' (Red Flower), and 'Winterglut' (Winter Glow), considering they come from a country whose citizens know a thing or two about getting through winter.

Cultural tips: Don't overfertilize bergenias or grow them in too much shade, which leads to flabby, floppy growth and reduces their winter coloration. Be patient if they look bedraggled during hot, dry periods; they'll perk up later, and the stress might actually improve their winter coloration. About the only cultural condition they won't tolerate is poor drainage. Plant them closely in containers for a fuller, more satisfying display.

BETA

beet, beet green, beetroot (*B. vulgaris*); Swiss chard (var. *cicla* or Cicla Group)

Family: Chenopodiaceae
Cultural group: annuals
Height: 6 in. to 2 ft.
Width: 6 in. to 2 ft.
Light: sun to limited partial shade
Temperature: cool to warm
Overwintering: no, unless you want to see it flower
Moisture: moderate to ample
Drainage of medium: well drained
Fertility: average to high (nitrogen to push growth)
Ease/speed of growth: easy/moderate to fast
Propagation: seeds
Problems: caterpillars, leaf miners, leaf spots, mildew, root rots (and bolting if too dry and/or hot)
Principal interest: foliage
Length of seasonal interest: moderate

Design attributes

Color: green to red-purple foliage (beets); red, red-violet, yellow, orange, or white petioles (Swiss chard)
Line: leaves radiate out or up

Eat your (container-grown) vegetables! The multicolored Swiss chard *Beta vulgaris* var. *cicla* 'Rainbow' can be harvested when tastefully small or allowed to grow larger and more visually assertive. Doesn't that pepper look a little lonely hanging there?

Form: bunchy-mounded to vase-shaped
Space: not much
Texture: medium to coarse

As we grow up, we learn to appreciate the stronger flavors of certain vegetables. As gardeners we make the same progression, from the sweet but often fleeting seduction of flowers to the more substantial and long-lasting charms of foliage. Growing (and eating) beets and other ornamental vegetables is therefore an opportunity for us to prove our maturity on two different fronts.

Yes, beets can be beautiful. The dark-veined foliage of most beets grown primarily for their edible roots (*B. vulgaris*) is reasonably eye-catching, but a few selections offer sumptuously dark, shiny foliage that combines beautifully with a great many other foliage and floral colors. Even more colorful is the taller and lusher Swiss chard (*B. vulgaris* var. *cicla*) and its selections (cultivars in the Cicla Group), whose leaf stalks add an unexpected stroke of genius to container plantings. Look

Most beets produce green leaves with dark stems, which are arguably attractive, but most people would agree that the foliage of *Beta vulgaris* 'Bull's Blood' puts on a much more memorable show. The combination of the rich purple with the electrified pink schizanthus above it (and the gray pot beneath) can't be beat!

BIDENS
fern-leaved beggar's ticks, burr marigold
(*B. ferulifolia*)

Family: Asteraceae
Cultural group: annuals
Height: 8–12 in.
Width: 1–2 ft. or more
Light: sun
Temperature: warm to hot
Overwintering: not usually; hardy in Z(8)9–10
Moisture: moderate to ample
Drainage of medium: well drained
Fertility: average
Ease/speed of growth: easy to moderate/moderate
Propagation: seeds
Problems: a plethora of leaf troubles in the books—
    I haven't seen them
Principal interest: flowers, foliage
Length of seasonal interest: long

Design attributes
Color: golden yellow flowers
Line: pendulous stems curve gently; foliage offers lots of
    little lines
Form: loose mass; distinctive starlike flowers
Space: quite a bit
Texture: fine

for 'Bull's Blood' beet and 'MacGregor's Favorite', which looks like a cross between a Swiss chard and a red-leaved beet to me. 'Ruby' and 'Rhubarb' chards (sometimes seen as common names) are red-stemmed. 'Rainbow' Swiss chard offers a broad mix of stem colors.

All are technically biennials, giving their best the first year and then bolting to less-than-exciting bloom in the second (sometimes the first if grossly mistreated). All are edible at some point during their lives. Grow (and eat) your vegetables!

Cultural tips: Encourage abundant leaf production by providing plenty of nitrogen. Leaf color and sturdy, erect growth decrease with increased shade. The "seeds" are actually multi-seeded fruits that will produce clusters of multiple plants unless separated by hand before planting. Keeping them together automatically produces a denser foliage display.

There's much to be learned from a scientific name, provided you know the parts and their meanings. For instance, *Bi-dens feruli-folia* literally means "two-tooth ferula-leaf." "Two-tooth" works for the whole genus, the seeds of which bear two fur- or cloth-adhering points, or teeth (the common names are references to those teeth). The "ferula-leaf" part harkens to this particular plant's foliar resemblance to *Ferula* species (giant fennel, *F. communis*, and others).

Many bidens are weeds, vigorous in growth and liberal in seed production but sometimes quite attractive. I pull plenty of them in my garden every year but always leave a few to admire in bloom and to provide a bit of bird food. The ones at hand in this entry, *B. ferulifolia* and its selections, behave like good citizens and won't try to take over your garden. They drape and weave attractively in any container setting, but their all-season, golden daisies and finely cut foliage look especially fetching in combopot hanging baskets, standing out no matter how many companions surround them. I've seen 'Golden Goddess', a free-blooming sort, but you might also find 'Bidi Compact', 'Golden Flame', 'Goldie', 'Goldmarie', 'Peter's Gold Carpet', 'Samsara', 'Solaire Compact Yellow', and others in catalogs and online.

Opposite: The sunny, starry flowerheads of *Bidens ferulifolia* can't be missed in this complicated assemblage. Yellow and gold (and bleached-clean white) are the colors that stand out dependably in the garden.

Cultural tips: The more sun, the more flowers. Occasional applications of a water-soluble bloom-boosting fertilizer will reap rewards.

BLECHNUM
hard fern

Family: Blechnaceae
Cultural group: tropicals
Height: 1–2 ft.
Width: 1–2 ft.
Light: partial shade to shade

Temperature: warm to hot
Overwintering: min. 50°F, water regularly but not excessively, bright light; generally hardy in Z10–11
Moisture: moderate to ample
Drainage of medium: well drained but tolerates standing water
Fertility: average
Ease/speed of growth: moderate/slow to moderate
Propagation: spores (if you're really dedicated), buying a plant
Problems: mealybugs
Principal interest: foliage, form
Length of seasonal interest: all year

Design attributes
Color: various shades of green (with red in some)
Line: energetic upward and outward, and the fronds are almost purely linear

Blechnum brasiliense emerges in an energy-filled rush from the base of this combopot, its younger, reddish fronds subtly picking up the dark, strappy foliage of the phormium and the rim of the pot. Also note how the little bit of blue-gray foliage near the lower left of this beautifully framed photograph echoes the mass of it in the upper right, and how the dark blue pot repeats the dark shadows of that big blue-gray cloud.

A small specimen of *Blechnum brasiliense* 'Silver Lady' (dwarf tree fern) associates pleasantly with a self-sown, fine-textured *Pilea microphylla*. Which one is more ferny in texture, the fern or the pretender?

Form: vase, to vase on a thick stick—or a martini glass
Space: plenty around "stem" and within foliage
Texture: medium

Such an unpleasant-sounding name ("blecch-numb") for such appealing-looking plants! However, some references point out that members of the genus harbor a degree of toxicity, so maybe the "blecch" part is apropos. In any case, I'll continue to appreciate the resemblance of some species and selections to tree ferns and to value them for their much smaller stature compared to *Cibotium*, *Cyathea*, *Dicksonia*, and their kin. Those of us who lack the cubic footage to grow even a young tree fern can probably accommodate a blechnum or two, admiring them all the more as their form morphs from nest to feather duster.

Because of their abundant design attributes, blechnums serve equally well in a monopot or a combopot. They often do their best when kept in standing water, though, so choose similarly tolerant companions. Of the several available species, I suggest you try *B. brasiliense*, whose new fronds emerge red and turn green, and the similar *B. gibbum*. 'Silver Lady', a miniature form of *B. brasiliense* (or *B. gibbum*), has an animated appearance and an unflagging vigor.

Cultural tips: Don't keep hard ferns wet in winter, but don't let them get too dry, either, especially young specimens. Try not to manhandle the roots when potting them up into an acidic, open potting mix. Some people are convinced that periodic dousings of cold tea help the plants—I suppose the tannic acid couldn't hurt.

BOEHMERIA
false nettle (they won't sting!)

Family: Urticaceae
Cultural group: perennials
Height: 1–3 ft.
Width: 1–3 ft.
Light: sun to partial shade
Temperature: warm to hot
Overwintering: min. 50°F, water occasionally, bright light;

Staring at this bird's-eye view into the center of a larger 'Silver Lady' might induce vertigo. Are you falling into the depths of the fronds, or is everything rushing out at you from a central point?

The bold foliage of *Boehmeria platanifolia* brings not-so-subtle interest to container plantings, provided you can get beyond its "weedy" first impression. Just look at those cutleaf edges and red petioles: there's plenty of color and activity going on here.

hardy in Z4–8(9) (*B. platanifolia*), Z6–9
  (*B. nipononivea* 'Kogane-mushi')
Moisture: moderate to ample
Drainage of medium: well drained
Fertility: average
Ease/speed of growth: easy/moderate to fast
  (*B. nipononivea* 'Kogane-mushi' slower)
Propagation: division, cuttings; seeds (*B. platanifolia*)
Problems: spider mites, whitefly
Principal interest: foliage
Length of seasonal interest: long

Design attributes

Color: foliage green, sometimes marked with white or
  cream; red petioles on *B. platanifolia*
Line: from stems, petioles, teeth on leaves
Form: shrubby
Space: ample throughout (*B. platanifolia*); limited but
  implied (*B. nipononivea* 'Kogane-mushi')
Texture: coarse (*B. platanifolia*); medium (*B. nipononivea*
  'Kogane-mushi')

Who needs flowers? The endlessly changing display of creams
and greens on the leaves of *Boehmeria nipononivea* 'Kogane-
mushi' are plenty colorful, while the spiraled leaves provide
some circular action and the long petioles suggest even more
movement.

Sometimes you've got to go against traffic and swim up-
stream to lead the pack. I'm violating the rule against mixing metaphors to make a point: you're not going to discover,
much less enjoy, new plants unless you open your eyes to
them and try them under your particular conditions. Like
their relative, the fiber-producing *B. nivea* (ramie), both taxa
presented here are not prized for their flowers (their membership in the Urticaceae, or nettle family, pretty much sees to
that). But their foliage, albeit "weedy" to many, does offer
certain charms to those who are willing to break from the
herd. A species that first intrigued me in my Morris Arboretum days (in its variety *megaphylla*), *B. platanifolia* offers
striking dark pink petioles on a vigorously growing, shrubby
mound; it reseeds gently in my open garden, and I'm always
glad to see a few of those "weeds" returning in spring. *B. nipononivea* 'Kogane-mushi' ("gold bug" in Japanese) slowly but
surely produces an attractive mass of leaves that emerge covered with creamy gold, turning completely medium to dark
green in time.

Cultural tips: Don't coddle them; they don't need abundant
fertilizer or water. While relatively hardy, 'Kogane-mushi' is
best overwintered in a warmish spot and appreciates a spot
out of strong sun. *B. platanifolia* can take full sun.

BOUGAINVILLEA
paper flower

Family: Nyctaginaceae
Cultural group: climbers and trailers
Height: to 6 ft. (much more in time, especially if left
  unpruned)
Width: depends on training
Light: sun and plenty of it
Temperature: warm to hot
Overwintering: min. 40°F, water occasionally, bright light
  (will probably drop leaves); generally hardy in Z9–11
Moisture: moderate
Drainage of medium: well drained
Fertility: average
Ease/speed of growth: moderate/moderate to fast
Propagation: cuttings, root suckers
Problems: whitefly, spider mites, leaf spots
Principal interest: flowers (bracts, actually), foliage
  (variegated selections)
Length of seasonal interest: moderate to long

Design attributes

Color: floral bracts in white, pink, red, red-violet, yellow,
  and orange; foliage green, sometimes variegated
  with cream
Line: branches cascade and twist

Form: bushy to rangy, depending on pruning
Space: not readily apparent unless intentionally created
Texture: medium

MAGENTA (sorry if the all-caps treatment frightened you), admittedly a potent color when saturated and a bit nauseating when washed out, isn't the easiest color to work with. But if you're looking to make a statement about the visual and emotional power of color, I invite you to experiment with the M word, and orange, and—bougainvilleas. For the color-venturesome, the genus *Bougainvillea* offers plenty of assertive shades. The color from a bougainvillea derives from the bracts, which are modified leaves associated with flowers (the red "petals" of a poinsettia or the white ones of many dogwoods are other examples of showy bracts). The true flowers are prim little cut-edged white spots, which don't last nearly as long as their extroverted consorts. Grow them as exuberantly spilling masses or as precisely trimmed standard topiaries, but don't be afraid of their colors or what your neigh-

All bougainvilleas evoke the Caribbean and other tropical spots. Most aren't shrinking violets. Shrieking violets, maybe (especially this uncompromisingly magenta selection). Take a deep breath, and then flip back and forth in this book to find other colors this bad boy might play with.

Bougainvilleas can be grown in pots (including small hanging baskets). The bigger the container, the greater the potential floral display, assuming you provide for their cultural needs. Just keep in mind that a big pot needs to be relocated on occasion . . . and you might need a friend or two to accomplish the move.

Not content with flaunting only its fulgent pink-infused orange bracts (the true flower is that shy white fleck), *Bougainvillea* 'Bengal Orange' sets its wild color against variegated foliage. Use with (some) care.

bors and gardening friends might think of them. Who knows, they might have already come over to the Bright Side.

There are plenty of bougainvilleas from which to choose, whether as named or (often) unidentified selections. While browsing at a nursery or admiring them in a garden or golf course/resort of the same name (check out the Web entries!), watch out for the thorns, which catch many people by surprise (white-bracted 'Ms. Alice' and lilac 'Silhouette' peacefully bear no arms). I've been impressed by the following: 'Afterglow' pink-orange, not shy; 'Barbara Karst' in powerful red-violet; 'California Gold' (aka 'Golden Glow' and 'Hawaiian Gold') in light orange; 'Easter Parade' (smoky lilac); 'James Walker' (hot pink); 'Miss Manila' (rich pink); 'New River' (lilac); the perfectly named 'Raspberry Ice'; 'Rosenka' (hot orange); and 'Scarlett O'Hara' (eye-popping, hot red-pink). The strident colors of some, as in 'Bengal Orange', are accompanied by equally vocal (some might say "loud") variegated foliage.

There are some white paper flowers among all this vivid color ('Shubra' would appear even whiter against some of its vibrantly colored kin), double-bracted forms (several beginning with the word "Mahara"), dwarf ones (such as the strong pink 'Helen Johnson'), and even some that bear bracts in two colors, one white and the other a shade of pink or purple ('Surprise' in white and lilac lives up to its name). Combine the pastel ones with more potent paper flowers at your peril.

Cultural tips: These are not plants for anyone who can't control their use of a watering can or hose. Wet bad, dry good, but don't keep bougainvilleas so dry that their evergreen foliage drops off completely. Keeping them potbound for a while and easing up on the fertilizer promotes abundant bloom. They flower on new wood, so chop them back before another growth cycle resumes.

BRASSICA
cabbage, kale, mustard, mizuna (and many more)

Family: Brassicaceae
Cultural group: annuals (sometimes biennials)
Height: 6 in. to 3 ft.
Width: 6 in. to 2 ft.
Light: sun
Temperature: cool (cold, even) to warm
Overwintering: not usually, although many tolerate frost and freezing temperatures well into winter; some will persist to produce moderately interesting flowers in their second year
Moisture: moderate to ample
Drainage of medium: well drained
Fertility: average to high
Ease/speed of growth: easy/fast
Propagation: seeds

Problems: Cabbage loopers, leaf and stem rots, and mineral deficiencies headline a long list of potential problems. Many things like to eat or otherwise interact with cabbage and their kin.
Principal interest: foliage, form, with flowers ranking a distant third
Length of seasonal interest: long

Design attributes
Color: foliage in shades of green, blue, purple, red, pink, red-violet, and white
Line: often most evident in the wavy and crinkled foliage; older plants will show straight or curving, bare stems
Form: precise or very loose rosettes; masses; shrubby-treelike; vase-shaped
Space: around bare stems (sometimes present with age) or between leaves
Texture: medium to coarse; waves and crinkles can suggest finer texture

Everything you see here is eminently edible: the so-called red cabbage (the mature head will appear red in time, and in cole slaw), the frilly green parsley, and the nearly obscured needle-leaved rosemary and yellow-variegated sage. Tasty. Colorful. And a superb study of form and texture.

Cabbage, broccoli, cauliflower, Brussels sprouts, kale, collards, kohlrabi, mustard, mizuna, bok choi, and more: all closely related, all heavy feeders, all good for you to feed on, all easy to grow … but not all the sort of thing you'd want or expect to see in a container garden, right? Wrong. Even a quick look at the photos here should convince you that all five design elements abound in the cabbage patch. Take advantage of their cold tolerance by featuring them in fall, winter, and early spring container plantings; they remain long after the annuals and other boys of summer have gone, and a dusting (or blanket) of snow won't faze many of them. Feed them well, and in turn they'll feed your soul as well as your more basic metabolic needs. A small sampling follows. They all look good enough to eat!

Cabbage: any big so-called red (they're usually more purple and blue in the garden) or Savoy (crinkle-leaved) cabbage looks imposing in a container, either by its monopotted self or in an envelope-pushing combopot. Even young transplants of the big ones (as well as full-grown plants of smaller selec-

tions) are eye-catching; try planting several in a roomy pot and watch what happens. If a plant gets too big for the pot, just eat it.

Ornamental cabbage: yes, those circular two-tone pillows and big flower-like things massed at the entrance of shopping malls and light-industrial parks can make fascinating, pleasant additions to a container garden, especially when featured as monopots. Choose from white, pink, and red-violet with ruffles, crinkles, and lace. The series names of Tokyo, Nagoya, and Osaka indicate the origin of some of the ornamental cabbages worth looking for. Older plants develop noticeable, sturdy-looking stems, which add to their sculptural appeal as they lift the pillows into the air. Take the time to inspect these close up: I dare you not to become lost in thought as you meditate upon their haunting coloration and impossibly complicated form.

Kale: 'Nero di Toscana' (dinosaur kale, aka 'Tuscan Laciniato' or 'Black Palm'—all describe it very evocatively if not precisely) is long-bladed and -petioled; its dark green, waxy-

A shiny blue pot plays off of the blue and purple shades in the cabbage. I like to picture it in a pale yellow pot or a medium to dark green one, too. Or, even better, a light to medium gray one to make the foliage stand out even more assertively.

"Frothy" comes to my mind when I look at a heavily frilled kale. Although coarse, the texture of the foliage is lightened up quite a bit by the frills. Please also notice the angular pattern of the brick surface, made even more obvious by the green "weeds" in between them. Sometimes you should spare the herbicide.

Some kales aren't heavily frilled, but their cut, colorful leaves still catch the eye. (Here, the serious frills are contributed by the bright green parsley.) Note how the square pot picks up on the rectangular bricks and how both contrast with the looser, rounder forms of the plants.

coated leaves build up into plants about 3 ft. tall. More conventional-looking 'Winterbor' (in hypercrinkled blue-green) and 'Winter Red' and 'Red Russian' (both green and red-violet) produce their gorgeous leaves on mounds that build up to 1 ft. or more. If they survive winter, some send up abundant yellow flowers that resemble earthbound showers of sparks.

Mustard and mizuna ("spider mustard"): mustard greens range from plain to intricately frilled and cut. 'Osaka Purple' and 'Red Giant' (aka 'Giant Red') grow big and bold. I think mizuna looks like gigantic, elaborate green crystals.

Cultural tips: Keep in mind the first letter of a fertilizer analysis (N, for nitrogen) when providing for cabbage and their kin. More nitrogen means more foliage, and making foliage is what the leafy brassicas are all about. Colder weather—around freezing and often lower—accentuates the colors (and often the flavors). Keep a sharp eye out for cabbage looper caterpillars and other creatures eager to turn these vegetables into lace or cole slaw without the dressing.

Many cabbage-family kin bloom—in a big way—if they survive to see their second growing season. That tall pot makes both the foliage and the flowers of the kale seem even more rocket-like, don't you think?

The deeply cut, lively green foliage of a mizuna selection offers crystalline textural excitement. Showcase this attribute by featuring it in a simply shaped, sympathetically colored pot.

Mustard greens aren't always green. Some selections are variably tinged with red and/or purple, the better to associate with the red-violet of, for instance, the jewel tones of violas. I'm not wild about the bright blue pot, though—how about you? Cover it up to judge for yourself.

This pot strikes me as more complementary to the red and purple shades of the mustard. It doesn't scream "blue!" but instead serves as a quiet but still visible companion.

BREYNIA

snowbush, foliage-flower, leaf-flower, calico plant, snow on the mountain, sweet-pea bush (*B. disticha*)

Family: Euphorbiaceae
Cultural group: tropicals
Height: 1–3 ft.
Width: 1–3 ft.
Light: limited partial shade
Temperature: warm to hot
Overwintering: min. 60°F, water occasionally, bright light
Moisture: moderate to ample
Drainage of medium: well drained
Fertility: average
Ease/speed of growth: moderate/moderate
Propagation: cuttings
Problems: spider mites; slow decline if overwintered under wrong assumptions

Principal interest: foliage (and soothing rustling when a big plant is shaken)
Length of seasonal interest: all year (if you know how to keep the foliage on the plant)

Design attributes

Color: green with white (sometimes also pink or maroon)
Line: many fine twigs moving up and out
Form: open-bushy (unclipped) to densely bushy (clipped)
Space: limited if unclipped, virtually none if clipped (but the clipped shapes can reveal the space around them)
Texture: fine

I like *B. disticha* because it makes a lush mass of pretty little, white-flecked leaves on wire-like stems, all of which rustle appealingly when shaken or stirred; it can be trained into precisely sheared topiaries (hedges, even) or left to bush out as it will; and it can bring some coolness to other heat-lovers in warm-season combopots. I also like it because it reminds me to remain humble every time I encounter it: I failed with this plant for a few years before I memorably discovered how to overwinter it successfully.

You see, at first I assumed it would tolerate the conditions I provided many other plants in a greenhouse during winter: reduced light and limited water and heat. My first attempt suffered a leafless, sad-looking, protracted demise, but I picked up another one in spring, kept it going nicely until fall, and then—because I assumed my first plant was flawed in some way (not that my approach to growing it could be flawed, certainly!)—gave victim #2 the same treatment. Funny, but #2 died before spring arrived, too. It wasn't until I paid a winter visit to Mrs. Samuel M. V. Hamilton's expansive greenhouses that I was made aware of my stubborn (and obviously incorrect) assumptions about its needs. Mrs. Hamilton's gardeners have maintained a splendid topiary of snowbush for several years, taking many ribbons and other major awards with it at the Philadelphia International Flower Show. Standing in front of it in admiration in a bright, warm greenhouse

in February, I was informed it receives periodic but not excessive, year-round drinks from the hose. Now I know.

Moral of the story: don't make assumptions about a plant's needs. Do a little research, which can take many forms and forums, such as books, magazines, online sources, nursery tags, TV and other electronic media, and (most important of all, I think) interaction with people. Ask your neighbors and gardening friends about the plant. Pose questions at gardening conferences and botanic gardens. Attend flower shows and hope that the owner of the plant in question is standing by his or her plant and might be willing to offer you some personal insight (trust me, it happens).

I've known and enjoyed two snowbushes, namely *B. disticha*, with finely white-spattered foliage, and *B. disticha* f. *nivosa* 'Roseo Picta', which mixes pink paint with the white. A recent online search turned up 'Atropurpurea', which reportedly bears maroon leaves. I bet if I look a little deeper I'll find more selections and also read of their basic needs as well as some tips to keep them happy.

How precise can the head of a standard topiary be? This precise, actually, but only when given some attention. You'd better believe that a superb specimen such as this *Breynia disticha* f. *nivosa* 'Roseo Picta' receives periodic "haircuts" and the other cultural attention it deserves.

When happy, *Breynia disticha* produces refreshingly variegated foliage on almost threadlike stems. When unhappy, all you see are barren stems (and plenty of cast-off leaves under them).

Cultural tips: Keep it warm, evenly moist (not wet), and in a bright spot in winter, as you've read in my confession above. Learn from my mistaken assumptions.

BROWALLIA
bush violet, amethyst flower, amethyst violet

Family: Solanaceae
Cultural group: annuals
Height: 1–2 ft.
Width: 6 in. to 2 ft.
Light: sun to partial shade
Temperature: warm
Overwintering: no
Moisture: moderate
Drainage of medium: well drained
Fertility: average
Ease/speed of growth: easy/moderate to fast
Propagation: seeds
Problems: whitefly, leaf spots, stunted growth if kept too dry when young
Principal interest: flowers
Length of seasonal interest: long

Design attributes

Color: white, blue, or purple flowers
Line: not much in *B. speciosa*; taller *B. americana* offers some
Form: mounded to upright-bushy
Space: little to none in *B. speciosa*; *B. americana* offers some between leaves
Texture: medium

Browallia speciosa makes a pleasant little addition to container plantings. Adding a few white-flowered plants (including a white-flowered browallia) here would pick up on the light centers of the dark blue-purple blooms, lightening the overall effect.

Years ago, I was trying to grow browallias from seed, in those compressed, mesh-encased peat pellets, when I learned something about dry peat's stubborn resistance to water. I followed the package directions to a T: soak the pellets in plenty of warm water before inserting the seeds. Check. Keep the peat moist but not wet as the seeds germinate and the plantlets grow. Check. Plant out the young plants and then enjoy your success. Not. What I failed to do was to make sure the top of the peat pellet was covered with at least a thin layer of soil to help the peat retain moisture. Uncovered and exposed to the drying effect of sun and moving air, every little mesh-contained wad of peat quickly dried—much more rapidly than the surrounding soil—and all my little plants wilted repeatedly and eventually died. Digging up the casualties, I discovered that no roots had grown into the soil. It wasn't that the mesh stopped them; it was the Saharan nature of the rapidly drying peat that prevented the roots from doing their thing. Yet another reason for using coir, bark, compost, or any number of other renewable, more ecologically defensible materials instead of peat.

Browallias not killed by extreme dryness at their roots are charming things. The white, blue, and purple flowers of the *B. speciosa* selections (several with the words "bell" or "troll" in their cultivar names) bring cheer to containers in sunny and partially shady spots over much of the season on little bushes about 1 ft. tall. Usually taller and more wild-looking (more open in habit and less flower-bedecked), *B. americana* offers blue-purple or white flowers in less abundance than *B. speciosa*, but you might like that.

Cultural tips: Browallias like quite a bit of moisture, especially when small, and tolerate high heat and humidity once established. They shrink at cold temperatures at either end of the season, so don't plant them out too early, and be prepared to watch them blacken before many other tropical plants do so in fall. Try to root cuttings of any particularly attractive plants before cooler weather sets in.

BRUGMANSIA
angel's trumpet

Family: Solanaceae
Cultural group: tropicals
Height: 2–6 ft. or more
Width: 1–6 ft. or more
Light: sun (partial shade for variegated selections)
Temperature: warm to hot
Overwintering: cut back hard, provide min. 40°F, water sparingly or rarely, keep in low light; or leave intact, keep at min. 50°F, water occasionally, bright light
Moisture: ample
Drainage of medium: well drained
Fertility: average to high to absurdly high
Ease/speed of growth: easy/moderate to fast
Propagation: cuttings, seeds

Problems: whitefly, caterpillars of various ilk, spider mites, leaf scorch (on variegated selections grown in too much sun)
Principal interest: flowers, foliage (in variegated selections), fragrance, form
Length of seasonal interest: sporadic during warmest weather

Design attributes

Color: flowers white, pink, yellow, and orange; foliage sometimes variegated with white or cream
Line: upright to arching stems; upside-down trumpet-shaped flowers provide so much linear interest that they appear to be flying or dancing
Form: bushy to vase-shaped
Space: quite a bit around the hanging flowers of larger plants
Texture: coarse

A small (2–3 ft.) brugmansia will play nicely with several other companions in a roomy pot, as at the splendid Chanticleer, a pleasure garden outside of Philadelphia. Stunning. But in time (often as soon as the following season) most will need to be in a monopot—that is, if you expect them to grow large and produce many trumpets.

This large specimen of *Brugmansia* 'Charles Grimaldi' gets along with the coleus at its feet only because everything in the pot receives plenty of water and fertilizer.

How can you not think of a mass of trumpets or fancy ballgowns or spouting gargoyles when looking at *Brugmansia* 'Charles Grimaldi' in full bloom? Too bad you can't smell those flowers.

The superbly variegated *Brugmansia* 'Snowbank' doesn't need to bloom, but it does anyway. The white flowers are often clumsily positioned over the foliage, but at least they smell good. You could remove the flowers if they bother you . . . but which kind of monster would do that?

First, let's get some commonly encountered confusion sorted out: both *Brugmansia* and the closely related *Datura* are commonly called angel's trumpets (and both may be called datura), but the *Brugmansia* angels play their instruments pointing down, while the *Datura* angels lift theirs up. Also, *Brugmansia* brass sections usually contain far more members in much larger assemblages than *Datura* can muster, and *Brugmansia* trumpets occur in more colors and forms than those of *Datura*. None of this is to disparage *Datura*, however; they too have their charms. A little seed quickly becomes a leafy mass, and the concert begins once evenings are reliably warm. The fragrance is magical, attracting human noses and lepidopteran proboscises as night falls.

Brugmansia provides all that, but in a stupefyingly big way on older plants. I've seen specimens several years old dripping with hundreds of blooms, bringing to mind an army-sized band of angels or a cotillion of floor-length gowns. Even a recently rooted cutting can bear several disproportionately large flowers before cold weather sets in. The more water and

fertilizer you give them (within reason), the more they reward you: Richard Hartlage, longtime friend and garden designer extraordinaire, mulches brugmansias with pelleted fertilizer. That and liberal doses of water-soluble fertilizer means even small plants will be flower-laden in one growing season.

Should I add that their scent transfixes me (and others) in high summer, when their olfactory Siren call floats for amazingly long distances on the warm, humid air of early evening? Do I wish that seduction could go on forever? You bet.

For several years I subscribed to the pleasant notion that angel's trumpets reliably bloom cyclically, their greatest numbers coinciding with the full moon. The summer of 2008, when the brugmansias at Atlock Farm bloomed in several impressive flushes dramatically out of lunar sync, killed that theory. Maybe the time was out of joint.

Many cultivars can be found with some effort, especially if you hook up with folks in the societies that admire them (check them out online). Here are some angel's trumpets I've heard performing live:

B. ×candida 'Double White' is the nicest double I've seen. Some of the flowers might have been carved out of Carrara marble by the likes of Michelangelo.

'Charles Grimaldi' and 'Grand Marnier', both in luscious, mouthwatering apricot, bring me to my knees (and my nose to almost giddy satiety) whether in abundant bloom or stingily offering a few flowers.

In full, over-achieving bloom, 'Cypress Gardens' resembles a host of angels in pure white robes. There's also a white one with flowers that look like wads of shredded tissue. Whatever.

'Ecuador Pink' blushes pink.

'Milk and Honey' is well named.

'Snowbank', with white- and cream-variegated foliage, is the most attractive of the variegated selections. Don't expect heavy bloom (although a specimen at Atlock bloomed itself silly during the cool, wet summer of 2009).

Cultural tips: Increase the pot size over a couple of years until plants become large; an established specimen can remain in a roomy pot for several years. Chop them back severely before growth resumes, which can occur as early as February, even in colder climates. That early growth can be allowed to remain until setting the plants out for summer, at which time the shoots should be cut back again. Water and fertilize very generously as the weather warms up and new growth expands rapidly. Big plants are usually top-heavy and almost always need to be provided with some sort of countermeasure to wind, such as a very heavy pot or sturdy metal frame. They can also be chopped back and overwintered in a warm (60°F or so), noticeably damp place with a little potting mix around their roots.

BUXUS
boxwood, box

Family: Buxaceae
Cultural group: woody shrubs and trees
Height: 6 in. to 3 ft. or more
Width: 6 in. to 3 ft. or more
Light: sun to partial shade
Temperature: cool to warm (but surprisingly heat tolerant)
Overwintering: min. 45°F, water occasionally, bright light; or keep outside in a protected spot where hardy (generally in Z6–9)
Moisture: moderate (reasonably drought tolerant when established)
Drainage of medium: well drained
Fertility: low to average
Ease/speed of growth: moderate/slow to moderate
Propagation: cuttings, grafting
Problems: miners, scale insects, spider mites, psyllids, leaf rots and spots, root rot

Principal interest: form
Length of seasonal interest: all year

Design attributes
Color: mostly medium to dark green; some variegated with white or yellow
Line: almost absent unless allowed to grow untrimmed
Form: mostly densely mounded; some upright; easily trained into a range of shapes
Space: usually not evident unless allowed to grow untrimmed
Texture: medium to coarse

There's something about boxwood, that's for sure. Just the word (as well as the look, feel, and, well, smell, of the plants) conjures up a garden full of personal memories and associations. But none of my many encounters with boxwood involved container gardening until recently, when potted spec-

Many boxwoods can assume large dimensions (usually after many years, and in the ground), but they can also be attractively maintained in pots for a few years. This *Buxus* 'Green Mountain', trained into a splendid spiral and showing no signs of container claustrophobia, had been in its 12-in. pot for about two years when the photo was taken.

imens began popping up at Atlock Farm. They've ranged from massive squat balls to elegant spirals as well as many free-grown, unclipped specimens waiting to be planted as a hedge. I long ago accepted the peculiar, feline-related fragrance they emit, especially on hot, humid days. But for me, even in a pot, they still exude an air of history and solidity, of elegance and grand gardens.

Boxwood magic comes with very little effort. You can't treat boxwoods like a petunia or workhorse juniper, but they don't need to be coddled, either. Give them a long-lasting (some real soil is often appreciated), well-drained potting mix in a roomy pot, don't be stingy with the water, and keep them out of drying winter winds. Occasional fertilizer will keep them happy, as will a trim, either by shearing (manual or powered in spring and/or summer, for the most precise shapes) or breaking (which involves reaching into the body of the plant and snapping out twigs or larger stems by hand at any time, usually for less formal shapes). Breaking avoids un-sightly cut-off leaves but requires more time and precision.

Most look and grow best as monopots (especially when trained into formal shapes), but larger plants in roomy pots will coexist nicely with a nonassertive companion such as *Sagina subulata* or smaller sedum.

Which to choose? Start with the grand dame, *B. semper-virens* 'Suffruticosa' (so-called English or edging boxwood), which has the ineffable boxwood "look" and mystique but grows very slowly, perhaps as little as 1 in. per year in a con-tainer. Prepare to pay appropriately for a large, grand, aged specimen. Variegated selections of *B. sempervirens*, such as 'Elegantissima' and 'Marginata', look even more elegant but need extra winter protection from sun and wind. 'Green Mountain' (thought to be a hybrid between *Bb. sempervirens* and *microphylla* var. *koreana*) combines desirable appearance with increased hardiness. Related hybrids, such as 'Green Gem' and 'Green Mound', are worth a try for their rich green foliage and increased hardiness. Also consider some of the selections of *B. microphylla*, such as 'Green Pillow' and 'Kings-ville Dwarf', which slowly make dense mounds.

Cultural tips: Remember that rootballs in pots are more susceptible to winter cold and damage than those in the open ground, so choose selections that can handle at least your av-erage winters and be prepared to provide extra winter protec-tion during more extreme cold. Wrapping the pots with bub-ble wrap works but isn't very attractive, but placing the pot inside a larger pot and filling the space between with bubble wrap provides a double dose of insulation and can be attrac-tive, to boot. If the pots can be easily moved, consider shut-tling them in and out of an unheated garage or shed during your most severe weather.

CALADIUM
elephant ear, angel wings, heart of Jesus, mother-in-law plant

Family: Araceae
Cultural group: bulbs
Height: 2 ft.
Width: 1 ft.
Light: partial shade to shade; some might handle stronger sun if kept constantly moist
Temperature: warm to hot
Overwintering: keep tubers totally dormant at 50–60°F, very little to no water, light not necessary; can be kept potted in their growing medium
Moisture: moderate to ample to constant
Drainage of medium: well drained (C. *humboldtii* tolerates standing water)
Fertility: average to high

The boldly (and unusually) marked foliage of a caladium holds its own against a few eye-catching orange impatiens blooms. More orange would probably force the pink markings into obscurity in spite of their shapes, which bring Rorschach patterns to mind.

Ease/speed of growth: easy to moderate/fast
Propagation: division of individual tubers or clumps
    (notably *C. humboldtii*)
Problems: various tuber and leaf rots and spots, slugs and
    snails, spider mites
Principal interest: foliage
Length of seasonal interest: long

Design attributes

Color: fantastic patterns of green, white, red, and pink;
    newer ones include yellow and near-purple
Line: long petioles, if visible; leaf blades often strongly
    V-shaped, suggesting movement
Form: mounded if grown well; random shields on sticks if
    given less attention
Space: very little if grown well
Texture: coarse

Here's an extreme example of tying a garden scene together
with color: flowers in three shades of blue-pink (plus some blue-
green from the variegated ivy at the bottom) in a blue pot on a
blue deck backed by a blue fence. Even the air seems blue. Don't
those caladium leaves look like kites flying above a crowd?

Do not skip this entry, please. Caladiums are no longer simply the big-leaved pink, red, and white things you (yes, you, I've seen it done) stick in corners and hope they'll do something. Recent developments in the caladium world have remade this genus. First, the use of tissue culture has led to rapid increase of newer selections (so no more waiting a long time for a choice selection to multiply into large-enough numbers to bring the price down) and in many cases to increased vigor. Second, lance-shaped, strap-shaped, and tiny-leaved caladiums have joined the familiar shield-shaped ones, remaking the overall appearance of the plants from a couple of colored shields to emphatic statements. Third, someone is waving a magic wand over caladiums in Southeast Asia, because 'Leung Pa Li Chart' and other cultivars in unimagined colors have arisen over there and have hit our shores.

Caladiums love heat, and even one well-grown pot can be the star of your summer parties. I pot up the tubers in June, when the air temperatures in New Jersey are usually quite warm if not downright hot—three to six tubers, shallowly planted into 10- and 12-in. clay azalea pots filled with a very open bark- and coir-based mix. I keep them in a very brightly lit, airy greenhouse, give them ample water and water-soluble fertilizer, and almost literally watch them grow. By early August (about seven weeks from the start date), those funny-looking tubers will have grown into lush masses of foliage. Party time!

Choose from among an ever-burgeoning number of worthy selections. These are my favorites . . . for now:

A dense white fog spreads over much of the dark green leaves on 'Aaron'; 'White Ruffles' is similar.

The old standby 'Candidum' is white with green veins, and 'Candidum Sr.' is even more white. 'White Christmas' is similar to these two.

'Carolyn Wharton' sports dark pink to red veins and white and lighter pink blotching against green.

Those in the Florida series have thicker leaves that give them a bit more sun tolerance. 'Florida Beauty', an excellent grower, offers a mosaic of light green, pink, and red splashes on darker green. 'Florida Cardinal' boasts a strong red center area (with the veins extending the red outward a little) on a green background. The red veins of 'Florida Fantasy' bleed a tiny bit into a white background, which also includes a precisely marked green pattern (as if the leaves had been soaked in green dye, like those carnations sold on St. Patrick's Day). 'Florida Red Ruffles' is mostly red with a green edge and is gently ruffled.

'Gingerland' has a green edge surrounding a white cloud, with red splashes flying out from where the leaf blade joins the petiole.

'Miss Muffet' in lighter green contains variable red-pink veining and red splashes within a white mist.

Do not adjust your sets: this is the actual coloration of *Caladium* 'Leung Pa Li Chart'. Keep this and other lighter-colored selections out of direct sun (or they will give the impression of a brown paper bag) but not in dark shade; their chlorophyll-starved foliage needs all the help (from benevolent, indirect light) you can provide.

A long-established pot of *Caladium* 'Gingerland' looks like a mass of banners flying in the breeze, or a flock of birds rising from the ground, or a green, white, and red gusher. The buttoned-down, almost black pot centers and stabilizes the kinetic mass.

The mass of foliage of a white, green-veined caladium—one of the group whose most recognized member is 'Candidum'— brings light and life to what otherwise might appear dark and harsh. Put your finger over the white leaves to see what I mean. Of course, you might think that the white is rather harsh, too.

'Pink Symphony' and 'Thai Beauty' produce elongated, widely variable netlike patterns of pink, green, and white.

The white on the pointed leaves of 'White Wing' melts into a green edge. A suggestion of pink at the petiole and (sometimes) faint pink veins increase its simply elegant and refined look.

The so-called Thai caladiums with exotic-looking names (such as 'Leung Pa Li Chart' and 'Parichat') or more familiar-looking ones ('Siam Sushi') will take you to a totally different caladium place. Many remain quite small and/or bear wild color combinations.

Last but most definitely not least is *C. humboldtii*, arguably the most gorgeous and fascinating of the entire clan. It sends up many smallish leaves, producing dense, almost decadent masses of refreshing-looking foliage. I've had great success starting with six tubers in a 10-in. plastic pot filled with nothing but long-fiber sphagnum and keeping about an inch of standing water at the base of the pot. The tubers wake up in July and are often memories by November, but what a display!

Cultural tips: Don't even think about starting the tubers until your weather is reliably warm or even hot (air temperatures remaining above 65°F). You might want to carefully remove ("de-eye") the central or largest new shoot on the tuber, then wait a day or two before planting to encourage more leaves from each tuber. Set them about an inch under the surface of the mix with the curved side down and the bumpy side up, or on their sides if you want to hedge your bets. Cut off the flowers; they're freeloaders on the ample fertilizer and water they need to produce masses of leaves. You can keep them in the same pot for a second year before repotting into fresh mix. When it's *hot*.

Left: Botanically, the leaves of 'Gingerland' are described as sagittate. More colloquially, they'd be called elephant ears, just like the foliage of their larger cousins in *Alocasia*, *Colocasia*, and *Xanthosoma*, all included in this book.

Below: *Caladium humboldtii* has small leaves, but it more than compensates for that "failing" by sending out masses of them, especially when several plants are massed in a pot and given plenty of water and nitrogenous fertilizer. Cool.

CALATHEA
peacock plant

Family: Marantaceae
Cultural group: tropicals
Height: 1–4 ft.
Width: 1–2 ft.
Light: partial shade to shade
Temperature: warm to hot
Overwintering: min. 60°F, water regularly but not
    excessively, bright light
Moisture: moderate to ample
Drainage of medium: well drained
Fertility: average
Ease/speed of growth: moderate/moderate
Propagation: division
Problems: spider mites, leaf spots, brown leaf edges
    (from low humidity)
Principal interest: foliage
Length of seasonal interest: all year

Design attributes
Color: leaves green marked with contrasting greens, white,
    pink, and purple; undersides often dark green or purple
Line: petioles and elongated leaf blades provide some line,
    but often the most visible lines are the leaf markings
Form: mounded to upright; sometimes loosely vase-shaped
Space: not much
Texture: medium to coarse

Here we have a great common name combined with undeniable good looks, so I ask you: why aren't calatheas grown more often? They're not difficult to grow—I had one in my basement-level dorm room at Penn State. Wait, I think I know why they turn up rarely, at least in containers: they're houseplants, and we all know houseplants belong in the house. Really? Let's think about this for a minute. Houseplants often do well in low-light areas, often tolerate extremes in temperature, can get by with some neglect but reward the growers who treat them well, and otherwise behave like plants in general, whether indoors or out. Don't you put some of your houseplants outside for the summer? So why not include "houseplants" in your container plantings, whether as monopots or combopots?

Houseplant-pigeonholed *Calathea* follows container-classic *Caladium* in this book, and when you look at them in terms of the Big Five design elements, they start looking almost interchangeable. They even have similar cultural requirements (except, most importantly, for the tuber-starting part). So how about joining me in my campaign to use more "houseplants" in our container plantings? Do you think we'll succeed? Yes

We Can. Start with these strutting beauties, presented here in order of size:

C. sanderiana is the big one of the bunch, eventually reaching 6 ft. tall. Its leaves are pink-lined (the pink stripes occur more or less in pairs) with purple leaf undersides, making it a memorable combination with pink impatiens, pink begonias, and other more conventional container plants.

Cc. lancifolia and *zebrina* are the midsized members of the genus, reaching 2.5 and 3 ft., respectively. Both produce long leaf blades on long petioles, and their respective common names of rattlesnake plant and zebra plant should give you an idea of their attractive markings.

C. makoyana (cathedral windows) is the compact model, maybe reaching 1.5 ft. tall. Most specimens I've seen remain under a foot and have a stratified (OK, flattened) look to them. Also purple on the leaf undersides, selections of this species usually look handpainted with splashes or brushstrokes … or like a stained-glass window.

Like so many strutting peacocks, the leaves of *Calathea sanderiana* (at the top) and two selections of *C. makoyana* show off their beautiful markings. They won't attract peahens (well, who's to say, actually?), but they should catch some eyes. Consider liberating these traditional houseplants by growing a few in containers outdoors.

Cultural tips: Calatheas like humidity, but don't go crazy and spritz them all the time. Summers in much of the United States are plenty humid. Bring them inside for the winter and treat them like houseplants if you're still not comfortable with this houseplants-as-container-plants thing. But your attitude will change in time. I hope.

CALENDULA
English marigold, pot marigold

Family: Asteraceae
Cultural group: annuals
Height: 1–2 ft.
Width: 1–2 ft.
Light: sun to partial shade
Temperature: cool to warm
Overwintering: not usually, but they often persist in
    cool-winter areas with light frosts
Moisture: moderate
Drainage of medium: well drained
Fertility: low to average
Ease/speed of growth: easy/moderate to fast
Propagation: seeds
Problems: slugs and snails, aphids, leaf rots and spots
Principal interest: flowers, fragrance
Length of seasonal interest: moderate

Design attributes
Color: flowers in cream, yellow, and orange; some marked
    with red-brown
Line: older, rangier plants have curving or floppy stems
Form: loosely mounded to nondescript
Space: increases with age and floppiness
Texture: medium to coarse

While not a top-shelf, must-have container subject, calendulas can make agreeable additions to herbal-themed pots or short-season flowering pots. The petals are edible, often given to chickens in their feed (it makes their flesh more appealingly yellow, I'm told), added to salads, and sometimes used as a saffron substitute in rice dishes. That's all very nice, but I grow them for their sunny daisies and for their sharp, clean fragrance (especially noticeable in the foliage). By the way, our British friends call these plants marigolds, a common name we Americans reserve for *Tagetes*.

Most calendulas thrive in cooler weather (they can bloom all winter where winters are cool), so expect your plants to start looking stressed out as the mercury rises. Where winters are not too Arctic (Z5–6, say), you can sow some in early fall, and the little plants might well survive through winter and start blooming early the following spring. Or not. Try it.

While not a classic, summer-blooming container workhorse (like, say, petunias or impatiens), selections of *Calendula officinalis* bring hot color to cooler times of the year. Their fragrance is worth checking out, too. Let a few of their seeds (which remind some of toenail clippings) ripen for fun and to germinate in the fall for next season's plants.

Single or double, brown-tipped or not, and in whichever color, they're all pretty. Any of the many selections, old and new, should please you as they do me. Just don't put too many in a salad unless you lean toward strong flavors in abundance.

Cultural tips: Remember that they like cooler weather. Pinch young plants once (maybe twice) to promote branching and more flowers. Cutting the flowers for whichever use you fancy, and removing the spent heads before the seeds become evident prolongs the bloom season. See what happens when you don't give them very much nitrogen. They reseed easily if not clipped, but most of the fancier selections will revert to much plainer-looking flowers in succeeding generations. They'll still offer that wonderful fragrance, though.

CALIBRACHOA
mini petunia

Family: Solanaceae
Cultural group: annuals
Height: 6 in.
Width: 1–3 ft.
Light: sun to limited partial shade
Temperature: warm to hot
Overwintering: no
Moisture: moderate to ample
Drainage of medium: well drained
Fertility: average
Ease/speed of growth: easy/moderate to fast
Propagation: seeds (mostly bought as plants from nurseries, though)
Problems: whitefly, root rot (if medium is too wet)
Principal interest: flowers
Length of seasonal interest: long

Design attributes

Color: flowers in white and jewel tones of pink, red, red-violet, yellow, orange, blue, and purple
Line: present but not dramatic in a mass; attractively cascading or branching-horizontal if grown individually
Form: usually an assertive mass
Space: not much unless grown individually
Texture: medium

Nope, this isn't a petunia; it's one of many selections of the red-hot genus *Calibrachoa*. Think of them as smaller-flowered petunias that come in a wide color range (wider than the mostly cool-tinted petunia spectrum). Then use them with abandon (or simpatico plants).

I remember seeing calibrachoas for the first time. "What are these nice little petunias?" I wondered—and that was even before I knew their common name. These are indeed cousins of petunias in the mighty Solanaceae, which includes a mother lode of ornamentals (as this book proves) and edibles (tomatoes, peppers, eggplants), not to mention Mr. and Mrs. Potato Head. If you like petunias (how can you not?), give these a try, and you'll be won over. Calibrachoas are in fact often touted as superior to petunias because they're not sticky, they don't fall apart in the rain (some petunias are guilty of this), and they remain compact while blooming their heads off, which they'll do all season if happy. Another plus: the little flowers seem to disappear after they fade. However, I've never caught any fragrance wafting from a calibrachoa. Score one for petunias.

Mini petunias make overwhelming monopot hanging baskets and tall footed pots, and they mix nicely with other plants in any combopot you might dream up. Cultivars occur in several series; it is safe to say that what hybridizers have given us since *Calibrachoa* selections first hit the market in 1992 ranks up there with Luther Burbank's Shasta daisies, Dan Heims's paintbox of *Heuchera* creations, and Bill Radler's

The colors of many *Calibrachoa* cultivars darken or lighten as the flowers age, which brings satisfying visual depth to the overall display. Note how the smaller, younger blooms look redder and a bit darker that the larger, older ones.

Often the featured soloist of a monopot, a calibrachoa can also play second fiddle in a container concerto. Here, a rounded, hot-colored mini petunia selection complements the starry coolness of a Swan River daisy (*Brachyscome*).

The pale-edged flowers of *Calibrachoa* 'Callie Painted Coral' add a little diversity to the general look of the genus, which bears mostly solid-colored flowers. The pale edge makes the flowers look much more starry and increases the fine texture of the plants in general.

Knock Out roses. New ones are no doubt waiting in the wings to join these:

Callie is a series with a mere fourteen members (get to work, already!).

Million Bells. Approximately twenty different selections, among them 'Crackling Fire', a beauty with variable spatters of several hot colors. But caveat emptor: the name of this series has been widely applied as a common name for the genus, and what you see billed as "million bells" might actually be a member of another series. Not that it will matter greatly.

Mini-Famous includes a double blue-purple selection, for those so inclined, among others.

Spring Fling series includes fourteen selections and counting. They all look super-callie-springfling-istic to me.

Superbells is a series of twenty-six different selections, last time I looked, and they all look like candy or jewels.

Cultural tips: Don't let the roots sit in water. They *will* rot. Forget deadheading; they don't need it, and most people would go crazy trying to keep up with the job.

Most of the more popular mini petunia selections bloom themselves silly, provided they receive the conditions they like (and their roots aren't drowning). *Calibrachoa* 'Superbells Apricot Punch' is the soloist here. The punch seems to have had some bits of cherries or strawberries thrown in for added temptation.

CALLISIA
variegated chain plant (*C. fragrans* 'Melnickoff')

Family: Commelinaceae
Cultural group: tropicals
Height: 1–3 ft.
Width: 1–2 ft.
Light: partial shade
Temperature: warm to hot
Overwintering: min. 50°F, water occasionally, bright light
Moisture: moderate to ample
Drainage of medium: well drained; might take shallow standing water
Fertility: average to high (nitrogen to push growth)
Ease/speed of growth: easy/moderate to fast
Propagation: cuttings, rooted plantlets
Problems: rots and spots

Principal interest: foliage, form
Length of seasonal interest: long to all year

Design attributes
Color: foliage light to medium green heavily striped with white, can have purple cast on undersides; little white flowers are supposedly fragrant (hence the specific epithet)
Line: instantaneously visible—omnipresent—unavoidable
Form: rosette to pagoda-like with streamers
Space: everywhere, especially with age
Texture: medium to coarse

I first clapped admiring eyes on *C. fragrans* 'Melnickoff' on an early-morning photo expedition with Rob Cardillo to Chanticleer, that cutting-edge celebration of a garden. It had that spiderwort-family (Commelinaceae) gestalt, with its thick leaves and stems and open architecture (check out *Rhoeo* and

An established specimen of *Callisia fragrans* 'Melnickoff' demonstrates the inspiration for the common name, chain plant: do you see the bracts that appear at each node of the gracefully cascading stems? The "chains" produce flowers as well as plantlets, which can be separated to produce new plants. "Many-legged alien plant" might also be apropos.

The finely striped foliage of *Callisia fragrans* 'Melnickoff' suggests a neatly tied bow on the top of its container. Note how the angel vine (*Muehlenbeckia complexa*) provides a potent textural contrast.

Tradescantia for other glimpses of the same family). Even though the plant was unlabeled, I was confident that the Chanticleer gardening wizards would put a name on the spiderworty thing I admired. Of course they did, and now here it is, strutting its stuff for you.

Let me take this opportunity to encourage you to engage in a practice I call Learning to Look. If you don't know the name of a plant before you, examine its various parts (stems, leaves, flowers, fruits, buds, bark, even the bugs and other maladies that visit it) and get a feeling for its general aura or appearance. I think you'll find that something will "click" inside your head, giving you at least an idea of what it might be or to which other plants it might be related. If nothing else, you might recognize the plant when next you see it, this time with a label in front of it or a helpful garden wizard standing by.

I suggest you try growing *C. fragrans* 'Melnickoff' in both monopot and combopot situations. It's stately and engaging enough to be featured as a specimen but also very combinable with its variegated leaves and eye-catching chains.

Cultural tips: Like many of its Commelinaceous kin, variegated chain plant (as well as the straight all-green species) takes nicely to moist soil and less than a full day of sun (morning sun does very nicely). Those chains root very easily (another family trait) to produce thoughtful presents for friends who first learn of this variegated beauty in your container garden.

CAMELLIA
camellia

Family: Theaceae
Cultural group: woody shrubs and trees
Height: 2–5 ft. or more
Width: 2–3 ft. or more
Light: partial shade (sasanquas and *C.* ×*vernalis* selections like sun)
Temperature: cool to warm (tolerates some heat if roots are cool and shaded)
Overwintering: hardy in Z7–8
Moisture: moderate (to ample, with care)
Drainage of medium: well drained
Fertility: average; they shouldn't be pushed
Ease/speed of growth: moderate/slow to moderate
Propagation: cuttings, grafting, air layering, seeds (if you're patient)
Problems: scale insects, spider mites, blossom rot, rots and spots, cankers
Principal interest: flowers, foliage, form (of both plant and flowers)
Length of seasonal interest: brief to moderate (flowers); all year (form and foliage)

Design attributes

Color: flowers white and entirely in (or variously marked with) red, pink, or purple, often with prominent yellow stamens; foliage medium to dark, glossy green
Line: not readily noticeable; sometimes from stems
Form: densely to more openly shrubby, sometimes lax to cascading; flowers in various forms, all worthy of meditation
Space: limited but can be implied by flowers against the foliage
Texture: medium (flowers sometimes add a coarse note, believe it or not)

Three signature plants come immediately to mind when I think of the gardening-rich American South: southern magnolia (*Magnolia grandiflora*, which regrettably can be grown to full splendor in only the most ridiculously outsized pots), gardenias (which can be grown in pots quite nicely: flip to the Gs), and camellias. So if you want to enjoy a bit of Southern presence and charm in your garden—wherever that might be—think about growing a camellia, and begin

A close look at a flower of *Camellia* ×*vernalis* 'Yuletide' reveals the central boss of stamens, which reminds me of a 4th of July sparkler. No impossibly double flowers here!

with the one I consider to be the cream of the crop: *C. ×vernalis* 'Yuletide'. No, it's not one of the large, flouncy-flowered selections of the more familiar *C. japonica*, and yes, it blooms in the fall (and often well into winter). You won't be able to pick and wear a great big flower on your bosom (as ladies once did, back in the day), and you will need to provide winter protection in areas colder than Z7. Believe me, after one long, admiring look at a 'Yuletide' in full bloom, you'll want to provide for its cultural needs.

For the most part, camellias look their best grown as monopots (with maybe a little groundcover at the base or a spindly climber clambering up a good-sized plant), which lets their remarkable stateliness shine forth: few plants can compete successfully with that rich, shiny foliage and those exquisite blooms. Just about any selection of *Cc. japonica, reticulata*, or *sasanqua*, or the hybrid types like *Cc. ×vernalis* and *×williamsii* (their numbers are legion) makes a splendid container plant, provided you can provide (and move!) a large pot. Choose one that appeals to you at a local nursery or garden and look into the ins and outs of camellia culture. If you fol-low the basic information presented here, you'll be off to a good start. Try one.

Cultural tips: Camellias like an evenly moist, acidic potting mix, occasional doses of acidic fertilizer (some are specifically blended for camellias), and a mulch or groundcover. Compulsively pick up and dispose of the dead flowers to help prevent flower troubles. Thoughtful pruning (after they bloom, and to a leaf or two above the base of the most recent growth) prevents them from growing out of bounds. A good, hard chopping back does the trick, too; an unwieldy camellia should rebound well if in good health and provided with good care.

Note: Good news, Northerners. A fair number of so-called winter-hardy camellias (many with "April" in their cultivar name) are increasingly available. They have arisen from intentional breeding programs that strive to combine the luscious forms and colors of *C. japonica* with the greater cold hardiness of species such as *C. oleifera*. Their progeny vary in beauty and hardiness (some have been doing well in the ground in parts of Z6), but they all have their charms.

Careful pruning and informed, diligent care should produce a stunning specimen like this one. Can you tell from a couple of the plants at its base that *Camellia ×vernalis* 'Yuletide' blooms in fall and early winter?

CANNA
canna

Family: Cannaceae
Cultural group: tropicals, aquatics
Height: 2–8 ft.
Width: 1–3 ft.
Light: sun to partial shade
Temperature: warm to hot
Overwintering: keep totally dormant at 45–60°F, water very occasionally, light not necessary; can be kept potted in their growing medium; generally hardy in Z9–11, Z8 with protection
Moisture: moderate to ample to constant (for the aquatics)
Drainage of medium: well drained (aquatic types perform better in standing water)
Fertility: average to high
Ease/speed of growth: easy/moderate to fast
Propagation: division (of rhizomes), seeds (if you want to have some fun)
Problems: Japanese beetles, slugs and snails, caterpillars (although they often produce intriguing patterns of holes in the leaves), leaf spots, leaf mosaic virus
Principal interest: foliage, flowers
Length of seasonal interest: long

Design attributes
Color: foliage in green, red, yellow, orange, and white; flowers yellow, orange, red, and pink

Line: upright (some seem to be reaching for the sky); linear
    variegation adds more interest
Form: lumpy-bushy; insouciant
Space: around and below flowers, sometimes around leaves
Texture: unapologetically coarse

True confession: I wouldn't include cannas in any Top 10 list (maybe even Top 100) based on their flowers. Yes, they're colorful and undeniably showy (plenty of cannas are sold based on flower color alone), but they often resemble wet tissue up close and don't last very long. But if I had to create a list of top-shelf foliage plants for summer containers, cannas would definitely have a place for their assertive red, variegated, or just plain big and burly, green foliage. Here's a sacred cow I'd like to tip over: not all cannas are gigantic, broad-shouldered thugs that swallow everything in their path or pot. The seed-grown 'Tropical Rose' usually tops out at only 2 ft., and many—no matter how stately their bearing in the open ground—reach only about 3 ft. in pots. Don't be afraid to use them in (big) combopots or to show your savvy by featuring their foliage in monopots. How much you value the flowers is up to you.

Attempt these for their foliage, mostly:

'Australia' has seductive, richly dark and shiny foliage and looks skinnier than some; it will reach 3–4 ft. I've never seen its pink-red flowers; they probably look stunning with the leaves but might not get along nicely with combopot companions chosen to coordinate with the foliage.

'Durban' sends out beefy purple-green foliage with pink and orange-red veining. I usually remove the orange flowers, because the combination with the foliage is too much for (even) me. Figure 3 ft. or so.

'Grande' lives up to its name by growing to 8 ft., and its rhyming common name (banana canna) is mighty fitting, too. Flowers? Never seen 'em. Don't need or want 'em.

'Pretoria' is the canna to grow if you're growing only one. The photo shows it far better than I can describe, except you can't see the thin red margin around the leaves.

'Stuttgart' is the one to grow if you like to be disappointed. I've never seen it without brown edges or patches on the foliage once the weather becomes reliably hot. Even with ample water and heavy shade, its pretty white-marked leaves look nasty with those brown blemishes. It produces orange flowers on skinny 5–6 ft. plants.

'Tropicanna' looks and performs much like 'Durban' except for its pink flowers, which to my eye play better with the foliage, so I usually let them remain on the plants.

Grow these for their flowers, mostly:

'Orange Punch' has medium to dark green foliage on 2–3 ft. plants with super-saturated orange flowers. Wow.

'Richard Wallace' offers striking, clear yellow flowers on lively-looking, light to medium green foliage on 3–4 ft. plants.

And yes, sometimes you can have it all. Savor the happy combination of both foliage and flowers on these cannas:

'Cleopatra' produces fascinating, highly variable maroon markings on the leaves and stems; the flowers are equally unpredictable offerings of red and yellow. This is a shorter grower, maybe to 3 ft.

'Intrigue' sends up abundant, cloudy purple-green, skinny foliage and similarly cloudy red-orange flowers. It easily reaches 6 ft. Allow the flowers to remain on this one to produce little bumpy-pointy fruit.

'Red King Humbert' (aka 'Roi Humbert') is an oldie with hot red flowers carried above purple-red leaves. Figure 3–4 ft. or so in a pot.

'Wyoming' has purple-brown-green ("bronze") foliage that makes a gorgeous contrast with the orange flowers on 3–4 ft. plants.

Cultural tips: Cannas can tolerate a surprising amount of water at their feet. Some species actually prefer an aquatic home, and that preference extends (to a point) to many of

Canna 'Grande' almost comically dwarfs many of its possible companions. The one (yes, it's all one) plant in this photo grew from a single clump of intertwined rhizomes that took some doin' to undo at the end of the season. Notice the masterful touches of the dark red highlights on the stems.

Opposite: Even the pyrotechnic orange flowers of *Canna* 'Pretoria' can't compete with its lush, powerfully coarse yet finely striped foliage. Put a finger or two over the flowers: which is more memorable, the flowers or the foliage? You know the answer. Some people consider the flowers a distraction and remove them.

their flashy hybrids. Also, cannas are hardier than many of us think. No, they won't survive here in central New Jersey (Z6–7) outdoors in containers, but they have lived in a greenhouse heated to 45°F that more than once dropped to freezing or below when the heat failed. Nor do cannas need to be totally separated from their growing medium and stored in boxes of vermiculite or whatever in a special place reserved for sleeping summer performers. They do just fine if overwintered in the growing medium in their pots. At 45°F or so. Light or dark. Just don't let them stay wet.

CAPSICUM
ornamental pepper, chili pepper, hot pepper
(C. *annuum*)

Family: Solanaceae
Cultural group: annuals
Height: 6 in. to 2 ft.
Width: 6 in. to 2 ft.
Light: sun to partial shade
Temperature: warm to hot
Overwintering: not usually, although some do reasonably well in a warm, sunny window with regular watering
Moisture: moderate to ample
Drainage of medium: well drained
Fertility: average to high
Ease/speed of growth: easy/moderate

If you do decide to snip canna flowers off, they make eye-catching if fleeting cut flowers. From the top, these are 'Intrigue', 'Richard Wallace', and 'Orange Punch'. Orange you glad the yellow flowers were placed in between the other ones? The leaf belongs to 'Intrigue' and combines nicely with the flowers of the other two selections, don't you think?

Students of color theory take note: placing the purple fruits of *Capsicum annuum* 'Numex Twilight' near an orange marigold (or anything orange, for that matter) creates a perfect triadic harmony of the three secondary colors (the green leaves provide the third). Love it or hate it, you must admit that there's lots of color happening here.

Propagation: seeds
Problems: spider mites, aphids, leaf spots, root rot
Principal interest: fruit, foliage
Length of seasonal interest: moderate to long

Design attributes

Color: fruit start mid-green and then turn lighter green, yellow, orange, red, purple, or black (sometimes progressing through several colors); some leaves variegated with white and light purple, others almost black

Line: fairly intricate branching patterns on some; fruit often elongated

Form: shrubby to congested-dumpy

Space: in some more open-growing selections; around clusters of fruit

Texture: fine (variegated selections) to medium

When most of us gardeners think of sources for color in our container plantings, we first turn to flowers. It's natural. Then the possibilities of foliage come to mind (I hope). Coming in a distant third are fruit. That's understandable, given that most offerings out there simply don't produce attractive fruit or berries (or whatever you choose to call them). In *Capsicum* we have a glaring and glorious exception to this situation in *C. annuum*. If you think you recognize the genus name but can't quite place what you're familiar with, you're probably channeling capsaicin, the compound that gives hot peppers their kick and is used in heat-producing creams and other medications.

So, back to the fruit. Once a capsicum starts setting fruit, the display often lasts for months, and it's usually an everchanging light show, of sorts. Green becomes yellow then orange and finally red. Or dark green becomes near-black and then dark red. The fruit shapes don't progressively change like their colors do, but their forms vary widely from one selection to another: balls, cones, caps, Christmas lights, and skinny fingers, among others, borne singly or in clusters. All this makes for great fun in containers, whether the plants are grown as single specimens or groups in monopots, or adding to the beautiful music in carefully composed combopots. As if all those showy fruit weren't a sufficiently embarrassing embarrassment of riches, the foliage of some ornamental peppers is so attractively variegated that the peppers almost become a distraction.

Scores of ornamental peppers are available, and new ones appear annually. Here is a tiny sampling of the diversity out there:

Who cares what the peppers on *Capsicum annuum* 'Tricolor Variegatum' look like, when the leaves look like this? I want to combine this rich tapestry with lavender- or lilac-colored heliotrope, petunias, or angelonias. Pink, gray, cream, dark purple, and pale yellow flowers and/or foliage would be worth a try, too.

Pepper fruits aren't always red, but these chartreuse fruits on *Capsicum annuum* 'Super Chili' did eventually turn red. Note how a couple of them in the middle are beginning to heat up. How will they look against the pot?

What else would you call this dark, shiny, beadlike pepper? *Capsicum annuum* 'Black Pearl' combines beautifully with pink (here) and chartreuse (in the next photograph). What doesn't go with a little basic black?

'Black Pearl' took the gardening world by storm as soon as it became available, and rightly so. Its dark foliage, purple flowers, and almost black fruit (they turn red in time) are a sultry contrast to many other colors. It reaches about 1 ft. tall.

'Blast' offers clusters of orange fruit.

'Chilly Chili' bears elongated, color-progressing fruit in clusters. The peppers are barely hot, hence the clever name. It grows much larger than many others described here (to 1 ft., or a bit more).

'Ignite' produces lots of skinny little fruit on 6-in. (or so) plants.

'Medusa' lives up to its name through its clusters of twisted, snaky fruit.

The fruits of 'Black Pearl' go through a Goth phase before settling down to their mature red coloration. The leaves also progress, but in the opposite direction, from leafy green to sultry purple-black (unless the plants grow in too little direct sun, which prevents the umbral shades from developing fully).

Capsicum annuum 'Chilly Chili' perfectly illustrates the color progression of many pepper fruits, from yellow to orange to red. That's hot! The fruits aren't (on your tongue). The colorist in me wants to remove the cool blue-pink in the background: a much redder or more yellow (therefore hotter) pink could do.

The clusters of the stubby fruit of 'Salsa Yellow' go through a magical, eerie green stage.

'Summer Snow' and other variegated selections are sometimes ethereally beautiful, their leaves painted with shades of green, white, and light purple … and sometimes not. Be prepared.

Cultural tips: Don't let ornamental peppers dry out or get a chill; the flowers can abort, and you'll end up with few if any fruit. Keep them growing without interruption in a sunny spot for the best fruit display. Some remain attractive for months if kept in a warm and sunny place over winter.

CAREX
sedge

Family: Cyperaceae
Cultural group: perennials, annuals
Height: 6 in. to 3 ft.
Width: 6 in. to 3 ft.
Light: sun to partial shade
Temperature: cool to warm to hot
Overwintering: min. 40°F, water occasionally, bright light; variously hardy in Z3–9
Moisture: moderate to ample to constant
Drainage of medium: well drained, although many tolerate standing water
Fertility: low to average
Ease/speed of growth: easy/moderate
Propagation: division
Problems: leaf spots
Principal interest: foliage, flowers, fruit
Length of seasonal interest: long (some all year)

Design attributes

Color: foliage green or brown, some including orange or variegated with white or yellow; flowers/fruit green to brown
Line: many are nothing but
Form: many are upright-arching bunches, others are flattened and wavy; flowers/fruit are variations of prickly-looking balls or tassels
Space: a great many individual spaces between leaves; also around stems
Texture: fine to medium

It took me quite a while to appreciate the beauty and versatility of ornamental grasses. "Weedy-looking bunches of nothing," I thought. "Where's the hay baler?" Now, grasses hold me in their thrall. Well, some—not all. And before you think I don't know a sedge from a grass, be aware that you can read about "true" grasses elsewhere in this book (*Arundo, Hakonechloa,* and *Pennisetum*); in this entry we'll examine grasslike plants, not true members of the grass family (Poaceae). Sedges and their kin in the Cyperaceae (*Cyperus* gives the family its name) look grassy and so are often used like grasses in containers. You want some linear interest? Look to sedges. Color? Ditto. How about curious-looking seedheads? Those are here, too. Sun? shade? wet? dry? evergreen? deciduous? tall? small? All here. *Carex* is a huge genus of probably 1,500 species and plenty of selections, with more appearing yearly. Hot stuff!

Try these, for starters:

Cc. buchananii (upright-arching and dense, 2 ft., Z6–9), *comans* bronze form (mounded and open, 1 ft., Z7–9), and *flagellifera* (mounded-tufted, 3 ft., Z7–9) at first glance (and sometimes with later examination) all look dead. They're brown and truly beautiful, once you look at them and start to realize how many colors (of plants and pots) look good in their company. They are all evergreen and tolerate a wide range of soil conditions in sun or partial shade.

C. elata 'Aurea' (upright-arching, 2 ft., Z5–9) is deciduous, making bright yellow-green foliage in moist to wet soil in sun or a little shade.

C. morrowii (mounded, to 1.5 ft., Z6–9) is a nice medium green evergreen in its own right, but its selection 'Ice Dance' really lights up the place with its arching white-striped foliage. It takes sun but looks its best in some shade, and don't be stingy with the water or fertilizer.

C. pendula (almost shrubby, to 4 ft. and often wider, Z5–9) stands out from the crowd when in flower, the inflorescences starting out erecta and then becoming pendula against the long, medium to blue-green leaves. Evergreen and happy with plenty of moisture in sun.

C. phyllocephala 'Sparkler' (mounded-spreading, to 2 ft., Z7–10) also makes itself known, this time by virtue of its umbrella-spoke-like foliage arrangement and snappy white linear variegation on evergreen, medium green leaves. Palm sedge, as it is sometimes known, does best in sites away from full sun and in fact performs quite well in considerable shade. Don't let the umbrellas fool you: it likes plenty of water.

Cultural tips: Don't assume anything about a sedge's cultural needs. Do your homework. Ask around. Observe them in your own garden.

You're familar with evergreens, but how about everbrowns? *Carex buchananii* remains a warm brown all year, mixing attractively with hotter colors . . . but sometimes not as perfectly with cooler ones, as here. Its extreme expression of line offers a dramatic contrast with almost anything, though.

How much more linear could a plant get? The bronze-leaved form of *Carex comans* appears to be erupting into a delicate fountain. Place this close enough to a traffic path to tickle the legs of your family, friends, and guests. They'll hate or love you for it.

Not all sedges are brown; plenty of them are green or mostly so. *Carex morrowii* 'Ice Dance' brings bright coolth to shady spots, along with a strong suggestion of activity.

Like *Carex morrowii* 'Ice Dance', *C. phyllocephala* 'Sparkler' brings light and a sensation of coolness to areas out of the full, blazing sun. Of all the sedges pictured here, this one seems to me to "move" the most, owing to the elongated, striped foliage.

CATHARANTHUS
annual periwinkle, bush periwinkle, Madagascar periwinkle, old maid (*C. roseus*)

Family: Apocynaceae
Cultural group: annuals
Height: 6 in. to 2 ft.
Width: 1–2.5 ft.
Light: sun to partial shade
Temperature: warm to hot
Overwintering: no (unless you want to try to root some cuttings)
Moisture: moderate
Drainage of medium: well drained
Fertility: average
Ease/speed of growth: easy/moderate
Propagation: seeds, cuttings
Problems: rots (root if kept too wet) and spots, whitefly, spider mites
Principal interest: flowers
Length of seasonal interest: long

The inflorescences of *Carex morrowii* 'Ice Dance' don't jump out at you like zinnias or marigolds, but their intricate beauty does reward close inspection. Then move on to something more emphatic, if you wish. Variety is the spice of life.

Catharanthus roseus produces crowds of cheerful flowers over a very long season. Flower colors run mostly on the cool side of red, pink, and violet (plus equally cool white), so they combine nicely with shades of blue and purple but not so happily with hot colors, such as scarlet (lower left corner of the photo), yellow, and orange.

Design attributes

Color: flowers in white, red, pink, red-violet, and lilac; I hear tell there's a selection with variegated foliage
Line: not much, really
Form: mounded-shrubby
Space: not much here either
Texture: medium

Some plants are divas: they command attention and deliver the flashy goods that crowds seem to crave, but they require plenty of maintenance to look their best and to get along with their fellow artists. Others serve as the supporting cast, working in the background, keeping the production going without the spotlight shining on them. But sometimes, if given a little extra attention, a member of the supporting cast breaks out to become a low-maintenance star, making everyone happy. The last scenario applies fittingly to *C. roseus* (aka *Vinca rosea*), I think. Not only can the older, tried-and-true selections emerge from the shadows of unrecognition if given a bit more fertilizer, water, and light (not to extremes, happily), but newer, larger-flowered, more glitzy selections have be-

Can you imagine what this breakthrough diva of a *Catharanthus roseus* 'Merry-Go-Round' would look like in a brand-new terracotta pot? Place (or imagine) something orange over the pot to see what I mean. The pale blue pot was a brilliant choice, as was placing the container against a gray-brown wall (instead of, say, a red brick one).

come available in recent years, lifting the entire cast of annual periwinkles to increased stardom.

I will admit a preference for the diva (monopot) role, where these plants have a chance to produce stunning, radiantly healthy, flower-bedecked specimens. They do well in combopot situations, too, but—as always—consider every plant's cultural needs and growth rates before mixing them up in a pot. Annual periwinkles take their time during early growth and might be overgrown by speedier companions.

Try these, among others:

The Cooler series comes in a wide range of colors and withstands cooler temperatures than most others; they grow to about 1 ft. tall.

The distinctive Mediterranean series offers a very wide range of colors on low-growing (to 6 in.), spreading (to 30 in.) plants, perfect for spilling over pot edges or from hanging baskets.

The Pacifica series blooms earlier than others on foot-tall plants; their 2-in. flowers are unusually large.

Cultural tips: Don't panic when a catharanthus wilts dramatically (remember, the diva can come out under certain circumstances; it should recover after a nice, long shower), but do your best to avoid water stress. You don't like it, and neither do plants. Being subshrubby, they can be rooted from cuttings taken before the nights turn cool.

CENTAUREA
dusty miller (*C. cineraria*)

Family: Asteraceae
Cultural group: annuals (usually)
Height: 1–3 ft.
Width: 1–2 ft.
Light: sun
Temperature: cool to warm to hot
Overwintering: min. 50°F, water occasionally, bright light; hardy in Z7–9, perhaps a bit colder
Moisture: on dry side to moderate
Drainage of medium: well drained
Fertility: low to average
Ease/speed of growth: easy/moderate

Gray by itself is a soothing color, but when mixed with other colors it can play the role of unifier or even peacemaker. Here, the mass of gray centaurea helps unite the composition by diverting your eye from the several colors vying for attention around it.

Propagation: seeds, cuttings
Problems: root rot (from overwatering), unkempt look (if
    dead foliage isn't removed from older, taller plants)
Principal interest: foliage
Length of seasonal interest: long

Design attributes

Color: gray to almost white foliage
Line: straight to curving stems and outwardly moving
    foliage (increasingly noticeable with age)
Form: mounded-shrubby; can become gently reclining to
    floppy
Space: lots within the lobes of the leaves; around stems
    and within "mops" of foliage in time
Texture: medium

Dusty Miller. Didn't I graduate from high school with him? Actually, the common name is supposed to evoke the image of a guy who grinds flour for a living at the end of a busy day. All the good forms of *C. cineraria* (aka *C. gymnocarpa*) certainly do look like they've been dusted with gray to almost white flour, and that is why they get along so well with their companions in a pot. They're not dazzlingly white, which is a potent, bellicose color (yes, white is a color) that combines reluctantly, if at all, with most others. In my experience, clean white is *not* a dependable peacemaker, at least in a garden setting, particularly in regions that receive brilliant sunshine in summer. However, less strident shades of white (those that contain a suggestion of another color) can often be used to tone down warring (or at least tussling) colors and bring them together visually, especially in the close confines of a container. Here is where dusty miller and other similarly gray plants (*Artemisia*, *Dichondra*) become valuable allies when combining plants and matching them to their container.

Another attribute Mr. Miller adds to the mix is his texture, which is usually fine to some degree. Fine texture often gets along more amicably with a range of other textures than does coarse. As in matters diplomatic, delicacy and the willingness to be appropriately assertive in the right context achieve more meaningful cooperation than brashness and "my way or the highway." Some accomplished diplomats, all selections of *C. cineraria*, follow:

A big pot of *Centaurea cineraria* 'Colchester White' looks like a grizzle-bearded wizard or maybe a cloud scudding across the sky. While this is an extreme example of the calming power of gray, even a few stems of a gray plant tones things down. The finely cut foliage helps create a soft touch, too.

'Cirrus' and 'Silver Dust', both of which can be raised from seed, appear almost blindingly gray.

'Colchester White' should reach about 1 ft. tall and wide in its first year. (The burly plant shown in the photograph was overwintered and chopped up for cuttings in spring, and then it grew out into a broad-shouldered monster.)

Cultural tips: Take it easy with the nitrogen. Too much of it often leads to soft growth and more green than gray. Ditto the water: excess can lead to root rot.

CHAMAEDOREA
parlor palm (*C. elegans*)

Family: Arecaceae
Cultural group: tropicals
Height: 3 ft., maybe more
Width: 3 ft., maybe more
Light: partial shade
Temperature: warm to hot
Overwintering: min. 50°F, water occasionally, bright light
Moisture: moderate to ample

I like the plain green, fishbone-like leaves of a small parlor palm (*Chamaedorea elegans*): they look full of energy. The palmy look in miniature appeals to me, too, but that feeling changes as the plant grows larger and more imposing.

Drainage of medium: well drained
Fertility: low to average
Ease/speed of growth: easy/moderate
Propagation: division
Problems: spider mites, scale insects, spots and rots
Principal interest: foliage
Length of seasonal interest: all year

Design attributes
Color: light to mid-green leaves, black fruit (maybe)
Line: arching stems and fishbone-like foliage
Form: open-mounded to treelike (in time)
Space: quite a bit within and between foliage
Texture: medium

Parlor palm (*C. elegans*) won't develop an impressive trunk like the big boys (*Cocos, Phoenix, Washingtonia*), but it does provide impressively feathery leaves. Even little specimens do, such as the one I picked up at the opening of the Sealtest plant in Pittsburgh many years ago. Why a dairy facility was giving out palms gratis I don't know; but I liked the palmy leaves, and the little one I took away with me grew nicely, in its pot, on a well-lit porch—for a time.

The point? Even plants that eventually grow large and unwieldy can be enjoyed for their attributes in a container for a while when still small. A huge number of plants could serve us well for one season. Why not include reasonably priced dumb cane (*Dieffenbachia*) or philodendrons in our summer containers, whether monopot or combopot? Box stores often carry them, and they won't set you back very much. "You see things and you say, Why? But I dream things that never were; and I say, Why not?" Thank you, George Bernard Shaw. This sentiment applies to container gardening and a whole lot of other things in life.

Cultural tips: Spider mites can't get enough of parlor palm. Keep the soapy water or insecticidal soap spray handy.

CHLOROPHYTUM
spider plant, ribbon plant, mother of thousands

Family: Anthericaceae/Liliaceae
Cultural group: tropicals
Height: 1 ft., plus another foot or more with hanging plantlets
Width: 2–3 ft.
Light: sun to partial shade to shade (depends on degree of variegation)
Temperature: warm to hot
Overwintering: min. 50°F, water occasionally, bright light
Moisture: moderate to ample
Drainage of medium: well drained

Fertility: low to average to high
Ease/speed of growth: easy/fast
Propagation: division (of mother plant), plantlets
Problems: spider mites, tip burn, overall leaf burn
Principal interest: foliage, form
Length of seasonal interest: all year

Design attributes

Color: foliage green (plus orange in *C. amaniense* 'Fireflash'), white stripes on variegated forms
Line: eruptively linear (plantlets add downward/outward movement and more eruptive/explosive action); *C. amaniense* 'Fireflash' linear but with fewer and broader lines
Form: bushy-mounded (plantlets add another dimension of forms); *C. amaniense* 'Fireflash' flat to palmlike with age
Space: abundant between mother and offspring; *C. amaniense* 'Fireflash' shows plenty of space between the leaves
Texture: fine to medium; *C. amaniense* 'Fireflash' medium to coarse (less so with age)

My rallying cry for using houseplants as container plants outdoors can easily be made here. Here's a genus of classic houseplants that perform superbly outdoors, whether as pompom-like monopot specimens or combined with other plants that can hold their own against the dramatic linearity of a spider plant. One thing that the photos here don't show, unfortunately, is the eponymous and beloved "spiders" (offset plants borne on elongated inflorescences), which can be produced in abundance. Everyone takes delight in the baby spiders that hang from the mother, and they can spark an abiding interest in propagation and gardening in general. Here's how to get kids (or anyone not yet in our green fold, for that matter) interested in gardening: cut off a spider and pin it down onto some potting mix in a little cup or pot. Tell the recipient to keep the mix moist but not wet and keep it in bright light away from direct sun. Wait a couple of weeks for the excited call or visit from the proud parent of the newly rooted spider. You've just planted a seed … so to speak.

C. amaniense 'Fireflash' holds me spellbound every time I

Two baskets of *Chlorophytum comosum* 'Vittatum' receive visitors as they enter this garden. Try to picture the different impression that side-by-side placement of these two striped spider plants might create (or if they flanked the window, or if there were only one hanging basket in this spot).

A close look at *Chlorophytum comosum* 'Vittatum' reveals the energy of the striped foliage. Would the solidly green-leaved species suggest this much action?

see it. It looks like a big flat spider with orange legs (but doesn't make little spiders). Grow it in a purple pot to create a triadic harmony of the three secondary colors. Then impress your friends with your knowledge of color theory put into practice. Figure this one to grow about 1.5 ft. tall (in time) and 1 ft. or so wide.

C. comosum is the all-green spider. Its selection 'Variegatum' bears white stripes on the leaf edges, and 'Vittatum' has one white stripe down the middle of each leaf (basically).

Cultural tips: All are very easy to grow, but keep the variegated forms out of strong sun. And speaking of "tips": brown leaf tips are the bane of many a spider-tender, and it's widely reported that fluoride in our drinking water is the culprit. Easy and green solution: allow tap water to stand for a day or two before using it, or use collected rainwater or well water. You might even boil some tap water and let it cool before watering your spiders. Non-green solution: use bottled water from plastic containers that will still be taking up space in our landfills a zillion years from now.

CHRYSANTHEMUM
mum

Family: Asteraceae
Cultural group: perennials
Height: 2–3 ft.
Width: 2 ft.
Light: sun
Temperature: cool to warm to hot
Overwintering: not usually; some can be placed in a cold frame and repropagated in spring; many are hardy to Z6
Moisture: moderate to ample
Drainage of medium: well drained
Fertility: average to high
Ease/speed of growth: easy (except for the fussier ones)/ moderate to fast
Propagation: division, cuttings, seeds
Problems: plenty—rabbits, groundhogs, deer, aphids, spider mites, viruses, rots and spots
Principal interest: flowers, form
Length of seasonal interest: brief but glorious

Design attributes
Color: flowers in just about every color but blue
Line: only in the (attractively) floppy ones
Form: shrubby to floppy; others mounded to shrubby to upright
Space: evident (but not assertive) to none
Texture: medium

Chrysanthemums occupy a significant and sizeable place in gardening. The reds, yellows, bronzes, lavenders, and whites of mums are everywhere, as is the sharp scent of their foliage. Their ubiquitous fall presence in gardens and containers over much of North America is undeniable, and stunning success with figuring out their precise and very manipulatable cultural needs has made it possible to buy mums at any time of year. Short, potted football mums accessorized to look like bunnies at Easter. Bunches of spoon mums in July. You name the time, you can have some mums.

Still, many mums require a level of cultural attention that many of us cannot (or choose not to) provide, no matter how impressive the results. While you can of course enjoy a cushion mum or even an exquisite spider mum in a container, I want to encourage you to explore mums that require little care and offer ample rewards. Those I list here require no pinching, no removal of side buds, no extensive spray or fertilizer programs, and no protection from rain and wind, which can wreak havoc on the bigger beauties. They can wilt repeat-

Mums come in many colors, shapes, and heights, but few look as perky in a container as *Chrysanthemum* 'Sheffield Pink' and similar open-looking selections. Instead of a solid mass of color (which has its own merits and usefulness), 'Sheffield Pink' offers the opportunity to enjoy the individual flower heads.

edly and bounce back with no apparent damage. Their sherbet-colored flowers appear very late in the season and withstand severe freezes until they finally succumb to winter's icy fingers of death. They make splendid monopots and associate nicely with other like-minded plants in combopots. Who could ask for anything more?

My favorite, without question, is 'Sheffield Pink' (aka 'Sheffield' and 'Single Apricot'—and indeed, it is more apricot than pink to my eye). You might also find and like 'Sheffield White' and 'Sheffield Yellow' (which might arise as sports on your Sheffield; try rooting the sported shoots, but keep your fingers crossed). These might also beguile you: 'Cambodian Queen' in light red-violet (yes, it borders on magenta); 'Clara Curtis' (pink with enough yellow in it to think it's peach or salmon); 'Duchess of Edinburgh' (red); 'Emperor of China' (more or less the same color as 'Cambodian Queen' but double); 'Mary Stoker' (light orange-yellow); and 'Mei-Kyo' (violet-mauve-pink).

Cultural tips: One pinch early in the season can't hurt. I feel that staking these robs them of much of their charm.

CISSUS
grape ivy, oakleaf ivy (*C. rhombifolia*);
rex begonia vine (*C. discolor*)

Family: Vitaceae
Cultural group: climbers and trailers
Height: 2–6 ft. or more
Width: depends on training
Light: sun (not *C. discolor*) to partial shade
Temperature: warm to hot
Overwintering: min. 45°F (*C. discolor* better at min. 60°F), water occasionally, bright light
Moisture: moderate to ample
Drainage of medium: well drained
Fertility: low to average
Propagation: cuttings
Problems: spider mites
Ease/speed of growth: easy (except *C. discolor*, at times)/ moderate to fast
Principal interest: foliage
Length of seasonal interest: all year

Design attributes
Color: foliage mostly green (*C. discolor* adds silver and purple), also bits of brown
Line: strongly vertical or cascading (different if trained on a form or stakes); tendrils
Form: bushy to elongated, depending on training
Space: nearly none to some, depending on training
Texture: medium to coarse

Grape ivy (*Cissus rhombifolia*) looks rather special when thoughtfully framed, doesn't it? Even plain Janes become starlets when seen in a complementary setting. The geometric pattern on the container adds to the visual action: the plant itself seems to be bouncing around, arranging itself into a mosaic. The background of rectangular bricks adds attractive diversity to the overall composition by contrasting with both the round container and the diamond-shaped leaflets.

I like challenges, so this genus appeals to me: one species is a challenge to display creatively (how to showcase a common plant? that's *C. rhombifolia*), the second is a challenge to grow (but deserves the effort—*C. discolor*), and the third is a challenge to find (*C. adenopoda*). Let the games begin.

The common one, *C. rhombifolia*, grows easily and fills many an office or mall planter or classroom hanging basket. Grape ivy tolerates just about everything, really, so it makes a good plant to start kids or newbie gardeners with, and it rolls with the punches in container plantings. Common, yes; ordinary, no. Seek out the selection 'Ellen Danica' if you like the look of more deeply cut leaves.

The tricky one, *C. discolor* (rex begonia vine), prefers constant warmth to heat, bright light but not much direct sun, and plenty of humidity, which is generally easy to provide in summer. But if you want a good-sized plant to play with, you'll need to overwinter a first-year plant and build it up over the

Just one leaf of *Cissus discolor* makes a powerful statement of color and pattern. The silvery spots seem to be moving in an orderly procession toward the top against the dark green background as the thin red-violet veins guide the marchers into their proper places.

A swarm of butterflies seems to be rushing from their gray confines. *Cissus discolor* can bring that (and your own images, I hope) to mind if you take the time to consider how the five design elements interact with each other.

The predominantly gray container allows the purple-tinged, bright green, three-parted leaves and purple tendrils of *Cissus adenopoda* to jump out and demand attention. Here, less is more: a surging mass of this foliage would obscure the details. The gray container is nice, but I wonder how these leaves would look against a pale yellow pot.

next year or two. Keep it warm, humid, and evenly moist, and maybe some of the leaves will remain on the plant until it's time to put it back outside. Most people understandably grow *C. discolor* as an annual, but where's the challenge in that?

The third species of interest, *C. adenopoda*, is quite new to me. It doesn't seem to be a tricky one to grow, fortunately (pretty much like *C. rhombifolia*, it appears to me), so maybe soon I'll enjoy this carefully purple-painted beauty.

Cultural tips: See earlier for the fascinating but temperamental *C. discolor*. For the others, enjoy the easy ride.

CITRUS
lemon, lime, orange, grapefruit (and many more)

Family: Rutaceae
Cultural group: tropicals, woody shrubs and trees
Height: 2–6 ft. or more
Width: 2–6 ft. or more
Light: sun to partial shade
Temperature: cool to warm to hot
Overwintering: min. 50°F, water occasionally, bright light;
    generally hardy in Z9–10
Moisture: moderate to ample
Drainage of medium: well drained
Fertility: low to average
Ease/speed of growth: moderate/moderate
Propagation: grafting, cuttings, seeds (for grins, mostly)
Problems: scale insects, mealybugs, spider mites, various
    rots and spots, chlorosis
Principal interest: fruit, flowers, fragrance
Length of seasonal interest: all year

Design attributes
Color: fruit in yellow and orange; white flowers; medium to
    dark green (sometimes variegated), often shiny foliage
Line: on more open, progressively more pendent older
    plants
Form: shrubby
Space: increases with age
Texture: medium

A small but stately specimen of a variegated grapefruit (*Citrus* ×*paradisi*) selection deserves a suitably ornate pot that might evoke images of the Orangerie at Versailles. Of course Miss Pamplemousse will grow in a plain pot, but the overall impression would be less regal.

While the foliage certainly catches the eye, this variegated grapefruit (*Citrus* ×*paradisi*) selection offers a surprise: even its fruit is marked with more than the "expected" color. Variegation can be fun!

I don't pretend to know a great deal about growing citrus, but I do want to encourage everyone to try to grow at least one. Gardening is as much about the process as it is about the results, right? I've watched plenty of citrus come and go at Atlock Farm; most of them remain healthy and happy enough to produce their brilliantly colored, sweet-acid, powerfully fragrant fruit (which arise from intoxicatingly perfumed flowers). They're not the prettiest plants in the garden (many are gawky, tangly, and a bit nasty-looking), but they do grow superbly in containers. Four huge, old (eighty-five years?) 'Ponderosa' lemons have been growing at Atlock for years, in the same (heavy!) pots, no less. They receive enough water and occasional fertilizer to keep them happy, obviously, because every year their stems groan under the weight of softball-sized, gloriously bumpy and wrinkled yellow fruit. They haven't been repotted in more than a decade, and they keep doing their thing with no complaints.

I think every patio, poolside, and other special spot deserves to showcase some sort of citrus in a pot during the warmer months, whether freely grown or trained into some approximation of a standard topiary. Grow a shallow-rooted groundcover at its base, if you wish; give it ample water and some fertilizer (and a dose of chelated iron every now and then will help keep the foliage from turning a sickly yellow); and overwinter it in your sunny but cool orangerie. What, you don't have an orangerie? Then put it in a cool but sunny spot, ease up with the watering, and don't get crazy when a fair number of leaves drop off. More will come in spring.

You could choose from an entire grove of different kinds (oranges, lemons, limes, grapefruit, tangerines, pummelos, tangelos, other portmanteaus), but here are a few that I've seen doing well:

C. limon (lemon) in its many selections seem to me the easiest to grow. 'Sun Gold' offers attractive variegation, as does 'Variegated Pink Eureka'. Make sure you point out the variegated young fruit to your garden visitors before the stripes fade.

C. ×meyeri 'Meyer' remains small (maybe 4 ft. high), makes a nice informal standard, and readily bears crops of smallish, bright yellow fruit almost bursting with juice. Probably a cross between *C. limon* and sweet orange (*C. sinensis*), it was brought to the United States from China by the intrepid USDA plant explorer Frank Meyer. It's often considered among the hardiest of all citrus, but that still means it only might survive outside in Z8 with ample protection and more than a little bit of luck.

C. ×paradisi (grapefruit) is a product of the union between *C. sinensis* and a pummelo (*C. maxima*). Grow the big-fruited ones if you have the inclination and the space, but I suggest you try the much more compact (and smaller-fruited) variegated forms. The one pictured attracts its share of attention at Atlock Farm when in flower and fruit (sporadically) and in foliage (always).

Cultural tips: Don't grow citrus if you can't tolerate impaling yourself on their spines every now and then. Watch for the "big three" of the bug set that likes to feed on them before we do: scale insects, mealybugs, and spider mites. I don't need to remind you to avoid thermonuclear pesticides if you're going to eat the fruit, do I? Growing citrus from seed is a fun project (especially for kids), but be prepared to wait a while for the fruit to appear, if it ever does.

CLEMATIS
Virgin's bower

Family: Ranunculaceae
Cultural group: climbers and trailers, perennials
Height: 2–4 ft. or more (perennials usually 2 ft. or so)
Width: depends on training (perennials usually 2 ft. or so)
Light: sun to partial shade
Temperature: warm
Overwintering: keep evergreens indoors at min. 50°F,
    water occasionally, bright light; generally hardy in Z6–9

Moisture: moderate to ample
Drainage of medium: well drained
Fertility: average
Ease/speed of growth: moderate/moderate to fast
Propagation: cuttings, grafting, seeds
Problems: wilt, spots and rots, spider mites
Principal interest: flowers, foliage, form (if trained), fruit
Length of seasonal interest: brief to moderate (sometimes
    repeated or sporadic)

Design attributes
Color: vast range of flower color (no bright orange . . .
    yet); some of the perennials have dark purple foliage;
    silvery fruit (especially noticeable when backlit) if
    produced and retained
Line: often nearly absent unless trained (and grown thinly)
Form: upright to rambling mass (perennials upright-shrubby);
    flowers often distinctively starry or lantern-like
Space: depends on training
Texture: fine to medium

Clematis will grow well in containers, but they seem particularly ravishing when allowed to climb over an attractive support, such as this bird-topped tuteur. The icing on the cake here, though, comes from the placement of the blue-violet flowers against the yellow-green foliage and the gray tree trunks. Very color-aware.

I've read in more than one place that clematis deserve the appellation "The Queen of Vines" (or "Climbers," if the publication is British). Admittedly those books on clematis were probably written by clematophiles, who were therefore preaching to the choir, but I tend to agree with the preachers. Clematis have it all: superbly crafted flowers in a wide range of artfully sculpted shapes and sumptuous colors, on plants that lift the flowers skyward (or at least a few feet up) among attractive foliage. Even the seedheads merit notice. I've been known to stop dead in my tracks before a particularly toothsome clematis, and I've seen other people do the same. Evocative. Ethereal. Transcendent. Real pretty. You should definitely try your hand at them in containers.

Many clematis have brittle stems that take very poorly to being handled or being tossed about in the wind, so I recommend growing them attentively supported and by themselves, as monopots. However, you might come up with a knockout combopot association with one or more other plants. The so-called herbaceous types—they don't climb but can grow tall and rangy enough to require some support—often need to depend upon the kindness of strangers (other plants) in the open garden and therefore seem suited to combopot situations with plants they can lean on. But best to avoid totally, as container garden subjects, are the more rambunctious clematis and their selections, such as the splendid evergreen *C. armandii* (but what a fragrance!), *C. montana* (they can devour big trellises, for Pete's sake), or the deliciously scented, fall-blooming *C. terniflora* (aka *C. paniculata*), which has used good-sized American hollies for support at the Morris Arboretum in Philadelphia. While you're saving up for a really big pot and a welded metal trellis or jungle gym, I suggest you try some of these:

C. alpina could be the most delicate of them all; a few bamboo stakes should make them happy. They bloom early in shades of pink and blue and probably won't reach much beyond 3 ft. in a pot.

My personal fantasy garden would display several pots of the impossibly beautiful *C. florida* var. *sieboldiana* (greenish white with a central, flat feather duster of purple). Good luck getting it to 2 ft.

The large-flowered (often 6 in. across and thickly petaled) pink/purple/red/white/blue hybrids and their kin (there's a million of them, including the one on the tuteur on page 129) can get fairly large, so be prepared for some staking and training. Not one member of this eye-candy gang is homely, from the starlike singles to the confectionery doubles. Check out 'Polish Spirit' in full bloom and tell me that an image of stars falling from the heavens doesn't come to mind. Most of these bloom in the middle of the clematis season (and sometimes later) and might reach 4–5 ft. in a pot.

'Odoriba' looks like a texensis but is actually a child of two North American species, *Cc. viorna* and *crispa*.

The sumptuous purple falling stars of *Clematis* 'Polish Spirit', a member of the late, large-flowered group of hybrids, make a stellar display. Give them a roomy pot (and a party when in bloom).

C. texensis is no doubt in the (blue-)bloodlines of the lantern-flowered 'Duchess of Albany', 'Étoile Rose', and 'Gravetye Beauty' (all in pink shades), among others. They generally bloom after the large-flowered hybrids but before the late ones. Figure 4–5 ft. for these.

C. viticella selections range from the single-flowered, such as 'Betty Corning' (lavender), 'Étoile Violet' (um, violet, and a star of the group), and 'Madame Julia Correvon' (red), to the almost ridiculously double 'Purpurea Plena Elegans', which is in fact purple, double (think "*plen*tiful"), and elegant. Most bloom in midseason on plants that range 2–5 ft. tall (most notably 'Betty Corning', which in the open garden can engulf a good-sized shrub, but it can be restrained in a pot).

The herbaceous species include *Cc. heracleifolia, integrifolia*, and *recta*, all of which can be treated like deciduous herbaceous perennials, which die to the ground for winter. My favorite is *C. heracleifolia* var. *davidiana* (aka *C. tubulosa*), which might grow to 2.5 ft. tall, by which time it will need some vertical assistance. The flowers are reminiscent of hyacinths but sure don't smell like them. Unlike many of the others here, it's hardy in the ground in Z3–8, so it should be fine in a pot in Z4 and certainly 5. That's pretty hardy.

Cultural tips: Don't be afraid to prune the climbers. A

You nativists out there might want to consider including *Clematis* 'Odoriba', the offspring of two species native to North America, in a container planting. Non-nativists will probably be blinded (or at least seduced) by the whispered beauty of the flowers and not even think about the bloodlines.

Don't be misled by the delicacy of the flowers of *Clematis* 'Betty Corning': a well-grown plant can easily reach 6 ft. tall and bear hundreds of lavender bells, even in a container. Keep the pruning shears handy if she gets too big.

Viticellas generally bear smaller, more open flowers than their large-flowered hybrid cousins. Here is 'Madame Julia Correvon'— as both flower and fruit.

Clematis heracleifolia var. *davidiana* and other herbaceous clematis can be grown in pots, just like their sky-aspiring relatives. Expect a subtler, more earthbound display of clustered flowers on shrublike plants.

general rule: prune the early bloomers after they bloom, and the others as the shoots emerge in spring. Take them back to vigorously growing buds. Relax. Observe. Learn. Remember. The medusa-like seedheads are well worth keeping on the plant for their fuzzy glory (especially when backlit by the sun, which turns them into delicate silver filigrees), but they will reduce the number or preclude the appearance of later-season flowers.

CLEOME
spider flower, spider legs

Family: Capparaceae
Cultural group: annuals
Height: 1–4 ft.
Width: 1–2 ft.
Light: sun
Temperature: warm to hot
Overwintering: no
Moisture: moderate to ample
Drainage of medium: well drained
Fertility: low to average
Ease/speed of growth: easy/fast
Propagation: seeds
Problems: caterpillars, whitefly
Principal interest: flowers, foliage, fragrance, form
    (especially the larger ones)
Length of seasonal interest: long

Design attributes

Color: flowers in white, pink, and red-violet (magenta!)
Line: everywhere (especially the larger ones), from the
    stems, petioles, leaves, stamens, peduncles, and fruits;
    not as much in 'Senorita Rosalita'
Form: upright and outward; bushy ('Senorita Rosalita')
Space: quite a bit with the larger ones
Texture: medium to coarse

The "spiders" we grew when I was a kid were the big ones, 4–5 ft. tall, with clusters of fragrant blooms attracting the sphinx moths that were always around on warm summer nights. The light magenta one was probably *C. hassleriana*; we also grew white, pink, and purple forms, including 'Helen Campbell' (white), 'Pink Queen', and 'Rose Queen' (the newer Sparkler series has a similar color range but is more compact, to less than 4 ft.). The foliage had a distinctive, almost skunky aroma; the stems bore sneaky little, surprisingly painful spines; and both stems and flowers were covered in sticky stuff that held the lifeless bodies of countless little insects by season's end, by which time the flowers had turned into masses of long-stemmed fruits (this is where the spideriness becomes obvious). Their abundant seeds, something like coffee grounds, fell to the ground naturally or were assisted by yours truly. Even the sound of them hitting the ground was pleasant.

We never thought to grow cleomes in pots, and I admit the idea never occurred to me until I discovered the much shorter ones becoming widely available. The new ones, such as 'Senorita Rosalita', are touted for their height challenges as well as for their thornless, unsticky, much less fragrant foliage, and

they make very attractive and long-blooming choices for a pot. Speaking of "pot," the leaves resemble the foliage of *Cannabis sativa*, but only to a man on a galloping horse. Don't let anyone scare you into pulling out your spider plants because of the resemblance, unless you're growing some pot, perhaps in a pot, inside a attention-diverting, red-herring grove of spider plants. You're on your own with that.

Cultural tips: Take it easy with the fertilizer; too much will encourage spindly growth and fewer flowers. Cleomes can wilt dramatically but will revive quickly after you rescue them. Transplant them when a few inches tall, or scatter some seeds in the pot where you intend to grow them. You might find "volunteers" in the pots growing from seeds dropped during the previous season (or on the ground, certainly), which will make a fine teachable moment for kids, grandkids, and newbie gardeners in your life about letting plants come up where they like (or not).

Unlike most others of its clan, *Cleome* 'Senorita Rosalita' stays on the short side, making it perfectly suitable for less than gargantuan containers. Take care with that magenta coloration, though; some people would recoil in horror at the color combination shown here.

COBAEA
cup and saucer vine, cathedral bells (*C. scandens*)

Family: Polemoniaceae
Cultural group: climbers and trailers
Height: easily 6 ft. (much more if overwintered)
Width: depends on training (which it needs to behave like a nice plant)
Light: sun to partial shade
Temperature: warm to hot
Overwintering: not usually, but if you want to try and grow it much larger, it can be kept at min. 45°F, water occasionally, bright light
Moisture: moderate to ample
Drainage of medium: well drained
Fertility: average to high
Ease/speed of growth: easy/fast
Propagation: seeds, cuttings
Problems: spider mites
Principal interest: flowers, foliage, form (if trained)
Length of seasonal interest: moderate

Design attributes
Color: flowers open light green, becoming purple; white in f. *alba*; foliage has suggestions of brown and purple
Line: depends on training; tendrils (arising from leaves) provide some linear interest
Form: usually upright-rambling, depends on training
Space: depends on training
Texture: medium

If you're looking for something different in a climber, I suggest you give *C. scandens* a try. It's not a small, shy little thing—in fact, its deep-rooted hegemonous streak can be managed only with a firm hand—but once you see the pretty, tendril-tipped leaves and those unique flowers (perfectly described by the common name), I think you'll want to look for ways to use it in a spacious pot with other big boys. It's the color progression of the flowers that really holds my interest. The typical form opens a misty greenish cream and gradually becomes purple—not a pale, airy purple but a rich, regal shade of it. The white form goes through a less dramatic transformation from green-white to more of a cream. Both forms will grab your attention, I bet. I'm looking forward to

Cobaea scandens f. *alba* bears its collared trumpets (or cups and saucers, if you follow the suggestion of the common name) against a busy mass of multi-parted leaves and questing tendrils. The white and pale green combination makes me want to enjoy some vanilla ice cream with a bit of lime sherbet . . . in a little cup on a saucer.

Cobaea scandens definitely requires some restraint in smaller containers, but its novel flowers make the effort worthwhile. They open light green and gradually turn purple. Intriguing, aren't they?

seeing the form with variegated foliage. Anybody have some of it to share?

Cup and saucer vine looks best when grown openly on a big trellis or sturdy, open host plant to show off the attractive pinnate (roughly feather- or fishbone-like) leaves, delicate tendrils, and bizarro flowers (which aren't borne profusely, but they don't need to be; too much of this good thing would dilute the impact of the individual little cups and saucers). Letting it have its own way often results in a mass of … no, make that a *mess* of stuff.

Cultural tips: Seeds seem to take forever to germinate, so have patience. The plants hate cool weather (the lightest frost at either the beginning or end of the season will make it and you sad), so sow the seeds in warmth and plant them out after every last little bit of frost danger has passed. Don't handle the seedlings roughly when transplanting them, and be sure to settle the plants in their final position before they get more than 1–2 ft. tall. Once they hit their stride they go like gangbusters, clambering onto anything nearby, so keep your eyes open and your fingers handy to direct the stems in the desired direction. Go back six hours later to make sure the plant is minding you.

COCCOLOBA
sea grape (*C. uvifera*)

Family: Polygonaceae
Cultural group: tropicals
Height: 4–6 ft.
Width: 4–6 ft.
Light: sun to limited partial shade
Temperature: warm to hot
Overwintering: min. 50°F, water occasionally, bright light; hardy in Z10–11
Moisture: moderate to ample
Drainage of medium: well drained
Fertility: average
Propagation: cuttings, seeds, air layering
Problems: spots and rots
Ease/speed of growth: moderate/moderate
Principal interest: foliage, form (of foliage and also plant, with age); flowers and fruit, maybe
Length of seasonal interest: all year

Design attributes
Color: dark green leaves with red veining, white flowers, purple fruit
Line: upright-outward with age
Form: shrubby; individual leaves are noticeable blobs
Space: with age, as stems become bare
Texture: coarse

Sea grape is not everyone's cup of tea. It doesn't bear showy flowers when small, the foliage is not overtly flashy, and it can become unwieldy in time. So why is it included in this book? Because sea grape (*Coccoloba uvifera*) makes a loud and clear design statement, no matter how and where it is used.

First, consider the *color* of the leaves: medium green with red-violet veins. That's not a combination you see every day, for sure. And adding the red-violet veins of sea grape to any combopot is a way of assuring that *line*, and therefore movement, exists in a planting. The rounded, blobby *form* of the sea grape leaves can almost always be counted on to add variety in size (as in the photo here) and contrasts sharply with pointy or cut-edged leaves. And yes, there is quite a bit of *space* between the individual leaves of sea grape. Finally, big, uncomplicated leaves and other plant parts suggest a coarse *texture*, which sea grape has in spades. My first impression of

Note how the red-violet veins of sea grape (*Coccoloba uvifera*) echo the colors in the coleus below them and relate to the darker, almost black sweet potato foliage. Much like the green of the sea grape, the little bit of yellow-green foliage on the right quietly contrasts with the darker colors. They and the leaves of the black sweet potato have a much finer texture and create a pleasing textural contrast with the beefy sea grape. The coleus sits in the middle of the textural range, adding more diversity.

this species came from big masses of it along the road from the airport to the heart of Key West; I still remember marveling at its beefiness.

So, it turns out that sea grape has more to offer than might immediately meet the eye. Try the above exercise out on other plants that don't impress you at first, and you might well discover some useful design potential.

Cultural tips: Expect sea grape to get big, especially if you give it a very well-drained mix. This is one tough plant (it grows in sand in the brilliantly sunny, hot tropics, after all), so you don't need to coddle it. If it does get too big, chop it back and start over again.

CODIAEUM
croton (*C. variegatum* var. *pictum*)

Family: Euphorbiaceae
Cultural group: tropicals
Height: 1–4 ft. (often looks better when kept lower and denser)
Width: 1–4 ft.

Light: sun to partial shade
Temperature: warm to hot
Overwintering: min. 60°F, water occasionally, bright light; keep away from cold drafts
Moisture: moderate to ample
Drainage of medium: well drained
Fertility: average
Ease/speed of growth: moderate/slow to moderate
Propagation: cuttings, air layering
Problems: mealybugs, spider mites, scale insects, rots and spots
Principal interest: foliage
Length of seasonal interest: all year

Design attributes

Color: foliage green with markings in red, yellow, orange, and purple
Line: explosive leaf arrangement, stems (in time)
Form: shrubby
Space: some, with age
Texture: medium

It's almost impossible to look at any croton without being a little blinded by the dazzling colors, but the other design elements are there, too. After your retinas recover, check out line, form, space, and texture.

Three different selections of *Codiaeum variegatum* var. *pictum* both contrast with and complement each other. Unlike many crotons, the one at the top sends out a strong linear (and spotty) impression, and maybe one of those qualities registers with you before the color does.

Although the orange daisy-like flower seems like an afterthought when seen with this vividly colorful *Codiaeum variegatum* var. *pictum* 'Petra', its intensity and dotty nature do bring something to the party. Note too how the grassy leaves at the top echo the elongated green markings in the croton foliage.

This is just wacky: yellow-green, red-violet, and blue-black, going every which way. Need I point out how many plants (and pots!) would combine sensationally with the strappy leaves of *Codiaeum variegatum* var. *pictum* 'Picasso's Paintbrush'?

From a distance, most crotons look more like splashes of paint (or psychedelic rock-band posters from the late '60s and early '70s) than plants, and therein lies the secret to using them successfully: think of them as colors, not plants. Give them what they want, and they'll satisfy your longings for the tropics, or at least for some mad tropical color in a pot.

Can you feel the energy that crotons suggest? Nothing remotely pastel or passive comes from these! All the leaf shapes (skinny, broad, spears, threads) and colors appeared to be yelling at each other or maybe passing each other around in a mosh pit. They're powerful, but don't be afraid of crotons. You like color, don't you? And they're not just colorful, they're unpredictable (unstable?), with every leaf on many selections somehow—subtly or blatantly or middlin'—different from its companions on the same plant. Don't even bother to look for flowers. They're little nothings, really, and completely superfluous in comparison to the foliage. Use crotons as stridently assertive monopots, or group several monopots into a wild display, or grow one croton with equally raucous (or diametri-

cally and contrastingly, croton-showcasing sedate) plants in a combopot.

Specific selections, you ask? Check out the many available in nurseries and online, and then buy the ones that burn your retinas or tweak your imagination and start painting with them.

Cultural tips: Crotons don't grow quickly in the first place, so treat them right. Rough handling when transplanting, too little water, poor drainage, cold drafts, and cool temperatures in general will make at least some of the paint (leaves) fall off, much like with poinsettias (*Euphorbia pulcherrima*), their relatives in the spurge family (Euphorbiaceae). Be wary of the sap, because it might cause dermatitis and other unpleasant reactions (there's yet another thing in common with many spurges).

COLCHICUM
autumn crocus

Family: Colchicaceae/Liliaceae
Cultural group: bulbs
Height: 6 in. (flowering); 1 ft. (foliage)
Width: 6 in. (when the flowers fall over) to 1 ft. (foliage)
Light: sun to partial shade
Temperature: cool to warm
Overwintering: those discussed here are hardy in Z4–9
Moisture: moderate
Drainage of medium: well drained
Fertility: average
Ease/speed of growth: moderate/moderate
Propagation: multiplication (of corms)
Problems: slugs
Principal interest: flowers, foliage
Length of seasonal interest: brief (but in two
   nonconsecutive seasons)

Design attributes

Color: flowers mostly red-violet (some white); medium to
   dark green foliage
Line: long perianth tubes; upright-outward foliage
Form: goblets, stars, and dense rosettes (flowers); little
   cornstalks, sort of (foliage)
Space: in between petals, under flowers and foliage
Texture: medium

Colchicum autumnale 'Pleniflorum' and a variegated ivy in a gray pot make a cool combination on a warm October day. Even though the flowers don't last very long (maybe ten days), the surprise of seeing autumn crocus and English ivy in a pot instead of in the ground might make an impression that lasts for years.

Autumn crocus: the seasonal opener of that common name should tip you off that we're not dealing with conventional container plants (plant them in spring, enjoy them until frost zaps them) here. Indeed not. Colchicums grow from corms, bulblike structures that have more stem tissue in them than do bulbs, which are mostly leaf tissue. But that's not what's odd about them. They need to be potted up soon after you receive them in late summer, and in a few weeks they'll be in bloom. In fact, they'll bloom quite nicely if left out on a windowsill or other place with no potting mix in sight, such as the shipping box they arrived in. So there's no waiting until spring to enjoy the flowers here, which brings us to another oddity: they send up their cornstalk-like foliage in spring (which dies down in summer), leave no evidence behind, and then the corms send up those flowers. I find their through-the-looking-glass nature a fascinating spin on the usual; taking advantage of a peculiarity keeps container gardening fresh and interesting for me.

Common name aside, autumn crocuses ain't really crocuses, botanically. Membership in the genus *Crocus* (which is part of the iris family, Iridaceae) requires that. Now take another, this time etymological, look at that genus name. Yes, the drug colchicine can be extracted from *Colchicum*, but please don't try to do so in your home lab or kitchen. Colchicine is potent and can lead to nausea and vomiting to shock, multiple organ failure, respiratory distress, and other woes if ingested. So take note, and avoid autumn crocuses if you have kids and pets and other little munchers around and about.

But do try them if you feel safe around them. The flowers remind me of waterlilies, but they don't require all that contained water to make them happy. Conveniently, there's a hybrid called 'Waterlily', and it's probably my favorite of the genus, in rich red-violet on lushly double blooms. Others worth trying include the numerous selections of *C. autumnale*, which send up neat little bunches of happy, starry, single and double blooms in lilac-pink, red-violet, and white. *C. speciosum* produces beautiful groups of goblet-like flowers of pinkish red-violet (white in the ethereal 'Album'). There are quite a few more, but start with these before you graduate to the choicer, rarer, and fussier ones.

Cultural tips: Remember their backward growth habit. Combine them with something that looks good all season, gives the often floppy flowers a bit of support, and can cover up the blank space that the foliage leaves behind. Some day I want to combine the red-violet of *C.* 'Waterlily' with the chartreuse foliage of *Lysimachia nummularia* 'Aurea'. Groundhugging Jenny won't prop up the blooms, but I don't care; it will be another way to draw attention to the idiosyncratic tendencies of autumn crocus.

COLOCASIA
elephant ear, taro, dasheen, cocoyam

Family: Araceae
Cultural group: tropicals
Height: 2–8 ft.
Width: 2–8 ft.
Light: partial shade to shade (sun if kept wet enough)
Temperature: warm to hot
Overwintering: min. 50–55°F, water occasionally but sparingly, bright light; you might try a darker site to force dry, leafless dormancy
Moisture: moderate to ample to constant
Drainage of medium: tolerates standing water
Fertility: average to high
Ease/speed of growth: easy/fast
Propagation: division (of tubers)
Problems: spider mites, rots and spots

Principal interest: foliage, form
Length of seasonal interest: long

Design attributes
Color: foliage green and purple, sometimes marked with white, light green, yellow, or purple
Line: upward, often eruptive; downward-hanging foliage
Form: bunches of big ears (leaves)
Space: plenty in between leaves
Texture: assertively coarse

*C*olocasia (another plant with the common common name of elephant ear) has been riding a rocketship in the popularity stratosphere recently, and with good reason. Like its *Alocasia* and *Xanthosoma* kin, taro enters a (garden) room, takes up residence, and renders just about everything else puny or at least mundane by comparison. Colocasias have it all from a design perspective, but don't expect flowers or fruit to write home about (except for *C. gigantea* 'Thai Giant', in my

The blue-green leaves of *Colocasia esculenta* and the sage green pot make a subtly stunning combination. Oxymoronic, maybe. Attractive, definitely. Even the dying yellow leaf plays a part.

The very large, coarse leaves of *Colocasia esculenta* 'Fontanesii' contrast strongly with the much smaller, finer foliage of *Lysimachia nummularia* 'Aurea'. The grassy leaves to the left of the colocasia make an equally strong contrast in size and texture. (Note how there's no mention of color here.)

experience). No matter: they often elevate the appearance of companion plants simply by association.

Colocasias grow from tubers, often great big things, most notably the ones produced by *C. esculenta*, the source of poi and an ingredient in a great many other foods consumed widely in the tropics (the leaves can be eaten, too). Tropical people learned long ago to cook taro thoroughly to remove the calcium oxalate crystals they contain (in structures called raphides, from the Greek word for "needle"). Eating an uncooked corm or leaf is like eating a big bunch of little needles.

Whether featured by themselves in monopots or integrated into combopots, all these elephant ears might put you in mind of the tropics (or Babar, Dumbo, Horton, Horatio, or Lucy):

C. affinis var. *jenningsii* produces 8-in., dark purple-green leaves with silvery centers that remind me of wagonwheels or octopi. It should reach 2 ft. or so when happy.

C. esculenta easily sends up 2–3 ft. leaves on plants to 5 ft. tall. Many selections are available, some with names and

The bright green and blue-black leaves belong to the same plant of *Colocasia esculenta* 'Black Magic' (the green one is younger, the dark one, older). Darker-leaved selections of colocasias often display color dimorphism; use it to your advantage.

Note how the light green veins stand out against the dark blue-black of the foliage of *Colocasia esculenta* 'Illustris'. But even the imperial taro strikes me as an afterthought in this combination: that shiny, rich blue pot filled with hot orange zinnias (and spiced with a bit of almost spooky chartreuse) is a *sensational* matchup. Cover the colocasia to see what I mean.

A deeply saturated color stands out against a much brighter one, suggesting a neon diner sign glowing against the night sky above a deserted interstate. Well, not exactly (neon is much brighter than this leaf of *Colocasia esculenta* 'Diamond Head'), but I think you get the idea.

The preposterously large leaf of *Colocasia esculenta* 'Ruffles' is the alpha male in this elephant herd. How many plants do you know that produce leaves larger than their very ample pot?

Colocasias do sometimes bloom, splendidly, and not just at Chanticleer, as here. The cluster of inflorescences on this *Colocasia gigantea* 'Thai Giant' vividly evokes the passage of time. (Is anyone else reminded of the "Seven Ages of Man" monologue from Shakespeare's *As You Like It*?). Wow.

The delicate ruffling and hairline-marked edge of a leaf of *Colocasia esculenta* 'Ruffles' help soften this elephant ear's imposing presence.

others sold as leaf- and stem-color variations. Use the bloomy dark purple foliage of 'Black Magic' to set off a wide range of colors, but be patient with this one; it sometimes pokes along for no apparent reason. Plenty of others make sultry leaves, including 'Black Knight', 'Jet Black Bead', and 'Jet Black Wonder'. Choose 'Diamond Head' to appreciate the rich red of its younger foliage. 'Fontanesii' quickly grows into a big green hunk. 'Illustris' (imperial taro) makes dramatically patterned, dark purple-green, 1-ft. leaves on plants to 3 ft. 'Nancy's Revenge' bears pale yellow "spiders" on medium green 2-ft. leaves; some say the pattern shows only at maturity, which usually means you'll need to overwinter a little plant to see the spiders. And 'Ruffles' is utterly captivating, as the photos show.

C. gigantea 'Thai Giant' will bowl you over, especially if you catch it in bloom. Specimens check in at about 3 ft. tall and considerably broader.

Cultural tips: A soil-based potting mix (a third to maybe even half by volume) makes many taros happy and provides a

Colocasia gigantea 'Thai Giant' towers over its companions, including a hot-colored coleus, setting off fireworks of textural contrast. Giant, indeed.

Think about spotlighting a spike near the rim of a pot instead of smack in the center. It avoids the all-too-familiar (sooo 19th century) placement and adds a bit of eccentric flair to the composition. This uncentered *Cordyline australis* 'Red Sensation' echoes the dark centers of the coleus while offering a startling contrast in form. And how about that apricot pot?

heavy counterweight to the massive plants (which helps keep them vertical when the wind blows). Impressive size results from extra helpings of water and fertilizer. Place pots where the morning sun can shine *through* the leaves to produce a display different from when light shines *on* them. Revisit the photo of *C. esculenta* 'Black Magic' to see what I mean.

CORDYLINE
cabbage palm, cabbage tree (*C. australis*);
ti tree (*C. fruticosa*)

Family: Agavaceae/Liliaceae
Cultural group: tropicals
Height: 1–5 ft. or more
Width: 1–4 ft.
Light: sun (all-green and dark-leaved forms) to partial shade (variegated, generally)
Temperature: warm to hot

Overwintering: min. 55°F, water occasionally, bright light; generally hardy in Z10–11
Moisture: moderate to ample
Drainage of medium: well drained
Fertility: low to average
Ease/speed of growth: easy to moderate/moderate
Propagation: suckers, air layering
Problems: scale insects, mealybugs, spider mites, spots and rots
Principal interest: foliage, form
Length of seasonal interest: all year

Design attributes
Color: foliage green, brown, red, and purple, many variegated with white, red, pink, and yellow
Line: very obviously and abundantly linear
Form: explosions, some on bare stems
Space: among and under the leaves
Texture: fine to coarse

often conclude my "Lots of Pots" program, which explores various aspects of container gardening, by inviting a few audience members to come up and combine live plants based on their design elements and/or their compatibility with other plants. Why are "spikes" (usually a cordyline of some sort) so often their choice? Don't they know that they are selecting a plant that is frequently despised as a container-gardening cliché? Probably not, but I think that the wealth of interest provided by a humble spike transcends fads and plant prejudice. To me, a spike presents one of the most potent subjects for container crafters. When young, the rounded cluster of colorful, linear foliage seems to erupt from the ground, and older plants lift up their explosive leaves on an intricately leaf-scarred trunk. Whether you find the texture fine or coarse depends on you; I think cordylines exhibit both at the same time.

Most people—devotees as well as deriders—quickly register the various forms of *C. australis* (cabbage palm, when not dubbed a spike) as familiar, including 'Red Star' and 'Red Sen-

Opposite: Two humungous specimens of *Cordyline baueri* bring drama to the red border at Atlock Farm in central New Jersey. Yes, they are in pots, and the one in the back is placed on top of an upside-down pot to make it appear even more imposing.

sation', both of which array themselves in rich red-purple-brown shades and slowly progress from 1 ft. tall or so to maybe 3 ft. (they will get larger if overwintered). 'Red Star' has narrower leaves with less purple in them than 'Red Sensation'; both are handsome.

Another cordyline that looks familiar to many people is *C. fruticosa* (aka *C. terminalis*), but not as a container plant: the ti or good luck tree is widely grown as a houseplant. However, since this book advocates strongly (and often) for houseplant liberation, I suggest you consider spiking your ti outdoors. A large number of selections are available and in a much broader color range than cabbage palms; some ti trees offer wider leaves, with many of them variously painted in green, red, yellow, red-violet, and sometimes white, as well as accented

I can't help but be drawn into the energy-filled form of a large specimen of *Cordyline australis* 'Red Star'. Do you feel the plant is moving outward or inward? However you see it, use something this powerful sparingly; otherwise, you risk overwhelming your garden visitors.

This selection of *Cordyline fruticosa* would catch anyone's eye. Be thoughtful in your use of this and other DayGlo colors, but don't be afraid to play with them, either. I picture this with dark brown-red (to echo the other color in the foliage) as well as potent, bright yellow-green. Uncle Peter, where are my smelling salts?

with copper and bronze. They grow more quickly than cabbage palms and might confuse a spike derider into thinking that you've got your finger on the pulse of cutting-edge container design.

But if you want to overwhelm your garden visitors, get yourself at least one specimen of *C. baueri*, which looks like a spike from the Land of the Giants, or maybe a chocolate fountain. Try to start with at least a three-footer.

Something as big as *C. baueri* looks best as a specimen; smaller spikes get along with a huge range of plants in combopots. You might also consider including more than one spike in a pot, or planting one or all of them sideways; they'll right themselves, making interesting crooked trunks in the process.

Cultural tips: All cordylines respond to generous but not excessive amounts of fertilizer and water but will tolerate the opposite treatment, almost to the point of abuse. The smaller ones root easily if they grow too tall; simply chop off the top and place it in water or (better) a well-drained, moist potting mix out of wind and sun and other stressors. The decapitated plant might regenerate at least one cluster of foliage; if it does, maybe you'd consider giving the newly rooted spike to one of your spike-deriding gardening friends and point out what he or she has been missing.

COSMOS
cosmos

Family: Asteraceae
Cultural group: annuals
Height: 1–4 ft.
Width: 1–2 ft.
Light: sun
Temperature: warm to hot
Overwintering: no
Moisture: moderate to ample
Drainage of medium: well drained
Fertility: low to average
Ease/speed of growth: easy/fast
Propagation: seeds
Problems: seldom seen; sometimes mildew, but not until the end of the season
Principal interest: flowers, foliage
Length of seasonal interest: long

Design attributes
Color: flowers in white, pink, red, orange, and yellow
Line: zillions of fine foliage lines on *C. bipinnatus* selections; long flower stems on both *Cc. bipinnatus* and *sulfureus*
Form: mounded to open-shrubby; rounded to starlike flowers, some with tubular "petals"

Space: abundant little spaces among foliage and stems (*C. bipinnatus* and taller *C. sulfureus*); not readily evident (compact forms of *C. sulfureus*)
Texture: fine to medium

These plants of *Cosmos bipinnatus* 'Sonata White' were allowed to flop over and then attempted to right themselves, forming a gently cascading mass of white stars against green mist. Nice.

The lower-growing selections of *Cosmos sulfureus*, such as this 'Cosmic Orange', bring warmth to container plantings. They might also bring goldfinches and other seed-eating birds if you let some of the flowerheads go to seed.

Mom grew "cause-moze" (her pronunciation) every year, partly (mainly?) because they reseeded and eagerly returned the next season. Cosmos seedlings might have been the first non-weed plantlets I learned to recognize, their delicately cut true leaves standing out against so many coarse or plain-looking other youngsters. The cosmos from my earliest days, cheerful-looking pink and white daisies, were always grown in the open ground, and I never thought much about growing them in containers until recently. I've observed them looking perfectly happy (albeit extremely floppy) while attaining an impressively large stature in small nursery pots (3 ft. tall in 4-in. pots!) and have seen them looking mighty fetchin' in larger containers. It's time to use them more frequently in pots. A caveat: the taller ones will fall over if you don't stake them, but that might look stiff, rigid, and forced in a pot. Either let them lean on sturdier, larger plants or—here comes the rabblerouser in me—let them flop and see what happens. You just might like the look.

You have two principal choices: the often tall, airily cutleaf ones with flowers in white, red, and purple (*C. bipinnatus*), and the often shorter-growing selections with fewer and less finely cut leaves and fiery flowers in red, orange, and yellow (*C. sulfureus*). Try these:

C. bipinnatus: the Sonata series grows about 2 ft. tall. Many others grow taller and can make a mess in pots, but their painted and brushed flowers are very appealing, especially 'Sea Shells', whose petals look like colorful rigatoni.

C. sulfureus can tower 6 ft. tall! Members of its Cosmic series offer hot colors and barely exceed 1 ft. tall. Ditto the Ladybird series.

Cultural tips: Cosmos grow quickly and can be set back if disturbed too much when transplanted, so try to settle them into their containers when young. If you don't heed the usual advice to assiduously remove the fading flowerheads to encourage more flowers, the resulting seeds might fill the stomachs of goldfinches and other birds. Any seeds the birds miss will drop to the ground and probably come up next year. Look for the seedlings.

CROCUS
crocus

Family: Iridaceae
Cultural group: bulbs
Height: 2–4 in.
Width: 1–2 in.
Light: sun to partial shade
Temperature: cool to warm
Overwintering: forced in cold conditions for advanced bloom, or at normal time; variously hardy in Z3–8
Moisture: moderate

Drainage of medium: well drained
Fertility: don't worry about it (low to average if you want to grow them on for another try)
Ease/speed of growth: easy to moderate/fast
Propagation: multiplication (of corms), seeds (if you're patient)
Problems: mice and other rodents, rabbits, storage rots
Principal interest: flowers
Length of seasonal interest: brief (but potentially in three seasons)

Design attributes
Color: flowers in white, yellow, blue, and purple, many with two or three colors
Line: very skinny, linear leaves; flowers sometimes lined
Form: cups, goblets, stars
Space: they look airy
Texture: fine to medium

I know, I know: crocuses aren't even remotely a staple of container gardening. They're not petunias or impatiens or geraniums, but you don't eat the same few things every day or wear the same clothes all week, do you? The same reasoning applies to growing crocus in containers. Among the first bits of color to familiarly dot the late winter and early spring landscape (but read on), their little goblets and stars look happy, and they make people smile, especially the parents of little children that receive tightly clutched bunches of them. As container plants, think of them as cherished delicacies that you might enjoy for a few days or during a special holiday or event. A few days is exactly how long they'll be with you, but I think you'll remember and talk more about your pots of cro-

I am drawn to the floppy insouciance of this petite pot of *Crocus speciosus*. A container of these will be the talk of a late summer or early fall event: how many times have you seen fall-blooming crocus growing in a tastefully ornamented gray pot?

cuses with your gardening buddies than about your pansies and vinca vine.

Here's another compelling reason to grow a few crocuses in containers: you can have them during three distinct seasons, namely winter (forced ahead of their normal bloom time), spring (when they normally bloom for you in your area), and fall (if you get your hands on some of the fall-blooming gems). Pot the spring-bloomers in fall—from September to early December—and then keep them cold, moist, and in the dark, and where you can check their progress, just as you would for any other forced bulbs. You'll see little bits of color inside the leaf sheaths when the crocuses are ready to bloom, and it can take as little as five days to bring those bits into bloom after being brought into warmth and light. So, remove some pots from cold storage beginning in January to start enjoying their cheery color indoors, but make sure the pots have been in cold storage for ten weeks or so. Other pots—especially those kept sheltered outdoors in the cold for most of winter but then kept in a very cold (a few degrees above freezing) refrigerator—can be timed to bloom when outdoor crocuses are blooming to create a moveable feast.

But the most exciting crocus bloom season, to me at least, is in fall, when you and everyone else least expect to see crocus. Almost all bloom in shades of purple and so contrast energetically with the ubiquitous warm reds, oranges, and yellows of fall. Think of it: you could combine a pot of purple crocus with another containing a rust-colored chrysanthemum. Stunning!

By the way, if crocuses don't receive enough light or are kept too warm during bloom, they will stretch out and fall over. For a flower-show competitor (like me), that spells disaster: the judges will walk right by a floppy pot of crocus or other bulb. But the iconoclast in me might let some pots bob and weave gracefully on a windowsill and never give those judges a chance to withhold one of those bits of colorful ribbon.

You can choose from plenty of spring-blooming crocuses, but I suggest you begin with the selections of the freely blooming *C. chrysanthus*, such as the blue and purple 'Blue Bird', pale blue-purple 'Blue Pearl', the well-named 'Cream Beauty', 'Gipsy Girl' in bronze-striped gold, and the purple-marked white 'Ladykiller'. For a more delicate look, try the selections of *C. tommasinianus* in white, purple, and rarely pink. If bigger and bolder appeals to you, then the many named forms of *C. vernus* are right up your alley, including purple-marked white 'Jeanne d'Arc', 'Pickwick' and 'King of the Striped' (light purple striped with darker purple), and 'Queen of the Blues' (purple-blue). Plenty of other species and their selections can be forced with varying degrees of success.

The fall-bloomers that you can find without too much effort—and which must be potted up as soon as you receive them in summer—include *C. speciosus*, in white, blue, and purple, and the purple *C. sativus* (saffron crocus). Challenge alert: *C. sativus* might not bloom the first year and could be a problem child during the next growing season, but you'll be very pleased when they do bloom. Harvest the stigmas to use a special dish, and do not fail to tell your lucky guests you grew the saffron yourself!

Cultural tips: Treat crocuses as annuals (discarding them after bloom), plant them out in the open garden when the foliage yellows, or keep them in their pots for a few years, making sure to give them plenty of sun and some fertilizer while the foliage is green. Let the foliage die off naturally and then store the pots in a dry spot until fall, when you can knock the corms out of the pots and replant them, or simply leave them undisturbed and begin another round of forcing. Include a few in winter-interest combopots and smile when they bloom after the depths of winter.

CUPHEA

elfin herb, false heather, Hawaiian heather (*C. hyssopifolia*); cigar flower (*C. ignea*); bat-face, Mickey Mouse plant (*C. llavea*, among others)

Family: Lythraceae
Cultural group: annuals, tropicals (*C. hyssopifolia*)
Height: 1–3 ft. or more (if trained)
Width: 1–2 ft.
Light: sun to partial shade
Temperature: warm to hot
Overwintering: min. 50°F, water occasionally, bright light; hardy in Z10–11 (*Cc. ignea* and *llavea*)
Moisture: moderate to ample
Drainage of medium: well drained
Fertility: average
Ease/speed of growth: easy/moderate to fast
Propagation: cuttings, a few from seeds
Problems: spider mites, whitefly, aphids, spots and rots (all are rare, in my experience)
Principal interest: flowers, form (if trained)
Length of seasonal interest: long

Design attributes

Color: flowers in white, red, yellow, orange, and purple (some with black)
Line: erect to arching stems (nearly horizontal in *C. hyssopifolia*)
Form: shrubby
Space: many are quite open, *C. hyssopifolia* much less so
Texture: fine to medium

The Gates of Hell garden I created when I first moved into my house was a splendid, infernal success, a flashy mix of annuals and tropicals in hot and dark colors. But my favorite memory of it relates to the little nectar- and insect-seeking visitors the garden received every day for weeks: several ruby-throated hummingbirds (the only hummers we have in the East) took up residence nearby, the males squeaking and whizzing around and bobbing with each other to defend their territories, and the females (I hoped) raising babies in their impossibly tiny nests woven from spider webs and imagination. On sunny days the gorgeous gorgets of the males flashed in the sunlight and added to the fire. Their favorite plants weren't the big, flashy bloomers like dahlias and hibiscus but instead the small, bright orange, tubular blooms of *C. ignea* (from the Latin for "fiery" or "glowing"). Garden visitors might have overlooked the genus *Cuphea*, but the hummers didn't.

Whether the hummingbirds visit your garden or not, I hope you'll consider including some cupheas in your container plantings, whether in monopots or combopots. All bear smallish flowers, often abundantly, on neat little shrublets that associate pleasantly with many other plants.

C. hyssopifolia carries its little white or pale purple blooms on spreading mounds of tiny leaves. The gold-leaved form packs more pizzazz, with its contrasting pale purple flowers. Both normally stay well under 18 in. tall or so, unless trained into a standard topiary. Sometimes the plants are covered in bloom and other times not, but there are always some flowers.

C. ignea, the hummingbird magnet, grows larger than *C. hyssopifolia*, perhaps reaching 2 ft. tall and wide, but it is far more open growing unless rigorously pinched back. The shiny foliage and red to orange flowers appear all season. 'Green Cigars' produces light green and orange flowers; 'David Verity', a hybrid offspring, looks just like the species to me (and to the hummers, probably).

C. llavea (aka *C. ×purpurea*) produces amusing red, dark-centered blooms that resemble bats or Mickey Mouse (hence its common names). Figure 2 ft. tall after a while.

C. micropetala looks like a larger *C. ignea* in all its parts and makes a fairly impressive topiary if kept dense and symmetrical with attentive pinching. Otherwise, it grows into a plant about 3 ft. tall. It too is a hummingbird favorite.

Cultural tips: These are easy plants. Pinch a couple of

The ember-evoking flowers of *Cuphea ignea* glow even more warmly against dark colors, such as the rich red-purple of *Hibiscus acetosella* 'Coppertone'. Equally hot and bright colors (red, orange, and yellow) would seem to put the little fires out.

Both the white- and light purple-flowered forms of *Cuphea hyssopifolia* look like green foam spangled with little stars. A larger plant, especially a single-stem standard, offers sheets of foam spilling from on high. Very cool.

Use the little but glowing flowers of *Cuphea* 'David Verity' to catch more than a few eyes (and attract at least a few hummingbirds) in container plantings. Individually they don't last long, but new ones constantly open up to replace the spent blooms.

The bat- and Mouse-evoking flowers of *Cuphea llavea* (here in its selection 'Flamenco Samba') are fun when viewed close up, adding a bit of humor to container plantings.

times when young (except attention-grabbing topiaries and *C. hyssopifolia*, which branches nicely all by itself) and then let them grow as they will.

CYATHEA
tree fern

Family: Cyatheaceae
Cultural group: tropicals
Height: 1–3 ft. or more (easily to 25 ft. in time)
Width: 2–4 ft. or more in time
Light: partial shade (sun if kept constantly moist)
Temperature: warm to hot
Overwintering: min. 50°F, water occasionally, bright light; hardy in Z10–11
Moisture: moderate to ample
Drainage of medium: well drained
Fertility: low to average
Ease/speed of growth: moderate/slow to moderate
Propagation: spores (for the very patient)
Problems: drought, root rot, blowing over
Principal interest: form
Length of seasonal interest: all year

Design attributes
Color: rich, dark to medium green
Line: nothing but lines (trunk, rachises, leaflets); irresistible movement
Form: upright to curving flattened feather duster (palmlike)
Space: abundant
Texture: fine to medium (by virtue of their imposing size)

Longwood Gardens, west of Philadelphia, is a must-see for every gardener, gardener wannabe, and their indulgent spouses and families. Beauty, theater, and magic abound, but to me the most special spot in the entire place is the tree-fern room in the conservatories, where I've watched a few generations of tree ferns grow very tall and then be replaced with smaller specimens. You don't need a massive conservatory or even a large outdoor area to enjoy the graceful architecture of a tree fern. You will, however, need to set aside a place to overwinter it where not hardy, in time giving it away when it gets too large. But do think about growing one if you'd like to feel how a dinosaur must have felt while roaming through and feeding in the primeval forests. They also make a visual substitute for an umbrella, but I don't recommend using a tree fern as one: the abundant, tiny hairs on the fronds will make you itch big time, and inhaling the hairs can cause breathing difficulties.

Both *Cc. australis* and *cooperi* make statuesque additions to

The younger fronds of *Cyathea cooperi* emerge bright green and in time turn darker, a process easily seen and savored only on smaller plants. You'd need a crane to watch the color progression on a 25-ft. specimen (and a very capacious pot to accommodate one!).

Anything dating back to the time of the dinosaurs deserves some kind of pedestal, even if it's an upside-down pot covered with "icky" algae. Wait a minute—algae are even older than cycads (such as this *Cycas revoluta*), so they're perfectly apropos in this case.

a garden or patio. You can grow them as specimens but can equally easily combine them with a groundcover or similarly low-growing companion(s). You'll probably start with a 2-ft. specimen and will in a few years begin looking for a suitably spacious, cozy winter home. As should we all in a perfect world …

Cultural tips: Being ferns, they're thirsty and take poorly to dry potting mix and low humidity. Cover yourself as much as possible when moving, pruning, repotting, or otherwise exposing yourself to those itchy little hairs.

CYCAS

cycad, sago palm, fern palm; Japanese sago palm (*C. revoluta*)

Family: Cycadaceae
Cultural group: tropicals, succulents (sort of)
Height: 1–3 ft., more in time
Width: 1–3 ft., more in time

Light: sun to partial shade
Temperature: cool to warm to hot
Overwintering: min. 50°F, water occasionally, bright light
Moisture: on dry side to moderate
Drainage of medium: well drained
Fertility: low to average
Ease/speed of growth: moderate/slow to moderate
    (although new leaves can expand remarkably quickly)
Propagation: suckers, seeds (if you can wait a long time)
Problems: scale insects, spots and rots
Principal interest: form, foliage
Length of seasonal interest: all year

Design attributes
Color: medium to dark green
Line: almost pure line (trunk, old leaf bases on trunk, leaves)
Form: thick-handled squally feather duster (palmlike)
Space: around trunk, within foliage
Texture: medium to coarse

This youngish *Cycas revoluta* hasn't yet developed a prominent stem (or "neck," if you wish). What neck does exist on this specimen is completely covered by a "scarf" of alternanthera, which, like it or not, does serve as a transition in color, form, and texture between the cycas and the elegantly carved container.

Many container plants are with us for a single growing season (and in the case of pansies and other cool-weather sorts, not even that long), while others can form the basis of a long-term commitment. Cycads, and for our purposes here just one of them, *C. revoluta*, are a prime example of the latter, with anecdotal evidence of fifty-year-old plants (and older) making their way around in gardening circles. That shouldn't be even remotely surprising, considering that cycads shared the Earth with dinosaurs. These are tough plants for less-than-optimal conditions, although attentive care will result in a faster growth rate and more attractive specimens.

Their magnificence calls for the star treatment in monopots, I think, although they shouldn't be overlooked as possibilities for combopots, provided their companions aren't overly large or vigorous. Note how both photos show *C. revoluta* with a smaller, non-aggressive plant at the base. Either way, the old guy will be the focus of attention.

No, they're not palms; pines and spruces are more closely related to them. Older plants produce cone-like reproductive structures, the males appearing on some plants and the females on others. If you have a specimen old enough to be of reproductive age, celebrate it. Let's hope, however, that your plant was not illegally removed from the wild, as some are. It takes years for one of these to reach a good size, and the temptation is strong to poach them from their native habitats (or steal them from reputable growers, whether in a nursery or on a front porch). Please, always ask about the source when thinking about buying a cycad or any number of other high cupidity-promoting plants, including orchids, cacti, and oth-

ers. If the vendor hesitates or gives you a song and dance, please rethink your potential purchase.

Cultural tips: *C. revoluta* is remarkably tolerant of low light and dry soil but equally able to perform well in high light and considerable moisture. The most toothsome plants grow in high light and a moderately moist medium, however. Repot every few years and refresh the top inch or two of potting mix in between.

CYNARA
cardoon (*C. cardunculus*); artichoke, globe artichoke (*C. scolymus*)

Family: Asteraceae
Cultural group: perennials
Height: 3–5 ft.
Width: 3–5 ft.
Light: sun

You might not see a magnificent flowerhead such as this on your cynara, unless you live in a Mediterranean climate or are lucky. Console yourself with the elegant foliage. Your bees have other food stations, I hope.

Temperature: cool to warm
Overwintering: min. 40°F, water occasionally, bright light;
     hardy in Z7–9 (*C. cardunculus*), Z8–9 (*C. scolymus*)
Moisture: moderate to ample
Drainage of medium: well drained
Fertility: average
Ease/speed of growth: moderate/moderate
Propagation: seeds, division, root cuttings
Problems: root rot, slugs, sudden crown rot and wilting
     (from root rot, drought, or who knows what)
Principal interest: foliage, flowers
Length of seasonal interest: long

Design attributes

Color: gray-green foliage, purple flowerheads
Line: lots of lines in foliage and involucres
Form: vase-shaped to clumping
Space: quite a bit around foliage and flowerheads
Texture: coarse

The silvery slashes of *Cynara cardunculus* are a powerful contrast (of color, line, form, space, *and* texture) to the dotted green shawl of *Verbena* 'Moon River'. Wouldn't it be nice to see this against the soothing blue-gray of a bluestone patio?

These silver fountains of *Cynara cardunculus* add their own distinctive touch to an already elegant setting. They would look equally splendid on a deck or patio, but be sure to give them enough room to spread out.

Trying to make sense of the relationship between artichokes, cardoons, and their wild ancestor(s?) reminds me of trying to sort out a handful of sand by color. Let's keep it simple by stating that artichokes (*C. scolymus*) make those big, painstakingly edible cone-like things on plants with greener, less finely cut foliage, and cardoons (*C. cardunculus*) produce edible petioles and midribs on plants with more silvery, more finely cut, more attractive (I think) leaves. I suggest you grow cardoons in your containers and artichokes in your open-ground areas such as a mixed perennial border or vegetable plot.

Both are big, imposing, hungry things that are best grown by themselves or with compatible, smaller-growing companions at their feet. One year at Atlock we combined cardoons with culinary sage (*Salvia officinalis*) in gray-green pots, and the result was mighty satisfactory. I've never grown artichokes and probably never will. I'm happy to be one of those that admires the fully developed flowers in photographs and their enormous buds on a plate, steamed and ready to be savored with some melted butter.

Cultural tips: Feed them with plenty of nitrogenous fertilizer to produce abundant, large leaves. Keep the watering can or hose handy.

CYPERUS
umbrella plant (*C. involucratus*); papyrus, paper rush (*C. papyrus*); dwarf papyrus (*C. prolifer*)

Family: Cyperaceae
Cultural group: tropicals, aquatics
Height: 1–6 ft.
Width: 6 in. to 6 ft.
Light: sun to partial shade
Temperature: warm to hot
Overwintering: min. 50°F, water occasionally, bright light; hardy in Z9–10 (*C. prolifer*)
Moisture: ample to constant
Drainage of medium: requires standing water
Fertility: average to high
Ease/speed of growth: easy/moderate to fast
Propagation: division, rooting inflorescences, seeds
Problems: brown leaf tips if not enough water, spider mites
Principal interest: form, foliage, fruit
Length of seasonal interest: long

Design attributes
Color: medium to dark green foliage, light green to light brown fruit
Line: almost nothing but—among the best for linear interest

The refreshing green sparklers of a cyperus quietly burn against the raging, crackling fire of 'Yalaha' coleus. Very cool. Very hot. Very easy to copy or use as inspiration for your own synesthetic composition.

Tall pots of *Cyperus papyrus* line both sides of a tranquil pool. Cleopatra would feel right at home here (except for the fountain at the end, which is very Second Millennium CE).

Form: bundles of umbrellas without cloth cover; fireworks;
threads on stems
Space: abundant
Texture: fine to medium

Whether you're cognizant of the ancient history surrounding papyrus (*C. papyrus*) or not, this plant and other members of the genus offer some mighty useful, image-evoking and mood-creating plants for container gardeners (one glance at the accompanying photographs should drive my point home). They're easy to grow—assuming you give them plenty of moisture—and just as easy to propagate, whether by division (most of them) or by the curious method of placing a trimmed-back inflorescence upside down in water and allowing it to root and produce new plantlets (*C. involucratus*).

The nomenclature for this genus is a bit jumbled, so look for these names or their synonyms when searching for these plants online or in nurseries and catalogs:

C. involucratus (aka *C. alternifolius*) is the midsize model of the species presented here, growing 2–2.5 ft. tall and determinedly spreading to 2 ft. or more across. Its inflorescences are the leafiest ("bractiest"?) of the bunch. I like to see just a few stems in a combopot, creating the impression of umbrellas thoughtfully shading their companions. A big monopot of this looks downright lush and evokes images of imperial decadence.

C. papyrus needs room: it easily reaches 4 ft. in a pot (6 ft. when very happy) and even a few stems take up at least a couple of horizontal feet. "Clouds of threads on sticks" describes *C. papyrus* to a T. Site it where you and garden visitors will be forced (or at least encouraged) to interact with it and think of the ancient banks of the Nile as you push the stems aside.

C. prolifer (aka *Cc. isocladus* and *papyrus* 'Nanus') is the little guy, usually topping out at about 2 ft. in a container. Like its kin, it spreads over time, and I think this one looks best as a good-sized clump, the better to allow the different stages of bloom to be visible at the same time.

A towering clump of *Cyperus papyrus* dwarfs its pot and the dangling chains of *Lysimachia nummularia* 'Aurea' spilling at its feet. While the plants at the rear offer some extra color, I could also picture this container against a plain red brick (or gray stucco) wall. Simple and straightforward.

An unusually dense cloud of *Cyperus papyrus* inflorescences floats above a pool of variegated plectranthus, spilling out of a classically ornamented gray pot. You might well see something else, but whatever the imagery, I think you'll agree that this container planting demands that its viewers conjure up something.

I see green frost patterns on windows or hear precious, very brittle glass artifacts shattering when I interact with the relatively small inflorescences of *Cyperus prolifer*. How about you?

Cultural tips: Water, water, water. Feed heavily if you want your plant(s) to grow fast and large in a hurry; otherwise, these are quite thrifty and will attain the typical size without a great deal of fertilizer. Overwintered plants often look terrible in late winter but will quickly improve with increasing heat and light.

DAHLIA
dahlia

Family: Asteraceae
Cultural group: bulbs
Height: 2 ft. (except *D. imperialis*, which can reach 10 ft.)
Width: 2 ft. (3 ft. for *D. imperialis*)
Light: sun
Temperature: warm to hot
Overwintering: keep totally dormant at 50–60°F, very little to no water, light not necessary; can be kept potted in their growing medium or in boxes filled with vermiculite or perlite
Moisture: moderate to ample

Drainage of medium: well drained
Fertility: average to high
Ease/speed of growth: easy/fast
Propagation: division (of tuberous roots), cuttings, seeds
Problems: cucumber beetles, spider mites, stem borers, caterpillars, slugs, powdery mildew, stem rot (but don't let this list stop you: I've grown dahlias since I was a kid and have seen lots of dahlias and dahlia problems come and go)
Principal interest: flowers, foliage
Length of seasonal interest: moderate to long

Design attributes
Color: huge range (except true blue); the ones considered here are mostly red, yellow, and red-violet (except *D. imperialis*, which bears flowers in white, pink, or lavender); green to almost black foliage
Line: not much, except from flower stems
Form: shrubby
Space: toward tops of plants around flowers and flower stems
Texture: medium to coarse

I grew up with dahlias. My Uncle Van grew a long row of the same red ones every summer as a hedge to his vegetable garden. They went in the ground around Memorial Day, luxuriated all summer, produced plenty of softball-sized flowers, and then were lifted out of the ground after the first frost turned the tops to black mush (the only good thing about their demise was the abundant release of the distinctive fragrance of the foliage and stems—there's a scent there all season, but freezing magnifies it). After being cut back, allowed to dry out for a week or so upside down, and then placed into bushel baskets and surrounded with vermiculite, the clumps spent the winter in the root cellar (people had root cellars in those days). They were split up into large fist-sized wads of tuberous roots bearing dark purple "eyes" (new shoots) in May, and the cycle began anew.

I'd never choose one of Uncle Van's red dahlias for container gardening, however. They grew much too large, the flowers were massive red blobs, and the foliage was green. How gauche, especially in light of the dark-leaved, smaller- and single-flowered dahlias available these days. Dahlias make excellent additions to containers, provided you choose the smaller ones (in plant size and flower), let the sun shine on them all day, fertilize and water them sensibly (not too much nitrogen, or you'll have lusher but less exuberantly blooming plants), and keep the stakes handy. Pinch them a couple of times early in the season, and then let them grow as they will. Cutting the flowers for arrangements, bouquets, or admiration as single stems in a bud vase encourages more flower buds to form.

Please enjoy a retina-stimulating posy of so-called black-leaved dahlias, all of which grow nicely in containers. From the top: 'Bishop of Llandaff' (red), 'Ellen Houston' (bright red-orange), 'Gallery Rosamunde' (pink), 'Roxy' (bright magenta), 'Bishop of York' (yellow), and 'Fascination' (light magenta-pink).

The yellow centers of 'Bednall Beauty' shine like beacons in the night against the dark red flowerheads and much darker foliage, provided you allow the flowerheads to develop fully. Sometimes I nip out the buds while they're still young to be able to enjoy an uninterrupted mass of the near-black leaves. Ghoulish? Maybe.

Here's a sampling of ones I've admired in containers; most reach 2–3 ft., tops: 'Bednall Beauty' (red); 'Bishop of Llandaff' (also red) and others with similar hot shades in the Bishop series, including 'Bishop of York' (yellow); 'Ellen Houston' (bright red-orange); 'Fascination' (light magenta-pink, usually more double than 'Roxy'); 'Gallery Rosamunde' (pink); 'Mystic Spirit' (peach-apricot); and 'Roxy' (bright magenta, much like 'Fascination', but usually single). 'David Howard' is a dazzlingly rich, light to medium orange—superb and worth the search. 'Yellow Hammer' is yellow, often with a good deal of orange thrown in. And just for grins, grow the preposterously gigantic D. imperialis, which can easily reach 12 ft. in a container. It needs a long season (longer than the ones in central New Jersey, that's for sure) to produce its cosmos-like blooms in white, pink, and red-violet, but they're not that exciting. The plant's imposing stature is, however. Many others are offered in catalogs; I'm sure they're all worth a try.

Cultural tips: Watch the nitrogen. Follow Uncle Van's method (slightly modified for container culture), or leave them

Dahlia 'Mystic Spirit' offers the rarely encountered, visually intriguing combination of girly peach-apricot with manly (almost) black. Stereotypes aside, this is an exciting pairing of colors that deserves a complementary pot, perhaps a dark, shiny one or even one in light terracotta. It would work.

Some people cringe at the sight of magenta. I hope this photo wins over some of you: how can you not be drawn to the vivid flowerhead of *Dahlia* 'Roxy' hovering above its own chunky, dark leaves and glowing against the bright chartreuse background?

The term "spectacle value" is sometimes used when evaluating flower show entries, but it could certainly come up in a conversation about *Dalechampia dioscoreifolia*. Wow. Talk about less is more, even when talking about a spectacle. Just one of these bow ties steals the show.

in their pots for two years before lifting and dividing them. They root easily from cuttings taken in spring as the new shoots elongate, and taking the cuttings helps encourage the plants to branch out and therefore make more flowers. Dahlia enthusiasts and publications can provide a great deal more insight into growing them for exhibition, should you be bitten by that bug.

DALECHAMPIA
bow-tie vine, purple wings, Costa Rican butterfly vine (*D. dioscoreifolia*)

Family: Euphorbiaceae
Cultural group: climbers and trailers
Height: 6 ft. or more
Width: depends on training
Light: sun to partial shade
Temperature: warm to hot
Overwintering: min. 50°F, water occasionally, bright light

(smaller plants; big ones can be difficult to manage and look messy)
Moisture: moderate to ample
Drainage of medium: well drained
Fertility: average
Ease/speed of growth: easy/fast
Propagation: cuttings
Problems: aphids
Principal interest: flowers
Length of seasonal interest: moderate to long

Design attributes
Color: flowers vivid red-violet with darker center; foliage medium green; stems can be tinged red
Line: usually twisting and spreading; depends on training
Form: long-reaching climber with bow ties on it
Space: plenty between leaves (but can be reduced or almost eliminated by training)
Texture: medium

In the few years I've observed *D. dioscoreifolia*, it has made quite an impression on me. Bow-tie vine looks like any other nondescript string of leaves when not in bloom, but when it starts producing its sensational flowers, no other plant can rival it. Actually, as with others in the Euphorbiaceae, what we see is an inflorescence made up of the little true flowers in the center and flamboyant bracts surrounding them. Think of a poinsettia, and you'll see the family connection. It doesn't take a great many of these purple bow ties to make an impression, which is a good thing, because I've never seen a specimen dripping in flowers. But there's no need to gild the lily here. "A picture says a thousand words." Take a look at the photo and tell me you're still a disbeliever. Go ahead. I dare you.

Make the effort to find one of these, and then decide whether to grow it as a trained specimen in a monopot (a big, bow-tie-studded hoop of this at Atlock Farm a few years back remains a vivid and cherished memory) or combine it with a supporting plant in a combopot (more recently at Atlock, a good sized eucalyptus provided a trellis on which a bow-tie vine twined up several feet).

When happy, bow-tie vine will grow quickly and can easily become entangled in neighboring plants, so keep it confined to its own space. Otherwise, you might need to painstakingly disentangle it from other plants and structures and could damage it in the process. They can grow quite large; a single season could easily see a container-grown plant 6 ft. tall and 2–3 ft. wide. I'd like to see (or perhaps grow) *D. dioscoreifolia* in a hanging basket and see what happens. I bet it would be a knockout, bringing to mind a tie rack brimming of purple bow ties.

Cultural tips: Be the first on your block to grow one of these! Monitor its hegemonous ways. I suggest starting with new plants each season (buy new ones or propagate and overwinter small plants). Older plants seem to lose vigor and become a tangle of brown stems.

DICHONDRA
silver ponyfoot, kidneyweed (*D. argentea*)

Family: Convolvulaceae
Cultural group: climbers and trailers
Height: 1–2 in. (when prostrate), 3 ft. or more
    (when hanging)
Width: depends on training
Light: sun to partial shade
Temperature: warm to hot
Overwintering: min. 50°F, water occasionally, bright light
Moisture: moderate
Drainage of medium: well drained
Fertility: average
Propagation: cuttings, seeds

Problems: I've never seen anything significant
Ease/speed of growth: easy/moderate to fast
Principal interest: foliage, form
Length of seasonal interest: long

Design attributes
Color: silvery, shining gray-green, especially in sunlight
Line: nearly none (if prostrate), readily obvious
    (if hanging)
Form: long strings of fuzzy little ears
Space: depends on training
Texture: fine

You've probably heard of the "thriller-filler-spiller" method of creating attractive container-plant combinations, in which showy plants ("thrillers") are mixed with less assertive but compatible ones ("fillers"), with trailing plants hanging over the edge ("spillers") to marry the plants visually with the pot and to provide some obvious linear interest. Well, *D. argentea* is a plant that cannot be pigeonholed: its eye-catching,

The variously sized beads on the necklaces of *Dichondra argentea* 'Silver Falls' ornament any pot it's put in. Its silver coloration allows this workhorse of a trailer to combine beautifully with just about any color, even raw terracotta.

abundant, gracefully suspended foliage is capable of playing all three roles.

In one season, plants started as a few rooted scraps of stem cuttings can spill out 3 ft. or more from a land-based pot or hanging basket. Cutting the stems back a bit early in the season encourages branching and density, but it's not necessary to keep pinching these; they will fill in on their own. Just for fun, try directing several gathered strands up and into the other plants in a combopot instead of allowing the stems to hang in the usual way. You'll be admired for your creativity.

Try to find a color that doesn't combine attractively with the silvery shimmer of 'Silver Falls'. Unlike white or gray, silver seems to go with everything. The specific name *argentea* and the color reference in the cultivar name (sometimes used as a common name) are no accident: the foliage is silver, not gray or gray-green or white, especially when basking in strong, mid-day sunlight. Some day I'm going to train 'Silver Falls' over a stuffed form in the shape of a medieval knight. Can you see its resemblance to the chain-mail used in armor?

Cultural tips: Increasing shade decreases the silvery foliage impact. Don't be alarmed if plants wilt in the hot summer sun; a timely offering of water almost always revives them. The tiny flowers are little more than a curiosity, but the seeds they produce might germinate next year in surprising spots.

DIEFFENBACHIA
dumb cane, mother-in-law's tongue

Family: Araceae
Cultural group: tropicals
Height: 1–3 ft., more in time
Width: 1–3 ft.
Light: partial shade to shade
Temperature: warm to hot
Overwintering: min. 55°F (60°F+ is better), water regularly but not excessively, bright light
Moisture: moderate to ample
Drainage of medium: well drained; tolerates minimal standing water
Fertility: low to average
Ease/speed of growth: easy/moderate
Propagation: stem cuttings, air layering
Problems: mealybugs, spider mites, rots and spots
Principal interest: foliage
Length of seasonal interest: all year

Design attributes

Color: green, almost always marked with white and/or shades of green and yellow
Line: upward and outward (increasingly so with age)
Form: vaguely palmlike
Space: in between leaves; not immediately apparent
Texture: coarse

Good old dumb cane: it's not just for office cubicles and shopping-mall planters any more. While I wasn't looking, plant breeders and other plantspeople were selecting and offering an astounding array of cultivars from this easily grown and too-easily maligned genus. The photos here give merely a tip-of-the-iceberg indication of what *Dieffenbachia* can bring to a container planting.

Yes, as with many other houseplants, you can grow dumb cane in containers for the summer. Try one on a shady porch or patio, or under a tree. You probably won't need to look far and wide for them, since they are often offered in abundance—and often in very generous sizes at very reasonable prices—at box stores, discount stores, nurseries, florists, and other vendors. If you hesitate to overwinter a large plant, think about picking up a new one next year. A large one probably won't set you back as much as a flat of annuals, and it

Any dieffenbachia can be a thing of beauty when given the right setting, as here on a porch at Chanticleer. Note that there are no flowers in this container planting, but the dumb cane provides more color impact than many flowering plants ever could.

could make even more of an impact in a compatible pot, perhaps with simpatico companions.

While there are many named selections (other reference books include specific ones, especially of *D. seguine*), dumb canes are often offered with no name, and that's fine with me. They all look cool and refreshing, whether grown as a single specimen, massed with other selections, or combined with other like-minded foliage and flowering plants. But don't think you're going to be literally refreshed by gnawing on a leaf or stem. Like other members of the Araceae, dumb canes contain calcium oxalate crystals, which will cause your tongue to swell if ingested. That's why they're called dumb cane, not because they're stupid but because they can make you mute ("dumb").

Cultural tips: Chop them back and root the leafy pieces to make more plants while the plants send out new shoots. Pieces of leafless stem 2 in. long can be rooted by half-burying them along their length or height in moist potting mix. Watch out for those spider mites, who love them and aren't struck dumb by them.

DRACAENA
corn plant (*D. fragrans* Deremensis Group); spikes (*D. marginata*)

Family: Dracaenaceae/Agavaceae
Cultural group: tropicals
Height: 1–6 ft.
Width: 1–3 ft.
Light: sun to partial shade to shade
Temperature: warm to hot
Overwintering: min. 55°F, water occasionally, bright light
Moisture: moderate to ample
Drainage of medium: well drained
Fertility: average
Ease/speed of growth: easy/moderate to fast
Propagation: stem cuttings
Problems: spider mites, scale insects, mealybugs, rots and
   spots, tip damage from fluoride in water

Dieffenbachia seguine cultivars are available in a dazzling range of leaf patterns, ranging from nearly solid green to almost all white, with many degrees of spots and lines and splashes in between. They can bring the illusion of benevolent light to shady places.

A dracaena gushes like a nozzled lawn hose above a multicolored bunch of plants in a container grouping. Even with all that color, your eye probably fell first on the dracaena's visually arresting explosion of line, didn't it?

Principal interest: form, foliage
Length of seasonal interest: all year

Design attributes

Color: green leaves, many marked with white and red
Line: noticeable to extremely evident in spiraling leaves
    and naked stems
Form: explosive or at least upward bundles (Deremensis
    Group) of strappy leaves
Space: ample, less so in Deremensis Group unless older
Texture: fine to medium to coarse

Whether you're an accomplished draftsperson or an all-thumber like me, it can be useful to sketch plants before combining them in plantings. At the very least you will have gone through the process of examining plants and trying to capture their essential design interest. The genus *Dracaena* (like the closely related *Cordyline*) offers the designer of container plantings line above all: they're not called spikes and corn plants for nothing. Even I could capture them on paper in a few seconds: all that would be required is a bunch of arching lines arising from one point or from along a thicker line.

In this genus we find, once again, several familiar plants commonly grown as houseplants. In the continuing spirit of houseplant liberation, I'd like to recommend you consider them as useful and attractive additions to your container plantings. They can often be found in considerably large sizes for not a whole lot of money and so may be considered expendable at the end of the season, especially if you're pressed for overwintering space.

D. fragrans Deremensis Group, the ones commonly called corn plants, do in fact resemble corn (but without the tassels and ears) to varying degrees. For many years the all-green 'Janet Craig' was a *sine qua non* of the interior plantscape industry. 'Limelight' glows in luminous chartreuse. 'Massangeana' produces medium green leaves with a yellowish center stripe. The handsome 'Warneckii Gold Star' is variably striped. All grow quickly to 6 ft. or so—they almost seem to sneak up when you're not paying attention if given even a decent amount of fertilizer—and provide a lush touch to any planting. As a general rule, the greener the foliage, the less light it requires to look its best ('Janet Craig' persists even under escalators). If they get too big, chop them back and let them resprout, producing a denser plant.

D. marginata selections, at least when young, are dead ringers for cordyline spikes and may be used in exactly the same way. Older ones with skinny bare trunks and topknots of foliage remind me of the Truffula trees from Dr. Seuss's *The Lorax* (I strongly recommend you read this tale to your children and grandchildren in this age of extinction … and take it to your own heart as well). 'Tricolor' is the familiar one with green leaves striped red and white, but you can also find a red-edged, green-leaved form (which more than likely is the species itself). Figure they'll reach 2–3 ft. in a growing season at most. These too can be chopped off like their *D. fragrans* kin if they become unwieldy, but the Truffula-tree look will be reduced.

For fun you might consider *D. sanderiana*, the ribbon plant included in many dish gardens and other plantings and sometimes seen in aquariums (yes, this is one water-tolerant plant). Think of it as a minimalist version (to 2 ft. tall) of a Deremensis Group type in light to medium green edged in white. It looks fresh and lively and should combine nicely with many other plants that prefer plenty of bright light.

Cultural tips: Dracaenas tolerate neglect, but more attention pays dividends in speedy growth and lusher foliage. Older plants are top-heavy and require a heavy pot with a low center of gravity to keep them vertical. Spider mites loooove them, so keep an eye peeled and the insecticidal soap handy.

Corn plant (*Dracaena fragrans* Deremensis Group) doesn't come in only building-lobby green ('Janet Craig', on the right): just imagine how the solidly chartreuse ('Limelight') or multistriped ('Warneckii Gold Star') selections shown here would brighten up a dark corner, say under a porch overhang or heavy-shade-casting tree in your garden.

DURANTA
golden dewdrop, pigeon berry, skyflower
(*D. erecta*)

Family: Verbenaceae
Cultural group: tropicals
Height: 6 in. to 6 ft. or more, depending on training
    and age
Width: 6 in. to 3 ft. or more, depending on training and age
Light: sun to partial shade
Temperature: warm to hot
Overwintering: min. 50°F, water occasionally, bright light
Moisture: moderate to ample
Drainage of medium: well drained
Fertility: average to high
Ease/speed of growth: easy/moderate to fast
Propagation: cuttings, seeds, layering

Problems: whitefly, spider mites, scale
Principal interest: foliage, flowers, fruit
Length of seasonal interest: all year

Design attributes
Color: medium green foliage, sometimes all yellow or
    marked with yellow or white; flowers in white, blue, and
    purple; yellow fruit
Line: basically absent to upright and cascading (if trained)
Form: shrubby
Space: quite open (sometimes dense, depending on
    selection and training)
Texture: fine to medium

You *must* get to know *D. erecta* and its several forms. The
bigger, blooming ones flower in at least three colors (and
they all attract butterflies, which seem happy to add even
more animated color to the durantas) and bear yellow fruit

The yellow-green duranta on the right brings an almost phosphorescent glow to this
container planting. Viewing the dark foliage behind it strengthens its impact, but how do
you think it would appear when seen from the other direction (against the gray foliage
currently in the foreground)?

The cool blue (hence skyflower) flowers of *Duranta erecta* mature into yellow fruit (hence golden dewdrop and pigeon berry). Don't picture yourself eating the berries, though, because they're toxic.

(which attracts birds). The foliage is a plain but lively green or beautifully variegated with yellow. Some forms barely reach 1 ft. tall if left to their own prostrate ways (the former epithet for this species was *repens*, meaning "trailing" or "spreading"), while others easily reach 6 ft. as free-grown shrubs or topiaries. That's *D. erecta* in a nutshell for you.

Can you tell I like these plants? My favorite—and the one I've known the longest—often goes by the name of "gold-leaf form" or something similar, such as 'Sheena's Gold', 'Gold Mound', 'Eureka Gold', and 'Squatter's Gold'. Then there are the variegated forms: 'Gold Edge' is well described by the name, and another, as yet unnamed, flips the color pattern (perhaps "Gold Heart" would fit?). All are worthy. Whatever the name, start with one whose foliage is some shade of yellow-green or even gold, depending on the light received, with shade favoring the green and full sun favoring the gold. I've never seen these flower, but they don't need to; they offer more color power than many flowering plants. Small plants are useful as fillers in combopots, but in time they turn into carpets about 1 ft. or so tall and wide and then build into smallish shrubs a few feet tall and wide. Try training one into a mopheaded topiary 1–2 ft. tall for a different approach.

Up close, *Duranta erecta* 'Gold Edge' appears as a mass of yellow-edged green leaves, but from a distance it looks like a mysterious, green, glowing blob. Neat.

Just one stem of *Duranta erecta* 'Gold Edge' brings a blast of light to the darker shades in the calibrachoa and coleus. Cover up the duranta to see how different the planting looks without it.

Yellow, chartreuse (yellow-green), and shades of orange stand out brilliantly against the gray-blue windowbox. Included among the plants is a mostly yellow selection of duranta in the upper left-hand corner; it is basically 'Gold Edge' reversed and just as powerfully colored.

Last are the big ones that easily reach 6 ft. tall (and are easily trained into 6-ft. topiaries). These bloom—in sky blue (well, more lilac-blue to my eyes, but there's that common name to deal with), or that same color edged in white, or a much darker blue-purple edged in white (which I've seen in a few places called 'Sweet Memories' or, more stingily, 'Sweet Memory'), or all purple-blue ('Sapphire Showers'), or all white ('Alba', among other names). There are more out there to tempt you, but you get the idea. All flower reasonably freely (no masses of bloom here, but they do make an impression), and then the intriguing open clusters of golden dewdrops (fruit) begin to form and color up. There's a white-edged foliage variant with lilac-blue flowers, too. Pinching these larger-growing plants back regularly would increase the flower and fruit display, but you'd postpone enjoying the graceful, arching habit for a while, and the plants would become quite large and perhaps unwieldy, as they can in the open ground where hardy. I saw some fifteen-footers in Texas that impressed me with their size and made me wish I could grow golden dewdrop in my New Jersey garden.

Cultural tips: Grow them. Chop them back hard to keep them in bounds. Watch out for the spines that can appear on some forms.

ECHEVERIA
hen and chicks

Family: Crassulaceae
Cultural group: succulents
Height: 2–6 in., more in flower
Width: 2–12 in.
Light: sun
Temperature: warm to hot
Overwintering: min. 45°F, water occasionally, bright light; I've had success treating them as winter-active
Moisture: on dry side to moderate
Drainage of medium: well drained
Fertility: low to average
Ease/speed of growth: easy to moderate/moderate
Propagation: offsets, stem cuttings, leaf cuttings, seeds
Problems: mealybugs, root rot, leaf spots
Principal interest: form, flowers
Length of seasonal interest: all year

Design attributes

Color: foliage in shades of green, including gray-green and blue-green (sometimes red), often marked with red or

A group of opalescent echeverias seems to float in their container. Which is more complimentary/complementary: the orange of the pot or the firesticks (*Euphorbia tirucalii*)?

black; some leaves are hairy and appear silvery; flowers in red, orange, and yellow

Line: linear from flower stalks, circular in outline

Form: rosettes (with fireworks emerging from them in flower)

Space: only around flowers and between leaf tips

Texture: medium to coarse

Many gardeners in colder climates know *Sempervivum* (also known as hen and chicks) quite well. The precisely—mathematically, even—sculpted forms and applied colors of that genus are impressive, certainly, but they pale in comparison to the diversity strutted by their New World cousins in the Crassulaceae, namely *Echeveria*. The beauties in this genus don't die after they bloom, and the flowers occur in orange, red, and yellow in addition to hen-and-chicks pink. It's a pity they're not as cold hardy as sempervivums, and most echeveria hens don't produce chicks as readily as the other ones, but we can't have everything, can we? Being succulents, they appreciate sunny, dry spots but tolerate a fair amount of shade and respond well to extra (not excessive!)

Two very different expressions of line from this echeveria contribute to a dynamic photograph: the leaves appear to be whirling around the center of the rosette, while the flower spikes seem to be rising up and uncurling.

Who says that heavy, massive containers must always sit on the ground? Placing one of the two containers of echeverias onto the bench lifts the container (and this part of the garden) to a new and thought-provoking level.

water. I've grown mine exclusively as single-specimen monopots, but I need to branch out and try them en masse and in combopots, as the photos here prove.

Tiffany or Fabergé could easily have designed these jewels, and their numbers are legion. I'll mention a few species and hybrids, but even a half-hearted search will turn up many more.

E. agavoides might be considered the plain Jane of the crowd, in medium green (although 'Ebony' has dark purple, almost black, tips and is far from plain). The flowers occur in shades of pink and orange in winter. Fibonacci would love the buttoned-down precision of the pointy-leaved rosettes, which for me offset reluctantly. Figure 6 in. tall and wide in three years.

E. elegans is pearly gray-blue, almost iridescent. I've seen it produce little rosettes to maybe 4 in. across, but some sources say they can be three or four times that wide. Hmm. I bet they're referring to the width of the clumps that can result from offsetting. The flowers strongly resemble those of *E. agavoides* but look far more gaudy against the shampoo-blue.

The fuzzy ones, such as *Ee. pilosa, pulvinata,* and 'Doris Taylor', look their frosty best when the early morning or late afternoon sun shines through them and transforms them into glistening silver or gold. *E. pilosa* and 'Doris Taylor' make 6-in.-or-so-high, erratically branched piles of fuzz. *E. pulvinata* can get twice as tall.

But the most fascinating of all are the big hybrids, which occur in sumptuous combinations of blue, purple, red, pink, and green, often bloom-coated, with the usually hot-colored flowers adding to the dazzle. Many are carunculate (that is, they have elaborately bumpy outgrowths on the leaves). I've grown 'Magma', in dark purple with blue and red shadings and pink-orange flowers. The rosette is about 1 ft. wide and in time terminates an artistically snaking, bare stem, 2 ft. in length. Wow.

A warning: the gorgeous bloomy (powder-coated) selections have an Achilles' heel of sorts: once that coating is rubbed off—whether by an eager thumb wanting to feel the leaves, or by rough handling—it's gone for good. Oil-based sprays have the same effect, so don't use them if you want to preserve and enjoy the mineral-like surface qualities. The fuzzy ones lack the bloominess and so can be rubbed (within reason), oil-sprayed, or shot with an arrow in the heel without suffering damage or death.

Cultural tips: Echeverias can be grown quite dry but appreciate a good drink every now and then, especially in summer. You can push them along in winter with extra water, too, but with care. When the big ones grow tall and threaten to fall over, chop off the rosette, leaving 3–4 in. of bare stem as a "handle." Place the cutting in a pot so that the leaves rest on the rim, and then leave it alone for a couple of months. The cutting will send roots out into the air and can then be in-

What do you think this little echeveria would say if it could speak? Simple compositions consisting of a single, exquisite plant within an uncluttered context often speak volumes relating to light and shadow, balance, and many other design elements.

The unusual forms of many succulents (including this carunculate hybrid echeveria and its less bumpy companion) remind many people of sea creatures. No doubt the creator of this clever composition was thinking along those lines: check out the accessories.

serted into a very open potting mix. You can directly insert the cutting into potting mix at the outset, but that won't be nearly as much fun as showing off a flat cabbage with a scraggly beard underneath.

EPIPREMNUM
devil's ivy, golden pothos

Family: Araceae
Cultural group: climbers and trailers
Height: indefinite (or so it seems for *Ee. aureum* and
pinnatum); *E. pictum* 'Argyraeum' to 6 ft.
Width: depends on training
Light: partial shade
Temperature: warm to hot
Overwintering: min. 55°F, water occasionally, bright light

Moisture: moderate to ample but tolerates drought
Drainage of medium: well drained but tolerates standing
water
Fertility: low to average
Ease/speed of growth: easy/fast
Propagation: cuttings
Problems: mealybugs, spider mites, scale insects,
rots and spots
Principal interest: foliage, form
Length of seasonal interest: all year

Design attributes
Color: foliage green with white, yellow, or silver markings
(sometimes solid yellow-green)
Line: twisty, zig-zag
Form: long chains of leaves (depends on training); mature
specimens of *Ee. aureum* and *pinnatum* have very large,
lobed leaves
Space: can be noticeable between leaves
Texture: medium to coarse

Can't tell an epipremnum from a philodendron? See the text for a mini lesson. This photo shows the glowing yellow-green *Epipremnum aureum* 'Neon' and white-splashed *E. pinnatum* 'Marble Queen' (plus a couple leaves of cream-slashed 'Brasil' philodendron). All three hold great potential for providing color and line, at least a couple feet of both.

Once upon a time there were *Pothos*, *Rhaphidophora*, and *Scindapsus*, all of which have been partially or wholly absorbed into *Epipremnum*. And then it gets worse: the climbing examples of *Epipremnum* (an Old World genus) and *Philodendron* (which hails from the New) resemble each other strongly (maddeningly) at first (or hundredth) glance. To the rescue comes Mr. Subjunctive of plantsarethestrangest people.blogspot.com; he offers a detailed explanation of the differences, but in the interest of brevity, here are the two most readily visible ones: the petioles are grooved in *Epipremnum* (they're smooth in *Philodendron*), and leaves in *Epipremnum* lack sheaths, whereas in *Philodendron* they bear them for a while before they wither and fall away. Now I can look back and proclaim that the endlessly long "philodendron" that grew on my grandmother's porch was actually an epipremnum. I can still see the grooved petioles.

Why grow these humble and rather mundane plants in a container? Because they're tough as nails and offer plenty of design interest, that's why, and they're part of my houseplant liberation movement. Speaking of which, to me they appear constantly in motion and seem to almost jump out of a container. Try the ubiquitous variegated *E. pinnatum* 'Marble Queen' (sometimes listed as a selection of *E. aureum*). Among selections of *E. aureum* (sometimes listed as selections of *E. pinnatum*!) look for the silver-marked 'Exotica', the yellow-variegated "golden pothos," an all-green form ('Jade'), the well-named 'Neon' (lime pothos), and the toothsome 'Silver Satin'. *E. pictum* 'Argyraeum' (aka *Scindapsus pictus* 'Argyraeus') has silver-marked leaves and is worth the search; it might grow 6 ft. long in time, but don't expect it to grow across your grandmother's porch three times.

Cultural tips: Sheesh, these are really easy, once you get past the nomenclature. They don't care much for cold temperatures, though.

EQUISETUM
horsetail

Family: Equisetaceae
Cultural group: aquatics
Height: 6 in. to 4 ft.
Width: few inches to indefinite
Light: sun
Temperature: cool to warm to hot
Overwintering: min. 45°F, water occasionally, bright light; hardy in Z3–11
Moisture: constant or variable
Drainage of medium: best in standing water but will grow in constantly moist medium
Fertility: low to average
Ease/speed of growth: moderate/moderate
Propagation: division
Problems: none I've seen
Principal interest: form
Length of seasonal interest: long to all year

Design attributes
Color: dark green with lighter green and almost black bands and brown strobili (flower/fruit equivalents)
Line: almost pure line
Form: open, mostly upright bunches of stakes with little cone heads
Space: everywhere when young, then decreasing with age as the clump thickens
Texture: fine to medium

Make no mistake: I realize there are powerfully weedy horsetails out there—inarguable garden scourges able to shrug off applications of herbicides that quickly dispatch their fancier, more highly evolved relatives and that return even after diligent persecution of their intricately beautiful stems. But I like to turn faults into assets, when possible. Any plant that can tolerate the extremes of moisture, drainage, light, temperature, and fertility that horsetails seem to take in their stride (and stride can be almost literally interpreted here: they spread quickly and deliberately) is a candidate for experimentation, not just confinement, in container gardening.

A freely growing pot of horsetails adds a strong linear presence to any garden setting, and growing them in a water-filled container offers double the impact if seen from an angle that includes their reflection. Look closely at the photo to get a suggestion of the possibilities. It clearly shows the stems and dark-

er nodes; what you can't see are the tiny reduced leaves that arise from those nodes (in some species the leaves are feathery and eminently noticeable) and the conelike strobili (at the ends of the stems) that produce the spores (no seeds in this ancient genus) that might eventually become new horsetails.

I'm directly familiar with only the 2–3 ft. *E. hyemale* in containers, but I get the feeling that any of them will happily grow thus confined. The diminutive *E. scirpoides* (to 6 in. or so) is worth a try. Those maddeningly vigorous weedy ones in your garden (such as *E. arvense*) might surprise you, too.

Cultural tips: You can be almost mean to them. Pots of *E. hyemale* survive with no protection outside in Z6–7 winters at Atlock Farm, and they are the same pots that might go for a long time without any additional water (or are grown constantly wet: they don't seem to care). Anything that's been around since before *Tyrannosaurus rex* and his buddies did their thunder-lizard thing on this planet is one tough cookie.

Which design attribute do you notice first: line or form (or perhaps another element)? This horsetail (*Equisetum hyemale*) provides a textbook lesson in learning to look beyond color to appreciate the other qualities of a plant (or of many other things, for that matter).

EUCALYPTUS
gum tree, ironbark; argyle apple (*E. cinerea*)

Family: Myrtaceae
Cultural group: tropicals
Height: 1–6 ft. or more
Width: 1–3 ft. or more
Light: sun
Temperature: cool to warm to hot
Overwintering: min. 45°F, water occasionally, bright light; generally hardy in Z9–10
Moisture: on dry side to moderate to ample
Drainage of medium: well drained
Fertility: low to average (can be pumped up to a point with higher fertility)
Ease/speed of growth: easy to moderate/moderate
Propagation: seeds, cuttings (might present a challenge, however)
Problems: scale insects, aphids, rots and spots
Principal interest: foliage, form, fragrance (of foliage)
Length of seasonal interest: all year

Design attributes
Color: mostly blue-gray-green
Line: lines puncturing circles, lines with more lines or rounded outlines coming from them
Form: open-shrubby to open-treelike; variable when young
Space: abundant
Texture: medium

A small specimen of *Eucalyptus cinerea* contributes big color to this cool combination. It can be argued, however, that the bleached whiteness of the small mass of petunias makes the loudest statement, overpowering the quieter gray-blue (of the eucalyptus) and mid-voiced green (of the grass).

What is my earliest memory of the Philadelphia International Flower Show? Oddly enough, it's the large bunches of eucalyptus branches, bought in the vendors' area and carried around by seemingly half the visitors. Their ubiquitous blue-gray color and nose-twisting fragrance filled the show. But color and fragrance are not the only virtues that attract me to these plants, which I now enjoy in my garden: how many other plants have round leaves joined at their bases and apparently pierced by the stems? *E. cinerea* (argyle apple), the species most frequently encountered, does. By the way, those round, blue-gray-green juvenile leaves are produced by young plants; older leaves are much more elongated (and more green than anything). Chances are you'll never grow a plant long enough to see the adult foliage, though, so no big whoop.

Include *E. cinerea* in larger combopots. Other skinny plants associate pleasantly with it, and it makes a great trellis for climbing plants that are not overly vigorous. Its open form allows other plants to poke through.

Cultural tips: Start with a little plant and try to overwinter it for at least one return show. After a while they look tired

The branches of *Eucalyptus cinerea* evoke strings of chips or wafers emerging from an almost subliminal haze of pink *Talinum paniculatum* flowers. Do line and form (as well as space and texture) overshadow color in dominance here?

and worn, and that's the time to start over with a new one. Don't let oil sprays reach the foliage, or the beautiful bloominess will vanish. Take time to smell the eucalyptus.

EUCOMIS
pineapple lily

Family: Hyacinthaceae/Liliaceae
Cultural group: bulbs
Height: 6 in. to 2.5 ft.
Width: 6 in. to 2 ft.
Light: sun to partial shade
Temperature: warm to hot
Overwintering: keep totally dormant at 50–60°F, very little to no water, light not necessary; can be kept potted in their growing medium; generally hardy in Z8–10
Moisture: moderate to ample
Drainage of medium: well drained
Fertility: average
Ease/speed of growth: moderate/moderate
Propagation: offsets (of bulbs), leaf cuttings, seeds
Problems: disbelief and incredulity from first-time viewers; falling over

Principal interest: form, foliage and flower stems, flowers, fruit
Length of seasonal interest: moderate

Design attributes
Color: foliage and flower stems green, sometimes marked with (or solidly) red or purple; flowers white or shades of green, sometimes edged with purple; fruit green (sometimes marked with purple) aging to brown
Line: abundant, flat to arching to upright leaves; erect to curvy flower stems; lines from bracts emerging from top
Form: like a pineapple arising from an octopus
Space: ample within foliage and around flower stems and flowers
Texture: medium

Why did it take me so long to discover these statuesque beauties? Pineapple lilies are hyacinths gone all arty, with their cowlick-topped flower clusters and often colorfully dyed or spotted foliage. They last surprisingly long in bloom and—if you can free yourself from the urge to deadhead flowers that are past their prime—their fruit can persist for months, prolonging the suggestion of pineapples and all their tasty associations. Don't worry; the fruit won't sap the strength

Take one quick look at this photo, and you'll immediately understand why members of the genus *Eucomis* are commonly referred to as pineapple lilies. While the starry flowers are attractive, the angular fruits remain on the plant much longer and create the impression of a swarm of chubby bees.

A pot of pineapple lilies (*Eucomis pole-evansii*), garnished with scaevola, welcomes garden visitors. Be prepared to move a pot of them to an out-of-the-way place after their attractive bloom and fruit displays have finished for the season, which could be well ahead of your first frost.

of the bulbs so much that they won't bloom next year. Speaking of which, references often state their bloomtime as late summer. Don't believe it. Many of them will be in bloom in June, not August or September, in most areas. Probably.

I hope a few quick glances at the photographs here will convince you to try some pineapple lilies as specimens in a monopot or associated with other plants in a combopot. Catalogs these days offer a burgeoning number of them, all the better for anyone who wants a little adventure in their container gardening. They can be challenging to distinguish from each other (I'm still puzzled by them) and might not be exactly what you were expecting when you ordered, but I bet you'll be pleasantly satisfied with them in any case.

Ee. bicolor and *comosa* (aka *E. punctata*) resemble each other, with differences in the amount of purple spotting on the leaves and flower stems and in the length (height) of the flower clusters. The latter will probably end up a little taller (2 ft. or so) than the former (1 ft. or so) in bloom. 'Sparkling Burgundy' is an almost potable, perfectly named, purple-red selection of *E. comosa* that combines beautifully with many colors, such

as pale yellow, chartreuse, and red, bringing to mind the colors of sangria.

E. pole-evansii can reach 6 ft. tall, so make sure the container is amply sized. The green flowers will impress your family, friends, and neighbors.

I call *E. vandermerwei* the "little spotted octopus" (one of its selections is 'Octopus', so I'm not the only one noting the cephalopodian resemblance), but you're free to come up with your own faunal or floral association and pet name. I've never seen it get much taller than 8 in.

Cultural tips: Keep specimens (single or massed) in their pots until they get crowded. If you need to stake the flowers, you're not giving the plants enough sun.

EUPHORBIA
spurge

Family: Euphorbiaceae
Cultural group: annuals, perennials, succulents, tropicals

A salt-encrusted terracotta pot can barely contain the exuberance of a pair of *Eucomis vandermerwei* at peak bloom. Even though they are barely 6 in. high, these two could command a great deal of attention if placed strategically, say on a patio table or in front of a large, contrasting but still plain pot.

You probably don't notice the dark red *Euphorbia cotinifolia* until you take in the bright colors and the almost white pots, but when you do, isn't your eye drawn up even farther into the background trees? That little trick ties the entire area together.

Height: 6 in. to 6 ft. or more

Width: 6 in. to 3 ft. or more

Light: sun to partial shade to shade

Temperature: warm to hot

Overwintering: succulents and tropicals, min. 50°F, water occasionally or rarely, bright light; perennials, variously hardy in Z4–10

Moisture: on dry side to moderate to ample

Drainage of medium: well drained

Fertility: low to average

Ease/speed of growth: easy to challenging/slow to fast

Propagation: division, cuttings, seeds, grafting

Problems: mealybugs, spider mites, rots and spots

Principal interest: form, foliage, flowers

Length of seasonal interest: moderate to long to all year

Design attributes

Color: they're all there somewhere in this largest of plant genera

Line: what would you like?

Form: ditto

Space: from nearly none to copious

Texture: runs the gamut

*E*uphorbia is an extremely large genus: many experts put the number at around 2,000 naturally occurring species, and that figure doesn't include the many, many cultivars that have arisen from the hand of selectors and hybridizers—of *E. pulcherrima*, the ubiquitous poinsettia, alone! In the interest of space and rationality, I'm going to restrain myself and cover just a tiny fraction of them here.

But first, the boilerplate stuff about *E. pulcherrima*, probably the best-known member of the genus. Poinsettias have milky sap that will cause painful itching and perhaps worse maladies if it gets into your eyes (or into cuts or your mouth, or those of your kids and pets). The true flowers are the little yellow things (cyathia, to the cognoscenti) in the center of the showy "flowers," which are actually composed of colored bracts (modified leaves). Poinsettias are lousy container plants, so says I, unless you're willing to give them exactly what they need to keep the bracts looking good, much less keep them on the plant. Sorry—you're not going to get that information here.

Now on to a few much more interesting plants. Without question the one euphorbia to grow on that desert island (not literally—this is a mental exercise) you might find yourself inhabiting is the annual *E. hypericifolia* Diamond Frost (= 'Inneuphe'). Never mind that some people consider this a member of *Chamaesyce*; it walks and quacks (again, not literally) like some euphorbias and so is included here. It seems to bloom forever, or at least for the entire growing season until frost zaps it, and it always looks good. The word that immediately comes to mind when I look at it is "froth." Take a look at the

A confetti shower of white-flowered *Euphorbia hypericifolia* Diamond Frost (= 'Inneuphe') and green-leaved *Muehlenbeckia complexa* falls from a tall gray pot. Would you agree that texture plays the dominant design role here?

A strongly backlit mass of *Euphorbia hypericifolia* Diamond Frost (= 'Inneuphe') seems to sublimate into the air. Producing this and other sublime effects is what this selection does best.

There's not a flower in sight here, and yet these colors seem to jump off the page. The rich darkness of *Euphorbia* Blackbird (= 'Nothowlee') makes the chartreuse of the *Jasminum officinale* Fiona Sunrise (= 'Frojas') (coming in from the upper right) and the coprosma (on both sides) shine brightly, and the light gray container offers a noncompetitive backdrop.

Red (*Euphorbia cotinifolia*), blue (*Pelargonium sidoides*), and yellow (*Lysimachia congestiflora* 'Outback Sunset') make a triadic harmony of primary colors. The green background turns down the volume a bit, but I'd like to see this combination in a dark green, brown, or gray pot to let the colors assert themselves even more.

photos to come up with your own word (I don't mind if you end up choosing "froth" as well). Think of it as a shorter (to 1 ft. or so), much easier, and far longer blooming baby's-breath (*Gypsophila*) that combines graciously with other plants in combopots and makes airy-fairy monopots (especially hanging baskets). It grows almost anywhere but appreciates a moist-ish, well-drained, organic potting mix.

Blackbird (= 'Nothowlee'), one of the many available herbaceous hybrids, offers dense mounds, to 2 ft. tall, of dark purple evergreen foliage, a color that combines beautifully with many others. It takes heat and drought in stride, but give it plenty of sun if you want to enjoy the dark foliage: increasing shade produces increasingly green leaves. It's hardy in the ground in Z6–9, but do provide winter protection when it is grown as a container plant in colder areas; protection will help keep the foliage on the plant and keep the roots alive.

E. cotinifolia (the specific epithet refers to its uncanny foliar resemblance to *Cotinus*, or smoketree) determinedly grows into a large shrub to 6 ft. tall (maybe more if you keep at it)

rather scantily clad in foliage fit for a king. The bright red of the new foliage in time takes on shades of green and purple, and backlighting (provided by early morning or late evening sun) sets the leaves on fire. It usually requires at least two growing seasons to raise a good-sized shrub from a small starter plant, but it's worth the wait. Give it an open, organic potting mix. You can start it out small in a combopot, but I suggest you grow it as a monopot once it reaches 3 ft. or so. Be sure to move it to its winter quarters before frost threatens. An established plant can be chopped back quite hard to keep it in bounds, but I've seen big plants die after that treatment, too. Roll the dice and hope for the best.

E. tirucalli (pencil tree) is worth growing for the common name alone; especially worth tracking down is its fittingly named selection 'Sticks on Fire' (which, not surprisingly, goes by the common name of firesticks). Grow these for their animated masses of line and color and for their tendency to produce specimens that each take on their own unique appearance. You can prune them to direct their growth, but why

Euphorbia tirucalii 'Sticks on Fire' truly resembles a conflagration when grown in nearly full sun and kept a little on the hungry side. I like how the color of this pot suggests ashes.

Many selections of *Euphorbia milii* (crown of thorns) make dense shrubs studded with dots (that are often red, but you have plenty of other colors to choose from). A trailing crassula conveniently hides the terracotta pot, whose color wouldn't play as nicely with the red dots.

bother? Go with what the plants wants to do, and I think you'll like them. Like *E. cotinifolia*, *E. tirucalli* makes a great combopot subject when younger but then appreciates its own space. It and its smokin' selection are more succulent than the previous euphorbias, so give them a very well-drained, succulent-suitable potting mix for best results.

What, no discussion of crown of thorns (*E. milii*, but do see the photo) or snow-on-the-mountain (*E. marginata*) or gopher purge (*E. lathyris*) or myrtle spurge (*E. myrsinites*) or cushion spurge (*E. polychroma*) or wood spurge (*E. amygdaloides*) or any of the thousands of other succulent, herbaceous, annual, or woody euphorbias, many of which do very well in containers? Nope. We've gotta get off this train sometime.

Cultural tips: It's impossible to generalize usefully and safely about a genus that includes thousands of members, but I will hazard this: herbaceous euphorbias do very well in a good organic mix and will likely do very poorly in a mix designed for succulents.

EVOLVULUS
dwarf morning-glory (*E. glomeratus*)

Family: Convolvulaceae
Cultural group: climbers and trailers
Height: 6 in.
Width: 2 ft.
Light: sun
Temperature: warm to hot
Overwintering: min. 50°F, water occasionally, bright light
Moisture: moderate to ample
Drainage of medium: well drained
Fertility: low to average
Ease/speed of growth: easy/moderate
Propagation: seeds, cuttings
Problems: rots and spots
Principal interest: flowers
Length of seasonal interest: long

Design attributes

Color: blue or lavender-pink flowers, medium to dark green
   foliage with silvery hairs

Line: curved lines noticeable on trailing plants

Form: low-spreading

Space: some between stems and leaves

Texture: medium

The abundantly produced flowers of *Evolvulus glomeratus* will
smack you in the eye with their stunningly pure, clear, rich blue.
Other flowers with more red in them (therefore having a purple
or lavender cast) might look sickly in comparison if too closely
juxtaposed with these.

What a difference a background makes! Note how the blue of
the *Evolvulus glomeratus* seems much bluer against this yellow-
green background than against the gray (and bluer green) in
the other photograph. The background has enough yellow in it
to create a strong contrast, pumping up the blue.

I like to use *E. glomeratus* (aka *Ee. pilosus* and often confused
with *nuttallianus*) and its selections, normally cascading
plants, as fillers or even coaxed into impressive topiaries,
keeping in mind that the intense blue of the flowers might not
play nicely with others in the pot (but, of course, you're free to
ignore my color sensibilities). Also, the flowers close in low
light, so don't expect to enjoy them on dull days or as sunset
approaches. While they might look shriveled, the flowers will
probably open again the next day, so take it easy with the
deadheading. Happy plants will continue to bloom without
you administering floral decapitations, anyway.

There are white- or pink-flowered dwarf morning-glories;
I've never seen them but I imagine they're pretty. Still, I'd
miss that intense October-sky blue of the more familiar selections, such as the widely circulated *E. glomeratus* subsp. *gran-
diflorus* 'Blue Daze' and the beautiful *E. glomeratus* 'Hawaiian
Blue Eyes'.

Cultural tips: These are thirsty plants, but they recover remarkably from drought once they receive a drink. In fact, I
suggest you err on the dry side, because excess water will almost certainly lead to root rot.

FARFUGIUM
ligularia

Family: Asteraceae

Cultural group: perennials

Height: 2–3 ft.

Width: 2–3 ft.

Light: partial shade (sun, if you like to water all the time)

Temperature: warm

Overwintering: min. 45°F, water occasionally, bright light;
   hardy in Z7–8

Moisture: moderate to ample

Drainage of medium: well drained

Fertility: average

Ease/speed of growth: easy/moderate

Propagation: division

Problems: slugs and snails

Principal interest: foliage

Length of seasonal interest: long

Design attributes

Color: foliage green, sometimes marked with white or yellow; yellow daisy flowers are interesting or a distraction

Line: circles perched on straight lines (and some wavy
   edges on the circles)

Form: mounds of umbrellas (or other shapes)

Space: decreases with increasing density of foliage

Texture: medium to coarse

A good-sized specimen of *Farfugium japonicum* 'Aureomaculatum' sits in a bucket, waiting to be planted . . . or is it already in its container? This might not be a practical assemblage from a maintenance standpoint (what a pain it would be to mow the grass!), but it certainly would attract attention.

I think it's fair to state that most gardeners begin their journey with flowers, then only over time do they begin to appreciate the beauty and usefulness of foliage plants. I'm well into the foliage phase of my gardening exploits, and some might say I'm over the edge: I routinely remove flowers and incipient buds on many container subjects, and *Farfugium* is no exception. All the ligularias I've observed send up ungainly bunches of golden daisies. They're pretty enough once cut and enjoyed in a vase, but to me they detract from the splendor of the foliage. When I look upon a mature ligularia, I see stately mounds of umbrellas, cookies, ruffled dresses, or crimped pie crusts. You might see other stuff. It takes a season or two to build a new division into a specimen, but it's worth the wait.

The plain-green-leaved species *F. japonicum* (aka *Ligularia tussilaginea*) is attractive in its own stripped-down right, but its selections are artworks. Every leaf of 'Argenteum' sports a different pattern of white and sometimes cream on green, while 'Aureomaculatum' (leopard plant) always appears to be changing its spots. 'Kinkan' should bear white-rimmed leaves

Even single leaves of *Farfugium japonicum* and its selections have a strong presence of form. From the top: *F. japonicum*, *F. j.* 'Argenteum', and *F. j.* 'Crispatum'.

Visions of starry nights (or moldy St. Patrick's Day bagels) are often conjured up by a specimen plant of *Farfugium japonicum* 'Aureomaculatum'. Leopards, too (hence the common name).

The coarse foliage of *Farfugium japonicum* 'Giganteum' is offset a bit by its carefully drawn white veins and highly polished surface. Try to picture this with a diametrically finer maidenhair fern (*Adiantum*) or an equally fine, powerfully linear *Cyperus papyrus*.

This specimen of *Farfugium japonicum* 'Crispatum' obligingly drooped a few of its lower leaves against the pot so that we could better appreciate the form of the bold, curly-edged foliage. It might have been tempting to remove the "wilted" leaves, but a more creative head prevailed. Getta load of them gams (petioles)!

(mine started out that way and then reverted to the all-green form, darn it). 'Crispatum' is the one that reminds me of pie crusts, and 'Ka Un' (Fire Cloud) adds a bit of red fruit (actually, dark red hairs) at the base of its even more fanciful crusts. The most imposing of them all, however, is 'Giganteum', with much larger, all-green, spit-polished, convex leaves.

Young plants provide interest to combopots, but in time you'll probably want to isolate ligularias in their own monopot. In time they will build up into mounds of glory that might well bring other gardeners over to the Foliage Side.

Cultural tips: Slake their thirst often; established plants fill their pots and will wilt dramatically (but usually not terminally) if not kept moist, especially in sunny spots. A spot in morning sun will be more to their liking and will reduce your watering time (and increase your number of missed heartbeats when you see those umbrellas and pie crusts pathetically slumped over). More nitrogen = more and larger foliage sooner.

×FATSHEDERA
aralia ivy, tree ivy, botanical wonder
(×*Fatshedera lizei*)

Family: Araliaceae
Cultural group: tropicals, woody shrubs and trees
Height: 4 ft., maybe more
Width: depends on training
Light: sun to partial shade (especially for variegated forms)
Temperature: cool to warm
Overwintering: min. 50°F, water occasionally, bright light; hardy in Z8–10
Moisture: moderate
Drainage of medium: well drained
Fertility: average
Ease/speed of growth: moderate/moderate
Propagation: cuttings
Problems: scale insects, mealybugs, spider mites, spots and rots
Principal interest: foliage, form
Length of seasonal interest: all year

Design attributes

Color: shiny medium to dark green foliage (sometimes variegated)
Line: moderately noticeable, increasing with age
Form: open-shrubby becoming spreading-sprawly
Space: not initially evident but increases with age
Texture: medium to coarse

What an unholy mess of plant name, you're probably thinking. What's that × doing in front of that multiple-vehicle collision of letters? Let me sort things out for you. The big black × in front of a genus name is a big red flag telling you that the genus is the product of at least two separate genera that came together (or, more precisely in most cases, were brought together by matchmaking humans) to create a new one. From *Fatsia* (Japanese aralia), these plants inherited their larger leaf size and urge to grow like a shrub, sort of (they flop around if not supported), and from *Hedera* (English ivy), their basic leaf shape and long stems. You can certainly see both sides of the family (figuratively and literally: both parents are from the Araliaceae) when you examine ×*Fatshedera*. (It's pronounced fats-head'-err-uh, by the way; the last two letters of *Fatsia* were the victims of downsizing in the merger.)

The original, all-green form is attractive in its dark green shininess, but to me the pick of the litter in this monotypic genus is ×*Fatshedera lizei* 'Annemieke' with its variable proportions of green and yellow-green. The finely white-edged foliage of 'Variegata' is nice, too. I guess I should say that I love them all equally, even though they're not my kids. By the way, these kids won't have kids of their own: the flowers are sterile, so they won't bear fruit.

Cultural tips: If plants are too rangy for your tastes, pinching the stems back before they get too long should encourage some extra branching. But don't chop back a big, established plant: it might die after bravely trying to send out some growth. I suggest you grow it as a minimally trained vine instead of trying to turn it into a bush.

Variegated plants don't need flowers to offer visual interest: the coloration of ×*Fatshedera lizei* 'Annemieke' packs plenty of punch, as do the form of the individual leaves and their medium-coarse texture.

FATSIA
Japanese aralia (*F. japonica*)

Family: Araliaceae
Cultural group: tropicals, woody shrubs and trees
Height: 3–5 ft.
Width: 3–5 ft.
Light: sun to partial shade
Temperature: cool to warm
Overwintering: min. 50°F, water occasionally, bright light; hardy in Z8–10
Moisture: moderate
Drainage of medium: well drained
Fertility: average
Ease/speed of growth: moderate/moderate
Propagation: cuttings, air layering, seeds
Problems: scale insects, mealybugs, spider mites, spots and rots
Principal interest: foliage, form, flowers
Length of seasonal interest: all year

Every one of the large, deeply cut leaves of *Fatsia japonica* 'Spider's Web' offers a different combination of medium green, yellow-green, and white. I think this diva looks best all by herself in a simple, dark pot, but please feel free to disagree with me.

Design attributes
Color: foliage shiny medium to dark green (sometimes variegated); white flowers become black fruit
Line: dramatically extending petioles, radiating leaf veins
Form: open, shrubby mass of fans on a hot day in church
Space: not obvious (hidden among leaves) but feels like it's there (provided by the coarsely cut leaves)
Texture: coarse

A single specimen of any fatsia can easily be the most elegant personage in your container garden. Even the non-variegated species would do the trick, with its church-fan leaves and dramatically outward-reaching form. Very evocative of a faraway spot, I think. And *F. japonica* 'Spider's Web' is simply beautiful, as the photo here shows. Japanese (and other) fatsiaphiles have discovered and preserved any number of other exquisite forms over the years, such as the yellow-marked 'Aurea', the grayer, more deeply cut, white-edged 'Marginata', and the cream-tipped 'Variegata'. Make room in your garden (and overwintering facility) for one. If it blooms for you, be prepared to appreciate it even more; the big, open balls of pushpins take Japanese aralia to a new level. Local birds may share your enthusiasm if the flowers turn into black fruit.

Cultural tips: Give your plant the respect it deserves by placing it where the leaves won't be (or have a small chance of being) torn up or otherwise damaged. You can't afford to lose very many of those big leaves before the plant begins to look bereft. Older plants will probably fill their pot with almost nothing but roots and so will need plenty of water until you sensibly move it into a larger pot.

FICUS
fig

Family: Moraceae
Cultural group: tropicals, woody shrubs and trees (*F. carica*), climbers and trailers (*F. pumila*)
Height: 1 in. (*F. pumila*) to 6 ft. or more
Width: 1–6 ft. or more
Light: sun to partial shade to shade
Temperature: warm to hot
Overwintering: min. 50°F, water occasionally, bright light; variably hardy in Z6–9 (*F. carica*)
Moisture: moderate to ample
Drainage of medium: well drained
Fertility: average (*F. carica* benefits from extra fertilizer)
Ease/speed of growth: easy/slow to moderate
Propagation: cuttings, air layering, seeds
Problems: scale insects, mealybugs, spider mites, rots and spots, cold damage (*F. carica*)

Principal interest: foliage, form (particularly of the foliage), fruit

Length of seasonal interest: all year (except *F. carica*, which is deciduous but otherwise offers long seasonal interest)

Design attributes

Color: leaves in green, red, and brown (some variegated with white, yellow, and shades of green); fruit yellow, red, black, and brown

Line: variable; prominent leaf veining and bare stems

Form: mostly shrubby to treelike; *F. pumila* cascading or climbing; leaf shapes variable but often eye-catching

Space: mostly sandwiched between leaves

Texture: medium to coarse

Unlike some container gardeners, I do give a fig about *Ficus*, and I can tell you why in two words: foliage and fruit. Don't grow figs if you're in love with flowers; instead, look to *Ficus* to provide subtle to bold foliage in a fascinating variety of forms, colors, and textures and a gustatory sensation in summer that is second to none, as far as I'm concerned (from *F. carica*). None are difficult to grow, and all should be considered go-to plants for container gardening.

I could stare at *F. aspera* 'Parcellii' (clown fig) for an embarrassingly long time: while every leaf has the same basic tile arrangement of white and shades of green, each one is different from the others (and it's fun to imagine things in the patterns). The crisply fresh-looking foliage colors combine nicely with just about any other color, and you don't need a big plant to make an impression. It'll take a few years for a small plant to reach a few feet tall and wide.

F. carica, besides providing the go-to garment for sudden attacks of modesty after major transgressions (you can read all about it in Genesis), gives us boldly drawn foliage and fruit so tasty and luscious as to almost justify committing sins in the quest to devour them. A generous mass of the foliage reminds me of an applauding audience, and the fruit ... well, only two fruits can turn me into a salivating, Pavlovian dog when I think of eating them directly off the plant in summer,

The mosaic-like pattern of the leaves of clown fig (*Ficus aspera* 'Parcellii') contrasts with the fine white striping of *Callisia fragrans* 'Melnickoff', and both plants pick up on the whiteness of the container. Nicely put together, isn't it?

I think the standout feature of *Ficus carica* (other than the sensual delights that their fully ripe fruits—fresh figs!—can provide) is their deeply round-lobed, lush foliage, which is most attractively displayed on smaller plants (big plants often look gawky and rangy).

namely figs and tomatoes. But figs are not just any old fruit, such as pomes (apples and pears) or drupes (stone fruits, such as cherries and peaches) or berries (grapes, bananas, oranges, and tomatoes—trust me on this). No, a fig is a complicated thing called a synconium, mostly inverted stem tissue that surrounds the remains of many little male and female flowers. The gritty "seeds" are actually the undeveloped ovaries of the female flowers' pistils. But enough of the fruity stuff. Grow edible figs primarily for their handsome foliage and be glad when they bear fruit. Give them big pots (they can easily reach 6 ft. tall and wide in a couple of years) and overwinter them indoors unless you really enjoy building structures and wrapping them in burlap. Not a pretty sight.

F. elastica (rubber tree) is another houseplant in need of liberation. They're tough as nails and will take just about anything Mother Nature can dish out in your garden, so I suggest you give one a try. Their ultra-coarse texture almost screams within a container planting, and their structure makes a nice framework for trailing plants to clamber over. If ultra-coarse

Ficus elastica 'Melany' grows much more compactly and densely than the large, open, familiar rubber plant residents of offices and commercial spaces, although it does retain the thick, shiny foliage of the big boys.

You can avoid the awkward-teenager look of larger fig (*Ficus carica*) plants by training them as single-stemmed standards. While not as elegant as myrtle or as colorful as a standard rose, a standard fig such as this one does command the space around it.

Swags of *Ficus pumila* 'Variegata' swing from the rim of a tall terracotta pot, giving a foretaste of what this plant (and especially the solid-green species) could do if given free rein. Confined to a pot, it will nevertheless continue to fill out determinedly.

is not your thing, try the more refined-looking 'Melany'. This noteworthy selection makes a convincing and far more compact substitute for *Magnolia grandiflora*, which does not make a realistic container subject. All are rather slow growers; figure 1–2 ft. at most per year unless given optimum conditions (which rubber trees almost never receive).

F. pumila (creeping fig) can be tiny and repressed (in a terrarium, at least for a while) or far-reaching and aggressive (covering castle walls and forming ropes of greenery in conservatories). In a container it usually tumbles appealingly over the rim after amiably combining with its companions. While the all-green type is pleasing, I find its white-variegated selection more refreshing, but note: 'Variegata' often produces reversions (see the photo), which should be carefully removed if you want to preserve its precise white-edged look. In time the mature foliage of creeping fig becomes much larger than the smaller immature foliage, but you probably won't encounter that in a container planting unless you keep the fig going for at least several years. Figure 1–2 ft. of growth per year for container-grown plants.

Other figs suitable for container gardening include mistletoe fig (*F. deltoidea*), notable for its rhomboidal leaves, and weeping fig (*F. benjamina*), the "ficus" of every enclosed public space, doctor's office, and reception room in North America.

Cultural tips: Don't make this complicated. They're easy.

FOENICULUM
fennel (*F. vulgare*)

Family: Apiaceae
Cultural group: perennials (sort of)
Height: 3 ft., maybe more
Width: 18–24 in.
Light: sun
Temperature: warm to hot
Overwintering: hardy in Z4–9
Moisture: moderate to ample
Drainage of medium: well drained
Fertility: low to average
Ease/speed of growth: easy/fast
Propagation: seeds
Problems: root rot, aphids, slugs, swallowtail caterpillars (but keep reading . . .)
Principal interest: foliage, flowers, fragrance (of foliage and seeds), insect life
Length of seasonal interest: long

Design attributes
Color: medium green foliage, some forms grayish, bronze, or bronze-purple; flowers yellow
Line: a zillion tiny lines with larger lines running through

them, plus more lines and bunches of dots when in bloom
Form: a cloud trapped by bare branches (and fireworks among everything when in bloom)
Space: can be more space than plant
Texture: about as fine as a plant gets, rivaling *Asparagus setaceus*

Much of what I've written about dill (*Anethum*) applies to fennel, with notable olfactory and gustatory distinctions: to my nose, fennel offers a sweeter fragrance, and to my palate, fennel tastes like very mild licorice (some say anise, which to me is pretty much the same flavor). As a container plant, fennel offers nearly the same design elements as dill.

My favorite fennel is bronze or purpleleaf fennel, *F. vulgare* 'Purpureum' (aka 'Bronze'); its ridiculously fine foliage begins a sultry brown-purple and in time progresses to dark green with a grayish, powdery bloom (think of the gray stuff on blueberries to understand this particular meaning of the

This bronze fennel (*Foeniculum vulgare* 'Purpureum') and chives (*Allium schoenoprasum*) are not growing in a pot. But they could, so why not give this a try? Take a design tip from the garden wall and grow them in a largish, light to medium gray pot. A crenellated edge is optional.

word). But by all means give Florence fennel (*F. vulgare* var. *azoricum*) a try; the thickened bulblike stem bases add a solid form to plantings and please the taste buds, whether devoured raw or gently braised or grilled. It appreciates the same cultural conditions as "regular" fennel.

Like dill, fennel normally becomes a lunch counter for caterpillars and predatory insects and birds looking to turn the larvae into their own lunch. Please think twice about persecuting the caterpillars; they become those butterflies that we all admire or miss, wondering where they've gone. Plenty of other insects—bees, syrphids (flower flies), butterflies, and others—visit the upside-down-umbrella yellow flowers for nectar, too.

Use fennel in monopots or combopots, gently staking it if you wish or allowing it to create eye-catching lines as it falls over or into other plants. It provides an excellent excuse to go out into your garden simply to stroke the foliage to release its scent, or to gather a few leaves for your favorite culinary use. (Mine: a little bit of finely chopped fennel adds a new dimension to chicken or egg salad.)

If you let the plants go to seed, expect plenty of volunteers to come up next season, although birds and other two-legged seed-eaters (such as yours truly) like to eat a few of the tasty seeds.

Cultural tips: Often best treated as self-sown annuals or maybe biennials. Sow a few seeds every week or so for a continuous display of fresh new foliage. Full sun encourages sturdier growth. Older plants, with their rather long taproots, often transplant poorly, so move them when small and more resilient.

FUCHSIA
ladies' eardrops

Family: Onagraceae
Cultural group: annuals, perennials, woody shrubs
    and trees
Height: 1–3 ft. or more
Width: 6 in. to 3 ft. or more

This *Foeniculum vulgare* 'Purpureum' isn't growing in a pot either, but the gigantic *Alocasia* 'Calidora' behind it is—and its pot is big enough to accommodate at least a few fennel plants. Notice how the flowers lose their bronze cast as they open into golden chalices.

Who spilled the box of crayons? The complementary pair of magenta (red-violet, more or less) and chartreuse (yellow-green) play off each other in this arresting image of a fuchsia backed by Hakone grass.

Light: sun to partial shade

Temperature: cool to warm (and sometimes rather hot)

Overwintering: min. 55°F, water regularly but not
excessively, bright light; generally hardy in Z8–10

Moisture: moderate to ample

Drainage of medium: well drained

Fertility: average to high

Ease/speed of growth: easy to moderate/moderate to fast

Propagation: cuttings

Problems: spider mites, scale insects, thrips, whitefly,
aphids, fuchsia gall mite (troublesome in western North
America), excessive heat, root rot, other rots and spots

Principal interest: flowers, form (plant and flowers), foliage

Length of seasonal interest: moderate to long, depending
on your climate

Design attributes

Color: flowers in white, red, pink, blue, and purple; foliage
green, sometimes yellow or variegated

Line: upright to cascading stems; some flowers elongated
(shooting stars), many with prominent threadlike
stamens and pistil

Form: shrubby to mounded to cascading, some vaselike
(Triphylla Group); flowers resemble fancy dresses,
earrings, petticoats, or clubs with starry tips

Space: nearly absent to fairly evident (*ff. magellanica* and
triphylla more so)

Texture: medium

Fuchsia 'Gartenmeister Bonstedt', a member of the Triphylla
Group, maintains the family resemblance (actually, the genus's,
but you get the idea) to earrings in closeup.

As a student at Longwood Gardens, I wrote a paper, the gist
of which was to explain how to (attempt to) pull off gargantuan hanging baskets and impressive topiaries of *Fuchsia*
(and please don't spell it "fuschia"—the ghost of Leonhart
Fuchs might haunt you) in areas with hot, humid summers,
such as those along much of the East Coast. Summary: anyone can succeed with fuchsias (the classic ones that look like
fancy earrings or petticoats, anyway) by paying attention to
their preference for coolish temperatures and moist soil.

Much later I discovered the far more heat- and humidity-
tolerant hybrids derived from *F. triphylla*, such as 'Gartenmeister Bonstedt' and others. Their sharply four-pointed flowers
offer plenty of interest, as does their dark foliage. They often
last through an entire East Coast growing season without too
much attention, long after the fancier ones have succumbed.
The triphyllas don't cascade as gracefully as the others, but
the flowers usually hang down, providing some downward
motion to a planting.

If you garden where summers are cool (or can steel yourself to watching them inevitably decline and prematurely
check out in hotter areas), grow the earrings and petticoats.
Give them shade during the hottest part of the day and make
sure they don't dry out. If you'd like more information on

The hot-colored, downward-facing flower clusters of *Fuchsia*
'Gartenmeister Bonstedt' are suggestive of the last few colorful
sparks from fireworks falling back to earth.

these fancier ones, I suggest you go online or check out the many books (often written in England, for England, I'll warn you) on them.

Otherwise, turn to the triphyllas, which tolerate more heat and strong sun and can handle dryer (but not dry) soil or medium; in addition to 'Gartenmeister Bonstedt' (red-orange flowers and dark red-purple-green foliage), try the lighter coral 'Coralle' or the much redder 'Mary' (but she's a sensitive girl, often behaving more like the earring and petticoat types by swooning in heat and drought).

Selections derived from *F. magellanica*, the hardy fuchsia (some plants have survived Z6 winters in the ground with plenty of protection), do well in pots, producing lots of smallish, pointy petticoats on (in time) big plants. 'Aurea', a yellow-to chartreuse-leaved selection, and 'Versicolor', with white-edged, gray-green leaves, are worth growing for their foliage alone.

All fuchsias lend themselves to monopots as well as combopots, which is convenient if the fuchsia calls it quits in the middle of the season: its companions can then grow in to fill the void.

Cultural tips: Don't let the medium remain wet, or the roots will rot. Watch out for spider mites, but plenty of other maladies might afflict them, too, especially in those Pacific Coastal areas, where the earrings and petticoats otherwise thrive.

FURCRAEA
striped agave (*F. foetida* var. *mediopicta*)

Family: Agavaceae/Liliaceae
Cultural group: succulents
Height: 1–3 ft.
Width: 1–4 ft. or more, especially if offsets remain attached
Light: sun to partial shade
Temperature: warm to hot
Overwintering: min. 50°F, water occasionally, bright light
Moisture: moderate
Drainage of medium: well drained
Fertility: average
Ease/speed of growth: moderate/slow to moderate

An established *Fuchsia magellanica* (hardy fuchsia) can produce thousands of these ballerinas/rockets/earrings in a single growing season, provided the pot is roomy enough. Even small plants bloom heavily, though.

A single plant of an extremely heavily white-marked *Furcraea foetida* var. *mediopicta* makes a spiky topper for a planting in a venerable-looking urn, suggesting a punk hairdo sported by an otherwise veddy traditional gent.

Propagation: division
Problems: scale insects, leaf burn
Principal interest: form, foliage
Length of seasonal interest: all year

Design attributes
Color: leaves green with white striping
Line: readily evident thick lines emerging from center, emphasized by the variegation
Form: open, pointy rosette (develops trunk with age)
Space: ample within leaves and hemispherical outline
Texture: coarse

If you've already read the entry on *Agave*, you know that I'm fond of those spiny beasts, but their tendency to bite can pose a problem, to say the least. However, in *F. foetida* var. *mediopicta* I can enjoy the bold, explosive look of a big agave without risking the potentially bloody results of a close encounter. So can you. Not only that, but this gem grows more rapidly than agaves, becoming a rosette at least 2 ft. wide and tall in a couple of years. The literature states that they send up

large clusters of diurnal flowers in summer, but I'm still waiting for that. I can wait, because the plants themselves look like giant flowers to begin with.

These plants pack a punch whether grown in combopots

Seen from directly overhead, the variegation pattern of *Furcraea foetida* var. *mediopicta* looks like flat ribbon candy being extruded from a central nozzle. Would a plant of the all-green species give the same impression?

Now here's what I call a focal point: a severely linear, coarse *Furcraea foetida* var. *mediopicta* in an imposing pot in the middle of a prairie planting of much finer cattails, grasses, and flowering perennials. Can you keep your eyes off the furcraea for very long?

or by their glorious selves, as the photos here attest. Use a small one as a focal point in a combopot, but be prepared to isolate it as a monopot the following year, assuming you can overwinter it and you're not working with very large pots, say more than 18 in. in diameter.

Cultural tips: Even though there's plenty of white tissue in the foliage, these plants can take full sun, at least in central New Jersey (and they will look just as splendid with some shade). When in doubt, start a plant (any plant, for that matter) out in less than full sun and gradually move it into it. Don't jump the gun and pull off the "pups" before they have several leaves.

GARDENIA
common gardenia, Cape jasmine (*G. jasminoides*)

Family: Rubiaceae
Cultural group: tropicals
Height: 1–4 ft., sometimes more
Width: 1–4 ft.
Light: partial shade
Temperature: cool to warm
Overwintering: min. 50°F, water regularly but not
    excessively, bright light; hardy in Z8–10
Moisture: moderate to ample
Drainage of medium: well drained
Fertility: average
Ease/speed of growth: moderate/slow to moderate
Propagation: cuttings
Problems: finickiness, scale insects, mealybugs, aphids,
    whitefly, rots and spots, chlorosis
Principal interest: flowers, fragrance
Length of seasonal interest: moderate to long and often
    intermittently

Design attributes
Color: white flowers; medium to dark green leaves,
    variegated with white, cream, and green in
    G. jasminoides 'Variegata'
Line: not much
Form: decidedly shrubby unless trained
Space: nope, unless the plant sends out gangly shoots
    (which you should cut back to promote bushiness and
    bloom)
Texture: medium

Gardenias make many people sing the blues. Not the flowers; they're strongly, sweetly, tropical-fruitly scented and appear to be made out of pieces of thin wax. It's trying to keep the plants happy. To state that they're finicky is to be almost hyperbolically diplomatic: they're Difficult. What can go

With care (and some luck), *Gardenia jasminoides* grows into a venerable specimen. Note how the one shown here appears to be tolerating the other plants in its pot: that isn't always the case.

Yes, gardenias do bloom, and not just for corsages. Personally, I tolerate their divadom for sentimental reasons: simply having one around, whether in bloom or not, reminds me of my grandmothers and evokes happy memories of the two special ladies who loved them.

wrong? Too much water, too little water, too much light, not enough light, too much humidity, not enough humidity, too hot, too cold, too much fertilizer, not enough fertilizer, pH too high, pH too low, location too drafty, location without enough air movement, and other factors all (too easily) lead to yellowing and dropping foliage and flower buds that heartbreakingly fall off just before they open. Plenty of bugs and diseases like them, too. If you don't have trouble growing them in a container, count that as one of your green-thumbed blessings.

So why have I included *G. jasminoides* (aka *G. augusta*) in this book? Because 'Variegata', one of its selections, isn't as difficult (for me) to grow as the all-green forms, and the variegated foliage kindasorta looks like flowers. I can get mine to bloom every now and then (although many of the beautifully variegated buds drop off) and easily trained it into topiary, which adds to its appeal. The unvariegated forms are willing topiary subjects as well; by far the most popular of these is 'Veitchiana', with its classically beautiful, double white blooms and heady scent.

Grow a gardenia as a monopot, and experiment with it. Once you think you've figured out what it wants, try to keep providing those conditions. Big specimens are worth including as the central feature in big combopots, but be prepared to start figuring out why the plant looks unhappy. Actually, most plants I've seen appear happy in summer; it's the rest of the year that can cause you to sing the blues.

Cultural tips: Be prepared to make adjustments (and be frustrated). Happy plants can be pruned back quite hard to keep them in bounds.

Every now and then, a happy plant of *Gardenia jasminoides* 'Variegata' will make a little magic by sending out a shoot that pretends to be a flower. Celebrate the moment.

As seasons and conditions change, so does the amount and intensity of its green and white shadings. Older leaves on *Gardenia jasminoides* 'Variegata' lose their shine, making the younger, light-reflecting ones even more noticeable.

GERBERA
Gerber daisy, Barberton daisy, Transvaal daisy

Family: Asteraceae
Cultural group: annuals, perennials
Height: 12–18 in.
Width: 12 in.
Light: sun to partial shade
Temperature: warm
Overwintering: min. 45°F, water regularly but not excessively, bright light
Moisture: moderate to ample
Drainage of medium: well drained
Fertility: average
Ease/speed of growth: moderate/moderate
Propagation: division, seeds, cuttings
Problems: leaf miners, spider mites, aphids, rots and spots, sudden wilt
Principal interest: flowers
Length of seasonal interest: long

Design attributes

Color: flowers in white, red, pink, yellow, orange, and sometimes purple

Line: long, often curvy flower stems

Form: low, loose mounds of good-sized leaves with big daisies above

Space: ample around flowers and flower stems

Texture: medium to coarse

Gerberas are the only florist crop I've grown. I was fresh (out of college) and so were the seeds, which germinated and grew easily, almost every one yielding a healthy plant, but I doubt I'll grow them from seed again: they are ubiquitous in nurseries, and the big box stores carry them, too, so let them do the work, I say. If you like the idea of including big, showy daisies in your container plantings, buy a few and include them in your combopots. Let their companions carry the show when the gerberas aren't in bloom, which can occur off and on throughout the season. If you can't resist the urge to cut the blooms for indoors (they are superb, long-lasting specialty cuts), make sure you condition them in plenty of almost-hot water and think about gently wrapping a thin wire around the stems for support, just like many florists do. Their leaves, while not particularly showy, do make an impression with their size and abundance, and they can provide an attractive foil for showier flowers and foliage.

It seems that a blue million seed strains have come and gone, always topping their predecessors in intensity of color, flower size, degree of doubleness, and fanciful arrangements of their "petals" (being composites, those things that look like petals are individual ray flowers that, along with the disc flowers in the center, collectively make up a flowerhead). Buy what appeals to you in bloom and enjoy the additional color the plants offer as the season progresses.

Cultural tips: Overwinter your favorites and divide them in spring. Gerberas are thirsty, so keep the water handy. Don't manhandle them when planting; the roots don't take kindly to it.

Usually seen as cut flowers (and occasionally as lonely potted plants), gerberas can also bring their diverse flower colors and forms to windowboxes and other containers. Keep water, fertilizer, and whatever you use for deadheading handy, though, if you want a display such as this one to remain in abundant bloom.

GLORIOSA
gloriosa lily, glory lily, climbing lily (*G. superba*)

Family: Colchicaceae/Liliaceae

Cultural group: bulbs, climbers and trailers

Height: 1–4 ft. (more if you're really paying attention to their needs)

Width: depends on training

Light: sun to partial shade

Temperature: warm to hot

Overwintering: keep tubers totally dormant at 50–60°F, very little to no water, light not necessary; can be kept potted in their growing medium to multiply

Moisture: moderate to ample

Drainage of medium: well drained

Fertility: average

Ease/speed of growth: moderate/moderate to fast

Propagation: division (of tubers)

Problems: aphids

Principal interest: flowers, form

Length of seasonal interest: brief to moderate

Design attributes

Color: flowers in red, orange, and yellow; shiny, light to medium green leaves

Line: twisting stems, tendrils, and dynamically wavy/curvy flowers

Form: clambering thing with fancy birds or butterflies on it

Space: in and around flowers and between leaves

Texture: medium

The first time I saw a glory lily I thought it was a fake, conjured up by a silk-flower designer on a personal flight of fancy inspired by some exotic bird or butterfly. At first glance the flower is reminiscent of a more typical lily (*Lilium*) or daylily (*Hemerocallis*) that has been grabbed by the petals and pulled back hard, leaving the stamens and pistil to wave freely in the air ... or maybe everything was caught in a really strong updraft. Whichever image comes to mind, these lilies will create a stir in any planting they inhabit.

This much pizzazz comes with a price, at least in the attention required: you can't simply plop *G. superba* into a pot like you would a petunia or impatiens. The brittle, sticklike tubers need to be started into growth and then potted into a more permanent home, handled carefully all the while (they can irritate your skin and really irritate your innards if you, for some reason, eat them). Once in growth, the shoots will begin seeking out a support of some kind, whether a stake, trellis, or other plant, clambering up by the tendrils at the leaf tips. In their own time—and over a fairly extended period of time— the flowers will appear. You won't get a mass of blooms from an individual plant the first year. However, if you grow glory lily as a monopot, in a few years the tuber(s) will have multiplied into a tangled mass that could produce a flock of flowers instead of a few. In the spring following a big display, turn the whole mass out of the pot, carefully separate the tubers, and then divvy them up among monopots and some combopots. Your good husbandry will be rewarded by the opportunity to experiment with these exotica: according to some references, the flower colors change with weather and soil conditions, so—after building up a nice stock of them—perhaps you'd like to provide various potting mixes and fertilizer regimes (or at least watch for weather-related changes, if any).

The one most commonly encountered and sought after is *G. superba* 'Rothschildiana' in inflammatory shades of red and yellow, cooled down a bit by the spidery green filaments, which themselves end in hot little spots of pollen-coated anthers. Plain old *G. superba* makes do with orange and yellow. 'Citrina' (yellow with a brushing of orange or dark purple) is worth looking for, as are 'Lemon Sherbet' (yellow and green) and 'Pradhan's Orange' (entirely orange, more or less).

Cultural tips: Don't forget to provide support. If you want to build up a satisfying mass of them, use a coarse potting mix (one with plenty of ground bark, coconut fiber, and other organic materials), which should hold up over at least a couple of seasons. Regular applications of high-phosphorus fertilizer will promote good bloom and build up the tubers for next year. Do not let them stand in water.

The flowers of *Gloriosa superba* visit gardens only for about as long as the birds and butterflies they resemble, but their sojourn is memorable. Note how the darker background lets the flower colors jump off the page.

GYNURA
purple velvet plant, royal velvet plant
(*G. aurantiaca*)

Family: Asteraceae
Cultural group: annuals
Height: 2–4 ft. or more
Width: 1–2 ft.
Light: sun to partial shade
Temperature: warm to hot
Overwintering: min. 55°F, water occasionally, bright light
Moisture: moderate to ample
Drainage of medium: well drained
Fertility: average
Ease/speed of growth: easy/moderate to fast
Propagation: cuttings
Problems: spider mites, aphids
Principal interest: foliage
Length of seasonal interest: long

Design attributes

Color: medium to dark green leaves heavily covered in purple hairs; orange flowerheads (eventually)

Line: upright to curving (increasing with age)
Form: open-shrubby to sprawling to cascading
Space: abundant between leaves
Texture: medium

This liberated houseplant grabbed my attention as a kid, when a neighbors of ours planted one out. Not only was the entire plant purple, but it was intriguingly fuzzy. It built up into a sprawly mass of leaves and stems, and then one day I spotted orange dots (flowers) beginning to appear. They reminded me of little paintbrushes (years later I learned that's a typical inflorescence for some members of the daisy family). Even without the orange, the purple can invoke passion; however, the passion is not immediate and overt: you need to catch *G. aurantiaca* (aka *G. sarmentosa*) from the appropriate angles to fully take in its purpleness, and the "passion" is more intense on younger leaves and often on the undersides.

If you're not afraid of purple, or purple and orange together, you'll find many ways to take advantage of this plant as a splendid monopot or assertive member of a combopot. Pale yellow and chartreuse look smashing with it, as does apricot, red, red-violet, blue-violet, orange (of course), and even darker colors, as well as gray and white.

References indicate that *G. aurantiaca* (the specific epithet refers to the orange flowers) grows to 2 ft. tall or so and has leaves to 8 in. long; its selection 'Purple Passion' can reach 10 ft. tall with leaves to about 5 in. I haven't sorted these two out yet to my satisfaction, but passion can't be neatly quantified or qualified, now can it?

Cultural tips: Plenty of light encourages abundant purple coloration, although full sun might be too much for plants to handle, causing them to wilt regularly, even in moist soil. Pinch the stems back every now and then to promote branching and bushiness (and therefore increase the impact of the purple fuzziness, albeit delaying or preventing the appearance of the orange flowerheads), or let the plant scramble and trail or loosely climb.

The passionate purple of *Gynura aurantiaca* 'Purple Passion' starts out strong but lessens with time. Does that remind you of anything? Periodic pinching (to encourage the plant to send out young, fresh shoots) will keep the passion alive.

HAKONECHLOA
Japanese hakone grass, Japanese forest grass
(*H. macra*)

Family: Poaceae
Cultural group: perennials
Height: 1 ft.
Width: 1 ft. or more
Light: sun to partial shade
Temperature: warm to hot
Overwintering: min. 35°F, water very occasionally, no light necessary; hardy in Z5–9
Moisture: moderate to ample
Drainage of medium: well drained
Fertility: low to average
Ease/speed of growth: easy/slow to moderate
Propagation: division
Problems: not in my experience—maybe mildew?
Principal interest: form, foliage
Length of seasonal interest: long

Design attributes
Color: blades green, often striped with white or yellow, tinged red in fall
Line: abundant upright-arching-flowing
Form: like water springing up and flowing over a rock in a little stream (really pronounced in a mass in the open garden)
Space: quite a bit at top and around foliage mass
Texture: fine to medium; the flowers are very fine, almost misty

These grasses would seem not to be suited to container gardening—*H. macra* and its selections don't ever appear to be in any way "contained." And that's their beauty. Several years ago I put a smallish *H. m.* 'Aureola' into a suitably sized pot, and in a few years the much larger specimen looked like it was rushing/surging/exploding/bubbling out of its 14-in. quarters. I often wondered how it remained in the pot.

Take the photograph of *H. macra* 'Nicolas'. Look at that vibrant color. All that line, and form, like a stream cascading over rocks, or a bunch of ribbons flying in the wind. The spaces between the leaves echo their shape, contributing to the overall texture. Not many other plants are this freely expressive of their qualities or as easy to feature in monopots (appearing almost frenetic, with all that line surging outward) or in combopots (making other plants look more interesting while often remaining the center of interest) over the entire growing season.

The species itself, *H. macra*, offers all-green foliage, if you can find it. Like many other grasses, it remains attractive into winter, the lively colors of spring, summer, and fall giving way to warm shades of beige and straw. Its colorful selections (which, understandably, are much easier to find) are equally worth your attention. 'Albostriata' produces leaves striped green and white. 'All Gold' is well described (although "all chartreuse" becomes more fitting as the amount of shade increases). By far the most celebrated is 'Aureola', in green and yellow/chartreuse striping; in fall, it takes on red shades, the amount and intensity relating to the amount of sun the plant receives. 'Beni-kaze' (Red Wind) is basically green until the cooler weather of fall sets in, painting red on the foliage. The chartreuse 'Nicolas' turns brilliant red, orange, and yellow in fall. 'Stripe It Rich' is striped white and gold (with some green) and sets itself apart from the others by tolerating full sun.

Cultural tips: Most selections will thank you for siting them out of strong, hot sun. Partial shade will preserve the coloration of variegation, but red fall color may be diminished. Even a small plant will do wonders for many combopots, except those that offer very dry or very wet living quarters.

Happily, the pot's color blends nicely with the cool, rushing yellow-green of *Hakonechloa macra* 'Nicolas' (terracotta doesn't play nicely with many colors). Are any other notable design elements making themselves felt here?

Like any hakone grass, *Hakonechloa macra* 'All Gold' brings the suggestion of rushing, boulder-filled streams to a container planting. Note how the *Lysimachia nummularia* 'Aurea' reinforces the illusion but in a gentler, bubbling sort of way.

HEDERA
English ivy (*H. helix*)

Family: Araliaceae
Cultural group: climbers and trailers
Height: 1–6 in. (laid flat) to 3 ft. or more (when hanging or trailing)
Width: depends on training
Light: sun (a few of them, mostly the dark green ones) to partial shade (the white-variegated and yellow-toned ones) to shade (again, the dark green ones)
Temperature: cool to warm
Overwintering: min. 45°F, water occasionally, bright light; variously hardy in Z5–10 (*H. helix* cultivars)
Moisture: moderate to ample
Drainage of medium: well drained; tolerates shallow standing water
Fertility: average
Ease/speed of growth: easy/moderate
Propagation: cuttings

Problems: spider mites, scale, mealybugs, spots and rots
Principal interest: foliage, form (of leaves and plant), rarely flowers and fruit
Length of seasonal interest: all year

Design attributes

Color: foliage in a wide range of greens, often marked with white or yellow, cold brings on red and purple shades; yellow-green flowers; usually black fruit
Line: curving stems; bird's foot types have decidedly linear look (and depends on training)
Form: dense ropes of leaves and (depending on training) adult forms shrubby to sculptural
Space: not much, unless intentionally trained (others have more space)
Texture: fine to medium (a few approach coarse)

Sure, English ivy is a vigorous groundcover—too vigorous, in fact: some states have declared it a noxious or invasive weed based on its penchant for smothering forest floors and the native plants that otherwise would grow there. English

Hedera helix 'Buttercup' sends its long tentacles over a gray-brown urn, accentuating the melange of foliage colors. Note how *Hakonechloa macra* 'Aureola', spilling over from the previous entry, keeps the action moving along at the urn's base.

Don't dismiss the potential of a plant as common as English ivy (*Hedera helix*). A single shoot dangling from an uncommonly colored pot will create a satisfying garden picture, especially when shadows become part of the composition.

ivy is widely maligned for its presumed ability to damage walls of all kinds (only if the wall is unsound to begin with) and to kill trees it grows upon. I won't take a side here in the Ivy War except to state that I keep a watchful eye on (and pruning shears at the ready for) the *H. helix* growing in my garden. (Have you ever noticed its fragrance? The next time you prune one—or rip up a half-acre of it—take a moment to take in the vaguely spicy aroma.)

But there's no arguing the value of *H. helix* as a container plant. Think of it as a garland of foliage—a necklace, if you will—that can be trained on just about any kind of support or allowed to gracefully droop from a pot. The diversity it offers—based on color and leaf shape, primarily—is nothing less than startling. An image search online will give you an extensive presentation of the attributes English ivy has to offer, as will a visit to the Web site of the American Ivy Society. But beware: cultivars are mixed up in the trade, and even correctly named selections can sport and/or revert (mutations, all) into other vastly different-looking forms. Also, cooler weather often brings on strong red and purple tones, which can be quite beautiful. But another caveat: just because you have English ivy surviving quite well outdoors in your Z5 (or 6) garden, don't assume every cultivar will survive year-round outdoors in a container. Some are reliably hardy only to Z7.

Most of the English ivy we cultivate is in its juvenile stage, making long shoots that generally lie flat against the ground or against a wall or fence (with plenty of help from clinging adventitious roots). Juvenility also brings with it the wonderful variations in leaf color and shape. However, like most other life forms, English ivy eventually matures, at which time it looks more like a shrub than a vine; the adventitious roots are no longer produced, and, sadly, it produces monotonously similar-looking foliage that lacks the fascinating colors and forms of youth. But mature forms do flower and fruit (attractively, I think), much to the benefit of wildlife that seek out the late-season pollen, nectar, and dark fruit. Growing up isn't all that bad.

All *H. helix* selections are attractive in their own way; even the plain green ones have appeal and design potential. Trust me. I offer but a few of my own favorites for your consideration:

'Amber Waves' is an easy grower and producer of chartreuse foliage when given plenty of light; otherwise, it might as well be called "Green Waves." How beautiful…

'Buttercup' will be bright yellow if given enough sun and quite green if not. Cold weather adds red to the mix.

'Calico' is arguably the most beautiful of them all. The white and green splatter-patterns vary from leaf to leaf and always refresh me, maybe not like a cool breeze or a cold brew might do, but in their own way.

'Glacier' has a blue cast to it, setting it apart from many others.

A small sampling of *Hedera helix* selections appears to be moving clockwise (or is it slowly drifting to the right?). Seen here are the chartreuse 'Amber Waves' (top), the variegated 'Glacier' (to its left), the heavily white-marked 'Calico' (center), and the tiny-leaved 'Spetchley' (bottom), among several other variations.

Ivy the cat does her feline thing among two eye-popping specimens of *Hedera helix* 'Amber Waves' at Atlock Farm. The hanging basket is about three years beyond its infancy (as a cutting), and the mass in the urn about two. Ivy *can* move quickly.

'Iantha' looks like it's made out of green needles. Small and slow growing, it looks and does best all by itself.

'Improved Needlepoint' and the pretenders to the name have noticeably pointy leaves and an active look to them.

'Manda Crested' offers twisted leaves that turn bronzy-coppery in cold weather.

'Spetchley' grows relatively slowly but deliberately, eventually sending long, deeply curved projections from its container. It can also be trained into remarkable little treelike specimens (call them bonsai if you like) to impress your friends and flower-show judges.

Cultural tips: They hate waterlogged potting media. Watch out for sports and reversions, and root the forms you like. Remain vigilant at all times for spider mites, which relish English ivy as much as deer are partial to hostas (among too many other things, sadly for us).

HEDYCHIUM
ginger lily, garland lily

Family: Zingiberaceae
Cultural group: tropicals
Height: 3–5 ft., maybe more with plenty of fertilizer
    and overwintering
Width: 2 ft. at least
Light: sun to partial shade
Temperature: warm to hot
Overwintering: min. 50°F, water occasionally, bright light
    (might go completely dormant or look terrible);
    generally hardy in Z8–10
Moisture: moderate to ample
Drainage of medium: well drained
Fertility: average to high
Ease/speed of growth: easy to moderate/moderate to fast
Propagation: division, seeds
Problems: spider mites, aphids, rots and spots
Principal interest: foliage, form, flowers, fragrance
Length of seasonal interest: long (foliage); moderate
    (flowers, if they bloom)

Design attributes

Color: medium green leaves, sometimes marked with white;
    flowers white, red, pink, yellow, and orange; I'd like to
    see the fruit I read about
Line: extremely linear—stems, leaves, flowers
Form: clusters of ladders, topped with flames or bottle-
    brushes in flower (or sometimes birds, as in
    H. coronarium)
Space: ample
Texture: medium to coarse

My Aunt Ginny and Uncle Bill took *their* kids to the New York World's Fair in the summer of 1964—and then presented those of us left behind with goodies from the souvenir stands. I, being little Mr. Gardener, was given a plastic bag with a couple of knobby things (they were thick rhizomes) in a bit of peat. "They called them flame lilies, and they were all over the place," said Aunt Ginny. I planted them in a pot that fall and put them outside next spring. One pointy shoot emerged, then another, then another. They unfurled into a big mass of ladder-like, leafy, lush things that grew at least 2 ft. high, but they never produced their flames. I did enjoy the foliage a great deal, proudly showing the pot off to all visitors, until I left it out during a hard frost, so that was the end of that. Another disappointment (no Fair, no flowers), but I got over it. Eventually.

Looking back, I suspect Aunt Ginny gave me something from *Hedychium*, a genus I've admired for a while now. If you're looking for easy and tropical-looking, grow one of these into a big monopot (as I did as an enthusiastic kid) or feature

Does the far greater height of the ginger lily bother you? I think the ladder-like shoots of *Hedychium* 'Vanilla Ice' lead the eye to a spot well above their companions, elevating the feeling and impact of the entire planting. It's fine if you disagree.

one in a dazzling combopot, such as the one shown here, photographed at Swarthmore College. Even if it never blooms (which is very likely in short-season areas), you'll still be able to enjoy the exciting form of the plant.

If yours does bloom, be prepared to be intoxicated by the various fragrances of the flowers, borne in sizeable, bottle-brush-like clusters. I think they look like a flock of butterflies or other flashy insects arranged in precision drill-team fashion. You might be inspired to make a lei out of them. Try these (but there are plenty more, including quite a few hybrids; go online to see for yourself):

H. coccineum flames in shades of red, orange, and white. *H. coronarium* produces flowers in white with yellow markings, and *H. densiflorum* and its selections appear in variations of orange. Grow *H. gardnerianum* for its yellow flowers with red stamens. *H.* 'Vanilla Ice' is a gorgeously variegated sport of *H.* 'Dr. Moy', a hybrid between *H. flavum* and *H. coccineum*. The flowers remind me of cantaloupe or orange sherbet or some other luscious edible. Too bad I've seen them only in pictures

…but the foliage packs plenty of punch, even if you never see the flowers (or get to the World's Fair…did I say I got over it?).

Cultural tips: They're so easy, even a kid can grow them. Give them lots of sun, water, and fertilizer, and they'll grow quickly and lushly. Overwinter a monopot, and maybe next year you'll enjoy the flowers. Bring them in well before your first frost date in fall.

HELICHRYSUM
licorice plant (*H. petiolare*)

Family: Asteraceae
Cultural group: climbers and trailers
Height: 1 ft. when trailing, 1–6 ft. when hanging
Width: depends on training
Light: sun
Temperature: cool to warm to hot

Linear variegation, such as that found on *Hedychium* 'Vanilla Ice', reinforces the impression of movement already implied by the elongated leaves running up the shoots. Patchy or dotted variegation wouldn't have the same effect. Think about it.

Two seasons of growth (plus overwintering in a cool greenhouse) resulted in this tour-de-force hanging basket of *Helichrysum petiolare*, which dwarfs the impressively large potted begonia beneath it. Who says that licorice plant must always be used as a few stems for accent?

Overwintering: min. 50°F, water (carefully) occasionally,
    bright light; hardy in Z(9)10–11
Moisture: on dry side to moderate
Drainage of medium: well drained
Fertility: low to average
Ease/speed of growth: easy/moderate to fast
Propagation: cuttings
Problems: caterpillars, root rot, spots and rots
Principal interest: foliage
Length of seasonal interest: long

Design attributes

Color: gray foliage, sometimes yellow-green or variegated
    with cream
Line: not obvious except when younger and thinner (hmm,
    sounds like people)
Form: spreading-shrubby
Space: not much, unless trained openly
Texture: fine to medium

Given some space and time, a little plant of *H. petiolare* (or any of its selections) will spread and carpet a good-sized area with a deep, plush layer of foliage. Whether wall to wall or just a long, thin remnant, this shag rug of a plant can bring a satisfying swath of color and texture to any planting, provided it receives enough sun. Until recently I would have recommended licorice plant exclusively for combopots, but an eye-popping hanging basket grown at Atlock Farm changed my mind forever. Take a look at the splendid mass of silver-gray in the photograph and tell me you wouldn't like to show off a similar basket (or earthbound container) in your own garden.

But here in New Jersey (and probably elsewhere), *H. petiolare* has one Achilles' heel: a nasty little caterpillar that chews the foliage and leaves ugly webbing and, well, droppings. One day the shag carpet looks great, and seemingly the next day it looks like a traveling frat party went through and trashed it. Keep an eye out for the chewers, but also keep in mind that the caterpillars will grow up to become pretty little orange

The slightly grayed, yellow-green foliage of *Helichrysum petiolare* 'Limelight' creates the unsettling feeling of simultaneous cold (from the gray) and heat (from the yellow). Even the mass of blue-gray foliage behind it can't completely quench the heat, but it does cool it down a bit. Against dark green or dark blue, the foliage would blaze.

The small, green-gray leaves of *Helichrysum petiolare* 'Petite Licorice' contrast strongly with the larger, dark purple-blue foliage behind them. Unusually, these shoots are growing upward. Maybe the gardener wanted it that way?

and brown American painted lady butterflies … so maybe you can let a few live. A tough call, I know, especially when you like your plants healthy and whole but also like to have your garden visited by butterflies.

The gray-leaved species is widely familiar for very solid reasons: it grows easily and lends its elegance to many other plants. It and its selections, beauties all, mix well in combopots (and should make splendid specimens):

'Limelight' glows in shades of yellow-green. The lower, inner foliage is usually greener than the top foliage exposed to more sun, creating more depth (and perhaps reminding you of sculpted shag carpeting).

'Petite Licorice' looks like a smaller, denser version of the species.

'Variegatum' decks itself out in the gray of the species with some cream thrown in.

Some references list 'Gold Leaf' and 'Silver Leaf' as well as other names. I'd like to compare them next to the standards just named. Another species you might run into and consider growing is the shrubby *H. italicum* (curry plant), the foliage of which comes in various skinny widths, basically; it smells just like commercial curry powder but is not its source.

Cultural tips: Provide plenty of sun, but don't worry too much about water (in fact, root rot can easily become a problem if the medium is too moist) and fertilizer. These plants are quite thrifty. Watch out for those frat-boy caterpillars!

HELIOTROPIUM
heliotrope, cherry pie (*H. arborescens*)

Family: Boraginaceae
Cultural group: annuals
Height: 1–2 ft., more if trained into a standard
Width: 1–2 ft.
Light: sun
Temperature: cool to warm to hot
Overwintering: min. 50°F, water occasionally, bright light; hardy in Z11
Moisture: moderate to ample
Drainage of medium: well drained
Fertility: average
Ease/speed of growth: easy/moderate to fast
Propagation: cuttings, seeds
Problems: whitefly
Principal interest: flowers, fragrance, foliage
Length of seasonal interest: long (all year if overwintered)

Design attributes
Color: flowers white, blue, and purple; foliage light to dark green (which can be vaguely purplish)
Line: from upright to inevitably floppy stems

Form: shrubby (if kept pinched)
Space: not much
Texture: medium

I rarely walk by heliotropes without bending into them to take a very deep, very satisfying intake of their soothing, flowery-fruity-powdery, roll-around-in-the-grass-on-the-most-gorgeous-day-of-the-year scent. They could bear the ugliest flowers on the face of the earth (right up there with double tigerlilies and space age irises), and I would still grow them for their fragrance. You might be asking yourself, "What's he on? I've never smelled a heliotrope that could make me generate florid prose (or malign double tigerlilies and space age irises) like that." To which I responded, "Perhaps you've never been fortunate enough to be in the direct presence of a heliotrope that smells like heliotrope should." Some of the *H. arborescens* forms out there smell as much like the heliotrope I know and love as ice smells like chocolate. If you should happen upon a particularly fragrant individual heliotrope, buy it, grow it well, and take cuttings of it for enjoyment next year and beyond and also for giving to your best

Plenty of purple flowers bloom out there, but nothing else smells like a well-scented selection of *Heliotropium arborescens*. Try to sniff a heliotrope in flower before adding it to your collection.

friends. That's how some of selections came to be offered at Atlock, specifically the magically fragrant one we call "Haskell's form" (for Allen Haskell, who supplied us with the original many years ago). It and 'Sally Reath' (named for the masterful gardener who kept a neat-as-a-pin, brimming-with-ultrachoice-things garden in Devon, Pennsylvania, where this selection arose) remind me of the brilliant and generous people behind them who are no longer with us.

Sometimes the flowerheads on heliotrope are so large that the stems flop under the weight, and whitefly love the plants, and they don't make perfectly round-headed topiaries. So what? Cut off the offending heads and enjoy them indoors, or accept the fact that they flop and let them cascade from a container. Whitefly happen. Not all topiaries must be made from myrtle or boxwood. Grow heliotropes for their scent, and overlook their peccadilloes. You'll thank me for it.

Grow the unscented or barely scented ones in combopots (their floral and foliage colors go nicely with many other plants, such as the sweet potato and jasmine in the photo here) and the scented ones as topiaries or in overflowing hanging baskets, the better and more easily to become lost in their fragrance.

Aside from the intensely fragrant "Haskell's form," look for the more widely available 'Alba' in pure white and often described as having the fragrance of baby powder. All the other selections, including the widely touted 'Iowa' and 'Marine', have not impressed me with their scent as much as the ones already described. They have beautiful flowers and often a more attractive (less floppy) plant habit, but my nose knows. But if you find a plant of one of these other selections and its fragrance pleases you, grow it and spread it around. The world could use more fragrant heliotrope.

Butterflies don't seem to care if a heliotrope is fragrant or not. Tiger swallowtails and sulphurs combine beautifully with dark purple selections, orange fritillaries and monarchs go nicely with the lilac and lavender ones, and they all look good against 'Alba'.

Cultural tips: They like sun. They make superb winter-blooming plants for greenhouses, conservatories, and the like. Chop them back every now and then at any time to control ranginess and to encourage more bloom. Take some time to smell the heliotrope.

HEUCHERA
coral bells, alum root

Family: Saxifragaceae
Cultural group: perennials
Height: 1 ft. (foliage only), 2 ft. (with flowers)

Coral bells have been transformed, with seemingly endless foliage colors now available to tempt you. The soothing coloration of *Heuchera* 'Amber Waves' adds some warmth to a container planting and coordinates surprisingly nicely with both the pink-edged spikes of the phormium and the terracotta pot.

Width: 1 ft.
Light: sun to partial shade
Temperature: cool to warm to hot
Overwintering: hardy in Z4–8
Moisture: moderate to ample
Drainage of medium: well drained
Fertility: average
Ease/speed of growth: easy to moderate/moderate
Propagation: division, seeds (species)
Problems: root rot (usually from poor drainage), other rots and spots
Principal interest: foliage, flowers
Length of seasonal interest: long (foliage); moderate (flowers)

Design attributes

Color: stupefying range of foliage colors: shades of green, red, orange, yellow, and purple, and some definitely have a blue feeling to them; white, pink, or red flowers
Line: from the many upright flower stems

Form: low mounds with delicate Roman candles going off from them
Space: abundantly captured above the foliage mounds, among the flower stems and flowers
Texture: medium, sometimes bordering on coarse (flowers fine)

I discovered *Heuchera* as a child, when a neighbor shared a few starts of her coral bells. They grew easily on the sunny side of the front porch, and we were more than entertained by the hummingbirds they attracted, which came to drink from the clouds of little pink (they didn't look coral to me) bells. Those coral bells were almost certainly *H. sanguinea* or one of the many selections made primarily for their red, pink, or white flowers (a few have variegated leaves that stray from the medium green norm). Since my first meeting with the genus I've encountered many other examples, most notably *H. villosa* f. *purpurea* 'Palace Purple', with its shiny, dark, abundant foliage that justifiably beguiled millions. Unfortunately, some growers succumbed to the temptation to raise seedlings of

All coral bells don't radiate heat: *Heuchera* 'Raspberry Ice' projects a feeling of, well, the frozen treat that inspired its name. Cool. However, combine it with hot red, yellow, and orange, and it would melt away.

Do you see how the blue-green and red-purple of *Heuchera* 'Crimson Curls' and the orange tones of the pot create a tertiary harmony? Flower buds are beginning to show, but these days most of the flowers on coral bells seem an afterthought: it's the foliage that steals the show.

'Palace Purple', from which have sprung too many pretenders to the crown, with less than regal-looking foliage coloration and plant habits.

But while some were foisting 'Palace Purple' impostors upon us, plant genius Dan Heims and his Terra Nova Nurseries crew near Portland, Oregon, were revolutionizing *Heuchera* (and the related *Tiarella* and the intergeneric cross of the two, ×*Heucherella*), expanding their foliage from green, dark purple, and silver into solids and patterns of fantastic, near-psychedelic orange, chartreuse, red, pink, red-violet, and near-black, with leaf shapes ruffled and laced and twisting like something not seen since the early '60s on *American Bandstand*. For a wider look at the eye candy, check out the Terra Nova candy store at www.terranovanurseries.com.

With all the dazzling new foliage on heucheras and an equally wide range of colorful glazes on containers, a gardener could spend more than a few hours these days mixing heucheras with other plants and pots. I'd like to set the yellow-green of 'Lime Rickey' against a dark blue or turquoise pot, or see the terracotta of 'Dolce Peach Melba' or 'Caramel' in an oxblood container, or the near-black of 'Obsidian' in a pale yellow or rich green pot. But good for you if you still grow the "original" coral bells (including the many beautifully flowering selections of *Hh. americana*, ×*brizoides*, and *sanguinea*). The hummingbirds need all the help they can get during these days of urban sprawl and other challenges.

Here's a tip: use heucheras and their kin (tiarellas and heucherellas) in fall and winter containers. Frost crystals magically transform their leaves into ice fantasies, and a dusting of snow looks great against all those colors. Don't be surprised if the foliage undergoes color changes with the increasing heat and light of summer; enjoy the changes that you like and wait patiently for the less pleasing incarnations to be replaced by the fresher, more vivid colors of fall. You can always remove any leaves that look the worse for wear. The show continues the following spring.

Cultural tips: Don't plant their crowns below the surface of the growing medium, or they will rot. Don't go crazy with fertilizer or keep them in poorly drained quarters. Don't grow them in too much shade (although they'll tolerate some), or their colors will never reveal themselves. Protect them from the worst winter cold with pine branches or something else that will look good with them. Don't expect every one to succeed dramatically for you (high humidity can send some into a tailspin, and some might not come back from an up-and-down winter), but do have a good time experimenting with them. (With thanks to Dan Heims and his informative Terra Nova catalog.)

The pale orange of *Heuchera* 'Dolce Peach Melba' appears even more spectral when seen with the electric purple of the aster. Combining this heuchera with hot shades would make the foliage appear weak and dull.

The complex coloration of *Heuchera* 'Caramel' reminds me of the last muted gasp of color in fall. Can you see the touch of frost suggested by the finely hairy edges of the youngest leaf?

HIBISCUS
mallow

Family: Malvaceae
Cultural group: tropicals, annuals
Height: 1–4 ft. or more, depending on training
Width: 1–4 ft.
Light: sun to partial shade
Temperature: warm to hot
Overwintering: min. 50°F, water occasionally, bright light
Moisture: moderate to ample
Drainage of medium: well drained
Fertility: average to high
Ease/speed of growth: easy/fast
Propagation: cuttings, air layering, seeds (for grins)
Problems: aphids, whitefly, scale insects, Japanese beetles, caterpillars, rots and spots

Principal interest: flowers, foliage, form (if trained)
Length of seasonal interest: long

Design attributes
Color: flowers in white and shades and combinations of just about every color (*H. rosa-sinensis*); foliage green or red, often variegated with white, red, pink, and purple
Line: upright to leaning stems, petioles, flower sexual structure, trunk (when trained)
Form: open to more densely shrubby
Space: generally under/around flowers
Texture: medium to coarse

I can recommend three species of *Hibiscus* for container gardening. One is *H. schizopetalus* (Japanese lantern), with lacy-looking, pendent red flowers that remind me of elaborately headdressed Vegas showgirls. Another is the similar-looking and -behaving *H. rosa-sinensis*, the inspiration for countless

An elegantly shaped and glazed container (plus that bit of a green-leaved trailer) create a complementary frame for a *Hibiscus rosa-sinensis* selection. The muted coloration of the pot lets the pink blooms stand out, while a more brightly colored one would be a distraction or perhaps clash with them, even though they are surrounded by peacemaking green leaves.

All the umpteen wildly colorful, voluptuous selections of *Hibiscus rosa-sinensis* evoke images of tropical islands. Most train easily into standards that might suggest tiki torches to you.

Hawaiian shirts (including two of mine), with flowers in a vast range of colors: purple and blue have been coaxed from the gene pool, joining white, red, pink, yellow, and orange. Check out the Web site for the American Hibiscus Society to appreciate the psychedelic diversity. While these often look their most impressive as standard topiaries or simply big shrubs

Hibiscus rosa-sinensis 'Aussie King' shows off its Type-A coloration. Even in the absence of the brilliant red flowers, the foliage rocks and rolls with vibrant color. One of these grown as a specimen would be the cynosure of all eyes!

Hibiscus acetosella 'Maple Sugar' is indeed a sweet, dark confection made up of metallically shiny, richly red-purple *Acer*-like leaves and equally tasty stems.

grown as monopots, they willingly accept roommates in a large enough pot. Don't expect them to cover themselves with flowers all season, but do enjoy the smattering of big, flashy blooms (single or double) that should decorate the plant almost every day for many months (and into the colder months if overwintered with enough heat and light). Regular applications of high-phosphorus fertilizer will help keep the show going. One selection to grow for its foliage (and boisterous red flowers, too) is 'Aussie King'.

Finally, should the look of Hawaiian shirts in your garden not hold any appeal for you, I suggest you discover the merits of *H. acetosella*. The selections most commonly grown produce impossibly rich-looking, iridescent, dark red foliage. Wow. Try this as a partner with or backdrop for anything red, pink, orange, pale yellow, gold, chartreuse, light blue, medium purple, or even magenta (are there any colors left?). The fullest, most compact plants result from a combination of plenty of nitrogen and attentive chopping back (and maybe a few strategically placed stakes). They grow speedily in the heat of summer, so it won't be long before a bushwhacked bush fills in again. Did you notice how I haven't mentioned the flowers? They're dark and essentially invisible, often not appearing until winter, and even then underwhelming me. Some selections are worth looking for, including 'Coppertone' and 'Maple Sugar' (beats me how they differ) and the slyly named 'Haight Ashbury', which ranges from a mixture of dark red, pink, and green to that iridescent dark red and vivid pink. Trippy, man.

Cultural tips: Diligently watch for scale insects and Japanese beetles. These hibiscus (unlike some of our native American species) hate poor drainage.

HOSTA
plantain lily, funkia

Family: Hostaceae/Liliaceae
Cultural group: perennials
Height: 2 in. to 2 ft., 1–3 ft. in flower
Width: 6 in. to 4 ft.
Light: sun (morning, please, except in the far North) to partial shade to shade
Temperature: warm to hot
Overwintering: hardy in Z3–8
Moisture: moderate to ample (but surprisingly drought tolerant)
Drainage of medium: well drained
Fertility: low to average
Ease/speed of growth: easy/slow to moderate to fast
Propagation: division, seeds (for those seeking to raise species or to add still more cultivars to the treasure trove)

Problems: slugs and snails, deer (hostas inspired the term "deer salad bar")

Principal interest: foliage, flowers, fragrance

Length of seasonal interest: long (flowers brief)

Design attributes

Color: foliage in a staggering range of greens, yellows, or gray-blues, many leaves marked with other shades of the principal color or white, yellow, or blue (a few have red-purple petioles); flowers in white and purple

Line: petioles, leaf outlines, flower stalks, and (sometimes) variegation patterns

Form: springs bubbling out of the ground, birds or other creatures rushing out from the center

Space: around edges of plant, mostly, although some among leaves

Texture: medium (not often) to coarse—hostas are the go-to example for the term "coarse"

For anyone out there who still hasn't added herbaceous perennials to your container plantings, I have one word: hostas. They're tough as nails, easily surviving harsh Z6–7 winters in smallish nursery pots at Atlock Farm. They take drought, they don't need lots of fertilizer, and plenty of them get by with precious little sun. Best of all, the challenges I've just described can produce some of the most dramatic foliage effects you've ever seen in containers.

Hostas provide linear interest and form, their simply drawn foliage and stately mounds either incorporating space within them or drawing attention to the space around them. There's plenty of texture: in general, hostas are the very definition of coarseness, yet some approach a fine "ferniness" with their small, drawn-out leaves and spaces between them.

And imagine this: a gentle breeze carries a sweet fragrance to your nose, and the only flowers you can make out in the garden's gathering gloom are a few white trumpets emerging from a clump of dark foliage. "That gardenia-y scent can't be coming from that hosta," you think. Well, it can indeed, if you

Hostas make excellent container subjects. Honest. They offer all five design elements in spades and can remain in pots for a few to several years, especially when grown as monopots. Decide for yourself about the merits of their flowers.

A young plant of *Hosta* 'Blue Sophistication' needs another couple of years under its proverbial belt before it attains its full splendor. In the meantime, it associates pleasantly with a collar of English ivies and a corsage of pink-marked *Hypoestes phyllostachya* in a cool off-white pot.

grow the ethereal, dreamy *H. plantaginea* (August lily). It likes more sun than most hostas, so site it accordingly. The flower stalks reach to about 2.5 ft., but growing August lily in a pot brings the olfactory delights that much closer to your nose. Aside from *H. plantaginea*, a few thousand more are worth a spot in your container garden. Start with the American Hosta Society to see the riches on offer. But don't get hung up trying to find a specific cultivar for a pot; instead, decide what you want the hosta to bring to your container party and then find one of the many that fills that particular bill. Hostaphiles will be happy to help you find the one, or hundred, of your dreams.

Smaller hostas and younger plants of larger hostas bring their abundant design interest to combopots, but they reach their zenith when allowed to develop as monopots. Mix in a few monopots with other pots in your shady to partly sunny garden areas.

Cultural tips: Slugs will find your hostas in low pots, and

Smaller hostas, such as this 'Feather Boa', grow well in shallow pots and often start a conversation, whether beside a gravel path, as here, or featured as a centerpiece on your dining table.

No optical tricks are being played on you here: *Hosta* 'Sum and Substance' really can become this big. Use larger hostas to direct attention to a spot out of hot, direct sun, and be prepared to answer lots of questions about them.

deer will find them no matter how high you site them. Divide tightly congested clumps in early spring; you'll need to bring out the heavy artillery (back-to-back digging forks pulled apart) to split big ones. Hatchets and heavy kitchen knives will work on the smaller ones. It usually takes more than few years for hostas to require division, however, especially if you want to let them become big, impressive specimens.

HUMULUS
hops, hop vine

Family: Cannabaceae
Cultural group: climbers and trailers
Height: 5–10 ft. or more
Width: depends on training
Light: sun to partial shade
Temperature: warm to hot
Overwintering: keep totally dormant at just above freezing, very little to no water, light not necessary; can be kept potted in their growing medium; hardy in Z4–8
Moisture: moderate to ample
Drainage of medium: well drained
Fertility: average to high (nitrogen to push growth)
Ease/speed of growth: easy/moderate to fast
Propagation: cuttings, seeds (*Hh. lupulus* and maybe *japonicus* 'Variegatus')
Problems: mildews, rots and spots
Principal interest: foliage, form (if trained)
Length of seasonal interest: long

Design attributes

Color: foliage dark green marked with white (*H. japonicus* 'Variegatus'), light to medium green (*H. lupulus*), yellow-green (*H. lupulus* 'Aureus')
Line: not readily visible (depends on training)
Form: a boisterous mass of grapelike leaves
Space: often absent (depends on training)
Texture: medium to coarse

Members of this genus are amenable to training, readily climbing up a support…maybe too readily, but restraining vigorous growth is one of the many reasons we invented pruning shears (and why we have fingers). Take *H. lupulus* 'Aureus' (golden hops). Give it a big pot in a big spot, and await the inevitable questions and compliments. "What is that thing that looks like a yellow-green grapevine?" "That combination with [name a color or plant] is a knockout!" Tell them that golden hops is a chartreuse selection of the lustily climbing species that (in its more widely cultivated green-leaved selections) produces the very hops that add pleasant bitterness to beer. Also point out that hops are the plants (well, actually,

Even though the plant of interest here, *Humulus lupulus* 'Aureus', resides in the background, its more assertive yellow-green foliage jumps out and demands to be admired first. Be careful when leaning in for a closer look, though: that cottonthistle (*Onopordum*) bites!

Enjoy the intricate and variable coloration of *Humulus japonicus* 'Variegatus' either up close or at a distance, where it dissolves into a soft, attractive gray-green.

the dried conelike inflorescences) stored in those eye-catching conical buildings in England, for instance at Great Dixter, among many other gardens and farms.

If you're looking for a "grapevine" with fascinatingly splash-painted foliage (perhaps to admire while enjoying a beer on the patio), give *H. japonicus* 'Variegatus' (variegated Japanese hops) a try. It's less rambunctious than golden hops (maybe 5 ft. tall versus 10 ft.) and offers a cool, refreshing contrast to brighter colors and denser forms. You can let both twine around another big plant in a combopot or give each a form of its own to clamber over.

If the conelike hops do appear on your plants (females only), you will at least want to make a point of pointing them out to your garden visitors. Whether you harvest them for your own microbrew is entirely up to you.

Cultural tips: Don't encourage golden hops (or the all-green ones, if you choose to grow them) with lots of fertilizer; it will grow large, especially in full sun, without much encouragement. Variegated Japanese hops, on the other hand, will appreciate a little extra food and protection from hot, strong sun.

HYACINTHUS
hyacinth

Family: Hyacinthaceae/Liliaceae
Cultural group: bulbs
Height: 8–12 in.
Width: 6–12 in. (including foliage)
Light: sun to partial shade
Temperature: cool to warm
Overwintering: forced in cold conditions for advanced
    bloom, or at normal time; hardy in Z(5)6–9
Moisture: moderate to ample
Drainage of medium: well drained
Fertility: don't worry about it
Ease/speed of growth: moderate (but easy as forced
    bulbs go)/fast
Propagation: nope, unless you want to score and scoop
    the bulbs and wait a rather long time
Problems: bulb rot
Principal interest: flowers, fragrance
Length of seasonal interest: brief but glorious

Design attributes
Color: flowers in white, pink, blue, purple, yellow, and
    orange; medium to dark green foliage
Line: linear leaves, starry flowers, oval outline of
    flower cluster
Form: oval wad of stars with a hand (leaves) holding it or
    fallen giants if not properly grown (or staked, if neces-
    sary); Roman hyacinths much more loose-looking

Even a few hyacinths in a rustic container will do the trick when you're impatient for winter to end. Can't you almost smell these three 'Pink Pearl'? If the stems become too tall and spindly and fall over, you can continue to enjoy them as cut flowers.

A few pots of forced hyacinths (such as deep blue 'Blue Jacket', white 'Carnegie', and rich pink 'Jan Bos', shown here) will bring cheer and fragrance to the dull days of late winter. Grow them as single colors, or mix them all up for a harlequin display. They probably won't all bloom at the same time, though, which could be a good or bad thing.

Space: not much (more in the Romans)
Texture: medium to coarse (Romans not coarse)

I really don't care that hyacinths don't last long in flower and that their leaves (and often clunky form) aren't anything to write home about. Other hardy bulbs (and plenty of other plants) fall short in these areas, too, and I'd give them all up (except daffodils—I have my limits) in favor of reveling exclusively in the scent of hyacinths. Nothing else smells like a hyacinth: sniff them once and remember the redolent fragrance forever.

Their flower colors are mighty fine too, in strong to pastel shades of spring: the familiar pink ('Pink Pearl' and 'Fondant'), blue ('Blue Jacket' and 'Sky Jacket', often with a strong influence of purple), and white ('Carnegie' and 'L'Innocence'), and (less commonly) yellow ('City of Haarlem'), apricot ('Gypsy Queen'), red-violet ('Woodstock'), and lilac ('Splendid Cornelia'). The multistemmed, so-called Roman hyacinths, Festival hyacinths, or multifloras are worth a try, too, in pink, blue, and white. They send up multiple, more open flowerheads from their bulbs (that look like flattened artichokes to me) and so appear much less weighty, but they cost more per bulb. However, you will get quite a bit of bang for your buck.

The bigger the bulb, the bigger (and more imposing-looking and heavier) the flowerhead. Big ones make impressive pots, but they will require a tight corset of stakes and string to keep them vertical.

You can buy them in bud and/or flower if you don't want to force them, but hyacinths are among the easiest of hardy bulbs to force. Oddly, even though they don't like poor drainage in the open ground, hyacinth bulbs can be forced with nothing but water (in a specifically made hyacinth glass or similar container) under them, and they take well to forcing in the same way as you would a daffodil or tulip.

Their big, colorful, often lumpy-looking flowerheads make a strong (some say "coarse") contrast with many other more delicate-looking spring flowers. Combine them as you see fit with other spring favorites in short-lived combopots or grow them as potent masses of color in monopots. You might also consider tucking a few into more permanent combopots (such as those maintained for winter interest), enjoying them in bloom, and then pulling them out after they fade (or flop over and literally fall out, which they might do). Just do it, somewhere and somehow. Your nose will thank you when the hyacinths bloom.

Cultural tips: After they bloom, you have three options: 1) toss 'em, 2) plant them out in the open garden, where they should return for at least a few years, or 3) keep them watered and fertilized in their pots, let the foliage mature and turn brown, and then store them dry in the pots until fall, when you can separate the bulbs and replant them in pots or in the open ground.

HYPOESTES
polka-dot plant, freckle face (*H. phyllostachya*)

Family: Acanthaceae
Cultural group: annuals
Height: 6–12 in.
Width: 6 in. or more
Light: partial shade
Temperature: warm to hot
Overwintering: min. 55°F, water regularly but not
    excessively, bright light
Moisture: moderate to ample
Drainage of medium: well drained
Fertility: average
Ease/speed of growth: easy/moderate
Propagation: seeds, cuttings
Problems: whitefly (maybe)
Principal interest: foliage
Length of seasonal interest: long

Design attributes
Color: medium to dark green to nearly black leaves with
    white, red, pink, or red-violet spots
Line: upright to leaning to cascading stems
Form: spreading, open carpet to weak shrubs
Space: between stems and leaves but not significant
Texture: fine to medium (the spotting lightens the texture)

One plant takes honors as a practically cinematic celebration of the polka dot: *H. phyllostachya*, the polka-dot plant (aka *H. sanguinolenta* "of gardens"). While the dots aren't as perfectly shaped as those in the kaleidoscopic finale of Busby Berkeley's *The Gang's All Here* (hit YouTube to see "The

Polka-Dot Polka" and what follows), it doesn't take much imagination to see the suitability of the common name. Happily, the pink-dotted green pattern of the species has been joined by several selections that Busby would appreciate, particularly those in the Splash Select series, which adds white, red, pink, and near-black to the dance.

Often spreading or low-shrubby, *H. phyllostachya* makes a pleasant, eye-catching addition to combopots as well as very appealing little monopots. Kids love it. So do adults who let their inner child speak up.

Cultural tips: While usually recommended for partial shade, polka-dot plant's coloration jumps out when grown in full sun, provided plenty of water is made available (although I doubt the white-dotted ones would tolerate so much sun). Regular applications of nitrogen encourage abundant foliage, and regular pinching keeps everybody shorter and denser. Pinching precludes the dumpy blue flowers from appearing, too, but don't wait until the plants are large and rangy to cut them back: severe chopping may bring the entire polka-dotted production to a premature and unscripted End.

IMPATIENS
balsam, busy Lizzie

Family: Balsaminaceae
Cultural group: annuals
Height: 6 in. to 2 ft.
Width: 6 in. to 2 ft. (to 4 ft. in *I. repens*)
Light: sun to partial shade to shade
Temperature: warm to hot
Overwintering: min. 55–60°F, water occasionally,
    bright light
Moisture: ample
Drainage of medium: well drained
Fertility: average
Ease/speed of growth: easy to moderate/moderate to fast
Propagation: seeds, cuttings
Problems: aphids, spider mites, rots and spots, wilting from
    drought
Principal interest: flowers, foliage, form
Length of seasonal interest: long

Design attributes
Color: flowers in white, pink, lavender, lilac, and blue-pink,
    plus all the hot colors; foliage in many greens (including
    reddish and purplish), some variegated with white or
    yellow; stems sometimes red (most notably in *I. repens*)
Line: almost absent (*I. walleriana*) to prominent (New
    Guineas, Africans, and *I. repens*)
Form: shrubby (*I. walleriana*) to treelike (Africans and *I.
    balsamina*), spreading (*I. repens*), intriguing flower forms

Take a close, considered look at *Hypoestes phyllostachya* 'Splash Select Pink'—what else could it possibly be called? Do you also see a darker selection of polka-dot plant, 'Splash Select Red'? It too is a fittin' name.

Space: absent (or only implied) to ample (Africans and
some New Guineas)
Texture: fine to medium

The sherbet-colored 'Jungle Gold', an African impatiens, offers its hungry-baby-bird flowers in unavoidably showy clusters. You might want to keep them away from some of their more familiar pink- and lilac-flowered walleriana relatives, however, lest a color war break out.

Impatiens. Impatiens everywhere. In shade, in sun, in the ground, in public spaces, in catalogs and nurseries, but are they growing in your pots? Why not? "Too common," you might say. "Overused." "Garish." "Uninspiring." Trust me; many people haven't seen the half of what can be done with this genus. And remember that impatiens are popular for good reason: they're easy to grow, wildly colorful, and surprisingly versatile.

Let's begin with *I. walleriana*, the Everywhere Impatiens. They are shrubby-looking, common as dirt, and come in a stupefying range of plant heights and flower colors (with new series introduced every year, it seems). Seed catalogs and nurseries are full of them, so I encourage you to check them out for yourself. While they do best in morning sun, many of them can take more sun if given plenty of water.

A strongly colored *Impatiens walleriana* selection holds it own against the dark blue of the container. The trailing stems of a variegated *Vinca minor* selection (perhaps 'Illumination') soften what might otherwise be a too-potent combination of color, form, and texture.

A roomy-enough cavity of a tree trunk makes a perfectly suitable container for a double-flowered *Impatiens walleriana* selection. Impatiens are very adaptable, lending themselves beautifully to creative culture such as this. Don't simply push the envelope or think outside of the box every now and then; smash them, I say.

But the genus *Impatiens* contains plenty of other jewels, including the so-called African ones (a mixed bag of tall and sometimes spreading plants with flowers that look like birds, such as 'Jungle Gold', the red, green, and gold-flowered 'Congo Cockatoo', and the richly red-flowered 'African King') and others that look like our tall, rangy, native jewel weed (*I. capensis*) but with purple and white flowers.

I. balsamina (rose balsam) grows rapidly and blooms abundantly. When I grew them as a kid, I imagined them first as little trees with roses on their trunks and then, once their seed pods began to develop, as cacao trees (yes, the fruits of *Theobroma cacao*, the source of chocolate, hang from the trunks, too). Rose balsams look sensational when lined up in a long, skinny windowbox or similar-looking container in morning sun. The dwarfer forms often lack the rose-clad tree look (to be polite about describing them), so beware.

The so-called New Guinea impatiens turned the gardening world on its ear when they exploded on the scene a few decades ago. Impatiens for sunny spots? And what's with those beautifully marked, pointed leaves and purple stems? Hybridizers have worked their magic with the original offerings, and now there are many heights, flower colors, and leaf patterns from which to choose. By far my favorite of the bunch is the vibrant orange 'Tango', whose flower color appears that much more vivid against dark bronzy-green foliage (instead of competing with yellow-splashed leaves, which is the case with many of the New Guineas).

But if I could grow only one impatiens, it would probably be *I. repens*, a spreading (or cascading), nearly flat mass of small green leaves and purple petioles and stems. For me, the shyly borne, bright gold flowers add a discordant note, so I'm always tempted to remove them. This species grows happily in full sun at Atlock, but it wants and so receives plenty of water. Try combining *I. repens* with an orange- or pink-flowered selection of *I. walleriana* to befuddle your straightlaced gardening friends.

Cultural tips: The stems are brittle, so keep impatiens out of windy spots and ideally away from soccer balls and large

A good-sized, rolled-rim gray pot barely contains *Impatiens* 'Jungle Gold', spiraling *Begonia* 'Escargot', and sugar-dusted *Boehmeria nipononivea* 'Koganc-mushi' (among others). Wow! Kudos to the cutting-edge gardeners at the Scott Arboretum in Swarthmore, Pennsylvania.

If an impatiens sports elongated, variegated leaves, it can probably take quite a bit of sun, such as *Impatiens* 'Sunpatiens Landscape' in the foreground. The solidly green-leaved, white flowered one is another Sunpatiens, and like all New Guinea impatiens it too loves the sun. Read the label.

The green and purple combination of *Impatiens repens* appeals to me (I could take or leave the gold flowers), as does watching the thousands of little leaves exuberantly build up and trail out of their pot. It's so satisfying to watch something different strut its stuff.

dogs' tails. They like moisture but not standing water, which frequently leads to root rot. Expect them to turn to black mush after the first good frost of fall.

IPOMOEA

moonflower, moonvine (*I. alba*); sweet potato (*I. batatas*); cypress vine, cardinal climber (*Ii. coccinea*, ×*multifida*, and *quamoclit*); morning glory (*I. tricolor*)

Family: Convolvulaceae
Cultural group: climbers and trailers
Height: 2–12 ft. or more
Width: depends on training
Light: sun (although *I. batatas* can take some shade, altering the coloration)
Temperature: warm to stinking hot
Overwintering: tubers of *I. batatas* can be kept totally

While not as rampant and voluminous as its morning-glory relatives, *Ipomoea quamoclit* 'Valentine Mix' still obeys its internal programming as a climber to clamber and wind its way around its support, whether a frame or another plant. But it does it so finely and delicately . . .

dormant at 50–60°F, very little to no water, light not necessary, potted in their growing medium
Moisture: ample
Drainage of medium: well drained
Fertility: average to high (for stupendous specimens of *I. batatas*)
Ease/speed of growth: easy/fast
Propagation: seeds, cuttings, tubers (*I. batatas*)
Problems: whitefly, aphids, rots and spots
Principal interest: flowers, foliage, form, fragrance (*I. alba*)
Length of seasonal interest: long

Design attributes
Color: flowers in white, red, blue, and purple; foliage medium green (rarely marked with white) or chartreuse, purple-black, brown, or light green with white and pink (*I. batatas*)
Line: long and cascading, upright and twisting, or hard to

find, depending on training; also noticeable in foliage of cutleaf forms
Form: leafy ropes to blankets of leaves to delicate green clouds
Space: absent to abundant
Texture: fine to medium to coarse

When I was a child, a red-flowered vine clambered up a temporary string-and-pushpin trellis by our front door. Whether we grew *I. coccinea* (with either plain or feathery leaves and yellow-centered red trumpets), *I. quamoclit* (with very deeply cut foliage and starry red flowers), or *I. ×multifida* I can't say, but the cardinal-red flowers on our vine lasted a day or two (during gray spells) and the hummingbirds visited them all summer. Shortly thereafter we moved on to morning glories (and a sturdier trellis), specifically *I. tricolor* 'Heavenly Blue', and I learned from my mom how to pop the faded, curled-up flowers that bloomed in *ante meridiem* profusion. She'd squeeze a collapsed flower between her thumb and in-

The fleeting, October-sky blue of *Ipomoea tricolor* 'Heavenly Blue' can be yours in a container, provided it's roomy enough. Also, you'll need to keep a watchful eye on the ever-questing stems: just because you've provided it with a trellis or other framework doesn't mean it won't try to throw itself onto its neighbors.

The sugary, caramely, butterscotchy colors of *Ipomoea batatas* 'Sweet Caroline Bronze' bring a rich, warm feeling to container plantings. I don't think I'd ever think to combine them with a breezy-cool, lilac-colored *Lantana montevidensis*, but this book's photographer, Rob Cardillo, did. Sweet, indeed.

dex finger while pressing down just a bit, and then would come the crack. Now I teach others how to pop the morning glories at Atlock Farm, and 'Heavenly Blue' still provides much of the ammunition. Also worth trying are 'Pearly Gates' (white), 'Scarlett O'Hara' (red), and 'Flying Saucers' (variously variegated). 'Roman Candy' flaunts variegated flowers as well as white-splashed foliage. I find that the variegated ones don't grow as eagerly as the others, which easily reach 6 ft. in pots.

I very clearly remember the sweet potato (*I. batatas*) that grew at the back of one of my grade school classrooms, sitting above some water in a glass jar, suspended by several toothpicks thrust into it, and sending out an ever-increasing mass of roots. That long-ago sweet potato was one of the edible, plain-leaved ones, but we gardeners may now enjoy a richly colorful range of foliage colors and shapes. How anyone gets by without at least one of these is a mystery to me. 'Blackie' is the one that (re-)introduced gardeners to sweet potatoes, not for eating but for marveling at the deep purple-green-black, assertively lobed foliage. What a color! Like other sweet potatoes, 'Blackie' trails instead of climbs but can be trained onto a form or other support with some effort. 'Ace of Spades' of-

fers the same color as 'Blackie' on (you guessed it) spade-shaped leaves. 'Lady Fingers' (aka '#99') produces deeply cut (fingered) green foliage with suggestions of purple; in my experience, it doesn't grow as vigorously as the others (with the exception of the poky 'Tricolor'). 'Margarita' is without question the most vigorous of the bunch, easily reaching 10 ft. in a season if kept watered and fertilized liberally. The coloration varies with the amount of light received, leaning toward yellow in sun and green in shade, while the perfect spot allows 'Margarita' to dress in electric chartreuse. 'Sweet Caroline Bronze' might easily be dismissed as "brown," but that would perpetrate an injustice on this autumnally colored confection in caramel, merlot, and equally tasty shades of green, depending on the age of the leaves and the light conditions; she makes just about any companion sing. Last to consider is 'Tricolor', in beguiling light green, white, and red-violet, but it needs special treatment to get it to grow more than 1 ft. or so. Once Poky does reach about 1 ft. in length, pin the stem(s) down onto the potting mix and sprinkle a little mix over the stems. New roots will form, prodding Poky to send out several more shoots that usually grow more quickly than the original. In time—usu-

Ipomoea batatas 'Blackie' introduced many gardeners to the amazing diversity to be found among ornamental sweet potatoes, and it's still the first-choice sweet potato for many of us. That impossibly dark color goes with nearly every other color, and its gentle droopiness almost requires it to be allowed to hang out of a container.

Whether you call this sweet potato *Ipomoea batatas* 'Lady Fingers' (or the thuddingly prosaic '#99'), you will appreciate its finely cut foliage and not-too-rambunctious growth habit.

A lone moonflower (*Ipomoea alba*) looks longingly into the sky, wishing it could join its brothers and sisters, the stars. Florid, huh? The look (and scent) of moonflowers could make your writing flowery, too.

ally over at least two growing seasons—'Tricolor' should make an impressive specimen. Give all these plenty of light, water, and fertilizer to help them reach their full potential. However, you might reach for the pruning shears if you don't give them plenty of room.

Finally, moonflowers (*I. alba*) are more than just big white morning glories that bloom at night. They're magic. Each evening, a few spiraled buds unfurl to release their clean, seductive scent. Give them smallish pots and don't give them very much nitrogen: I'm convinced that tight, lean quarters encourage them to bloom (other garden writers take the opposite point of view). Full sun also helps but isn't necessary.

Cultural tips: Isolate all the twiners (everybody just described except for sweet potatoes, *I. batatas*) if you don't want them to invade and conquer nearby plants. Some of the sweet potatoes can overwhelm other plants, simply by growing over (or outgrowing) them, so keep an eye out for them, too. Cardinal climbers are the least hegemonous of the lot. Give morning glories a sturdy framework—living or constructed—to engulf, and take it easy with the nitrogen.

IRIS
flag

Family: Iridaceae
Cultural group: perennials (*Ii. ensata* 'Variegata' and *pallida* 'Variegata'), bulbs (*I. reticulata* and kin)
Height: 2–3 ft. (*Ii. ensata* 'Variegata' and *pallida* 'Variegata'), 3–12 in. (*I. reticulata* and kin)
Width: 2 ft. or more (*Ii. ensata* 'Variegata' and *pallida* 'Variegata'), 2–3 in. (*I. reticulata* and kin)
Light: sun to partial shade
Temperature: cool to warm

Overwintering: *Ii. ensata* 'Variegata' and *reticulata* (and kin) hardy in Z5–8; *I. pallida* 'Variegata' hardy in Z5–9
Moisture: moderate to ample (*Ii. ensata* 'Variegata' and *pallida* 'Variegata'), moderate (*I. reticulata* and kin)
Drainage of medium: well drained (*I. ensata* 'Variegata' tolerates standing water when in bloom)
Fertility: average
Ease/speed of growth: easy to moderate/moderate
Propagation: division, offsets (of bulbs of *I. reticulata* and kin)
Problems: iris borer, soft rot, leaf spots, slugs and snails (previous four on *Ii. ensata* 'Variegata' and *pallida* 'Variegata'), bulb rot (*I. reticulata* and kin)
Principal interest: foliage (*Ii. ensata* 'Variegata' and *pallida* 'Variegata'), flowers (all three), fragrance (*Ii. pallida* 'Variegata' and some *reticulata*)
Length of seasonal interest: long (foliage on *Ii. ensata* 'Variegata' and *pallida* 'Variegata'); brief (flowers)

Design attributes
Color: flowers in blue, purple, and red-violet with yellow markings
Line: classic swordlike foliage (*Ii. ensata* 'Variegata' and *pallida* 'Variegata'), skinny-linear foliage (*I. reticulata* and kin)
Form: fans with intricately geometric shapes above them (*Ii. ensata* 'Variegata' and *pallida* 'Variegata), dry spaghetti with intricately geometric shapes at their base (*I. reticulata* and kin)
Space: abundant at tops of and between foliage, within the flower outlines
Texture: fine (foliage on *I. reticulata* and kin), medium (the rest)

The genus *Iris*—so appropriately named for the goddess of the rainbow, given the vast range of flower colors—contains many, many garden-suitable examples (provided you are aware of and can provide for their needs, of course), but as far as I'm concerned, only three have earned their chops as container worthy. Two are foliage plants that grow from ground-hugging rhizomes and happen to bloom for a little while, and the other is a charming lot of little bulbous baubles grown for their flowers (which also don't bloom very long, but living beauty is temporary, isn't it?).

I. ensata 'Variegata', one of the variegated Japanese irises, stops me in my tracks every time I see it. I think a good-sized clump of it looks like a 4th of July fireworks grand finale just before the shells explode (think of the spark trails), or maybe a whole lot of green swords coated in cream. Being a Japanese iris, it likes plenty of moisture and sun and surprises its grower with a few gold-marked, flattish, rich purple flowers. It's odd that something so showy in leaf would be so shy with its bloom production, but even extroverts have their quieter sides.

A good-sized clump of *I. pallida* 'Variegata' doesn't bring fireworks and swords to my mind; instead, I see an elaborately spiky, green and cream Mohawk haircut blown around by the wind. The blue-violet flowers have the classic three-petals-up/three-petals-down look (standards and falls) shared by most other bearded irises and emit a pleasant grapey scent (to my nose). The fragrance motif continues if you dig up, dry, and grind up the rhizomes to make orris root, a reputedly violet-scented fixative used to preserve the scent of potpourri. Nice, but a bit of a bother. Unlike *I. ensata* 'Variegata', this one prefers a dryish, well-drained potting mix but shares its affinity for sun. Both make unforgettable color and linear contrasts with just about anything that shares their cultural preferences.

And now for something (not exactly) completely different: *Ii. reticulata, histrioides, danfordiae*, and several other species and many hybrids in the so-called rock garden iris crowd. Force them (like a tulip or daffodil) once, enjoy their intricacies and delicate fragrance up close and personal for a few days, and then discard them or hope that maybe some of them will persist after you plant them in the open ground. All the ones most commonly grown (save for the green-golden *I. danfordiae*) come in shades of blue and purple (a few might be described as white, but they're pale blue, really) with spots and streaks to varying degrees on the falls, which often sport a flash of gold. If I could grow only one it would be the elusively turquoise 'Katharine Hodgkin', but I'd be almost as happy with the super-reliable rich blue 'Harmony' or deep purple 'George' (all reticulatas). Keep these irises cool, moist, and in plenty of sun (or bright light, say under fluorescent tubes) as you're waiting for the flowers to pop out, which can be as little as four days after being removed from cold storage.

Cultural tips: The dreaded iris borer (and its vile cohort, bacterial soft rot) can make smelly sludge out of rhizomatous irises, so keep an eye out for little cuts in the foliage and goo running out of them. Divide the tangles of rhizomes every three years or so, cut the leaves back by at least half, and repot them. For a splendid display, put as many of the bulbous ones in a single layer in a pot as you can manage.

White-striped swords of *Iris ensata* 'Variegata' rush out of a black pot. No matter where and how it's used, this iris always appears to be in a frenzy. The flowers slow down the pace, so I remove them. Quickly.

Shorter and more broadly leaved than its relative, *Iris pallida* 'Variegata' still packs an energetic visual punch. I'm merciful with the classic-looking flowers on this one (as opposed to those on *I. ensata* 'Variegata'), for two reasons: their gentle but somehow potent blue-violet color and their Concord-grape fragrance.

JASMINUM
jasmine

Family: Oleaceae
Cultural group: climbers and trailers
Height: 2–6 ft. or more
Width: depends on training
Light: sun to partial shade
Temperature: cool (to induce bloom) to warm to hot
Overwintering: min. 50°F, water occasionally, bright light; hardy in Z9–10
Moisture: moderate to ample
Drainage of medium: well drained
Fertility: average (high phosphorus to promote heavy bloom)
Ease/speed of growth: easy/moderate to fast
Propagation: cuttings, layering (not air layering)
Problems: aphids, scale insects, mealybugs, rots and spots

Principal interest: foliage, flowers, fragrance
Length of seasonal interest: all year

Design attributes
Color: medium green leaves (sometimes marked with white, pink, yellow, and/or gray-green), chartreuse in *J. officinale* Fiona Sunrise (= 'Frojas')
Line: long and upright or cascading (depends on training)
Form: strings with Matisse paper-cut leaves (depends on training), and sometimes with stars
Space: ample at edges of plant, depends on training
Texture: fine to medium

Without question, jasmines emit some of the most hypnotizing floral fragrances, so of course they're worthy container subjects, right? Well, as far as I'm concerned, most of the truly fragrant ones aren't much to look at (such as the often-straggly *J. sambac* and its mythical selection 'Grand Duke of Tuscany'), and the showy, flower-laden ones (*Jj. offici-*

These few shoots of *Jasminum officinale* Fiona Sunrise (= 'Frojas') set against a quiet background could inspire an extemporaneous lecture on the five design elements. But I won't launch into one, because you can pick out and appreciate the obvious presence of all of them, right?

Suggesting the business ends of a couple of gigantic lightning bugs, two columns of *Jasminum officinale* Fiona Sunrise (='Frojas') electrify a patio. Two good growing seasons should be enough time for small starter plants to cover the forms.

nale, polyanthum) require precise—some might say incantation- and sacrifice-dependent—care to bring them into bloom. So grow jasmines for their foliage, and if flowers do appear, accept your good fortune humbly.

The leaves of *J. officinale* are pretty enough in their own right, but it's the variegated ones that steal the show in containers. 'Argenteovariegatum', as the name tells us, is silver-variegated (well, it's more like cream or milk), and 'Aureum' bears gold-marked foliage (more yellow, really, but the suggestion of gold carries more weight, even in the plant world). Both make pleasing additions to containers if restrained to a few long, weaving stems. But if "pow" is more your style than "pleasing," give *J. officinale* Fiona Sunrise (= 'Frojas') a try. Whether playfully restrained in combopots, or given free rein as a tour de force trained specimen, Fiona's pervasive chartreuse foliage will make an impression. No one will wonder where the flowers or fragrance is.

When properly grown, *J. polyanthum* suggests a fragrant white cloud in late winter (giant hanging baskets of it can stop traffic), but "properly grown" means carefully managing temperature and moisture at the right times, usually in a greenhouse or other structure. Join me as an iconoclast and let the strings of fine-textured foliage (managed as you would *J. officinale*) weave through other plants or let it billow and serve as a foil for coarser textures and/or showy flowers.

Cultural tips: These are easy to grow when you're not stressing out over what they need to bring them into bloom. Treat them as you would a meat-and-potatoes foliage plant, and I think you'll find you don't miss those smelly flowers.

JUNCUS
rush

Family: Juncaceae
Cultural group: perennials, aquatics
Height: 1–2 ft.
Width: 1–2 ft. or more
Light: sun to partial shade
Temperature: cool to warm to hot
Overwintering: min. 50°F, water occasionally, bright light; hardy in Z4–10 (*J. effusus* 'Spiralis'), Z4–11 (*J. ensifolius*), Z6–11 (*J. patens*)
Moisture: moderate to ample
Drainage of medium: well drained but tolerates standing water
Fertility: average
Ease/speed of growth: moderate/moderate
Propagation: division
Problems: rots and spots
Principal interest: form, foliage

Length of seasonal interest: long (evergreen except in very cold areas)

Design attributes
Color: green to dark green
Line: nothing but (curls in *J. effusus* 'Spiralis')
Form: sketched, a zillion lines coming from a spot in the ground
Space: everywhere
Texture: fine to medium

Gary Larson is a genius. His Far Side cartoons always bring a smile, especially the one with the mother stick figure standing over her kid's bed and addressing the stick figure physician who's just arrived: "Thank goodness you're here, Doctor! … I came in this morning and found Billy just all scribbled like this!" Brilliant.

If you want to get a good idea of what Billy looked like (apart from his frowny-face head), check out the photo of *J. effusus* 'Spiralis'. This plant certainly looks like it was scrib-

Green scribbles in a streamlined urn: this is as pure, abstract, and quintessentially expressive as container design gets. About all *Juncus effusus* 'Spiralis' asks for is a sodden potting mix in (at least) morning sun.

bled by a gardener who wanted a plant with immediately obvious linear interest. Give it wet conditions—not just moist, but wet—and it will keep scribbling away. Set its green lines against the colors and shapes of other aquatics, such as the colorful starry flowers and round leaves of waterlilies (*Nymphaea*) or the evocative clusters of water lettuce (*Pistia*). An out-of-the-ordinary container shape, such as a cube or cone or other clean, stripped-down form, will make a corkscrew rush appear even more exciting and arty. Of course it will look good in a more mundane container, but why set a diamond in tin?

Beware: *J. effusus* 'Spiralis' and a few other rushes (*Jj. filiformis* 'Spiralis', *balticus* 'Spiralis') are mixed up in the nursery trade and in gardens. All look scribbled, so the true identity won't make much difference to you or anyone admiring your creativity, I bet.

Plenty of other rushes might tempt you along the way, especially if you find yourself browsing in a good water-gardening nursery, from the well-described flat sedge (*J. ensifolius*) to the hair-like *J. patens*.

Cultural tips: Rushes like moisture; a very moist potting mix will do, but a wet one—or one under 1–2 in. of water—will make them very happy.

KALANCHOE

felt bush, velvet leaf (*K. beharensis*); flapjacks, paddle plant (*K. thyrsiflora*); panda plant, pussy ears, plush plant (*K. tomentosa*)

Family: Crassulaceae
Cultural group: succulents
Height: 4 in. to 2 ft. or more
Width: 3 in. to 2 ft. or more
Light: sun to limited partial shade
Temperature: cool to warm to hot
Overwintering: min. 50°F, water occasionally, bright light
Moisture: on dry side to moderate
Drainage of medium: well drained
Fertility: average
Ease/speed of growth: easy/moderate
Propagation: stem cuttings, leaf cuttings, offsets
    (*K. thyrsiflora*)
Problems: mealybugs, aphids, rots and spots
Principal interest: foliage, form, flowers
Length of seasonal interest: all year

Design attributes

Color: gray-green, blue, and brown foliage (*K. beharensis*), gray-green edged with red (*K. thyrsiflora*), gray edged with brown (*K. tomentosa*)
Line: varies widely but always interesting

Three different selections of *Kalanchoe beharensis* softly but insistently demand attention. At the lower left is an unusually deeply cut selection, above it hovers the perfectly named 'Fang' (check out the leaf undersides), and to the right a compact form performs a balancing trick with its pot.

How many colors can you find in this compact selection of *Kalanchoe beharensis* (and can you see how they develop as the leaves enlarge and age)? All those colors, plus all that fantastic, pastry-chef-gone-wild crimping, occur on a plant that might reach 1 ft. tall.

Form: shrubby pagodas (*K. beharensis*), sideways stacks of
  pancakes (*K. thyrsiflora*), nests of fuzzy little animals
  (*K. tomentosa*)
Space: between and around leaves, around flowers
Texture: fine to medium to coarse

Succulents of just about every stripe fascinate me, and not
just because so many are absurdly easy to grow. (Kids
grow them on their bedroom windows. Office workers keep
them on their desks.) The only difficult thing about this particular genus of succulents is getting more than three people
to agree on the pronunciation of the name. Kal'-an-cho. Kal-
an-cho'-ee. The succinct, clipped klank'-oh. And ka-lank'-oh-
wee (my choice). Say it as you will; everyone will know what
you mean.

Three kalanchoes really push my buttons, in a good way
(and none are the ubiquitous *K. blossfeldiana*). First is *K. beharensis*, which is soothing in all its forms. You might find that
an odd judgment, based on a quick glance at the photos: how
can those cut-up, jagged edged things be soothing? Two ways.
For one, their foliage comes in shades of sage green and light
slate blue and Earth Mother brown, colors that are often referred to as "colonial" or "traditional," which implies propriety
and safety and correctness, reinforcing their comfortable nature. Second, their leaves are sedatively fuzzy and invite tactile interaction (hence the common names). I'm familiar with
four forms of this living security blanket: the species itself,
which produces lance-shaped or triangular, cupped leaves in
shades of silver-blue and brown and grows as an open shrub
to 3 ft. or so; a more pronouncedly cut-edged but otherwise
similar form; 'Fang', with its smile-inducing teeth on the leaf
undersides, on a plant that grows more densely than the type;
and a so-called compact form, which in my experience has
never reached more than 1 ft. tall, but whose coloration and
exquisitely precise, rippling form are worthy of meditation (or
at least admiration). All quietly implore you to include them in
succulent combopots or to raise them into specimens.

While felt bush calms me, flapjacks (*K. thyrsiflora*) excites
me, conjuring up images of, well, pancakes (I don't call them
flapjacks, nor have I ever been served by a man called Cookie
while on a wagon train), paddles (hence the other common
name), clapping hands, and those billowing skirts that feature prominently in some Mexican dances. In time (and if
grown with protection from excessive rain), the red-edged
green leaves become heavily coated in gray bloom (powder),
and then the even more heavily coated flower spikes rise up to
2 ft. and command attention. They last for months—without
bowling you over with their yellowish flowers—and should
elicit enthusiastic questions and ooh-ahs from every garden
visitor (except for succulentophiles, who if even remotely
thoughtful and polite will admit they know the plant and rave
nonetheless). I've seen it as a specimen (try it in a beautifully

complementary mustard-colored pot) and in wildly colorful
combopots with other succulents. Splendid either way.

As you might guess by its common names, *K. tomentosa* ex-
erts the same sedative effect on me as *K. beharensis*—until I
catch sight of its frenetically dotted leaf edges. They remind
me of chase lighting from disco days, or the aisle lighting on
airplanes. However, the yin-yang interaction of the sedative
and the stimulant ends up creating a mighty appealing plant
for both monopots and combopots. It's so willing to grow that
healthy leaves that fall from the plant will in time root and
make new shoots, even if the leaves fall on a windowsill or
desk. This little trick, and its super-easy culture, make panda
plant an ideal hook for introducing kids to gardening. I think
I'll go to sleep (or maybe head out to a disco) now.

Cultural tips: All three get by with very little water but will
grow more quickly and attractively with more attentive watering. Don't keep the soil constantly moist, however. Do not
let oil-based sprays fall onto the leaves of *K. thyrsiflora*, or the
bloominess will vanish.

The silvery companion foliage surrounding this *Kalanchoe thyrsiflora* gives an impression of the powdery bloom that normally
coats much of the plant, especially the flower stems. I suspect
heavy rain washed a good bit of the bloom from this specimen.

LABLAB
hyacinth bean (*L. purpureus*)

Family: Fabaceae
Cultural group: climbers and trailers
Height: 6 ft. or more
Width: depends on training
Light: sun
Temperature: warm to hot
Overwintering: no
Moisture: moderate to ample
Drainage of medium: well drained
Fertility: average to high
Ease/speed of growth: easy/fast
Propagation: seeds
Problems: starting the seeds too soon or in cool medium
Principal interest: flowers, fruit, fragrance, form
Length of seasonal interest: long

Design attributes

Color: foliage medium green (often purple-toned) with purplish petioles; flowers purple, sometimes white; fruit purple
Line: twisting, but depends on training
Form: lots of triangles on strings with flowers and flat, purple bananas
Space: plenty among foliage, flowers, and fruit
Texture: medium to coarse

I like to grow annual climbers in containers because they quickly turn into lines. Long, sinuous, active-looking lines. If not managed—meaning watched with an eagle eye, thinned out, and thoughtfully trained onto a support or other plant—many in time become tangled blobs (think of morning glories and cup-and-saucer vine) of stems and leaves that threaten to overwhelm anything nearby, including slow-moving garden visitors. However, usually by that time some eye-seducing floral color has been added to the mix, making me forget how much I enjoyed the exuberant linearity.

As you can tell from the distinctively shaped flowers, *Lablab purpureus* belongs to the pea family. Those tiny, almost black things will become large, flattened, showy, purple, edible, adjective-inspiring pods.

Although the white support looks cool and clean, growing *Lablab purpureus* on a yellow-orange tuteur would create a stunning triadic harmony with the blue-green foliage and red-violet flowers. Maybe next year?

Not so with hyacinth bean, *L. purpureus*. Even before the fragrant and colorful red-violet flowers appear, its lines (stems) become vehicles for carrying triangles: each triangular leaf is itself made up of three separate and distinct, blob-defying triangles. The purple shades of its stems and leaves add interest, too, and then, as the flowers realize their fate in life, the headliners of the show (the fruit) begin to enlarge into pieces of purple stained glass. The big, flat pods don't always look like stained glass, though; it's only when the early morning or late afternoon sun shines on the younger, highly colored pods that the organ music begins to swell. I strongly encourage you to grow a few hyacinth beans to see for yourself. Just make certain to site the pot where light will hit the pods. If it doesn't, move the pot to where it will. There is a white-flowered form, but I seem to remember that it comes up short in the amount of purple in the stems, leaves, and pods.

Cultural tips: Being beans, basically, they need a warm medium to germinate; otherwise, the seeds rot or simply fail to get moving until the temperature reaches 70°F or so. My Grandpa Marsh planted beans only after the soil felt summery-warm, not springy-cool, on his bare feet. That old folk method still guides me in planting anything that likes it hot (coleus, caladiums, and other ultra-tropical stuff), but it sure is hard to stay barefoot and balanced on the medium in a pot, even if it's a big one.

Note: The pods are edible. I've never cooked with them, but I'm told that they should be picked when young and still flat, tender, and tasty. Leave some on the plants for the light show, though.

LACTUCA
lettuce

Family: Asteraceae
Cultural group: annuals
Height: 6–12 in.
Width: 6–12 in.
Light: sun to partial shade
Temperature: cool to warm
Overwintering: no
Moisture: ample
Drainage of medium: well drained
Fertility: average to high (especially nitrogen)
Ease/speed of growth: easy/fast
Propagation: seeds
Problems: slugs and snails, rots and spots, variously legged
    munchers, high heat (causes bolting, but that can be
    ornamental, too)
Principal interest: foliage, form
Length of seasonal interest: moderate

A salad bowl of lettuce in your garden will elicit chuckles and the occasional knowing aha, too. Start by sowing a package of mixed lettuce seed directly into the bowl and then thin the potentially comeliest seedlings to about 6 in. apart. You can eat the thinned-out seedlings. Before the plants bolt, eat them, too.

If growing lettuce in a bowl-like container isn't edgy enough for you, try your hand at making a hanging basket filled with them. You might also want to include other greens, such as the kale and mizuna here. You're bound to receive some questions and compliments, and keep the salad dressing handy.

Design attributes

Color: leaves green, sometimes with red
Line: mostly from leaf edges or elongated leaf shapes
Form: loose to tight bunches of, well, lettuce
Space: varies with density of head
Texture: fine to coarse

Let us consider lettuce, not so much for its edible qualities but for its visual ones. I think you'll agree that it comes in appealing shades of green and red, with some white thrown in. The looseleaf types offer plenty of line with their elongated, wavy, cut, and/or twisty foliage, and the loosely heading types make appealing rosettes with circular outlines containing other lines. Their forms, while approaching lumpy in most cases, are still often worth a second look. Lettuce in general doesn't offer a whole lot of spatial interest, but it can be created by leaving space between individual plants or growing them between plants with contrasting colors. Their textures range from coarse (most of them) to fine (such as the dandelion-like 'Emerald Oakleaf' and the red-brushed green 'Prizeleaf').

So why isn't lettuce grown more in containers? OK, an individual lettuce doesn't normally live very long, but lettuce can be successively sown over a season (except during the hottest parts) and they don't need to be overwintered. Bolting (the horticultural term for sending up flower spikes) pretty much ruins their good looks, but it's easy enough to remove the plants (or eat them) before they bolt.

Enough hard sell. Here are a few of the (to me) more toothsome ones. Whether or not they taste good is another matter, but you'll determine that for yourself as you grow some of these in containers.

'Emerald Oakleaf' resembles a dandelion plant, but without the cheerful flowerheads.

The highly ruffled 'Green Ice' beguiles in rich emerald green.

You could convince yourself that the dark red of 'Majesty' is actually regal purple and the tight rippling and ruffling is embroidery.

'Prizeleaf' suggests red-topped green waves.

'Royal Oak Leaf' does resemble the leaves of the white oak group with their rounded lobes.

By the way, the genus name *Lactuca* (from the Latin *lact-*, "milk") refers to the milky sap that flows from the larger veins of older plants. It can be quite bitter, not at all like a nice big glass of milk.

Cultural tips: Plenty of water and nitrogen in sun or partial shade is all they need, but do keep an eye out for two-, four-, six-, and eight-legged lettuce munchers.

LAMIUM
deadnettle

Family: Lamiaceae
Cultural group: perennials
Height: 6 in. to 2 ft.
Width: 1–3 ft.
Light: sun to partial shade
Temperature: cool to warm
Overwintering: hardy in Z4–8
Moisture: moderate to ample
Drainage of medium: well drained
Fertility: average (to restrain their rambunctiousness, if desired)
Ease/speed of growth: easy/moderate
Propagation: division, cuttings
Problems: slugs and snails, spots and rots
Principal interest: foliage, flowers
Length of seasonal interest: long (foliage); brief (flowers)

Design attributes

Color: foliage green (sometimes yellow), often marked with silver; flowers in white, pink, and red-violet (yellow in *L. galeobdolon*)
Line: not readily evident unless cascading (although some of the silver foliage markings provide a linear look)
Form: mostly boisterously carpeting or cascading
Space: not much
Texture: medium

We gardeners toss the word "silver" around with imprecise abandon, using it to describe a great many plants with, more realistically, gray foliage. But some plants *do* offer the exciting metallic glint of silver, not the calmer, softer shades of gray (which, to be honest, often contain a fair amount of green or blue). Notable examples include many begonias, some of the newer selections of *Heuchera*, and even some squash (the leaves, not the fruits, unless some crafty person came along with a can of spray paint). And, of course, the genus before us here.

Most people turn to *Lamium* for groundcovers, but as long as we're open to growing groundcovers from *Hedera*, *Liriope*, and *Sedum* in containers, then why not *Lamium*? The more vigorous (read: invasive) ones might better be restrained in containers, anyway, where we can admire them less anxiously for their positive qualities.

L. galeobdolon is the bad-boy invasive miscreant of the group, and most of its selections need a firm hand to prevent them from (in a manner of speaking) beating up their neighbors, especially in containers. The selections 'Hermann's Pride' and 'Silver Angel' are worth a try. Their yellow flowers

The silver-spotted necklaces of *Lamium galeobdolon* 'Emil Tramposch', a deadnettle, trail gracefully from their pot. If they reach open garden soil, they might root and take off in a hurry.

Lamium maculatum 'Beacon Silver' and several of its relatives add metallic-looking silver flashes to container plantings. Even though they are hardy herbaceous perennials, they can be grown with annuals and tropicals. No one says they can't.

add interest, but some (including yours truly) find the yellow and silver combination a bit discordant. 'Emil Tramposch' is described as a clump-former, but to me it looks like it sends long runners out from a central point. If that means "clump former," then I suppose it is.

L. maculatum offers several silvery beauties among its selections, including 'Beacon Silver', the nicely contained 'Cosmopolitan', 'Chequers', and 'White Nancy'. Its white blooms distinguish Nancy from the others, which bear flowers in shades of pink and purple. Unique among the maculatums is 'Anne Greenaway', with medium green foliage very variably marked with chartreuse (yellow in plenty of sun) and silver.

All these selections make impressive hanging monopots, and their silver foliage contrasts very nicely with pink, blue, and purple foliage and flowers in combopots.

Cultural tips: Thin or chop them back if they threaten their neighbors; in fact, in hotter areas, many of these will slump in heat and drought. Giving a midsummer buzzcut (not just a trim) along with extra water and fertilizer should bring them back for a second show in fall.

LANTANA
shrub verbena

Family: Verbenaceae
Cultural group: annuals, tropicals
Height: 1–2 ft. (*L. montevidensis* to 4 ft.)
Width: 1–3 ft. (*L. camara*); depends on training
    (*L. montevidensis*)
Light: sun
Temperature: warm to hot
Overwintering: min. 50°F, water occasionally, bright light
Moisture: moderate to ample
Drainage of medium: well drained
Fertility: average to high (to promote heavy bloom and
    produce growth for training)
Ease/speed of growth: easy/moderate to fast
Propagation: cuttings, seeds (for fun)
Problems: whitefly (sadly a magnet for them, like others in
    the verbena family), spider mites, rots and spots

Principal interest: flowers, form (especially if trained)
Length of seasonal interest: long

Design attributes

Color: flowers white, red, pink, orange, and yellow
(*L. camara*) and white and lavender (*L. montevidensis*);
foliage sometimes marked with yellow (*L. camara*)

Line: from stems (angular in *L. camara*, cascading in
L. montevidensis)
Form: shrubby (*L. camara*) to spilling over (*L. montevidensis*),
and bearing brooches
Space: not readily noticeable unless trained
Texture: fine to medium

Please take a little time to study the intricate beauty of the unopened flower clusters of this *Lantana camara* selection, or indeed of any plant. Many of their subtler, less celebrated features will go unnoticed unless you take the time to appreciate them.

I don't normally let strong orange and light pink get too close, but they don't seem to be at war with each other in this assortment of *Lantana camara* selections. Why? Take a close look at which color appears in the center of the pink blooms.

A small plant of *Lantana montevidensis* quickly transforms from a few leafy, skinny sticks into a threadbare but colorful, spreading sheet or hanging curtain of white or lavender (such as here, with 'Lavender Cascade').

The hot yellow flowers and cooler green and greenish cream of the foliage of *Lantana camara* 'Samantha' create a frisson of chromatic tension. A slightly edgy interaction can appear far more exciting than one composed of colors with approximately the same "heat" or other quality, such as brightness or saturation.

If you like the smell of marigolds (*Tagetes*), you'll love the sharp, strongly scented foliage of *Ll. camara* and *montevidensis*, as well as appreciate how quickly they take on the filler role in container gardening. One late May when I was a kid, we planted a few specimens of *L. camara* 'Radiation' (or similar selection) in full sun up against the house, and over the next four months they went from little 6-in. starts to wide, low-spreading shrubs spangled with eye-catching flower clusters in fiery shades of red, yellow, and orange and bouncing with butterflies.

As container plants, both *Ll. camara* and *montevidensis* are hard to beat, with the former weaving through its companions in combopots and the latter cascading below them. Both make splendid topiaries, *L. camara* offering its irregularly shaped, color-dotted heads (that remind me of brooches or millefiori paperweights) for the butterflies that still flock to them, and *L. montevidensis* suggesting lavender or white fountains rushing from a tall pipe. One caveat: both species are scourges in some tropical areas of the world, spreading widely from the fruits eagerly eaten by birds or simply dropped to the ground. I suggest you do a little research before adding any lantana to your frost-free garden.

As the group photo suggests, the flowers of *L. camara* run mostly hot, with pink and white thrown in for fun. I've seen many selections come and go, but 'Samantha' has been around for a while and will probably be with us well into the future, valued for its sunshiny blooms and refreshingly variegated foliage. 'Irene' reminds me of the lantana from my childhood; the flowerheads interact combustively with other hot-flowered plants and resemble embers against dark foliage.

L. montevidensis comes in white and lavender. That's it. But the long-reaching, almost needle-thin, interwoven branches produce a spreading or cascading scrim of clean color, and a lot can be said for (and done with) that.

Cultural tips: Heat doesn't bother them, but make sure they receive plenty of water. Topiaries can be cut back hard in spring and pinched a few times to restore a big head (or cascade) of foliage and flowers.

The hot yellow and orange in the flower clusters of *Lantana camara* 'Irene' make the cantaloupe-colored pot seem almost cool in comparison. Which color(s) do you see in the clusters of flower buds?

LEONOTIS
lion's ear, lion's tail, lion's tooth (*L. leonurus*)

Family: Lamiaceae
Cultural group: annuals (usually)
Height: 3 ft. or more
Width: 2 ft. or more
Light: sun
Temperature: warm to hot
Overwintering: min. 50°F, water occasionally, bright light; hardy in Z10–11
Moisture: moderate to ample (recovers amazingly well from severe wilting)
Drainage of medium: well drained
Fertility: average to high phosphorus
Ease/speed of growth: easy/moderate
Propagation: cuttings, seeds
Problems: whitefly, spider mites
Principal interest: flowers
Length of seasonal interest: brief, in most areas

Design attributes
Color: bright orange; medium green foliage
Line: very noticeable in bloom; otherwise, only from elongated leaves
Form: shrubby (with nests of energetic orange baby birds when in bloom)
Space: around flowers and flower stems
Texture: medium

And now for something a little different. I've found a plant that blooms during the mum season, produces flowers

Of course you can't help but notice the bright orange and green of *Leonotis leonurus*, but please put on your black-and-white-vision glasses and study the line, form, space, and texture that lion's ear offers.

Notice how the energetic, whorled leaf and flowerhead arrangement of the potted *Leonotis leonurus* echoes the form of the in-ground *Euphorbia lathyris*. Please don't be afraid of siting container plantings in garden beds, or you might miss out on powerful combinations such as this one.

in autumnal orange, grows well in containers, doesn't fall prey to a wide variety of maladies, and it isn't available on a 24/7/365 basis (like mums). *L. leonurus* looks like a pleasant-enough shrubby mound for much of the growing season, and then, when tree leaves begin to turn color, out come the orange (or white, in the never-seen-by-me 'Harrismith White') buds and flowers. I've seen this species grown only as a specimen in monopots: Atlock farms them every year, starting them from cuttings, pinching them a few times for bushiness, and advancing their bloom season a bit by raising them in geometrically laid-out precision—on black plastic. I suspect it would make a companionable member of a spacious combo if grown unpinched. A single stem of lion's ear in bloom suggests a skyrocket in multiple-explosion flight, a green arm wearing several orange cuff bracelets, or a troupe of orange-wigged acrobats standing on each other's shoulders. No doubt you can come up with your own fanciful associations. Try that with a chrysanthemum.

Cultural tips: Water liberally and fertilize with plenty of phosphorus, even if you are conservative in other aspects of your life.

LEUCANTHEMUM
butter daisy, annual marguerite, miniature shasta daisy (*L. paludosum*)

Family: Asteraceae
Cultural group: annuals
Height: 12–18 in.
Width: 12–18 in.
Light: sun to minimal partial shade
Temperature: warm to hot
Overwintering: no
Moisture: moderate to ample
Drainage of medium: well drained
Fertility: average
Ease/speed of growth: easy (when they want to be)/moderate

Propagation: seeds
Problems: unpredictability, sudden wilt (probably from root rot)
Principal interest: flowers
Length of seasonal interest: long

Design attributes

Color: gold flowers, medium green leaves
Line: stems, rather hidden among foliage and flowers
Form: shrubby
Space: not a great deal
Texture: medium

If you haven't grown butter daisy, start doing so ASAP. Even though its foliage borders on the weedy-looking (a trait common to many in the daisy family), this species cranks out cheerful flowers that begin appearing early and keep coming all season. Plants stay dense and compact, and bugs and bigger critters stay away. The combination of fresh green and

Leucanthemum paludosum (aka *Melampodium paludosum*) happily bears its starry flowerheads in masses that conjure inevitable associations with constellations and 1960s decorative motifs. Give them all the starlight (in this case, that from Sol) you can provide.

bright gold glows wherever it's used, whether in splashy mono-pots or combopots, so long as it's cast with plants in equally assertive colors (bright red, orange, blue, and purple flowers, as well as dark foliage); that same brightness comes across like a screech when put together with pure white, gray, yellow, pink, or magenta.

'Show Star' has been around for a while and continues to please. I've never grown 'Million Gold', but it appears to be more compact than 'Show Star' and so deserves a try. I hope the hybridizers are trying to pull more diversity from butter daisy's genetic pool, such as yellow (not gold) flowers, and maybe double ones, and perhaps white ones. We shall see.

Cultural tips: All of the praise given here assumes that butter daisy receives full sun in a reasonably fertile, moist, well-drained potting mix. Too much shade (as in even a couple of hours of it) often leads to floppy growth, and poor drainage will rot the roots. Plants will withstand considerable drought but won't be quite so generous with doling out the gold. Also, plants given perfect quarters sometimes mysteriously collapse and die, but keep that under your hat. Shhhh… it happens.

LIRIOPE
lilyturf, monkey grass, spider grass

Family: Convallariaceae/Liliaceae
Cultural group: perennials
Height: 6–12 in.
Width: 6–12 in. to indefinite (in the case of *L. spicata*)
Light: sun to partial shade to shade (which reduces flower production)
Temperature: cool to warm (tolerates hot)
Overwintering: variously hardy in Z7–10 (*L. muscari* from Z6, *L. spicata* Z5)
Moisture: moderate (tolerates drought)
Drainage of medium: well drained
Fertility: average
Ease/speed of growth: easy/moderate
Propagation: division, seeds (if you'd like to maybe raise new variations)
Problems: rots and spots, slugs
Principal interest: foliage, flowers
Length of seasonal interest: long, maybe nearly all year

Design attributes

Color: flowers white, blue, and purple; foliage mostly dark green, often marked white or yellow
Line: abundant arching lines of foliage, upright flower stems
Form: arching circular to spreading mass (grasslike, for sure) with little, long, skinny bunches of grapes above

Space: abundant in *L. muscari*, less so in *L. spicata* (flowers give impression of space around them)

Texture: fine to medium

As a kid, I famously mangled the pronunciation of a few words while reading aloud in school ("misled" was mize'-uld—cue laughter from classmates and correction from

Up close, *Liriope muscari* 'Pee Dee Gold Ingot' resembles arching sprays of green and gold water surging in a grand, illuminated fountain display. From a distance it looks more like greenish yellow grass. However you see it, it's worth a try.

Just because *Liriope muscari* 'Big Blue' is almost always used as a groundcover doesn't mean you must grow it in the open ground. Give your monkey grass a new place to play by growing some in a container.

teacher—and "calliope" was cal'-ee-ope). And so, class, we skip over Penelope and come to the genus *Liriope*. Repeat after me: leer-eye'-oh-pee. You know, the grassy-looking plants named after the Boetian naiad who fell for the river god Cephissus. The two of them became the proud parents of Narcissus, who fell for himself (see *Narcissus*).

Lilyturf most often serves as a capable and attractive groundcover, but I think of it as a scaled-down version of a clivia, crinum, hippeastrum, or other irresistibly eye-catching, strappy-leaved plant. Instead of requiring at least a 12-in. pot and plenty of space, a good-sized clump of liriope will fit nicely in a 6-in. pot. Those bold, arching lines suggest movement, creating exciting monopots and providing some action to combopots, especially when moving against a mass of larger, simpler leaves. The flowers are nice, too, but they definitely play second fiddle to the foliage.

Any selection of *L. muscari* (or the similar-looking *L. exiliflora*) should perform splendidly in a pot: choose from nearly evergreen, all-green or white- or yellow-variegated foliage and flowers in white, blue, and purple on plants to around 1 ft. tall. Even one division will make a statement. If you want to create the illusion of a lawn in a pot, turn to *L. spicata*, which spreads like crazy wherever it grows.

Cultural tips: Cut them back in spring as you would plants in the ground (unless you use your lawnmower on them, in which case I suggest you use scissors on your container plants). New, fresher-looking foliage will replace the winter-worn leaves from the previous season. If you want to encourage the production of flowers, give them plenty of sun. You could also insert some rock candy formed on sticks for pretty much the same look.

LOBELIA
blue lobelia, edging lobelia (*L. erinus*)

Family: Campanulaceae
Cultural group: annuals
Height: 4–10 in.
Width: 4–12 in., sometimes more
Light: sun to minimal partial shade
Temperature: cool to warm
Overwintering: no
Moisture: moderate to ample
Drainage of medium: well drained
Fertility: average to high phosphorus
Ease/speed of growth: easy/moderate to fast
Propagation: seeds (might reseed)
Problems: excessive heat, slugs, rots and spots
Principal interest: flowers, form
Length of seasonal interest: moderate to long

Design attributes

Color: flowers in white and pastel to rich, jewel-like shades of red (more pink than red, really), red-violet, blue, and purple; foliage medium to dark green to almost black

Line: lots of little lines from leaves and flower lobes

Form: tight, running, cascading, or frothy mass of insects or tiny birds

Space: not much literal space but can seem cloudlike

Texture: fine

Way back when, I raised some *L. erinus*—probably 'Crystal Palace', maybe 'Sapphire'—from seed and planted them out in the Pittsburgh-area garden in which I cut my gardening teeth. They dazzled me with a few of their impossibly rich blue, insect-like flowers, and then that was it. Finito. Kaput. Dead. All of them. The June heat did them in. Over the years, I spotted pathetically struggling lobelias in public and private gardens all over the East Coast. But then I made my way to England (in late spring) and to Alaska (in late August/early September) and was nearly knocked off my feet by big, billowing baskets of sapphire blue and amethyst purple. I recognized *L. erinus* and immediately turned emerald green with envy. Goaded by a desire to figure out where I and others had gone wrong, I did a little research. The answer? High temperatures and low soil moisture quickly send *L. erinus* to the big compost pile in the sky (or the one at the far end of your garden). England and Alaska, among other spots, usually don't see those extremes, so their lobelias bloom for months.

Happily, some selections of *L. erinus* show better heat tolerance, and hybridizers are working on pushing the envelope even further. Try the Moon series and the Regatta series (including 'Regatta Sky Blue') if you've tried and failed with the beguiling but heat-shy 'Crystal Palace', Palace series, 'Sapphire', or others. If you do succeed with them, enjoy them in big monopot hanging baskets (to suggest colorful clouds or mist), or add these jewels to combopots. The richer, stronger colors hold their own against equally potent red, yellow, gold, and white, and the medium to pastel shades mix nicely with lighter colors as well as with dark-toned and gray foliage.

Cultural tips: Provide a well-drained but moist potting mix,

Lobelia erinus and its selections offer some of the purest, cleanest blue shades available to us container gardeners. Surrounding them with a bit more blue-tinged white and fresh green (which is already present on the leaves, thereby creating an echo) would intensify the blues.

Gardeners in favorable areas can grow *Lobelia erinus* into great big masses of color without needing to worry about constantly providing water and waiting for excessive heat to smite them. Lucky. (Color-oriented readers will want to cover and uncover the bright yellow spots to see how they rule over this composition.)

and site them out of the strongest sun. That and cooler than normal temperatures should prolong their bloom (as will growing some of the heat-tolerant selections—or moving to England or Alaska).

LOBULARIA
sweet alyssum (*L. maritima*)

Family: Brassicaceae
Cultural group: annuals
Height: 2–8 in.
Width: 6–12 in.
Light: sun
Temperature: cool to warm
Overwintering: no
Moisture: moderate
Drainage of medium: well drained
Fertility: low to average
Ease/speed of growth: easy/moderate to fast

Propagation: seeds
Problems: root rot, aphids
Principal interest: flowers, fragrance (variable)
Length of seasonal interest: long (can be interrupted)

Design attributes
Color: flowers white, pink, red-violet, and purple; medium to gray-green leaves
Line: circular flowerhead outlines; flower stems if allowed to get too old; maybe stems if cascading
Form: frothy mass
Space: not much, but can imply it
Texture: fine

One spring, as he tended the rows of purple and white that lined the walk to his front door, our neighbor Charlie Snyder stopped to give me a lesson in transplanting sweet alyssum. "Always take a ball of dirt with the roots and water the plant in good." He gave me a few little plants, each with a ball of dirt; I carried them home and watered them in (good);

White sweet alyssum foams out of its container. Please note the slight bluish cast of the pot: in a more typically orange- (think red-) toned container, the alyssum would be serving as a peacemaker between the pot and the cool-colored flowers above it.

and for years afterward, long after Charlie transplanted his family to parts unknown, his alyssum came up in our garden, for *L. maritima* reseeds prolifically.

'Carpet of Snow' has been around for a while (perhaps this was Charlie's white one), as has 'Snow Crystals', which grows taller than most. 'Royal Carpet' blooms in purple, and 'Rosie O'Day' is…rose.

I think they look nothing like cabbages (notwithstanding their family connection) and look their best when used as carpets and waterfalls in combopots or windowboxes. I suggest you grow at least a few in a hanging basket, the better to inhale the sweet but delicate fragrance of the tiny flowers, which resemble snow or little snow cones (in the case of the syrupy colored ones). No doubt some are more sweetly scented than others, so get out there and sniff.

Cultural tips: Sow them where you want them to grow, or transplant them carefully (you will have plenty of seedlings) into your pots. Shear them back after the first big flush of bloom, give them some fertilizer and water, and watch them come back for a second show (often after the heat of summer passes). Poor drainage and/or excessive moisture leads to root rot and death.

LOTUS
parrot's beak, pelican's beak, coral gem
(*L. berthelotii*)

Family: Fabaceae
Cultural group: climbers and trailers
Height: 6 in. to 3 ft. or more
Width: depends on training
Light: sun to limited partial shade
Temperature: cool to warm to hot
Overwintering: min. 40°F, water occasionally, bright light
Moisture: moderate to ample
Drainage of medium: well drained
Fertility: average
Ease/speed of growth: moderate/moderate
Propagation: cuttings
Problems: leaf drop (from dry medium), spider mites
Principal interest: foliage
Length of seasonal interest: long (all year if overwintered)

You could throw several handfuls of blue-green needles into a mesh bag and let everything hang over a pot, or you could grow a plant or two of *Lotus berthelotii* instead. Do you have any doubt about which of this plant's five design elements makes the biggest impression?

Design attributes

Color: blue-green foliage; rarely (in my experience) red-orange flowers, but I bet it blooms nicely in other areas

Line: almost pure line from stems and foliage

Form: spreading-cascading mass of needles

Space: around edges, mostly; can imply space by its cloud-like appearance

Texture: fine up close; none from a distance

Beware the red herrings that are some genus names. Here we have *Lotus*, whose foliage couldn't look anything less like the umbrellas of sacred lotus (*Nelumbo nucifera*) if it tried, but whose flowers very much look like other members of the pea family (seriously, check them out, if you get the chance). What a well-grown specimen of *L. berthelotii does* look like is a hundred thousand needles falling to the ground. Some might say that if you look at a plant closely, you can hear those needles falling, too. Put that remarkably fine texture to work in a combopot with just about any other plant that shares its cultural preferences, or celebrate it—perhaps by literally putting it on a pedestal—in a monopot. Can you see a specimen falling from a gray, dark blue, rusty, or oxblood urn or other tall container?

I've seen the sizzling, red-orange and black flowers only once. They explain the common name of parrot's beak, but I think they strike a discordant (or is it a masterfully contrasting?) note with the foliage. If you'd like to see the flowers, take this under advisement: cool temperatures in spring promote bloom, but high summer heat (day or night) will prevent the parrots from flocking.

Cultural tips: I grew an *L. berthelotii* trained to a 2-ft. single stem, and the multiple stems rushing down from where the leading shoot was pinched out did bring to mind fountains, waterfalls, a very elaborate chenille scarf, and those needles dropping. At least until I let the potting mix get too dry, after which the plant looked more et than wet. Too much water will achieve the same sad result. Full sun promotes the full expression of the vaporous blue-green of the foliage.

LUDWIGIA
mosaic plant (*L. sedoides*)

Family: Onagraceae

Cultural group: aquatics, annuals (culturally)

Height: none, essentially—floats on surface of water

Width: 6 in. to 2 ft., maybe more

Light: sun to partial shade

Temperature: warm to hot

Overwintering: min. 55°F, keep wet (or at least quite moist), bright light; hardy in Z11

Moisture: constant

Drainage of medium: requires standing water

Fertility: average

Ease/speed of growth: moderate/moderate

Propagation: division

Problems: theft, loss over winter

Principal interest: form, foliage

Length of seasonal interest: moderate (seems to take a while to get going)

Design attributes

Color: yellow-green leaves turn red with age; yellow flowers

Line: stems, but who notices them?

Form: a floating, very precise mosaic

Space: strictly implied between the leaves

Texture: fine

Whenever I gaze upon *L. sedoides*, I am transported back to first grade and a colorful set of thin, diamond-shaped wooden tiles I played with (often!) during rainy recesses. While this beautiful species can't be stored neatly in a box, as those tiles were, it does grow readily in an aquatic container, its precise radiating patterns reappearing every morning after being closed overnight. A plant this worthy of close examination (meditation, even) deserves to be grown by itself in a plainly colored pot, one that coordinates with the foliage, say in yellow-green, red, or perhaps dark brown or shiny black, to pick up on the reflections and silvery patches of the water and add to the magic. Put the pot on a table, column, plinth, or similar piece that will lift the mosaic closer to the eyes of its admirers, who at first glance probably won't comprehend what they're seeing. I've never seen the bright yellow flowers, which look remarkably like evening primroses (*Oenothera*), a relative in the Onagraceae.

"Look at my comely form," *Ludwigia sedoides* appears to say. This isn't just any old shape we're looking at here, though; it's a very regular, draftsman-drawn version of a rosette. You'll find other rosettes in this book, but none quite as precise and evocative as this.

I wonder if those tiles are still made …

Cultural tips: Mosaic plant grows quickly once the water warms up, so be patient (or put a heater in the water). I'm guessing that fish could ruin the mosaic, so beware.

LYSIMACHIA

loosestrife; golden creeping Jenny (*L. nummularia* 'Aurea')

Family: Primulaceae
Cultural group: perennials, climbers and trailers
Height: (when creeping) 4–6 in. (*L. congestiflora* 'Outback Sunset'); 2 in. (*L. nummularia* 'Aurea')
Width: (actually length, when trailing) 1–2 ft. (*L. congestiflora* 'Outback Sunset'); 1–3 ft. (*L. nummularia* 'Aurea')
Light: sun to partial shade
Temperature: cool to warm (tolerates hot)
Overwintering: min. 50°F, water regularly but not excessively, bright light (*L. nummularia* 'Aurea'); hardy in Z6–9 (*L. congestiflora* 'Outback Sunset'), Z4–8 (*L. nummularia* 'Aurea')
Moisture: moderate to ample
Drainage of medium: well drained
Fertility: average
Ease/speed of growth: easy/moderate to fast (*L. nummularia* 'Aurea')
Propagation: division, cuttings
Problems: aphids
Principal interest: foliage, form, flowers (*L. congestiflora* 'Outback Sunset'; more a curiosity on *L. nummularia* 'Aurea')
Length of seasonal interest: long (foliage and form); brief (flowers)

Design attributes

Color: medium green leaves with yellow markings and red stems (*L. congestiflora* 'Outback Sunset'), golden-yellow

Emerging from the radiant point near their eponymous constellation, hundreds of Perseid shooting stars light up the night sky … one might say. It takes about a year for a few pieces of *Lysimachia nummularia* 'Aurea' to turn into a meteoric dazzler like this one, worthy of the finest (or simplest) pedestal.

The yellow flowers of *Lysimachia congestiflora* 'Outback Sunset' bring a spot of warmth to an otherwise cool composition of gray and shades of green. Remember (when matching this up with companions) that its flowers don't last very long.

Several strands of *Lysimachia nummularia* 'Aurea' glow against the dark purple-red alternanthera and the gray container. Too much shade would have snuffed out the glow, producing a much less chartreusey green.

Drip . . . drip . . . drip. To increase the visual and suggested auditory effects, thin out every other shoot or so of this *Lysimachia nummularia* 'Aurea'.

to chartreuse to yellowish green leaves (*L. nummularia* 'Aurea'); yellow flowers (both)

Line: from stems (especially noticeable in *L. nummularia* 'Aurea' when cascading)

Form: carpeting to cascading

Space: very little to quite noticeable (especially *L. nummularia* 'Aurea' if thinned out)

Texture: medium

Some plants truly merit the appellation "green thug," with their overly questing roots or rhizomes, rampageous growth habits, and resistance to eradication. Every gardener knows some. Normally I avoid thugs (green or otherwise), but I've embraced one, so much so that I make a point at some of my speaking engagements and other horticultural fora for a more sensible approach to *L. nummularia* 'Aurea', the golden creeping Jenny. Yes, it can skulk out from a garden bed into your lawn, but it pulls up easily and cries uncle after being mowed and outcompeted (and rained upon by herbicides).

But that admirable vigor qualifies it as a superb container plant, whether as a manageable few strands in a combopot or as a breathtaking hanging basket or tall pot, its chartreuse coif cascading Rapunzel-like from on high. I rank chartreuse high on my list of colors for container plantings, and golden creeping Jenny offers it abundantly. Its golden flowers are an afterthought, really, and thankfully don't last long.

Another member of the genus, definitely not a thug, takes the look of its cousin Jenny in a different direction. *L. congestiflora* 'Outback Sunset' starts with chartreuse, adding darker green to its variegated foliage, which is borne on red stems. The golden flowers (more or less the same as Jenny's) look appealing, not jarring, against the varied background colors. It doesn't grow as vigorously as Jenny (and appreciates a winter rest), but that makes it more manageable in combopots, whether composed of hardy plants carried over from one growing season to another or enjoyed as an annual in single season pots.

Cultural tips: Yearly division of both keeps the plants (and the colors) looking fresh. Too much shade dulls the colors; give overwintered golden creeping Jenny a sunny spot to keep the color up.

MANDEVILLA
Brazilian jasmine, dipladenia

Family: Apocynaceae
Cultural group: climbers and trailers
Height: 1–6 ft. or more
Width: depends on training
Light: sun to limited partial shade
Temperature: warm to hot
Overwintering: min. 50°F, water occasionally, bright light
Moisture: moderate to ample
Drainage of medium: well drained

Fertility: average to high nitrogen to push growth, phosphorus to push flowering
Ease/speed of growth: easy/moderate to fast
Propagation: cuttings
Problems: mealybugs, spider mites, whitefly, rots and spots
Principal interest: flowers, form (if trained)
Length of seasonal interest: long

Design attributes
Color: white, pink, or red flowers; shiny, medium to dark green leaves
Line: from stems (depends on training) and leaves
Form: ropes or masses of leaves and flowers
Space: depends on training
Texture: medium to coarse

A flock of birds escapes from a barely visible wire cage. Note how both the white flowers of the mandevilla and the fresh greens of the sweet potato on the left and the asparagus fern on the right stand out against the pot and the perfectly color-matched architecture in the back. I wish the bright blue bits of the evolvulus stood out more, though; a blast of blue would complete an eye-popping combination.

Sometimes it's fun to let a plant find its way up a support and then go its own merry way. The informal self-expression could please you far more than the look of a more rigidly trained formal shape. Here, *Mandevilla* 'Bride's Cascade' uses a teepee of stakes to pursue its own insouciant agenda.

Mandevilla ×*amabilis* 'Alice du Pont' standards echo the shape of the potted grasses at the left, and both solid forms contrast sharply with the purple ground fog of *Verbena bonariensis*.

The sunny-side-up flowers of *Mandevilla* 'Bride's Cascade' bloom over a long season. Pity they have no scent.

Mandevilla 'Red Fury' and other newer hybrids bloom when quite small, making them ideal subjects for a reasonably sized hanging basket. The shiny green foliage of their rangier kin is still there, but it's smaller and more closely spaced along the stems.

For a long time I noticed mandevillas here and there, most memorably at Longwood Gardens, where big (10–15 ft.) specimens of the tried-and-true *Mandevilla ×amabilis* 'Alice du Pont' bore their cheerful pink stars. But my big *Mandevilla* moment didn't occur until I discovered the colorful Sun Parasol collection: instead of rangy, almost burly plants with some flowers, these hybrids are much more compact (reaching 3 ft. in their first season if well grown, and certainly when overwintered and grown on for at least one more season), and happy ones bloom abundantly for months. 'Red Fury' demonstrates the most appealing traits of this new generation: they make gorgeous additions to hanging baskets and get along nicely with their companions, no matter the sort of pot.

The boisterous pink- and white-flowered selections of *Mm. ×amabilis* and *splendens* (or whatever they're classified as these days) are still worth growing as form-trained specimens in big pots, which allow for plenty of growth (and provide space for a companion plant or two). But it's those Sun Parasols (now available in at least nine variations of flower color and plant size) and their doppelgangers that offer a world of possibilities for containers: grow them singly in a small pot or hanging basket, or in multiples in bigger quarters, whether trained onto a small form or allowed to spill over the edge. Combine them with sun-loving flowering annuals and/or foliage plants, playing with their colors and textures as you will. Note: to my eye, the pink and red ones carry a blue tinge, so you might want to mix these with cooler and darker shades of yellow and orange as well as just about anything blue or purple (or in their blue-tinged shades of pink and red).

Cultural tips: They all appreciate plenty of water and high-phosphorus fertilizer. Be careful where you site the big ones; they can quickly climb into low-hanging trees or give smaller neighbors an anaconda-like squeeze treatment. Chop the big ones back hard during growth or after being overwintered (they bloom on the current season's growth). In time the smaller ones might need some attention from your pruning shears, too. Don't panic when the leaves fall off during winter.

MELIANTHUS
honey bush (*M. major*)

Family: Melianthaceae
Cultural group: tropicals, woody shrubs and trees, perennials
Height: 1–3 ft.
Width: 1–3 ft.
Light: sun to partial shade
Temperature: cool to warm to hot
Overwintering: min. 50°F, water occasionally, bright light; hardy in Z8–10
Moisture: moderate to ample

Drainage of medium: well drained
Fertility: average
Ease/speed of growth: moderate/moderate
Propagation: cuttings, seeds, suckers
Problems: whitefly, spider mites
Principal interest: foliage, form
Length of seasonal interest: all year (unless treated as a cutback perennial)

Design attributes
Color: blue-gray-green foliage and red-tinged petioles, sometimes with hints of purple
Line: upright to leaning to curving stems; petioles; pinnate leaves with "pinking"
Form: like a bunch of peacocks' tails or showgirls' headdresses

Forget about color here for a minute. The intricately pinked leaves of *Melianthus major* 'Antonow's Blue', the chunky chains of *Helichrysum petiolare* 'Limelight', and the dotted mass of boxwood offer a prime example of how the interplay of texture can be as visually arresting as a color combination.

Opposite: Like a couple of Vegas showgirls, two shoots of *Melianthus major* liven up the stage. Which combination is more colorful, the big feathers paired with the yellow-green tradescantia, or the ones backed by the dark phormium?

Space: abundant and intricate
Texture: medium warring with fine and coarse

The exciting, sharp-toothed look of honey bush could have been created by my craft-y Grandma Rogers and her pinking shears. Few other plants pack the visual punch of *M. major*, and it's not difficult to grow. However, obtaining a good-sized specimen means either spending big for an established plant or starting with a small one and overwintering it for at least one season. It responds to regular doses of nitrogen by growing steadily to an impressive 3 ft. or so in one season. Established plants, cut back almost to ground level in spring, should easily reach 3 ft. again by season's end. If not cut back, mature specimens produce strongly scented, shaggy spikes of dark red flowers that make a superb contrast to the blue-green foliage in spring. Do you want one now? They can be grown from seed (if you can find them) or suckers separated from the parent plant, and they root (unpredictably) from cuttings, so start looking. Seed-grown specimens might show some variation from the usual cool blue-green.

Be ahead of your time by featuring *M. major* or one of its selections (such as 'Antonow's Blue') prominently in your container gardening, whether as a monopot specimen or in a thoughtfully composed combopot. A plant this richly blessed with all five design elements deserves to be grown, experimented with, savored, and celebrated. Just for fun, keep a pair of pinking shears next to your honey bush and watch as garden visitors try to decide whether you used them on the leaves.

Cultural tips: Keep a younger plant coming along to replace an older one, which might suddenly go into a dramatic decline. Resist the urge to stake the branches that gracefully slouch and lean.

MENTHA
mint

Family: Lamiaceae
Cultural group: perennials
Height: 1–3 ft., can cascade 3–4 ft.
Width: 6–12 in. or much more
Light: sun to partial shade
Temperature: warm to hot
Overwintering: variously hardy in Z3–9
Moisture: moderate to ample
Drainage of medium: well drained but tolerates standing water
Fertility: low to average (but you can really push these with high nitrogen)
Ease/speed of growth: easy/moderate to fast
Propagation: division, cuttings, seeds

Problems: invasiveness, whitefly, rots and spots
Principal interest: fragrance, foliage, form (if allowed to cascade)
Length of seasonal interest: long

Design attributes
Color: foliage green, sometimes marked with white, yellow, and purple; stems sometimes reddish; flowers white, pink, and light purple
Line: from stems
Form: shrubby to spreading mass to cascading
Space: scarce, usually
Texture: medium

I have a love-hate relationship with mint. Love the fragrance and taste, hate how mints spread too aggressively and take over a garden bed in no time. I bet you've heard of the classic way to contain mint in the garden by planting them in a bottomless container of some sort buried to within a few inches of the rim. Um, why not grow mint in an unburied pot, where the questing rhizomes can cascade gracefully from the pot (and be cut off before they reach the ground)? Even better, tease mint by growing it in a hanging basket placed high above ground level; only the most determined (and unwatched) mint will be able to reach the soil and run away. A hanging basket of mint also provides abundant opportunities for brushing against it to release the minty freshness.

The light green would look refreshing by itself, but those deftly applied, creamy white edges make this *Mentha* selection seem even cooler. Even a few stems would bring the sensation of a cool breeze to many container plantings.

Mints are a nomenclatural and taxonomic mess, but I can recommend a few that don't seem to travel under a bunch of names:

M. ×piperita (peppermint, the child of water mint and spearmint) generally has pointy, hairless leaves and a sharp scent. Grow a big pot or hanging basket of it to meet the demand all season.

M. requienii (Corsican mint) produces flat, running masses of tiny, potently fragrant leaves; they're pepperminty, with the strong scent of pennyroyal mixed in. Small, low pots of it make a very pleasant addition to a patio or dining table.

M. spicata (spearmint) has broader leaves than peppermint and has that sweeter, spearmint-gum fragrance. Grow it anywhere, in any pot, simply to be able to smell it. This one sprints (so to speak); a little starter plant took three years to run the length of my childhood home. Uphill.

Plenty of other mints will beguile you, including the cold-water-fresh-looking variegated ones and those supposedly scented with apple, lemon, pineapple, and other olfactory delights. Every one is worth a try. Practically speaking, it makes sense to grow them all by their sprinting selves as monopots, but you might try them in combopots; just keep an eye on them as they relentlessly conquer more territory.

Cultural tips: Mints are thirsty; most can be grown in shallow standing water to reduce your maintenance time. The more nitrogen fertilizer you give them, the more lushly they grow, but the potency of the fragrance might be diminished. Root a favorite from a cutting (or pull up a runner and plant it) and don't worry about the correct name.

MUEHLENBECKIA
angel vine, wire vine, maidenhair vine (*M. complexa*)

Family: Polygonaceae
Cultural group: climbers and trailers
Height: 1–2 in. when trailing, 1–3 ft. or more when trained
Width: depends on training
Light: partial shade
Temperature: cool to warm to hot
Overwintering: min. 50°F, water regularly but not
   excessively, bright light; hardy in Z8–10
Moisture: moderate to ample
Drainage of medium: well drained but tolerates shallow
   standing water
Fertility: average
Ease/speed of growth: easy/moderate to fast
Propagation: cuttings, seeds
Problems: letting them dry out more than once, mealybugs
Principal interest: foliage, form (especially if trained)
Length of seasonal interest: all year

Yes, mint can run amok in a garden, but it can't if it's hanging in the air. An abundant basket of mint releases its mesmerizing scent when anyone brushes past the foliage, whether accidentally or with premeditation.

Like most mints, the numerous pairs of leaves set at right angles to each other up the stems of peppermint (*Mentha ×piperita*) create a sensation of vertical activity.

Design attributes

Color: dark green leaves on dark stems, insignificant light green flowers, white fruit

Line: abundant, depends on training

Form: wires or threads with little beadlike leaves (and sometimes crown-like fruit); depends on training

Space: abundant, no matter what

Texture: fine

Several years ago, Atlock Farm came upon angel vine, and it has since taken the nursery (and the customers) by storm. And no wonder: it grows rapidly and easily, provided it receives plenty of moisture in a not-too-sunny spot. It can be trained easily to just about any form, such as metal hoops, globes, spirals, hearts, chairs, jewelry trees, squash, and corset-like structures made from twigs. For those not inclined to training plants into "unnatural" shapes, angel vine naturally forms veils, clouds, and other airy shapes when allowed to grow freely in a container.

Do you own a pot whose color is a bit potent, but you still want to plant it up? Use angel vine as a hanging screen to soften the color while still letting it partially show through. Would you like to tone down the coarse texture of a specimen plant? Grow it with angel vine. How about an area that cries out for a hanging basket, but not a big, wildly colorful one? Angel vine again. Is there a big, shallow pot in a shady to brightly lit spot that needs a quick filler/groundcover? You guessed it.

For most of the year, angel vine looks pretty much the same, like a mass of thin-gauge black wire with green confetti stuck to it. If you look closely in spring, however, you'll see little bits of light green stuff, which are the flowers. Soon after and often through much of summer, those bits mature into bizarre little five-peaked white crowns with a tiny black "jewel" at the center; you're correct if you guessed these are the fruit. To me they look like they're made out of white Gummi bears, but don't eat them, please, or let kids munch on them, either. Even though angel vine is in the same family as buckwheat, it's not a good idea to graze on their fruit (or on anything unfamiliar and untested, for that matter).

Muehlenbeckia complexa will climb anything that allows the wiry stems a chance to weave through it, or the green cloud can be allowed to sublimate out of a pot, hanging basket, windowbox, or other container.

A delicate veil of the green beads and brown threads of *Muehlenbeckia complexa* partially obscures its mellow-toned container. How would angel vine look against a green pot? How about a dark brown one?

Let's consider Fine v. Coarse: not a Supreme Court decision, but instead the interplay and visual impact of two very different textures. Here, the exhaled puffs of *Muehlenbeckia complexa* contrast sharply with the thick stem bases and massive pot (softened a bit by the lines of blue glaze dripping down the side).

Make a point to look for and enjoy the tiny fruit of *Muehlenbeckia complexa*. Honestly, they don't offer much design interest, but they fascinate anyone possessing even the slightest bit of imagination. Can gardening be pursued satisfyingly and well without it?

Both *M. complexa* 'Nana' (aka *M. axillaris*) and var. *trilobata* are described as having violin-shaped leaves; I'd like to see them in the flesh, so to speak. In the meantime I'll continue to enjoy the one example of angel vine I know.

Cultural tips: Angel vine will allow you to let it almost completely dry out once. It's curtains the next time. Sad yellow curtains, and soon even the yellow will drop off, leaving only the little black wires. Pieces of stem root easily if stuck into a little (constantly!) moist potting mix.

MUSA
banana

Family: Musaceae
Cultural group: tropicals
Height: 2–6 ft. or more
Width: 2–6 ft. or more
Light: sun to partial shade
Temperature: warm to hot

Here's a closer look at the younger foliage of *Musa* 'Siam Ruby'. The mostly brown-red leaves look mighty fetching with the light shining on them, but they are transformed into warm sheets of caramel (or perhaps bananas Foster?) when backlit by the sun.

Opposite: The broad blades of *Musa* 'Siam Ruby' languidly stir the humid summer air in Silas Mountsier's New Jersey garden. Note the potent textural contrast that designer Richard Hartlage set up between the coarse musa and the very fine *Carex comans* bronze forms that flank it.

Overwintering: min. 45°F, remove leaf blades down to the pseudostem, water sparingly
Moisture: moderate to ample
Drainage of medium: well drained
Fertility: average to high
Ease/speed of growth: moderate/moderate
Propagation: removal of sideshoots
Problems: spider mites, mealybugs, rots and spots, leaf shredding
Principal interest: form, foliage (sometimes flowers and fruit)
Length of seasonal interest: long

Design attributes

Color: medium green leaves, sometimes marked with white, often tinged or marked with red, orange, or purple
Line: from pseudostem and elongated leaves, sometimes from flowers and fruit
Form: a fountain going up and out; a bunch of paddles or oars
Space: ample all around
Texture: coarse

Time flies like an arrow … fruit flies like a banana. Plenty of other creatures do too, but (alas) most container-grown *Musa* never flower and fruit. They do produce sideshoots, however, which provide nice new plants to separate and pot up or give to friends.

I like bananas a whole bunch. You can grow any banana in a pot (assuming it's big enough; the large fruit-producing

Do you see a mirror image here? No? Put on your black-and-white glasses to see how the upward reach of *M. acuminata* 'Zebrina' echoes the downward-pointing fronds of *Nephrolepis exaltata* 'Rita's Gold' (golden Boston fern).

Note how the midrib on the leaf of *Musa* 'Siam Ruby' echoes both the color of the brick and the terracotta of the pots, while the lime-green splashes pick up on similar shades beneath. The dark brown-red-purple mass of the leaf centers and anchors the entire composition. Kudos to designer Richard Hartlage, who arranged the elements of this magnificent color harmony, and to photographer Rob Cardillo for capturing it.

ones will require a very spacious container), but my practical side compels me to tell you to go with the smaller ones. "Smaller" is a relative term; some bananas recommended for container culture can in time top out at 10 ft. However, you can always pull off some of those sideshoots, pot them up, and discard the big shoot to keep things under control. Ask a friend to help you when contemplating that task, and afterward offer him or her a sideshoot (or maybe a banana) as a token of your gratitude.

Let's consider a few examples of *Musa*, grown for their paddle-resembling, tropics-evoking, garden-transforming foliage gathered into impressive bunches. Start with the easily managed *M. acuminata* 'Zebrina' (blood banana). The red-splashed foliage and red pseudostems are wildly attractive and combine well with just about any sun-loving tropical plant you might get your hands on. Underfed and otherwise held back, it will reach 3 ft. or so in a season, but providing plenty of fertilizer and water should produce at least a six-footer. All *M. acuminata* selections (including the one most often offered as "green-leaved banana") are worth a try. All create the illusion of the tropics in a pot.

'Siam Ruby' (which Richard Hartlage included in Silas Mountsier's inspiring garden) is still quite new to gardening. Thanks go to Tony Avent of Plant Delights Nursery for finding this gorgeous hybrid in Thailand in 2005, giving it an English name, and offering it. Tony has never seen it taller than 8 ft. (it should be less lofty in a pot) and says it loves intense heat and humidity.

Cultural tips: Bananas grown in windy spots often end up with dramatically shredded leaves (although some seem to shred themselves). Do you like them big? Provide lots of sun, water, and nitrogenous fertilizer, and hope the weather stays hot.

MYRIOPHYLLUM
milfoil, parrot feather (*M. aquaticum*)

Family: Haloragaceae
Cultural group: aquatics
Height: often emerges above water to 6 in.; under water can reach 1–3 ft. or more
Width: 2–3 in., but usually in masses
Light: sun
Temperature: warm to hot
Overwintering: min. 50°F, keep wet, bright light; it might die back to the base; hardy in Z9–11
Moisture: constant
Drainage of medium: requires an aquatic environment
Fertility: low to average
Ease/speed of growth: easy/fast
Propagation: cuttings

Problems: hungry fish, irate politically correct plant-code enforcers (concerned about potential invasiveness), algae and duckweed smothering them
Principal interest: foliage
Length of seasonal interest: long

Design attributes
Color: light to medium green leaves
Line: from stems above and below water surface, finely linear foliage (can look like they're crawling out of the container)
Form: bottlebrushes; almost green hair
Space: ample
Texture: fine

Yes, I know that milfoil (*M. aquaticum*) has invaded many waterways in warmer parts of the world, wreaking havoc with small-boat navigation and irrigation systems, altering the physics and chemistry of the water, outcompeting native

Myriophyllum aquaticum can become a scourge of waterways, but it behaves itself nicely in a garden setting, especially when its gardener can muster the courage to thin it out every now and then. Otherwise, the feathery (my use of that adjective was inevitable), animated stems might become a threatening-looking surge of green.

flora and fauna, and providing excellent habitats for mosquito larvae. This is also the plant that, if left unchecked, turns an aquarium into a green mess. However, we're gardeners—tenders of the Earth, if you will—and we can easily confine milfoil to an aquatic pot and keep it thinned out, the better to appreciate its impossibly fine leaves and animated form.

Milfoil is one of the easiest of all container plants to maintain: stick a pot of it into an aquatic container when the water warms up, maybe add a tiny bit of water-soluble fertilizer every now and then, and enjoy the show as the underwater "pine trees" lift themselves up to break the water surface and go over the edge of the pot. Grow it all by itself in a beautifully glazed pot and enjoy the serenity, or add it to an aquatic combopot as you sincerely pledge to keep an eye on it as the season progresses. One look at the photograph should make you want to grow a bit of milfoil—aren't you tempted now?

Cultural tips: Too much fertilizer in the water will probably lead to algae and/or duckweed proliferating and coating the milfoil. Not pretty.

NARCISSUS
daffodil, jonquil

Family: Amaryllidaceae
Cultural group: bulbs
Height: 6 in. to 2 ft.
Width: depends on the size of the pot
Light: sun to partial shade (as much light as possible when forcing)
Temperature: cool to warm
Overwintering: generally hardy in Z3–9
Moisture: moderate to ample
Drainage of medium: well drained but tolerates shallow standing water
Fertility: none if forced; average afterward, if bulbs are kept going
Ease/speed of growth: easy (forcing a bit more challenging)/moderate
Propagation: offsets (of bulbs), seeds (got five years or so to wait?)
Problems: slugs and snails, basal rot, large narcissus bulb fly, viruses, drought during rooting and/or active forcing period; (exclusive to forcing) too-short period of cold, no acclimatization, bad timing
Principal interest: flowers, fragrance
Length of seasonal interest: brief but can be extended through a variety of bloom times and forcing times

Design attributes
Color: flowers white, red, pink, orange, yellow, and green; green leaves

Line: leaves and flower stems; some flowers have a linear look
Form: skinny leaves with precisely cut flowers above; a bunch of flowers in a pot to artistry
Space: at tops of leaves/clumps and around flowers
Texture: medium, mostly (some jonquils are fine)

Yes, gentle readers: some of the daffodil bulbs you buy for planting in the ground in fall can be forced in containers to savor their late winter cheer, weeks ahead of the beauties growing outdoors. You might even try forcing your own in-ground bulbs after digging and dividing them. Just be sure to use the biggest ones. I've forced daffodils in pots for twenty years; what I've learned along the way can be boiled down to four basic steps, which apply (with appropriate tweaking) to other hardy bulbs:

1. PICK
  • Use healthy (clean and heavy) bulbs of more or less the same size.
2. POT
  • Don't be afraid to plant closely or high, and use a well-drained potting mix. The "noses" should poke a bit above the potting mix.
  • Arrange in single, double, or triple layers (single layers for bulbs other than daffodils).
3. STORE
  • Provide a cold period—ideally in the range from just above freezing to about 40°F—of an appropriate length. Twelve to sixteen weeks is ideal for daffodils.
  • Keep the pots in a spot that will provide shelter from temperature extremes, excess moisture, and hungry animals (such as a cold frame, deep hole with a covering, roomy crawl space, or window well).
  • Check the pots during the cold period for heaving (lifting out of the pot) and watering needs.
4. GROW
  • Allow enough time after removal from cold storage until bloom time. Force at moderate temperatures (50–65°F is ideal). Generally, the later in the season the bulbs are removed from the cold, the less time it will take to bring them into bloom.
  • Acclimatize (gradually raise the heat and light) the bulbs for a few days before providing full light and warmth.
  • Figure one to four weeks from acclimatizing to bloom.
  • Keep a careful eye out for watering needs (daffodils like plenty of moisture; I try to keep about 1 in. of water in saucers under them) and pests (mainly aphids and thrips).
  • Cooler temperatures (to just above freezing) prolong the life of the flowers.

Sorry, those of you in warmer areas: the procedure just outlined won't work, because you don't have sufficiently cold winters. But there are ways around that, such as using pre-cooled bulbs (prepared to bloom without the cold treatment) and growing kinds that don't need a cold period, such as paperwhite narcissus. The paperwhites (which are included in Division 8, tazettas, for those of you who are counting along with the American Daffodil Society classification system) mustn't freeze; the best-looking pots of them are forced cool. My favorite paperwhites, 'Ariel' and 'Ziva', are fragrant (but not overwhelmingly so, as some are) and can produce at least a dozen flowers per stem.

But if you can provide the cold forcing conditions just described, go for it. There's excitement to be had in watching the leaves elongate and realizing that the flower buds are coming up through them. All that is merely a prelude to the pulchri-

Opposite: How can you not smile when you look at a bunch of daffodils? Their cheerful colors and active lines (of the leaves, flower stems, and sometimes nodding flowers) create a happy, positive feeling. From the top, they are *Narcissus* 'Flower Drift' (a double), 'Itzim' (on the bench), birdlike 'Peeping Tom', bunch-flowered 'Martinette', and diminutive 'Tête-à-Tête'.

Below: Bright yellow *Narcissus* 'Tête-à-Tête' combines with anemones and pansies to create a colorful welcome to spring. Note how the daffodil foliage repeats the upright lines of the blue fence while the more circular outlines of the flowers less obviously echo the row of circles behind them.

tude of a pot of daffodils in full flower, when Old Man Winter still rules outdoors with his cold, icy, gray grip. You can also grow daffodils (and other hardy bulbs) in pots that are left outside for winter decoration; those bulbs will bloom at the same time as the ones in the open ground. And no one is stopping you from buying some bulbs in bloom and plunking them into a more attractive container with or without other plants. I've always forced daffodils as monopots (I prefer to force everything separately and then display the pots together), but maybe some day I'll try some combopots with tulips, grape hyacinths, and other hardy bulbs.

Now, which daffodils force well? Here are the ones I'd want to take to that proverbial (but rather cold) desert island with me, ordered numerically by horticultural division (although note that not all thirteen divisions are represented in my short list).

Division 1 Trumpet: 'Bravoure' has white petals and a golden yellow trumpet. 'Little Gem' produces teeny flowers (about 1 in. across, officially a miniature) in all gold.

Division 2 Large-cupped: 'Brackenhurst' produces yellow and orange, long-lasting flowers. 'Ice Follies' opens cream and yellow but fades to all cream; it's one of the best of all daffodils to force, without question.

Division 4 Double: 'Cheerfulness' (mostly white) and 'Yellow Cheerfulness' produce multiple rose-like flowers per stem and emit an intoxicating fragrance.

Division 5 Triandrus: The miniature 'Hawera' blooms

profusely—bearing up to six flowers on a stem— in medium yellow.

Division 6 Cyclamineus: Try 'Jetfire', a midsized flower in yellow and orange, and the all-yellow 'Peeping Tom'.

Division 7 Jonquilla: 'Quail' produces brilliant yellow-gold fragrant blooms, two or three to a stem.

Division 8 Tazetta: The intoxicatingly fragrant 'Falconet' is my favorite tazetta for forcing, in gold and orange-red and at least three to the stem.

Division 12 Miscellaneous: 'Tête-à-Tête', a golden miniature, is the most widely forced daffodil in the world, I'm told. It's easy. Start with this one.

By the way, the genus is named for Narcissus, who in the short version of the Greek myth comes to a bad end after becoming unhealthily fixated on his own handsome reflection. The extended version deals with unrequited love, remorse, revenge, incest, and death (of course—this is mythology). You'd never know from looking at them that all that drama went into making these beautiful flowers. Daffodils will infect you with a benign sort of yellow fever. Give in to it; resistance is futile once you've grown them in the open ground, forced them in pots, or (and this really sets the hook) won blue ribbons with them in flower shows. Trust me.

Cultural tips: Keep forced bulbs growing in their pots until the foliage looks really sad. Stop watering them, place them on their sides, and don't think about them again until fall, when you can plant the bulbs in your garden.

NELUMBO
lotus

Family: Nelumbonaceae
Cultural group: aquatics
Height: 2–4 ft. (above water surface)
Width: 3 ft. to indefinite
Light: sun
Temperature: (warm to) hot
Overwintering: min. 40°F, keep moist, low light; hardy in Z4–11
Moisture: constant
Drainage of medium: requires standing water
Fertility: average
Ease/speed of growth: moderate/moderate to fast
Principal interest: foliage, form, flowers, fruit
Propagation: division, seeds
Problems: caterpillars, Japanese beetles, spending too much time staring at them
Length of seasonal interest: long (foliage); moderate but intermittent (flowers)

Lights, camera, action: the exquisite bloom of *Nelumbo* 'Mrs. Perry D. Slocum' is *slowly* opening and expanding, but it certainly suggests motion. How many colors do you see here?

Circles, ovals, and other curvaceous shapes, plus straight, curved, and wavy lines interact in a simple composition worthy of your deepest consideration. Yes, the colors (again, of *Nelumbo* 'Mrs. Perry D. Slocum') are nice, but you've got to admit that form and line play leading roles with lotus.

Design attributes

Color: medium gray-green leaves; flowers white, red, pink, and yellow (rarely lavender)

Line: petioles, rounded leaf outlines

Form: umbrellas (leaves); onions (buds); cups to chubby tutu-ed ballerinas to expanding stars, or artichokes (flowers); showerheads (ovaries and fruits)

Space: abundant around the petioles (under the leaves)

Texture: coarse, in reality, but often not in perception

There's something transcendent about a lotus that can take you beyond what you see. When I look at one in its summer glory, I see umbrellas, artichokes, and showerheads. I've never seen an unattractive lotus, but beauty is in the eye of the beholder, so check out the many available hybrids online (some of the offerings will make you gasp), in a catalog, or (best of all) in a garden before making your own choices. 'Momo Botan' produces semidouble pink and white flowers and is somewhat smaller overall than many of them and so makes a good starter lotus. 'Mrs. Perry D. Slocum', one of whose parents is our native yellow *N. lutea* (American lotus), is full-sized and gorgeous, with pink flowers turning yellow. The double-flowered ones often produce wavy, intriguingly molded showerheads (and nice flowers, too, but they last a few days, and the heads last for years as dried keepsakes).

You don't need a pond to enjoy the glories of a lotus, but don't think you can grow one in a little pot, either. At Atlock they grow in aquatic pots about 3 ft. tall and wide, which allows them to reach impressive dimensions. While they will grow in smaller containers, the proportion of big plant to puny pot might make the lotus look clumsily large and looming. No way should a transcendent plant be allowed to look like that.

All lotuses—not just the conducive *N. nucifera* (sacred lotus)—provide opportunities both for meditation and for some interactive fun for you, kids, and every gardening visitor: 1) Dribble a little bit of water onto a leaf, and watch as the water seems to be flung off, not just passively fall off. 2) Stand in front of a plant during a rainstorm and see the previous phenomenon repeated 1,000 times. 3) Note how the petals and stamens suddenly, noisily fall off, leaving behind the ovary/showerhead, and watch over the next few weeks as the showerhead turns into a sculpted piece of dark chocolate with holes and little balls that rattle when you shake them. 4) Add that botanical wonder to your collection of treasures for contemplation (or for remembering one of summer's high points in the middle of winter).

Cultural tips: Grow them in roomy pots filled with soil or a 2:1 mixture of soil and potting mix (not pure potting mix; much of it will float and make a mess) covered with coarse gravel. Place them just below the surface of the water at first; gradually drop them down to 1–2 ft. below the surface as the leaves get bigger. Fertilizer tablets inserted into the soil every few weeks will reap big rewards. Remove dead leaves and flower parts that fall into the water.

NEPHROLEPIS

lemon button fern (*N. cordifolia* 'Duffii');
Boston fern (*N. exaltata*)

Family: Nephrolepidaceae
Cultural group: tropicals
Height: 1–3 ft.
Width: 1–4 ft.
Light: partial shade
Temperature: warm
Overwintering: min. 50°F, water occasionally, bright light; variously hardy in Z9–11
Moisture: moderate to ample
Drainage of medium: well drained
Fertility: average

Nephrolepis exaltata 'Rita's Gold', a golden selection of Boston fern, fan-dances among its companions in a combopot at Swarthmore College, where container gardening has been taken to the level of fine art.

Ease/speed of growth: easy/moderate
Propagation: division, spores
Problems: spider mites, scale insects, mealybugs, rots and
    spots, brown pinnae (from drought or insufficient
    humidity)
Principal interest: foliage, form
Length of seasonal interest: all year

Design attributes

Color: medium green fronds, sometimes yellow, chartreuse,
    or variegated
Line: arching rachises and abundant pinnae, some more
    linear than others
Form: mostly gushing masses or balls, plenty of variation
    in pinnae
Space: prominent (*N. cordifolia* 'Duffii') to limited
Texture: fine to medium

Just about any fern can be grown in a container (admittedly
with some effort for the tiny, choice ones), but it's *Nephrolepis* that offers the most versatile ferns of them all. Grow them
indoors as houseplants and then let them summer outdoors
in a brightly lit spot, such as under a high-canopied tree or on
a covered porch. In the spirit of houseplant liberation, you
could also grow them as annuals, using and enjoying them as
you would other foliage plants and then discarding (or merci-
fully relocating) them at the end of the growing season. They

Close up, the individual pinnae of *Nephrolepis exaltata* 'Tiger
Fern' look like individual slices of a delectable lime cheesecake,
while an entire frond of them elicits inevitable comparisons to
an exotic feather (*pinna* does mean "feather," you know).

A mass of green crumbs and a twisted tower of little knife blades
represent the two textural extremes found among selections of
Boston fern (*Nephrolepis exaltata*). They're all ferny, though,
and deserve to be tried out in your containers located in
(mostly) shady spots.

The precisely two-ranked pinnae ("leaflets") of lemon button
fern (*Nephrolepis cordifolia* 'Duffii') march outward in random
directions. Not orderly, but very active. Does this look like a
conventional fern to you?

bear no flowers (they reproduce from spores, remember), but they offer plenty of design interest.

Start with the most familiar of them all, namely Boston fern (*N. exaltata*), which reminds me of a green accordion. That foot-wide and -tall plant you start with can easily turn into a five-footer when attentively grown as a specimen in a monopot, but you could include a small plant in a combopot and remove any fronds that encroach on its neighbors. Why not? You selectively prune other plants, don't you? Boston fern can take it. You can still find 'Fluffy Ruffle' (which I grew as a kid in my north-facing bedroom window), but plenty of other fanciful selections of Boston fern are now available. Try the appealingly variegated 'Tiger Fern', which probably won't become as large as the all-green Boston, and don't pass up a plant of 'Rita's Gold' when you see one. The sensational Rita brings her shades of yellow (gold, given plenty of light) and chartreuse, as well as an almost nervously energetic form, to innovative containers everywhere.

Another one to try is *N. cordifolia* 'Duffii' (lemon button fern), with rounded, buttonlike pinnae (no, not leaflets; these are ferns, and they have their own lexicon of terms). A mature specimen will measure 2 ft. across but not as high, and the fronds may carry dagger-shaped pinnae instead of button-like ones, but the plant will still look ferny.

Cultural tips: These ferns don't need large pots, but keep an eye on them to make sure they stay moist. Many tolerate a surprising amount of morning sun, so move yours around to see how much sun they can take before the fronds begin to turn brown. New fronds will emerge to replace the damaged ones.

NYMPHAEA
waterlily

Family: Nymphaeaceae
Cultural group: aquatics
Height: above water, 3–6 in. (hardies), 1 ft. (tropicals)
Width: 2–4 ft. or more
Light: sun
Temperature: warm to hot
Overwintering: min. 50°F, keep moist, bright light in their containers, or keep leafless rhizomes/tubers in damp sand; tropicals are hardy in Z10–11, hardies in Z4–11
Moisture: constant
Drainage of medium: requires standing water
Fertility: average
Ease/speed of growth: moderate/moderate to fast
Propagation: division, seeds, plantlets (from leaves of viviparous ones)
Problems: aphids, China-mark moth, leaf miners, waterlily beetles, spots and rots, hungry fish

Principal interest: flowers, foliage, form, fragrance
Length of seasonal interest: moderate (flowers); long (foliage and form)

Design attributes
Color: flowers white, red, pink, yellow, blue, and red-violet; foliage medium to dark green, sometimes variegated with red and purple
Line: from submerged petioles and elongated petals
Form: a dance or crowd of notched circles
Space: implied between leaves and flowers, literal under flowers of tropicals
Texture: medium (when seen as a dance) to coarse (when a crowd)

Waterlily. The very word is mellifluous, soothing, lush. I admit that most waterlilies need a pond or at the very least a good-sized pool to accommodate them, but a few of them fit obligingly into manageably sized aquatic containers. They make captivating focal points for a patio or even a balcony (provided the balcony can support the combined weight of the container, water, and plant), so if you can provide a sunny spot and a little specialized care, you too, like Monet, can contemplate a serene waterlily in your garden (and perhaps paint it *en plein air*).

Catalogs and other references refer to hardy and tropical waterlilies, but the differences extend beyond their abilities to withstand cold: while the flowers of the hardy ones float on the surface of the water and bloom during the day, the tropicals usually rise several inches or more above the water and open diurnally or nocturnally. Some have red-splashed foliage, and all fashion geometrically arranged patterns with their iconic lilypads (unless they outgrow the surface area of their container, which often happens, or their caretaker fails to muster the courage to remove the older leaves; both situations create leafjams). Another fun note: some waterlilies are viviparous ("live-bearing"), a reference to the little plantlets that develop at the spot where the petiole joins the blade (the pad, in this case). They're fun to watch develop and even more fun to raise to blooming size.

Here are a few, less widely spreading waterlilies (referred to as miniatures or dwarfs in references and catalogs):

The flowers of 'Aurora' (hardy) display an ever-changing parade of yellow, orange, and red shades as they age. The dark red-spotted foliage adds interest.

'Chromatella' (hardy) bears bright yellow flowers and leaves marked with purple and coppery bronze.

'Helvola' (hardy) is a yellow-flowered hybrid involving *N. tetragona* and is equally teeny.

'Hermine' (hardy) has white flowers and withstands water temperatures to about 15°F.

Nymphaea 'Perry's Baby Red' grows contentedly in a half-barrel or similarly sized container. Just make sure Pac-Man doesn't eat all the flowers.

An ethereal bloom of *Nymphaea* 'Surfrider' serves as the focal point that unites several disparate shapes (including reflections; don't forget them as integral elements of water gardening) in a small aquatic container.

'Perry's Baby Red' (hardy) varies from deep pink to purple-red.

The blooms of 'Solfatare' (hardy) progress from yellow to orange to red, and the red-marked foliage adds more pizzazz.

The viviparous 'Surfrider' (tropical) bears blue flowers.

The hardy *N. tetragona* is a Gulliver compared to its Brobdingnagian kin, barely spreading its circle of purple-marked leaves a foot wide under the white blooms.

Cultural tips: Give waterlilies basically the same summer care as *Nelumbo* (lotus), except that 1 ft. of water above them should suffice. It's not a bad idea to bring in the hardies (and of course the tropicals) for the winter. Don't include even a tiny fountain in a waterlily's container: they *hate* moving water and will sulk.

OCIMUM
basil

Family: Lamiaceae
Cultural group: annuals
Height: 6 in. to 2 ft.
Width: 6–12 in.
Light: sun
Temperature: warm to hot

A pot of *Ocimum basilicum* 'Marseille' provides plenty of basil for pesto and other delights, and it looks appealing in an herb garden or other garden setting. This potful is begging to be thinned out, which will allow the remaining plants to grow large and leafy.

Overwintering: min. 55°F, water occasionally, bright light

Moisture: ample

Drainage of medium: well drained

Fertility: average to high

Ease/speed of growth: easy/moderate to fast

Propagation: seeds, cuttings

Problems: whitefly, aphids, slugs and snails, rots and spots, jumping the gun in spring

Principal interest: foliage, fragrance

Length of seasonal interest: long to all year

Design attributes

Color: foliage medium to dark green often with purple, sometimes variegated with white or cream; flowers usually white or purple (especially bracts), but you might want to pinch these out

Line: usually not obvious except on upright forms

Form: shrubby

Space: usually not much

Texture: fine to medium

An upright selection of *Ocimum basilicum* makes a hedge in a pair of rectangular pots. A brief session with a pair of scissors, pruning shears, or hands (skip the hedge shears, please) would result in a more formal-looking wall of basil (and a very pleasant olfactory experience).

Frank and Anita DeCesare, our neighbors back in the day, had three things in their vegetable garden: tomatoes; those long, yellow Italian peppers; and a weedy-looking green plant with a powerful, sweet-spicy-soapy fragrance that my young nose deemed unappealing. Wow, what five decades will do. The DeCesares' weed was basil, and I've since made up for lost basil-enjoying time by seeking it out in food (Italian and Thai, mostly) and by rubbing the leaves just about every time I walk by a plant of it.

Basil has been liberated from the vegetable garden in a big way. One look at the photo of the three selections of *O. basilicum*, sweet basil (by far the most familiar species), and *O. ×citriodorum*, lemon basil (aka *O. b.* var. *citriodorum*), should give you plenty of ideas for combining basils with all sorts of plants in containers, exploiting their rich coloration, ample form, and various textures. The one we at Atlock call "hedging basil" offers more linear interest than most of them, especially when grown lined up in a pot and sheared once or twice (like a hedge). You can complete the quintet of design elements by making a standard topiary from many basils, where the head of foliage calls attention to the empty space below it.

Start basil from seed later than your tomatoes, and plant it out when both the soil and air temperatures are dependably warm. Plenty of sun, water, and nitrogen fertilizer encourages vigorous growth and production of those fragrant leaves. If pesto is your goal, pinch out the incipient flowers as you see them to keep the leaves coming; many of the all-green, pesto-suitable selections have boring white flowers. However, others with attractive colors, pleasing forms, and distinctive fragrances produce very pretty pink or purple blooms and dark bracts, so please let at least a few plants (pesto-bound or other-

So you think all basils are medium green and have big, floppy leaves . . . well, think again. *Ocimum ×citriodorum* 'Pesto Perpetuo' offers pastel, white-edged foliage; *O. basilicum* 'Osmin' cloaks itself in regal purple, and *O. b.* 'Siam Queen' echoes the theme here of pointy (not puffy) foliage. All three will fill your nostrils with perfume when brushed or rubbed.

wise) go to flower. Bees, butterflies, and other nice bugs will thank you for that, as will hummingbirds.

Start with any of the many selections of *O. basilicum*, such as 'Genovese', 'Green Ruffles', 'Marseille' (touted as the best-flavored variety by more than one reference), or 'Napolitano', and then branch out into the many others that offer differences in color, form, and fragrance, such as iridescent, variably purple-tinged 'Dark Opal', the almost black-leaved 'Purple Ruffles', and the well-named 'Spicy Globe'.

One you won't be able to resist is 'African Blue' (*O. basilicum* 'Dark Opal' × *O. kilimandscharicum*), with dark green, dark purple-veined leaves, lavender-mauve flowers that open from dark bracts, and a deep, assertive spice-rack fragrance. Larger and shrubbier than many basils, it is worth trying to overwinter once, if only for cuttings for next year's plants (it won't come true from seed).

Cultural tips: Basils insist on plenty of sun, heat, and drainage. Don't deny them, and they won't deny you. Let a plant or two of a particular cultivar bloom before deciding whether you want to suppress flowering in favor of pesto/foliage.

There's nothing subtle about *Ocimum* 'African Blue': besides rich color, it delivers active lines, unapologetically shrubby form, abundant space within its parts, and fine texture. Check off all five elements, and then add delectable fragrance to the list.

OXALIS
shamrock, sorrel, sourgrass

Family: Oxalidaceae
Cultural group: annuals, bulbs, tropicals
Height: 6–12 in.
Width: 6–12 in., maybe more
Light: sun to partial shade
Temperature: cool to warm to hot
Overwintering: min. 55°F, water occasionally, bright light; or keep totally dormant at 50–60°F, very little or no water, light not necessary; can be kept potted in their growing medium; variously hardy in Z8–10
Moisture: moderate to ample
Drainage of medium: well drained
Fertility: average
Ease/speed of growth: easy/moderate to fast
Propagation: division (of bulbs or clusters), cuttings, seeds
Problems: aphids, spider mites, rots and spots
Principal interest: foliage, form, flowers
Length of seasonal interest: long to all year (shrubby types)

Design attributes

Color: foliage green, often marked or entirely in shades of red, yellow, or purple (sometimes nearly orange); flowers white, red, pink, yellow, and purple
Line: from stems on older plants, petioles, flower stems
Form: mounded to shrubby to cascading heaps of shamrocks or cartwheels without rims (or little palm trees); flocks of butterflies
Space: throughout plant or limited to edges; around flower stems and clusters
Texture: fine to medium

I'm fully aware of the monsters that lurk in the motley crew that is the genus *Oxalis*, having ripped out countless stems and leaves of them (note I didn't mention roots) over the years. The weeds grow quickly (often running underground), go to flower just as rapidly, and then eject their seeds when the wind, an animal, or a weeding gardener disturbs their explosive pods. But don't let the pernicious members of the genus prejudice you against the rest of the bunch. Over the years I've discovered some choice ones for container gardening, grown as monopots as well as combopots.

'Coppertone' makes low (less than 1 ft. tall), spreading, almost shrubby mounds of everchanging foliage in shades of chartreuse, yellow, green, red, and even orange (increased light and heat accentuates the orange) on equally colorful and mutable stems. It combines well with many summer annuals that pick up on its colorful foliage, but I've also seen it as

Not all oxalis are weeds. *Oxalis* 'Coppertone' plays nicely with others and offers a wide and often shifting palette of colors. Here the chartreuse incarnation glows alongside a satisfyingly vivid alternanthera.

Late-day light brightens a cluster of miniature palm trees, er, *Oxalis lasiandra*, set against a dark red-purple alternanthera. What do the leaves suggest to you? Did you perceive their shapes before their color?

a killer monopot, in a low (3–4 in.) but wide (about 16 in.) bonsai container. The yellow flowers appear sporadically and are pleasant enough. This cultivar, which propagates easily from cuttings, grows year-round at Atlock.

O. lasiandra (palm tree oxalis) produces long-petioled, medium green, sometimes purple-shaded leaves—reminiscent of horse chestnut leaves, palm trees (hence the common name), or wagon wheels—that are upright for a while and then gracefully lean over. The pink flowers go nicely with the foliage. Increase this one from the little bulb clusters it makes.

The long-petioled green leaves of *O. peduncularis* give it a very open, dynamic look, even when young, but an old plant looks like it's literally spinning while crawling out of its container. Give it a year or so to reach its full, idiosyncratic self (reaching perhaps 1 ft. above and below the rim of its container). Yellow flowers appear abundantly or not. I suspect it grows from rhizomes or other underground structures, but it propagates easily from cuttings.

O. tetraphylla (aka *O. deppei*) 'Iron Cross' makes large, four-parted, clover-like green leaves with dark brown-purple cen-

Oxalis is from the Greek *oxys* ("sharp"), referring to the taste of some leaves in this genus. *Triangularis* refers to the three-sided shape. *Papilionacea* is the Latinization of the French word for "butterfly." *Atropurpurea* is a combination of the Latin qualifier *atro* ("dark") and *purpurea* ("purple"). Now you know the etymology of the official name for this cloud of dark purple butterflies.

ters, reminiscent (to someone, obviously) of the German military medal. The common names of good-luck plant and lucky clover (as well as its pink flowers) help lighten the mood that might otherwise be suggested by a foot-high handful of Eisernen Kreuzes. It too grows from bulbs.

O. triangularis subsp. *papilionacea* 'Atropurpurea' decks itself out in three-parted, rich purple foliage and light purple-pink flowers. The open mounds easily reach 1 ft. wide but are not as tall. It's splendid as a monopot, but even a small, few-leaved plant makes a strong statement in a combopot with gold, yellow, chartreuse, light purple, and magenta companions. Share some of its little bulbs with friends.

O. vulcanicola (aka *O. siliquosa*) 'Copper Glow' resembles 'Coppertone' in habit and culture but is much more heavily shaded with copper-purple. The flowers add yellow, which might or might not be a good thing.

O. vulcanicola 'Zinfandel' also looks and behaves much like 'Coppertone' except for the deep, rich purple-red foliage (as in the wine of the same name). I like the yellow flowers on this one, which offer the possibility for a powerful combination with other yellow flowerers. It is reputedly sterile and non-invasive, which should recommend it to anyone who might still be hesitant to grow anything bearing the name "oxalis."

Cultural tips: Poor drainage will slay them quickly. They tolerate extremes of sunlight remarkably well, but a nice spot in morning sun encourages the finest coloration, I think. Don't be alarmed if you notice the leaves closing up toward the end of the day; many open and close on a quotidian schedule.

PASSIFLORA
passionflower, granadilla

Family: Passifloraceae
Cultural group: climbers and trailers
Height: 5 ft. or more
Width: depends on training
Light: sun to partial shade
Temperature: warm to hot
Overwintering: tropicals min. 50°F, water occasionally, bright light; others variously hardy in Z6–9
Moisture: moderate to ample
Drainage of medium: well drained
Fertility: average (high phosphorus should push bloom)
Ease/speed of growth: easy/fast
Propagation: cuttings, seeds
Problems: spider mites, scale insects, rots and spots (sometimes resulting from iron deficiency)
Principal interest: flowers, form (of flowers), foliage, fragrance
Length of seasonal interest: long but sometimes intermittent (flowers); long (foliage)

Design attributes
Color: flowers white, red, and purple; foliage light to dark green, sometimes marked with silver or contrasting greens
Line: from stems, tendrils, leaf lobes, petals, stamens, stigmas, and coronas
Form: underwater or extraterrestrial life forms have landed in your garden
Space: can be abundant, depends on training
Texture: fine (some parts) to mostly medium

The Doctrine of Signatures, in the elaborate rendition offered by Jakob Böhme (1575–1624), purports that God marked ("signed") natural objects with visible clues about their usefulness to mankind—for example, the lung-shaped, spotted leaves of lungwort (*Pulmonaria*) could be used to treat spotty diseases of the lungs, and the liver-shaped leaves of liverwort (*Hepatica*) point to their efficacy in treating liver ailments. The doctrine met with varying degrees of acceptance over the centuries (there are American Indian and Oriental

The intricate flowers of passionflowers (such as this *Passiflora caerulea*) suggest different things to different people. Some are reminded of various items and players in the passion of Christ. I see a colorful, line-filled, uniquely formed, space-defining, finely textured beauty that must be admired and put on display.

versions of it as well), but it's safe to say, I think, that 17th-century Jesuit missionaries in South America took it to its zenith with their take on passionflowers.

It wasn't carnal passion the Jesuits were focusing on but rather the suffering, or passion, of Christ on the cross. Every part of the passionflower plant symbolized (or bore the signature of God pointing to) an aspect of the crucifixion, and the Jesuits used passionflowers to present the story to the local residents as they attempted to convert them to Christianity. (They employed other methods, but we won't get into that here.) The flower itself bore witness to the ten faithful apostles (minus Judas and the denying Peter, in the ten petal-like tepals), the crown of thorns (the fringy corona), the five wounds (the stamens), and the nails (the three parts of the stigma). Not wanting to omit the bad guys, the missionaries saw the hands (or spears) of the crucifiers in the leaves and their whips in the tendrils. I've not read of the part that the egg-shaped fruit plays in the passion (the stones that the crowd threw, perhaps?). Interesting.

However you might view passionflowers, I think you should give yourself the opportunity to enjoy their unique beauty by growing at least one in a pot. Sure, they can easily reach 10 ft. in the open ground, but the confines of a container (and providing some pruning and training) can bring them down to a more manageable size. The most efficient solution of all is to train one onto a hoop or sphere, but you can also send them up, down, and around a trellis or weave them through other plants. A hanging basket of any passionflower might make me want to convert (to that approach to growing them, that is). Every one of them is mesmerizingly beautiful (or at least intricate), so pick your favorite from these or from others you might encounter. Note that some are tropical, while others are actually quite hardy.

The flowers of the hybrid 'Amethyst' bloom in the color of fine examples of their semiprecious mineral namesake. Tropical.

P. caerulea (blue passionflower) looks just like the photo. Its selection 'Constance Elliott' is the all-white version, although sometimes the corona (the fringe) can be pale blue. Z6–9.

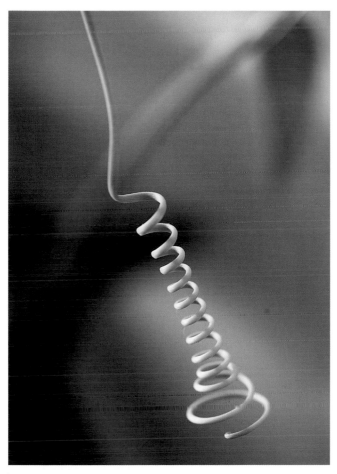

An unfulfilled (unattached) tendril of *Passiflora ×decaisneana* rewards close inspection. You will inevitably be seduced by the scene-stealing flowers, but I think you'll agree that this bit player offers a subtle allure.

The aliens have arrived to beam me up into their spaceship and take me to Potof IV, their home planet. On second thought, I'm about to be ingested by a jellyfish. No, *there's* that wacky lampshade I thought I'd thrown away. Wait, I have it now: it's a fanciful bloom of *Passiflora ×decaisneana*.

P. coccinea (red granadilla) has a puny corona, but the tepals couldn't be any more red. As in blood. Tropical.

P. coriacea (batwing passionflower) could defensibly be grown only for its silver-marked foliage, which does suggest bats on the wing. The flowers are missing seven apostles but still have the unmistakable passionflower look to them. Z8 and up.

P. ×*decaisneana* can grow very large and has boring foliage, but those flowers will get you thinking. Give it a big pot, cut it back, and train it. Tropical.

P. edulis (passionfruit) is widely grown in frost-free parts of the world for its edible (hence the specific epithet) fruit. The flowers are nice, too, but can't hold a candle to its heavenly-scented selection 'Incense'. Z8 and up.

P. incarnata (maypops) grows shorter than many others (maybe to 6 ft.). The flowers strongly resemble those of *P. caerulea* and have a sweet-musty fragrance. Bumblebees really work these over. Z6–8.

The flowers of *P. trifasciata* look like an entangled bunch of long-legged spiders, while the foliage (its container-gardening *raison d'etre*, I think) reminds me of light purple- or silver-veined goose feet. Tropical.

For a detailed trip into the intricacies of *Passiflora*, check out the Web site for the Passiflora Society International, or take a little time to play with Google. Passionflowers are a cure for dispassionate container gardening.

Cultural tips: Expect them to grow quite large in time. Deal with it. They flower in the current season's growth, so don't be afraid to cut them back hard.

PELARGONIUM
geranium

Family: Geraniaceae
Cultural group: annuals, climbers and trailers, tropicals, succulents
Height: 6 in. to 2 ft. or more
Width: 6 in. to 2 ft., sometimes more (depends on training for ivy types)
Light: sun to limited partial shade
Temperature: cool to warm to hot
Overwintering: min. 50°F, water occasionally to liberally, bright light . . . or upside down in a root cellar; basically hardy in Z10–11, some to Z7 during mild winters and with protection
Moisture: on dry side to moderate to ample
Drainage of medium: well drained
Fertility: average to high (if pushing growth in winter, especially, or pushing flowers)
Ease/speed of growth: easy (except those fussy little zonals)/moderate

Propagation: cuttings, seeds
Problems: whitefly, thrips, caterpillars, mealybugs, rots and spots, root rot, galls, edema, and those nasty, disguised flower caterpillars (they become the color of the petals they feed on, more or less)
Principal interest: foliage, flowers, form (especially if trained), fragrance
Length of seasonal interest: long to all year (foliage); long (flowers, if allowed to bloom)

Design attributes
Color: foliage green, often marked with white, red, orange, yellow, and purple-brown; flowers white, red, pink, orange, and red-violet (rarely yellow)
Line: abundant in the ivy types and scenteds, less so in others; some variegation patterns, leaf lobes, and flowers add line
Form: shrubby, colorful puffs against bushes; scarecrows (old zonals); waterfalls (ivy types); carpets (especially *P. tomentosum*)
Space: usually not readily apparent (sometimes almost nonexistent)
Texture: fine to medium to coarse

The genus *Pelargonium* (commonly known as geraniums, not to be confused with *Geranium*, the hardy geraniums) is a smorgasbord, offering an abundance of selections for diverse appetites, tastes, and combinations. Translation: there are so many geraniums I could write a book-length treatment on them, but I don't have room, so here's a sampling of the feast.

By far the most familiar of the bunch—the meat and potatoes, if you will—are the zonal geraniums, bushy plants with lush leaves (marked, or zoned, in various colors) and rounded clusters of often vibrantly colored flowers. These are the so-called bedding geraniums, but they certainly don't need to spend their lives in bed. Most perform extremely well in containers, as long as you keep an important point in mind: many require far less water than you might think in summer and respond very positively to plenty of water in winter. So take it easy with the watering can in summer, but give your overwintering zonals plenty to drink (and a corresponding level of fertilizer). I suggest you grow them as specimens in monopots, grouping them with other pots as you see fit. While many zonals are grown for their flowers (offered by the legion in nurseries each spring), I go for the ones with variegated foliage, especially the miniature and dwarf ones that remain low and compact, especially if pinched back occasionally. Favorites include the eventually trailing 'Alpha', with yellow-green leaves marked with dark red, plus scarlet flowers; 'Bird Dancer', a pointy- or starry-leaved (stellar) selection in green and almost black foliage with light salmon flowers; and

A row of *Pelargonium* 'Vancouver Centennial' (a zonal geranium) in neatly matched pots creates an eye-catching lineup. Serendipitously, the line of brightly colored flowers doesn't run parallel to the line of plants but instead dives into it, adding a dash of energy.

Who wouldn't revel in the yellow-green foliage and red-orange flowers of *Pelargonium* 'Crystal Palace Gem'? Combining them with some purple foliage in a blue pot *almost* produces a perfect complementary tertiary triad. Stepping back a little from the pot causes the blue and purple to merge, and then complementary perfection is achieved.

This leaf collection merely scratches the surface of the tremendous diversity the genus *Pelargonium* offers. If you think you've seen 'em all (referring to many things in gardening and life), you ain't seen nothin' yet.

An unexpected setting can take an attractive container planting and lift it to an even higher level. Placing a squarish pot of the almost round, neatly black-lined leaves of *Pelargonium* 'Distinction' and the wispy strands of *Muehlenbeckia complexa* against a gently curving mass of softly colored trunks creates Art.

Sometimes there aren't enough flowers on a plant of *Pelargonium* 'Crystal Palace Gem' to make a significant contribution to the overall display, so I remove them and enjoy the yellow-green foliage all by itself (or look for other plants and objects that might bring out the best in the foliage).

'Vancouver Centennial'. The last is a real knockout if grown in high light, where the leaves assume sumptuous shades of gold and maroon (less light diminishes the punch), plus its orange-red flowers always catch the eye. Larger ones worth trying—not quite full-sized zonals but bigger than the miniatures and dwarfs, in both plant and leaf size—include 'Crystal Palace Gem' (yellow-green foliage, red-orange flowers), 'Distinction' (finely ruffle-edged leaves with a thin black line near the leaf margins and completely superfluous red flowers), and 'Turkish Delight' (red-orange flowers and leaves triply banded in gold, maroon, and light to medium green).

Tip: If the flowers of a particular geranium don't appeal to you—for example, the flower color is boring or doesn't play well with its foliage or the flowers and/or foliage of a companion—remove them. The plant won't think any less of you for doing that, and your containers will look that much better for it. The plant will appreciate it if you learn how to remove the flower stalks before they bloom, though: carefully bend the stalk back and to the side at its swollen base and snap it off. Practice on a less-cherished plant to get the hang of it. You can also cut them off just above the swollen bases, which will soon dry up and fall off.

I live in an area where the trailing ivy-leaved geraniums don't bloom well—certainly not like they do in cooler-summer areas such as the Pacific Northwest, Maine, or the Alps, where they spill forth like so much candy-colored paint from a bucket. If you can grow them for their flowers, seek out the Balcon series. Otherwise, enjoy the foliage display from the likes of 'Sunset' (which displays pinkish purple markings when kept cool and dry, as does 'L'Elegante') or 'The Crocodile', which produces finely gold-netted, dark green leaves during

Thinking outside the pot involves (among other things) growing a plant in an unconventional way. Usually seen in windowboxes or more traditionally shaped pots, this narrow-necked urn provides a pleasantly unexpected setting for shyly blooming ivy geranium (*Pelargonium peltatum*) selection.

Most ivy geraniums are grown for their cheerful, strongly colored flowers. Be careful where you place them, however, because they might end up being seen against colors that turn the volume up to deafening.

Some ivy geraniums don't need flowers to make a design statement: their leaves say plenty. The variegation pattern and trailing stems of *Pelargonium peltatum* 'Sunset' bring new meaning to the term "falling stars," and seeing the plant against a contrasting gray-brown background accentuates the space between the leaves. Stellar.

A scented geranium strategically stands watch at a corner of an old stone wall. Many species and cultivars easily grow into splendid specimens when given their preferred cultural conditions and some attentive pruning, which encourages branching and denser growth.

A mass of the smallish, rumply, blue-gray-green leaves of *Pelargonium sidoides* helps brighten a rich but dark assortment of foliage, as do the nearly white pot and vividly magenta verbena. Just for fun, see what happens when you cover the verbena's blooms.

cooler weather. The foliage from a few stems of any ivy geranium adds an elegant, gentle touch to almost any combopot, just like a side of vegetables makes a sensible companion to meat and potatoes.

While the zonals and ivies comprise the majority of items on the groaning *Pelargonium* smorgasbord, don't fill up on them: save room for dessert! To me, the scented-leaf geraniums offer the most satisfying experiences of the entire genus. Many bear the fragrance of foods and flavorings, which you want to imagine as you rub the leaves to release the scent: apple (*P. odoratissimum*), apricot (*P.* 'Paton's Unique'), coconut (*P. grossularioides*), lemon (*P. citronellum* 'Mabel Grey', *P. crispum* 'Variegated Prince Rupert'), lime (*P.* 'Lime', oddly enough), nutmeg (*P.* 'Fragrans'), orange (*P.* 'Orange', aka 'Prince of Orange'), and peppermint (*P. tomentosum*). Others—such as *P. abrotanifolium* (southernwood), *P.* 'Citronella', and *P. sidoides*—have sharper, less mouthwatering odors, or floral scents, including eucalyptus (*P.* 'Lady Plymouth') and rose (*P.* 'Attar of Roses'). Their plant habits run the gamut from shrubby to floppy and from tiny to towering (relatively), but they're all worth growing as monopots (including as topiaries, especially 'Mabel Grey' or 'Variegated Prince Rupert') or in combopots.

By the way, many zonals have a distinctive scent, too, but they don't have an obvious marketing advantage by being associated with lemons, peppermint, and other fragrant comestibles.

There are many, many others in the genus, but I think we're all full from our multiple visits to this particular smorgasbord. Check out offerings online and in other references, and be sure to observe them in local nurseries and gardens.

Cultural tips: Poor drainage kills them, but so does prolonged drought, so grow them in a very well-drained mix and water appropriately. Afternoon shade is beneficial in hot areas or during unusual hot spells, which often suppresses bloom. Look for heat-tolerant selections if you garden in a hotter climate. Don't be afraid to pinch them (or chop them back) every now and then to keep them in shape.

PENNISETUM
fountain grass

Family: Poaceae
Cultural group: annuals (*P. setaceum*), perennials
(*Pp. alopecuroides* and *purpureum*)
Height: 2–4 ft. (*P. alopecuroides*), 2–3 ft. (*P. setaceum*),
3–4 ft. (*P. purpureum*)
Width: 2–3 ft. (*P. alopecuroides*), 1–2 ft. (*P. setaceum*),
2–3 ft. (*P. purpureum*)
Light: sun to very limited partial shade
Temperature: warm to hot
Overwintering: min. 50°F, water occasionally, bright light

(*Pp. purpureum* and *setaceum*), just above freezing, no water, light not necessary (*P. alopecuroides*); hardy in Z6–9 (*P. alopecuroides*), Z7–11 (*P. purpureum*), Z9–10 (*P. setaceum*)
Moisture: moderate to ample
Drainage of medium: well drained
Fertility: average to high nitrogen if pushing the annuals
Ease/speed of growth: easy/moderate to fast
Propagation: division, seeds
Problems: rots and spots
Principal interest: foliage, form, flowers, fruit
Length of seasonal interest: long (foliage and form); brief to moderate (flowers)

Design attributes
Color: foliage green, red, pink, and purple; flowers whitish to gray-brown to red-purple

Few other grasses include this much deep pink in their paintbox. Note how the green in the center of this well-grown specimen of *Pennisetum setaceum* 'Fireworks' brings some diversity to what otherwise might be a monotonous burst of pink and dark purple. Also note how nicely the colors associate with the brown pot and the gray bluestone.

Line: unavoidable
Form: a gusher with feathers or tails when in bloom/fruit
Space: ample within and around entire plant
Texture: fine to medium

I can't draw very well. Never could, really. But I can look at a plant and size up which sort of linear interest (or not) it can bring to a container planting. In fact, I try (and encourage the audiences at my container-design programs) to look at a plant in terms of line before being seduced by that shameless temptress, color. The next time you are thinking about composing a container planting, try this exercise regarding line: take out a piece of paper and something to draw with. Quickly sketch the lines you see in a given plant; if it takes you more than a few seconds to do so, the linear nature of the plant is either too complex or too obscure to make a readily perceivable contribution to a container planting. That doesn't mean you can't

include that subject in a planting, of course, but it should encourage you to look for other quickly sketchable candidates if line is your goal.

Most grasses can be sketched in a couple of seconds, and members of the genus *Pennisetum* are no exception. Look at the photos here to see for yourself (better yet, take out that piece of paper and something to draw with). Can you see how they appear to be moving, leading your eye from one spot to another? No wonder the common name for the genus is fountain grass.

If you're looking for green lines, choose *P. alopecuriodes* (easily to 3 ft. tall) or its selections 'Hameln' (2 ft. tall) or the even shorter (to about 1 ft.) 'Little Bunny'. The fuzzy-looking flowers and seedheads provide more interest but frequently come back to haunt the garden in the form of volunteer seedlings everywhere, including garden beds and even the lawn. (You might prefer a meadow, after all.)

A closeup of *Pennisetum setaceum* 'Fireworks' gives a better feeling of the space contained within its arching and spreading foliage.

Trails of beige sparks (very noticeable flower spikes) rush out of a dark red cloud (*Pennisetum setaceum* 'Rubrum') and fall back to earth. A puff of gray centaurea furthers the lively illusion of smoke and fire. Can you see how static this combopot would appear without the fountain grass? Covering it with your hand will show you.

Most grasses look like they're in constant motion, and this *Pennisetum purpureum* 'Prince' is no exception. Please note the bluish cast at the base of the central, more mature shoot: it's a bloomy coating that gives another dimension to the rich coloration. Kinda like gray hair on many older heads.

PENTAS
Egyptian star cluster (*P. lanceolata* and presumed hybrids)

Family: Rubiaceae
Cultural group: annuals
Height: 2 ft., maybe more (except the California and Graffiti series, to about 1 ft.)
Width: 1–2 ft.
Light: sun
Temperature: warm to hot
Overwintering: min. 55°F, water occasionally, bright light; variably hardy in Z10
Moisture: moderate to ample
Drainage of medium: well drained
Fertility: average
Ease/speed of growth: easy/moderate
Propagation: cuttings, seeds
Problems: whitefly, spider mites
Principal interest: flowers, butterflies
Length of seasonal interest: long

Design attributes
Color: flowers white, red, pink, red-violet, and purple; medium green foliage, rarely marked with white
Line: stems, foliage sticking out (with pale midribs), starry flowers (individually)
Form: upright shrubby starbursts with butterflies attached
Space: not much except that implied between flower clusters
Texture: medium

But if red-purple lines are your desire, then choose from the selections of *P. setaceum*. 'Rubrum' is the old standby, to about 2.5 ft. 'Fireworks', which adds pink and green to the festivities, will reach about 2 ft. tall; its flowers and seedheads are strongly tinged with the red-purple of the foliage.

And if you like 'em big, *P. purpureum* 'Prince' will fill the bill, easily reaching 4 ft. tall and half that wide. Ditto 'Princess', which has broader leaves and grows more densely than 'Prince'. I haven't observed the flowers.

Draw, pardner. Or at least sketch.

Cultural tips: The more sun, the better the color on the red-purple ones; it's not as much of an issue for *P. alopecuroides*. Poor drainage knocks them out in a hurry. Drought doesn't, but it will slow them down.

I admire plant breeders. They focus on a genus and play around with it, turning out something different. Sometimes, the new kid on the block is better than its predecessors: it blooms more freely or over a longer period, grows more compactly, shows more disease resistance, expands the color range. The other side of the coin comes up, however, when this year's model doesn't improve on the existing horde. I'm happy to report that the former is the case with *Pentas*, a genus of pleasant-enough plants with cheerful flower clusters (but with a tendency to grow tall and floppy and skimp on the blooms) that has been transformed by the release of still-pleasant plants with more of those clusters on more compact, shrubbier mounds. Or maybe you like the taller, more "wild-looking" habit of the more familiar pentas. Go for it; that's what freedom of choice is all about. You could be totally inclusive and grow both. But whichever you choose, rest assured that you will have visitors: butterflies are irresistibly drawn to pentas flowers, flying from one cluster to another, poking them excitedly with their proboscises.

Plopping flowers (or other plant parts) into a jar (or other container) will help you decide which colors (and other design elements) go with each other. Would you combine all four of these *Pentas lanceolata* selections in the same pot? Which would you omit? How about using much more of one color and "spotting in" one or more of the others?

This bowl of *Pentas* 'Graffiti Red Lace' must be wondering when the butterflies will arrive. In the meantime, the plants offer their unapologetically red flowers for our admiration. Cover the terracotta to see what happens.

The cream-variegated, red-flowered *P. lanceolata* 'Stars and Stripes' stands out from the crowd, but it needs plenty of pinching to contain its rangy ways. You'll find other older, taller pentas out there—some named, some offered only by color—so choose your own favorites. Pinch them a few times if you want them to grow more compactly, or start with the shorter California and Graffiti series (credit breeders for these), which shouldn't need more than one pinch to keep them low.

I think you'll want to grow taller pentas in combopots and the more compact ones as monopots. And please don't call one plant a "penta." It is still a pentas. You don't have a single agapanthu, cactu, or iri, do you?

Cultural tips: Pentas tolerate drought remarkably well and take full sun and heat in stride.

PERILLA
beefsteak plant, shiso (*P. frutescens*); curly perilla (var. *crispa*)

Family: Lamiaceae
Cultural group: annuals
Height: 2–3 ft.
Width: 1–1.5 ft.
Light: sun to limited partial shade
Temperature: warm to hot
Overwintering: no
Moisture: moderate to ample
Drainage of medium: well drained
Fertility: average
Ease/speed of growth: easy/moderate to fast
Propagation: seeds (*P. frutescens*), cuttings ('Magilla')
Problems: rare—maybe variability of 'Magilla'
Principal interest: foliage, fragrance
Length of seasonal interest: long

Design attributes
Color: medium green foliage, sometimes marked with or solidly red-purple (*P. frutescens*) or mixtures of green, red-violet, purple, and white ('Magilla'); flowers blue
Line: upright flower and fruit stems
Form: shrubby
Space: on edges of plants
Texture: medium

My brother John looks more like our mother; I favor our father. He's an elephant (always has been); I'm a donkey (ditto). John has kids; I have cats. Yet we are both highly competitive. We both like to travel. We love wordplay, and we both can recall all kinds of useless but entertaining information. Sound familiar? Much as two siblings can differ yet share similarities, so too can a pair of plants in the same genus. And so we come to the *Perilla* boys. *P. frutescens*, familiar to consumers of Japanese cuisine as shiso, could be described as a vigorous, shrubby annual grown for its edible, scented (variously described as cinnamon, lemon, mint, fennel, or basil) foliage. The blue flowers are more of a distraction than an attraction. It might just as easily be dismissed as a maddening weed, scattering its seeds everywhere. Those descriptions would likewise extend to its two selections, the dark maroon 'Atropurpurea' and the equally dark, sometimes iridescent var. *crispa*, with heavily cut, wildly wavy leaf margins. Despite their prolific reproductive habit, all three make excellent container plants, their foliage combining easily with their companions or standing alone in monopots, and their dead skeletons providing interest in fall. The dark-leaved selections are especially versatile, providing contrast for just about any light or bright color in your proverbial paintbox. Caveat emptor: I've seen *P. frutescens* and its kin offered for sale as basil (see *Ocimum*). Shiso might resemble basil, but I wouldn't make pesto with it.

Shiso's little brother (so to speak) has recently upstaged his sibling. Like shiso, 'Magilla' perilla quickly becomes a shrubby mass of foliage, and its blue flowers likewise won't launch a thousand ships; but unlike shiso, 'Magilla' seems sterile or is very rarely capable of setting seed, so you don't need to worry about those flowers launching a thousand seedlings, either. Like shiso, 'Magilla' can be combined or allowed to stand alone, but don't expect its list of potential companion plants to be as long as shiso's: the strident magenta of 'Magilla' (or the even showier 'Fantasy') offers a challenge to creating combopots. (Try to picture 'Magilla' with brassy gold or apricot without shuddering.) One genus that does offers likely playmates for 'Magilla' is *Solenostemon* (coleus); many coleus echo the wild foliage coloration of 'Magilla' (magenta, dark red-pink, dark purple, and medium to dark green).

Unfortunately, 'Magilla' has its dark side, too: variability. Like many coleus, 'Magilla' is genetically unstable, producing shoots that differ from the rest of the plant, and new plants propagated from those shoots will retain the different coloration, for good or ill. Sometimes the combinations are pleasing,

Pretty leaves. Pretty flowers (if you look verrrry closely). Pretty much a volunteer seedling bomb waiting to detonate, but you can easily pull out the seedlings if you don't want them. So sit back and enjoy the iridescent dark purple, cut-edged leaves of *Perilla frutescens* var. *crispa* and deal with the abundant progeny later.

A well-grown plant of 'Magilla' perilla contributes bright red-violet (OK, magenta) to the other strong (and not so strong) colors playing here. Don't you want to see what would happen if you remove the pale pink flowers of the impatiens? What if the exciting contrast with the chartreuse leaves were absent?

'Magilla' perilla is a chameleon, varying the relative amounts of the colors on the leaves, sometimes adding a color or dropping one entirely, depending on where it is growing (and sometimes on its mood). This tendency has given rise to other worthy selections, such as 'Magilla Purple', shown here.

as in its polar-opposite 'Magilla Vanilla', in light to medium green with, yes, vanilla centers. But I've seen seriously ugly, muddy-looking plants of 'Magilla' turn up. Look for good-looking specimens of 'Magilla' for sale in spring and remove any shoots that seem to be heading toward mud and gloom.

Cultural tips: Shiso can be kept quite small through starvation (don't fertilize it) and water deprivation, but 'Magilla' won't like that treatment. You won't need to pinch shiso to encourage it to branch, but a pinch or two will benefit 'Magilla'.

PETUNIA
petunia

Family: Solanaceae
Cultural group: climbers and trailers
Height: 6–12 in.
Width: 6 in. to 3 ft.
Light: sun
Temperature: warm to hot
Overwintering: min. 50°F, water occasionally, bright light
Moisture: moderate to ample
Drainage of medium: well drained

Below: Many petunia flowers look like they've been cut from a bolt of velvet or other sumptuous fabric, and their companions need to be equally saturated to stand up to their rich colors. Note, for example, how here the lighter, veined double petunias pale beside their strident red-violet, dark purple, and wine red companions.

Fertility: average to high (high phosphorus to promote
flowering)
Ease/speed of growth: easy/moderate to fast
Propagation: seeds, cuttings
Problems: aphids, whitefly, root rot, rots and spots,
rain damage
Principal interest: flowers, form, fragrance
Length of seasonal interest: long

Design attributes

Color: flowers white, red, pink, yellow, red-violet, and purple, often two or more colors in various patterns; medium green leaves
Line: from upright to cascading stems and sometimes from
star-patterned flowers
Form: carpets to waves to balls of color; trumpets and
fancy crinolines; less desirable forms look like straggly,
semi-upright, sparsely leaved ladders
Space: usually only implied (and even then hard to find in
the heavy bloomers)
Texture: medium

Our Pittsburgh-area garden almost always had petunias,
whether carried home from a nursery or self-sown volunteers. I remember being dazzled by the bright, rich colors
(some in star patterns or picotee-edged) and large, ruffled
trumpets of the fancy ones we planted. I also recall their pa-
thetic progeny: little magenta or white flowers borne on the
edges of rickety "ladders." But they all had two pleasant characteristics in common: a light, sweet-clean fragrance and the

ability to grab onto any nose that tried to inhale it. To this day,
any petunia I encounter must undergo the sniff test, for both
scent and nose-clingability. Those that pass remind me of
long-gone, soft summer nights and the erratic flight paths of
hawk moths and hummingbirds to come.

Petunia Surfinia Sky Blue (= 'Keilavbu') represents another step
closer to a truly blue petunia. Keeping it away from noticeably
purple flowers will accentuate the blue.

This seductive, overstuffed bloom of *Petunia* 'Pirouette Red'
won't stick to your nose when you sniff it, but the raspberry-
ripple coloration might stick in your mind. Double petunias
remind me of the rococo abundance of a Fragonard painting
or cancan dancers at the Moulin Rouge. How about you?

Somebody's not afraid to use color! Bright red-violet *Petunia*
'Suncatcher Pink Vein' jumps out from between the yellow-green
of the foliage behind it and the warm brown (almost orange) of
the furniture. Cover the yellow-green to see a different overall
color effect.

Today's petunias deserve a top spot on anyone's list of favorite container plants. Many have foliage that disappears under the flowers, and new trumpets or petticoats appear constantly to replace the fading ones. The plants resemble blankets or waterfalls (or an umbrella-carrying parade walking down a city street) and don't require pinching or deadheading to keep them dense and neat. Many stand up to rain instead of appearing to melt in it. Whether in a hanging basket or combopot, they keep on comin'. Super.

The only problem is trying to choose from a bewildering array of available selections (and more arrive every spring, like the swallows at Capistrano). I say if you like the color, buy it. There's always next year (gardeners always say that) if a petunia fails to live up to your expectations this year. Start your exploration with the many permutations to be found in the Wave series (look for Shock, Double, Easy, and Tidal in their names), which embraces a party full of flower colors, sizes, and forms on plants that range from low and spreading to taller and more confined. The vigorous Supertunias have impressed me, too, especially the starry 'Raspberry Blast' in very vocal shades of pink and red-violet. Many more will beguile you.

Not so long ago, a very unlikely-looking petunia was the object of a Beatlemania-like craze. *P. integrifolia* was propagated by the thousands at Atlock Farm and elsewhere, but no one could completely meet the demand for the small-flowered, black-throated magenta petunia that grew like a weed in containers and in the open ground. Everyone wanted a piece of it, but then the winds blew differently; it wasn't even propagated at Atlock in 2009. Fickle humans. But don't think that *P. integrifolia* has disappeared: its genes have been incorporated into many modern hybrids, the most pleasing of which do stick to my nose when I sniff them.

Cultural tips: Observe the Big Three for petunias, namely sun, water, and fertilizer. Older, stringier plants can be rejuvenated by cutting them back and providing the Big Three. Don't be surprised if your petunias hold on through the first frosts of fall or if volunteer seedlings come up next year.

I really like how the flower color of *Petunia* 'Shock Wave Denim' ages from dark blue purple to almost white. From a greater distance, this and other Waves do seem to undulate. Honest.

Petunia integrifolia grows like there's no tomorrow, bringing its potent color and surging lines to containers. Believe it or not, the overall effect is subtler than that of many of its Wave petunia progeny: the flowers are smaller, and more green from the foliage appears between the blooms.

PHILODENDRON
philodendron

Family: Araceae
Cultural group: tropicals, climbers and trailers
Height: 1–6 ft. or more
Width: 1–3 ft. or more (depends on type, and on training for the climbers)
Light: partial shade to shade
Temperature: warm to hot
Overwintering: min. 55°F, water occasionally, bright light
Moisture: moderate to ample
Drainage of medium: well drained (although the trailing types can remain in water)
Fertility: average
Ease/speed of growth: easy to moderate/slow to moderate to fast

Propagation: division, cuttings, air layering
Problems: mealybugs, scale insects, spider mites, root rot, rots and spots
Principal interest: form, foliage
Length of seasonal interest: all year

Design attributes

Color: foliage green, often marked or tinged with or entirely in shades of red, pink, yellow, orange, and purple
Line: from trailing stems, petioles, elongated leaves and lobing, and/or noticeable midribs
Form: trailing to cascading, open mounds, ropes of hearts or shuffling cards, flights of geese
Space: abundant to limited, depends on training
Texture: medium to coarse

If any genus deserves to become the standard bearer for houseplant liberation, it's *Philodendron*. Philodendrons don't (normally) bloom, but they offer plenty of color in addition to the other four design elements. The trailing ones grow quickly, and the shrubbier selections, while not speedy, soon become meaningfully sized additions to container plantings.

Start your campaign with that most familiar species (in look if not in name), *P. hederaceum* (aka *Pp. oxycardium* and *scandens*; heartleaf, sweetheart ivy), in sturdy, sensible medium green (often red- or bronze tinged when young). Include it wherever a string of hearts or clapping hands might bring interest to a pot, hanging basket, or windowbox. Just for fun, train a few of the stems up and into a larger companion plant instead of letting them find their normal way downward. You'll discover other vining philodendrons along the path of liberation, including *P. pedatum* (aka *P. laciniatum*), a reluctant climber with bold, deeply cut leaves that remind me of a flock of birds in flight, and the equally avian-evoking and even bolder *P. bipennifolium* (panda plant, fiddleleaf).

The fun continues with the erratically variegated hybrid 'Brasil', which appreciates some bright light or even a bit of early morning sun to keep the colors bright and abundant.

Hanging high above another member of its clan, a rollicking basket of *Philodendron* 'Brasil' brings its colorful, curvy energy to a screened porch. Note how the leaf coloration ranges from solid green to solid yellow-green, with almost as many creamy splash patterns as there are leaves in between.

The trowel-blade leaves of *Philodendron* 'Moonlight' unfurl a vibrant yellow, then progress through lively shades of yellow-green before settling into a quiet medium green. Do you see the pointed orange structures in the center of the plant (that almost exactly match the color of the pot)? They are cataphylls, leaflike sheathes that fall off the plant as their companion leaves mature. That's a new word to me, too.

Rich caramel shades of a shiny pot bring out the warmth of the yellow-green areas of the leaves of *Philodendron* 'Brasil', while the blue-gray of the base picks up on the cooler green shades. Cover the pot or the base to see for yourself, then see how everything works to produce a harmonious combination. Yes, it would be safer to eliminate the blue-gray, but why not push that envelope a little?

Watch for all-green shoots, which make a pleasant contrast to the splashed foliage but can become too much of a good thing if allowed to burgeon. Cut them out, root them (easily) in water, and enjoy the all-green abundance.

But the genus offers the strongest possibilities for the houseplant-liberation cause in its nonclimbing species and selections. I've known the broad-shouldered *P. bipinnatifidum* (aka *P. selloum*) for years, admiring its deeply cut, fishbone-like leaves on long petioles. If you have plenty of space, include one outdoors among your container plants and be prepared to hear plenty of superlatives from garden visitors.

Similar-looking but much more easily accommodated hybrid philodendrons have been introduced over the past few decades, including all-green 'Xanadu' and the breathtaking 'Xanadu Gold' in gradations of yellow and chartreuse. Other shrubby philodendrons lack the deeply cut foliage of these but make up for that in their boldly outlined, brightly or richly colored leaves, including eerily yellow-green 'Moonlight' and 'Prince of Orange', the latter unfurling in rich orange and

The outline of a large *Philodendron* 'Xanadu' echoes the ragged edge of the other circle: a solitary *P.* 'Prince of Orange' encircled by a group of 'Moonlight' philodendrons.

gradually aging through shades of bronze and dark green. 'Prince Albert' offers regal-looking, dark red leaves, and 'Red Empress' looks similar but with gently cut leaf edges. 'Pink Princess', in black-green and pink, will catch more than a few eyes.

Once your philodendrons have escaped house arrest, I hope you'll look around to find other likely subjects for liberation. The International Aroid Society, Inc. (www.aroid.org) is a great place to continue your exploration of the family.

Cultural tips: Philodendrons hate the cold; they'll be happy outside as long as night temperatures remain above 60°F. A quiet spot will help retain the high humidity they enjoy. The selections with colorful leaves can be badly damaged by pesticides, so keep a diligent watch for pests and treat them carefully. I've seen 'Xanadu' wilt to the point of flat-out collapse and recover within half an hour of being watered, but try not to let yours get to that desperate state.

PISTIA
water lettuce, shell flower (*P. stratiotes*)

Family: Araceae
Cultural group: aquatics

Height: 4–6 in.
Width: individually 4–6 in.
Light: sun to partial shade
Temperature: warm to hot
Overwintering: min. 50°F, keep in shallow water, bright light
Moisture: constant
Drainage of medium: requires standing water
Fertility: low to average (they're very thrifty)
Ease/speed of growth: easy/moderate to fast (they sneak up on you)
Propagation: division
Problems: I've never seen any
Principal interest: form
Length of seasonal interest: long

Design attributes
Color: foliage light to medium green, sometimes tinged with red or purple
Line: not immediately obvious, but movement is implied
Form: it's called water lettuce for a very good reason
Space: limited between leaves (but plants can imply a great deal of space)
Texture: medium to coarse

Is this a salad bowl of head lettuce waiting to be doused with a little balsamic vinegar and olive oil? No, it's an aquatic container filled with the rosettes of *Pistia stratiotes*. Do you see how the lines on the water lettuce's leaves echo those on the hostas?

Sometimes you need to do something conspicuously different to make people rethink their preconceived notions. Something like growing water lettuce (*P. stratiotes*) all by itself in an attractive aquatic container instead of the usual waterlily or miniature cattail. Better yet, integrate the plants and pot into the rest of your garden, as shown in the photo, then be ready to answer some questions:

Q: What is that?
A: *Pistia stratiotes*.
Q: Is there a pot of dirt I can't see?
A: No, they float on the water.
Q: Does it bloom?
A: Yes, but the flowers aren't going to jump out at you.
Q: Are they related to lettuce?
A: Nope. They're in the same family as philodendrons.
Q: Are you kidding me?
A: Would I kid you?
Q: May I play with them?
A: Knock yourself out.

Yes, play with them. Before they make a thick floating mat (which they do in bodies of water in warmer areas, where they may be considered noxious weeds), individual plants can be pushed around the surface of the water. In fact, if you swirl the water in just the right way, they might suggest the teacups ride at your favorite amusement park. They won't need a deep container; one as shallow as 8 in. will meet their needs and make them look good.

Cultural tips: The warmer the water (within reason), the faster they grow and multiply, sending out stolons to make more plants. A little water-soluble fertilizer added to the water every now and then will keep them happy if they are growing by themselves; no extra fertilizer should be needed if other potted plants share their quarters.

PLATYCERIUM
staghorn fern

Family: Polypodiaceae
Cultural group: tropicals
Height: 1–3 ft. or more
Width: 1–3 ft. or more
Light: partial shade to shade
Temperature: warm to hot
Overwintering: min. 50°F, water occasionally, bright to subdued light; hardy in Z9–11
Moisture: moderate to ample
Drainage of medium: well drained (if there's any medium at all)
Fertility: low to average

Ease/speed of growth: moderate/slow to moderate
Propagation: division, spores
Problems: scale insects, mealybugs
Principal interest: form
Length of seasonal interest: all year

Design attributes
Color: dark or silvery green and brown
Line: from lobes on fertile fronds, immediately visible, arching, reaching, cascading, flowing
Form: trophy heads, fountains, ribbons, spurting green lava
Space: abundant when young, becoming less evident with age
Texture: medium to coarse

So you won't grow staghorn ferns because you've seen them displayed at public gardens, hanging on a wall like so many moose heads in a hunting lodge. "Way too big for the likes of my garden," you say. Well, I'll bet you grow a lot of plants that could become hulking giants in time (just about any palm, many citrus, and cordylines, to name a few). So why not try a platycerium? Even single slab-mounted specimens of staghorn ferns can serve as a focal point for a wall, but let's go one step further and think about more creative ways to use something that *eventually* gets too big for you to handle. Imagine how four of them would look, their slabs joined to form a cubical "hanging basket." Two steps further: mount them on sturdy poles and stick them into the ground like you might a tiki torch (and weave hot-colored ribbons through the fern fronds to simulate fire). It's time to enjoy playing with a few staghorn ferns while they're young; deal with their size if and when they become staggeringly large.

However you display them, don't forget that they are ferns, and as such they like moisture (but can tolerate drought far better than many other ferns) and prefer not to be grown in hot, sunny spots. Like many other ferns, they produce fertile and sterile fronds; the fertile ones are the green banners (which eventually bear brown spore-bearing patches), and the sterile fronds are the shallow, bowl-like papery green things at the base that in time turn brown and build up into permanent mounds. In nature as well as in gardens, those mounds trap organic matter and water and should not be messed with. Plus, they create the head part of the mounted trophies.

Here's how to mount a small staghorn fern: start with a slab (of wood, plastic, marble, whatever strikes your fancy, but remember that you're going to need to attach a hook to it at the end of this process) about 1 in. thick and no more than 1 ft. square. Place it flat on a work surface, then put a mound of spaghnum moss the size of a softball in the center. Carefully remove the fern from its pot and place it on top of the spaghnum, then press down gently. Snugly but not too tightly wrap some twine, raffia, or fishing line around the sterile

These young stags (or fawns, if you wish) remind me of green banners flying in the wind, or a kickline of Rockettes. They're still in plastic pots filled with a very open potting mix, awaiting the day they'll be mounted onto wooden slabs or a hanging basket. In the meantime, these four little specimens of *Platycerium bifurcatum* add an informal touch to a formal setting.

fronds and the slab, then tie it off. Don't go crazy with the wrapping; a healthy staghorn fern should make more of those sterile fronds that will attach themselves to the slab before the wrapping breaks down. Finally, attach a hook or some other hanging device, and then go look for a clever place to hang your trophy.

Doubtless the most commonly grown staghorn is *P. bifurcatum* (aka *P. alcicorne*). You might find some variants, such as the selection 'Netherlands', which supposedly grows more compactly and fully. Plenty of other species, with their own variations on the trophy look, are worth searching out, such as the well-named *Pp. grande* and *superbum*, and the few- but hugely fronded *P. wandae*.

Now go find a clever way to display a few small potted specimens. Here's an idea: mount a small one on a hook and hang it off the side of a pot that contains [fill in the blank].

Cultural tips: Staghorn ferns are epiphytes. They grow on trees in the wild, so air movement up high makes them happy, and they prefer to be where rain (or water from a hose) can fall on them and be trapped in their sterile fronds. They don't require much fertilizer but will respond to it with surprisingly

It might take a little while to figure out that the pointy, bright green structures belong with the long green "horns" of *Platycerium bifurcatum*. Seen as a whole, this big staghorn fern looks like the king of the forest walking among his subjects . . . or sticking out from a trophy-hunter's wall with a bunch of other majestic heads.

rapid growth (assuming their other cultural requirements are being met).

PLECTRANTHUS
Swedish ivy

Family: Lamiaceae
Cultural group: tropicals, climbers and trailers
Height: 4 in. to 2 ft. or more
Width: 4–12 in. or more, depending on type and training
Light: sun to partial shade
Temperature: warm to hot
Overwintering: min. 55°F, water occasionally, bright light
Moisture: moderate to ample
Drainage of medium: well drained, although *P. verticillatus* can live in water for a long time
Fertility: average
Ease/speed of growth: easy/moderate to fast
Propagation: division (of rooted stems), cuttings, seeds
Problems: whitefly, spider mites, mealybugs, rots and spots

This genus offers plenty of foliar interest, and a few taxa offer the added attraction of flowers, such as *Plectranthus* Mona Lavender (= 'Plepalila') in the upper left. Reliable old *P. verticillatus* sits at the top right, and a single leaf of indispensable gray-green *P. argentatus* is at the bottom. The real multitaskers release powerful scents when their foliage is gently rubbed or brushed, including the two selections of *P. amboinicus* in the middle.

Plectranthus forsteri 'Marginatus' trails gently from its container. The paint-dipped leaf edges bring a bit of dazzle to what might otherwise be an indefensibly dull display.

Backlighting always adds excitement, transforming the potentially bland into grand. Check out the light-filled hairs on the petioles of *Plectranthus forsteri* 'Marginatus'! A walk around your garden in early morning or late evening will reveal many other light delights.

Principal interest: foliage, form, flowers, fragrance
Length of seasonal interest: long to all year

Design attributes

Color: foliage green, sometimes heavily gray-green or
     shaded with blue or purple, often marked with white,
     contrasting green, yellow, dark purple, and silver;
     flowers white, blue, red-violet, and purple
Line: mostly from upright to spreading to loosely
     cascading stems
Form: shrubby, cascading, scrambling mobs of leaves,
     depending on training
Space: generally scarce, except maybe with *P. argentatus*
     or loosely hanging ones
Texture: borderline fine to medium to coarse

Swedish ivies are the cozy afghans of the plant world, fling-ing themselves out and over the containers (or beds) they grow in, quickly bringing color and coverage to monopots and combopots. Take, for example, what is probably the most commonly grown species of them all: *P. verticillatus* (aka *P. australis*), the iron-clad resident of office cubicles, shopping malls, and dorm rooms everywhere. As plain and familiar as dirt or vanilla ice cream, it nonetheless provides a pleasant mass of green (and is another perfect standard bearer for the cause of houseplant liberation).

But most of us prefer some variety in our afghans and container plants, so let's look at some variations on the theme. Begin with *P. hadiensis*, which offers all-green, thick, scalloped, fuzzy leaves on long stems that seem to pour out of a tall container or hanging basket. *P. forsteri* 'Green on Green' has similar leaves in light and medium green on denser plants. *P. forsteri* 'Marginatus' and *P. madagascariensis* (aka *P. coleioides* 'Variegatus'; mintleaf) are very similar: both offer medium green foliage edged in white. And then there's *P. amboinicus* (Cuban oregano), which has thick leaves, heavily

As many gray-foliage plants do so very well, *Plectranthus argentatus* brokers the peace among warring strong colors and also lets similarly colored plants show off their differences (for example, in form or texture). Not surprisingly, I have an urge to cover the terracotta pot. No, wait, let's get rid of the red-violet spots in the lower left. May you experience similar cognitive dissonance when you think about your own container plantings.

Lavender, medium green, dark purple, gray, dark blue, and yellow-green: can you find them all in this photo of a potted *Plectranthus* Mona Lavender (= 'Plepalila')? Can you imagine if all the colors appeared in roughly equal amounts? Using some colors in larger quantities and others as scattered bits helps make a potentially bewildering number of colors come together attractively.

scented of mint/eucalyptus/chest rub. Plectranthus are often confused or mislabeled; my advice is to grow several of them and then root cuttings of the ones that appeal to you (or take photos of them and show them to nursery folk next year to see if *they* can identify them).

Fortunately, some plectranthus are unmistakable. One is *P. argentatus*, which offers large, soft, gray-green leaves on similarly endowed, purple-tinged stems. It grows less densely than many of its relatives, but giving it a few pinchings while still young will thicken it up (if you wish). Stop pinching as the season moves toward fall, though, which will allow the long spikes of light purple flowers to develop and bloom.

P. ciliatus won't be easily confused with others, either. Its foliage, medium to dark green on top and rich, dark purple underneath, shows off best when allowed to trail out of its container. Use it to soften the harsh orange tones of a new terracotta pot, creating a triad of the secondary colors (purple, green, and orange) in the process. Very designer-minded of you.

While a good number of the trailing plectranthus eventually flower (mostly in purple shades ranging from Barely There to Should I Care?), there's a new group of much more upright, shrubby hybrid plectranthus coming onto the scene, and I would be remiss to omit them. The first one I noticed, Mona Lavender (= 'Plepalila'), grabbed my attention with its dark green and purple leaves and abundant flowers in Look at Me lavender. It can be brought into flower while still small or be held back until the foliage mass under it is quite large (at least 2 ft. high and gently spreading out), when the entire plant can resemble a lavender-fogged thundercloud. Other cultivars, with blooms in white, red-violet, and purple, offer the same potential. Tuck a small plant into a combopot, or let three or four plants fill a large hanging basket. Wowee.

Cultural tips: Many plectranthus are quite brittle, so keep that in mind when handling them. They respond quickly and dramatically to extra dollops of fertilizer.

PLUMBAGO
Cape leadwort (*P. auriculata*)

Family: Plumbaginaceae
Cultural group: annuals, tropicals
Height: 1–4 ft., maybe more
Width: 1–3 ft.
Light: sun
Temperature: warm to hot
Overwintering: min. 50°F, water occasionally, bright light; can be chopped back and pretty much abandoned; hardy in Z9–10
Moisture: moderate to ample
Drainage of medium: well drained

Fertility: average
Ease/speed of growth: easy/moderate
Propagation: cuttings
Problems: spider mites, mealybugs
Principal interest: flowers, form (if trained)
Length of seasonal interest: long

Design attributes
Color: flowers in classic sky blue or impossibly clean white
Line: from stems, depends on training
Form: shrubby or cascading or half-heartedly climbing
Space: ample—and that blue just adds to the feeling
Texture: medium

Some plants don't need to be "sold" to customers at Atlock Farm. They sell themselves. Shredded-looking 'Butter Kutter' coleus, showy bleeding hearts (*Dicentra spectabilis*), every epimedium, yellow calibrachoas—all are happily carried off by the flat. They all have "It." And then there's *P. auriculata* (aka *P. capensis*) and its sublime f. *alba*, which is as white and

I hope *Plumbago auriculata* grows on that proverbial desert island we sometimes talk about, because I wouldn't want to be deprived of the almost sedative quality of its pure and elusive color. I'd need something to fill the hours . . .

Picture the almost blinding whiteness of *Plumbago auriculata* f. *alba* next to the pure blue of the more familiar type: cool, in two senses of the word. However, be careful when combining pure white with other darker or lighter colors: it can make them look deadly dull in comparison.

wonderful as the species is blue and beautiful. Take a look at the photographs—do you see "It" there? That clear, pure white or October-sky blue. The way the starry flowers, set perfectly against the medium green of the foliage, tumble down the gently arching stems. Aaaaaaaaah. What you can't see is the plant's dogged determination to bloom for months and its appeal to butterflies.

So do you think *P. auriculata* is a self-seller at Atlock? Not on your life. It has a little problem that makes people think more than twice about buying it: the form of the plant itself. The stems on young plants seem to go in too many directions, not all of them attractive. There's a lot of empty space contained within the plant, and the foliage is sometimes gathered into messy-looking lumps. At least I think those are the reasons for the initial resistance from customers, many of whom will go on to buy a young plant after they get one look at a larger specimen. Those larger plants have It, by George, and the hope (and perceived challenge) of transforming the squashed cabbagey leafiness of a small plant into a dazzling standard topiary in full bloom no doubt seals the deal. Not that all those young plants will become 5-ft. fountains of blue or white, cascading from a single sturdy stem; it takes work (and informed direction) to train a stem upward and then encourage it to produce a spectacular head.

Smaller plants bring It to combopots (where they will thank their companions for disguising their youthful gangliness), but larger plants need their own monopot quarters. Arrange a few by a pool, set one into a garden bed in need of a summer lift, or try your hand at producing a traffic-stopping standard topiary, set like the Hope Diamond as a focal point.

Cultural tips: Provide plenty of sun, water, and fertilizer for ample bloom, but even less well-treated plants will grow and

bloom nicely. Cut back a small plant a few times and then let it send out long, arching shoots. Don't coddle it over winter; it can be almost abandoned and will return for more in spring.

POLYGONATUM
Solomon's seal

Family: Convallariaceae/Liliaceae
Cultural group: perennials
Height: 6 in. to 3 ft., mostly
Width: 6 in. (individually) to 2–3 ft. or more
Light: (sun to) partial shade
Temperature: cool to warm
Overwintering: keep just above freezing, little water, light not necessary; variously hardy in Z3–9
Moisture: moderate to ample
Drainage of medium: well drained
Fertility: average
Ease/speed of growth: easy to moderate/slow to moderate
Propagation: division, seeds
Problems: slugs and snails, deer
Principal interest: foliage, form, flowers
Length of seasonal interest: long (except flowers, which are brief)

Design attributes
Color: foliage green, sometimes marked with white, cream, or yellow; flowers almost always white or cream (a few are pink); dark blue globular or elongated fruit, maybe
Line: from stems, linear leaves, markings, flowers
Form: arching ladders with (mostly) broad rungs, sometimes with hangers-on; those scary hanging roller coasters
Space: quite evident to scarce
Texture: medium

Plenty of hardy herbaceous perennials can be grown in containers, but Solomon's seals almost literally call out for it. A single stem looks like a ladder reaching for the stratosphere (think Jack and the Beanstalk, but less prosaically), while a clump of them reminds me of a flock of birds suddenly disturbed into flight. A ladder or two in a combopot provides irresistible lines to draw the eye, and that flock of birds rising from a monopot can make an unusual specimen or focal point.

You'll need to wait for the flock to take shape, however, because most members of the genus take their sweet time building up from a shoot or two to a large, thick clump. They're not fussy, though; a sparsely stemmed plant can grace a combopot for a few years (or even be reduced every year to individual stems) and then in time be moved to solitary quarters to assume stately maturity. I speak from experience: my 14-in. pot of *P. odoratum* var. *pluriflorum* 'Variegatum' (there's a mouthful of a moniker) began as a little division and now sends up dozens of shoots every year.

Although you will enjoy the flowers for the short time they are present, precisely marching their way up the stems (and with luck, they will become beadlike black fruit), you must choose and celebrate these plants for their foliage and overall form. But which ones? While the low-growing species (such as *P. humile*) or the tiny ones (such as the exquisite, pink-flowered *P. hookeri*) can look spot-on perfect in a woodland or rock garden, they seem lost in any but a small pot. I suggest you try any of the larger-growing species (*Pp. biflorum, falcatum, ×hybridum, multiflorum, odoratum,* or *verticillatum*), all offering variations on the ladder or flock-of-birds theme. Watchful eyes and skillful hands have led to the availability of some variegated selections, especially of *P. odoratum,* that look like masterfully painted silk wall hangings come to life. Look for them, dig deeply into your pockets, grow them lov-

Usually woodlanders, Solomon's seals (here, *Polygonatum odoratum* var. *pluriflorum* 'Variegatum') take very well to container gardening. As with many hardy herbaceous perennials, the flowers are ephemeral, so keep that in mind as you combine them with other plants.

ingly in a container, and dole out a few divisions to your best gardening buddies.

Cultural tips: Since they can remain in the pot for a long time, provide a good-quality potting mix containing plenty of ground bark, coconut fiber, and other coarse-textured organic matter. Regular doses of nitrogenous fertilizer will speed them along. Give them a long, cold winter in a protected spot; they are hardy herbaceous perennials, after all.

RHIPSALIS
mistletoe cactus

Family: Cactaceae
Cultural group: succulents
Height: 1–3 ft. or more
Width: 6 in. to 2 ft. or more, depends on training
Light: partial shade (*not* full sun, like for most cacti)
Temperature: warm to hot
Overwintering: min. 50°F, water sparingly, bright light
Moisture: on dry side to moderate
Drainage of medium: well drained
Fertility: average
Ease/speed of growth: easy/moderate
Propagation: cuttings, seeds
Problems: mealybugs, scale insects, rots and spots
Principal interest: form, sometimes flowers and fruit
Length of seasonal interest: all year (form); variable (flowers and fruit)

Design attributes
Color: stems in light and medium green, sometimes bluish; flowers mostly white or pale green; fruit white, some red or pink-tinted
Line: these plants *are* lines, except for the flowers and fruit
Form: waterfalls, wigs
Space: from abundant to basically absent
Texture: fine

Mistletoe cacti are oddballs. No thick, globular, spine-covered "classic" cacti here. Also, they don't occur naturally in hot, dry deserts but instead in much moister, forested regions, where they quite literally hang out in trees and on rocks (like their epiphytic cousins, the holiday cacti of *Hatiora* [aka *Rhipsalidopsis*] and *Schlumbergera*). As far as we can tell, *Rhipsalis* contains the only species of the cactus family possibly native to the Old World, *R. baccifera* (which is also a widely distributed resident of tropical areas in the New World). But if you look closely at a mistletoe cactus, you'll find multi-petaled, stamen-filled flowers that look like reduced versions of the larger, showier blooms of their relatives, and many have little spines, just as you'd expect from a cactus. The little, white (sometimes pink or red), mistletoe-like berries (hence the common name) are smaller versions of bigger cactus fruits, and many persist for months.

Neat, huh? All the aforementioned facts are nifty little tidbits to toss into gardening conversation, but the most fun comes from watching a mistletoe cactus progress from a few lines to a small rush of water to a spaghetti mop and finally into a green version of Cousin Itt (from the Addams Family, not the cactus family). Take advantage of a small plant's extreme linearity in combopots, and then move it into a pot or hanging basket of its own as it slowly but steadily becomes a major conversation piece (automatically providing an opportunity to use those tidbits of information).

Some of the more commonly encountered species include *Rr. baccifera* and *floccosa*, with thicker, less abundant stems than some of the others, and the much finer-looking *capilliformis* and *pilocarpa*. All look like they've been quickly sketched with a green pencil or crayon.

Being epiphytes, they want the conditions they'd receive in their native habitats, up in trees and on rocks, so give them a very well-drained potting mix that holds onto frequent splashes of water for just a little while. Barad mix, named for cactus superstar Dr. Gerald Barad, fills the bill very nicely. It's made up of equal parts coarse organic potting mix (one that contains plenty of bark, coconut fiber, and other chunky or fibrous plant remains) and porous mineral matter, such as pumice, turface (similar to cat litter but more highly fired to make it last longer), diatomite, or heat-expanded shale. Though I've seen it happen, don't expect a mistletoe cactus to thrive in garden soil, peat-rich potting mix, or sphagnum moss.

Cultural tips: Try to remember that these are cacti with both "normal" cactuslike and non-cactuslike qualities and cultural needs. They root easily from pieces of stem inserted into their potting mix.

Green spaghetti (or seaweed, or a shower of sparks) pours out of a whimsical pot. Many rhipsalis can be reduced to green lines, pure and simple. Simply beautiful. By the way, this mistletoe cactus trails no more than 3 ft. downward but is at least twenty years old.

RHOEO
Moses in the bullrushes, cradle, or basket (he gets around); oyster plant

---

Family: Commelinaceae
Cultural group: tropicals
Height: 6–8 in., maybe more (but might be a result of too little light)
Width: 6–8 in. (more if allowed to clump)
Light: partial shade
Temperature: warm to hot
Overwintering: min. 55°F, water occasionally, bright light
Moisture: moderate to ample
Drainage of medium: well drained but tolerates shallow standing water
Fertility: average
Ease/speed of growth: easy/moderate to fast
Propagation: offsets
Problems: slugs and snails
Principal interest: foliage, form
Length of seasonal interest: all year

Design attributes
Color: foliage striped white and green with red-violet tinges, undersides more heavily (to predominantly) red-violet
Line: elongated leaves, accentuated by linear striping
Form: exploding rosette
Space: abundant when young and at edges, progressively less as offsets enlarge
Texture: medium

"What's in a name? That which we call a rose / By any other name would smell as sweet" (*Romeo and Juliet*, Act 2, Scene 2). For me, trying to figure out the correct name

It's hard to contain the chromatic and linear oomph of 'Tricolor' rhoeo, unless you step several feet back from it. Then it becomes an eerily glowing, disembodied specter, especially if backlit.

The raggedly circular, kinetic outline and striped foliage of an established cluster of 'Tricolor' rhoeo makes an eye-catching focal point. This specimen was soon after split up into almost two dozen individual plants, all of which became clusters of similarly lively rosettes in less than a year.

for a particular plant in this genus (or *is* it in this genus?) has become a bit of a drama. Some sources consider 'Tricolor' a selection of *R. bermudensis*; others claim it should be referred to as *R. spathacea* 'Nana Variegata'. Still others accept the *spathacea* part of the name but include it in the genus *Tradescantia*, as *T. spathacea* 'Vittata'. Talk about an identity crisis! At least we can all agree there are three colors involved.

Whichever its correct name, this beauty makes a sweet container plant, that's for sure. Not only is the combination of green, white, and light red-violet unusual and refreshing, but the elongated leaves and multiple rosettes create the impression of bustling activity. It doesn't take long for a single rosette to become a crowd in a small pot. A smallish cluster adds an exclamation point to a combopot (especially when combined with mostly green companions that let the rhoeo stand out), and a specimen-sized monopot of many rosettes can create a focal point on a table or among a group of other potted plants.

Cultural tips: This is easy and undemanding, but do keep it out of strong sunlight and make sure it stays moist. Its trailing cousins (or are they siblings?) in the genus *Tradescantia* prefer similar cultural conditions.

ROSA
rose

Family: Rosaceae
Cultural group: woody shrubs and trees
Height: 6 in. to 2 ft. or more
Width: 6 in. to 2 ft. or more
Light: sun to partial shade
Temperature: warm to hot
Overwintering: keep totally dormant at just above freezing, very little to no water, light not necessary; variously hardy in Z3–10; most container types Z7–9, with protection to Z6
Moisture: moderate to ample
Drainage of medium: well drained
Fertility: average to high (to push bloom)
Ease/speed of growth: easy to moderate/moderate
Propagation: cuttings, grafting, seeds (rarely)
Problems: aphids, spider mites, Japanese beetles, rose chafers, caterpillars, cane borers, thrips, rose slugs, deer, blackspot, powdery mildew, rust, viruses, crown gall, canker, dieback, cold damage, suckering
Principal interest: flowers, form (spreader-hangers and standards), fragrance (don't get your hopes up—they don't all smell like a rose)
Length of seasonal interest: long but sometimes intermittent (flowers)

Design attributes

Color: flowers in white, red, pink, orange, yellow, and
  red-violet
Line: noticeable in spreader-hangers and standards
Form: shrubby to carpeting to cascading to climbing;
  depends on training
Space: practically absent to abundant, depending on
  training; can also be implied by and between flowers
Texture: fine to medium

D on't put on your rose-colored glasses when contemplating growing roses in containers, but don't dismiss the
idea, either. Their often very long bloom season and wide
color range make them worth a try. So does their power to
conjure up a lifetime of memories and cultural references. Valentine's Day. June weddings. Any wedding. Birthdays and an-
niversaries. Potpourri. Rosewater. Rose windows. "Rosebud."
"Lo, how a rose e'er blooming." Get the picture? Of course you

Opposite: Shades of yellow (including that contributed by
another member of the Flower Carpet series) and yellow-green
subtly contrast with the coolly colored stone wall and birdbath
in the background. The simple, dark brown pot and gray birdbath encourage your eye to stop and rest in an otherwise
active, detail-filled setting.

do. Our lives are permeated with the sight and scent and imagery of roses. Lucky us.

But then there's the other side of roses, which anyone who
has ever grown them knows too well. They are often beset
with thorns, bugs, diseases, and other baggage—pick one
from column A and one from column B. If you limit your use
of pesticides (or eschew them entirely), many modern (and
some of the older) roses are off limits unless you can bear to
watch the bad guys occasionally turn your roses into shreds,
holes, and spots. Stay away from the huge shrub roses and
far-reaching climbers unless you garden on a very grand

Yes, roses can be grown quite successfully in containers (but
you need to bone up on your rose culture first). A pale pink
member of the Flower Carpet series floats between the lime
green of the plants at its feet and the backlit foliage above it,
and the gray pot adds to the light, airy feeling. What would a
dark pot do for this garden scene?

A strong pink selection from the Flower Carpet series of
groundcover roses stands up to the strong purple of the spiky
salvia and groundhugging yellow-green sedum nearby. The
brown-gray pot and muted brick walk offer some quiet among
the noisier colors.

scale. What's left, you ask? Plenty: miniature roses, patio roses, Flower Carpet roses, maybe even the revolutionary Knockout series, and standard (topiary) roses, all of which bloom repeatedly without asking for too much extra or special care. Some are remarkably resistant to pests and diseases. All can be kept quite small to reasonably contained, but some will require chemical attention to keep them at their best.

Miniature roses bear small flowers, sometimes on anything but miniature-sized plants, so caveat emptor. Many do, however, bloom on satisfyingly small plants to 2 ft. or less. Even the ones that get large (including some of the climbers) can be managed with pruning shears, so give them a try. Keep the pesticides handy if you want blemish-free plants. Surprisingly, their generally small stature and thin stems belie their hardiness: they often stand up to cold Z6 winters (without protection) and other adversity. Like their larger cousins (the hybrid teas, floribundas, and other groups), new selections appear on the market every year, so I suggest you do a little research, beginning with the American Rose Society and continuing online, in catalogs, and at local nurseries.

Patio roses are generally larger than the miniatures in flower and plant size but not as large as floribundas. Like miniatures, they often require chemical attention to lessen damage from disease. It seems to me that these are about as hardy as hybrid teas and floribundas, which means winter protection (indoors) will be required in Z6 and colder.

The Flower Carpet series can reach 3 ft. in both directions; they don't create a flat carpet, as the name might suggest. Disease often leaves their foliage alone or nearly so. Their introducer says they are hardy in Z5–10 (in the ground), so container-grown plants will benefit from winter protection in Z5 and colder.

The Knockout series will reach 4 ft. in both directions, but they are tough as nails and can be cut back severely to keep them in bounds in a container. Like the Flower Carpets, they laugh at disease and cold (but protect them in Z5 and colder).

If you like a challenge (and the rewards that come along with a tree covered with roses), try maintaining a hybrid tea or floribunda standard topiary in a pot. Be prepared to attend to their pruning and disease-management needs, and make sure to provide a sturdy stake. Some might require winter protection in Z7; all will require it in colder areas.

Cultural tips: Most roses are hungry and thirsty. Japanese beetles and other insects will devour just about any rose flower, so prepare yourself for them. Chemicals will kill the beasts, but so will knocking the larger ones into a jar of soapy water.

ROSMARINUS
rosemary (*R. officinalis*)

Family: Lamiaceae
Cultural group: woody shrubs and trees
Height: 6 in. to 3 ft. or more
Width: 6 in. to 2 ft.
Light: sun
Temperature: cool to warm to hot
Overwintering: min. 45°F, water occasionally, bright light or sun, and keep the air moving (to combat mildew); hardy in Z8–10 (except 'Arp' and 'Salem' to Z7)
Moisture: on dry side to moderate
Drainage of medium: well drained
Fertility: low to average
Ease/speed of growth: easy to moderate/moderate
Propagation: cuttings, seeds (rarely)
Problems: mealybugs, powdery mildew, rots and spots
Principal interest: foliage, fragrance, form, flowers
Length of seasonal interest: all year (flowers brief; sometimes repeat)

Design attributes
Color: dark green foliage, occasionally marked yellow; flowers blue, rarely pink or white
Line: stems upright to arching to cascading, needle-like leaves
Form: shrubby to cascading, depends on training
Space: basically nonexistent in older shrubby plants, can be very noticeable in cascading forms
Texture: fine to medium

Though I certainly tasted and smelled rosemary in Italian food as a kid, I don't remember the first time I saw a rosemary plant or a sprig of it. Now I cannot pass a specimen without touching it to release its scent. That clean, sharp pine-lemon fragrance ranks right up there with chocolate chip cookies, baking bread, and heliotrope on my Top Ten Sniff List. I've also learned to enjoy the flavor in roast lamb and chicken and still savor it in marinara and other sauces.

But you aren't required to appreciate the fragrance or taste of rosemary to enjoy the look of it in a container. The dense, dark "needles" and sturdy branches suggest a shrubby, upright, or weeping pine tree or other conifer; in fact, you might want to grow a rosemary as a "bonsai" that won't require the pruning and training for producing an authentic bonsai. Blue (sometimes pink or white) flowers add to the appeal, especially toward the end of winter. Add a smallish plant to a combopot herb planting or any other sun-loving group; your senses will thank you. But be prepared to move it into a pot all by itself as it grows (assuming you can overwinter it).

I've never met a rosemary I didn't like, and there are a bunch of them. 'Arp' and 'Salem' are referred to as the "hardy" rosemaries, often pulling through winters in Z7; both are best described as bushy. Upright forms include 'Fastigiatus', 'Miss Jessopp's Upright', and 'Pyramidalis', among others; a group or row of them makes a strong statement anywhere. Several selections offer rich blue flowers, including 'Benenden Blue' (aka 'Collingwood Ingram') and 'Logee's Blue' (which reputedly resists powdery mildew better than many others).

My favorites, however, are the weeping, creeping, active-looking prostrate forms, such as 'Lockwood de Forest' and 'Prostratus' (of which there are multiple forms all traveling under this name, I'm willing to wager). No two plants look the same, but they all look like they're twisting and shaking as I watch them.

Cultural tips: Being Mediterranean, rosemary can handle strong sun and poor, dry soil; some think the fragrant oils are more abundant in stressed plants. Maybe. When overwinter-

Left: The sinuous green arms (tentacles?) of *Rosmarinus officinalis* 'Lockwood de Forest' reach well beyond the confines of their container. Note how the simple pot lets the plant show off its one-of-a-kind form (and lets your imagination kick in).

Below: The frenetic needles of a trailing rosemary compete for attention with the parachuting, conelike inflorescences of an ornamental oregano (*Origanum* 'Kent Beauty'), while the delicate little leaves and insect-like flowers of a pelargonium rise above the fray.

ing rosemary, provide the sunniest spot you can and try to keep the air moving; otherwise, powdery mildew will probably develop. A bad case will kill your plant, as will poor drainage at any time of year.

RUTA
rue, herb of grace (*R. graveolens*)

Family: Rutaceae
Cultural group: woody shrubs and trees
Height: 1–2 ft., maybe to 3 ft.
Width: 1–2 ft.
Light: sun to partial shade
Temperature: warm to hot
Overwintering: min. 45°F, water occasionally, bright light; or keep totally dormant at just above freezing, very little to no water, light not necessary; hardy in Z5–9
Moisture: on dry side to moderate
Drainage of medium: well drained
Fertility: low to average
Ease/speed of growth: easy/moderate
Propagation: seeds, cuttings
Problems: photodermatitis (a potentially big problem for you, not the plant)
Principal interest: foliage, flowers, fragrance
Length of seasonal interest: long (foliage); moderate (flowers)

Design attributes
Color: foliage grayish blue-green (marked with pale cream in 'Variegata'); flowers yellow
Line: stems, rachises, and elongated leaflets
Form: shrubby
Space: progressively less as plant bulks up
Texture: fine to medium

I really like the look of rue. The bloomy blue-gray-green, maidenhair-ferny foliage and yellow flowers complement each other beautifully, and its shrubby habit creates an impression of healthy, carefree exuberance. Beneficial (and good-looking) insects like it as well. As a subject for container gardening, rue combines very pleasantly with many other plants, and its sharp, dense scent (sometimes described as bitter, acrid, or pungent) pleases my nose, too.

So pretty. So beguiling. And so very dangerous, I'm rueful to relate. Once upon a time, in a backyard in New Jersey, an initially small rue became a big, handsome bush, seeding freely. So one hot, sunny, humid summer day I decided to pull most of the seedlings and chop the parent plant back. There was so much stem and leaf mass that I ended up carrying a few big armloads back to the compost pile. A few hours later,

my forearms had developed a bright pink-red rash, and it felt like a voodoo priestess was sticking a thousand little pins in me. The next day the rash was angry red, blistering, and intensely itchy. Long story short, I had offered textbook conditions for rue-caused phytophotodermatitis: oil (actually a complex mixture of several aromatic hydrocarbons) from the leaves readily entered my pores, opened wide by that hot, sunny, humid summer day, igniting an allergic reaction that made every case (a big number) of poison ivy I've ever had pale in comparison.

I view rue differently now, but I still garden with it, *very* cautiously. Cloudy, cool days allow me to pot it, trim it, and do whatever else I need to do, but on sunny, warm to hot days I shrink from rue like a vampire flees from sunlight. Unless you know for a fact that you do not react to rue, I suggest you do the same.

Also worth trying are the lower-growing, bloomier-leaved 'Jackman's Blue' and the randomly pale cream-splashed 'Variegata'. References like to point out that it is one of the few variegated plants that can be dependably propagated from seed.

The denser the plant of *Ruta graveolens*, the less you will notice the intricate, lacelike construction of the foliage. Don't be afraid to thin out some stems and even leaves if your rue has become a thick, solid mass (but see the text for a cautionary tale).

Cultural tips: A dry, sunny spot encourages more compact growth, more richly colored foliage … and probably a higher oil content in the leaves.

SAGINA
pearlwort, Irish moss, Scotch moss (*S. subulata*)

Family: Caryophyllaceae
Cultural group: perennials
Height: 1–2 in., give or take
Width: 6–8 in.
Light: sun to partial shade
Temperature: cool to warm
Overwintering: min. 40°F, water occasionally, bright light; hardy in Z4–7
Moisture: moderate
Drainage of medium: well drained
Fertility: low to average
Ease/speed of growth: moderate/moderate

Propagation: division
Problems: spider mites
Principal interest: foliage, form, flowers
Length of seasonal interest: long (flowers brief)

Design attributes
Color: medium green leaves, chartreuse in 'Aurea'; white flowers
Line: none from a distance, zillions of them up close
Form: a tuft, a mat, a carpet, a strip(e), a flow—you can almost paint (or sculpt) with this
Space: none, although 'Aurea' can give the impression
Texture: fine up close, none from a relatively short distance

Quite a few relatively low-growing plants serve usefully as groundcovers (or carpets, if you will) in a container, but only a few appear flat enough to approach "paint." Pearlwort (*Sagina subulata*) provides an opportunity to think of plants and container gardening in near-abstract terms; instead of focusing on leaves, flowers, stems, and such, you can reduce

Color echoes link a cleverly planted garden ornament (we can't call this tour de force a pot, can we?) to its setting. Green *Sagina subulata* picks up on the green foliage to the left, while chartreuse *S. s.* 'Aurea' exactly repeats the foliage to the right. The grassy foliage in front adds a bit of variety. Kudos for the corner-forward placement relative to the wall!

them to flat planes of color. Long, thin plantings become lines in the width you choose. Forms might include precisely regular circles (easily achieved by growing low round pots of pearlwort) or squares (in square pots) or free-form pieces that suggest Matisse's cutouts. While space is nonexistent in a single clump of pearlwort, it can be implied by setting a bit of it against more brightly or darkly hued plants (in the tour de force photo, the light and dark versions create the illusion of space). Up close, pearlwort's texture ranks among the finest of them all (a zillion tiny leaves will do that), but from even a small distance, fine transforms into very coarse as the little bits merge into a solid mass. While most of pearlwort's design elements might not be immediately obvious, a little abstract thinking will reveal them.

As far as I'm concerned, we have two pearlworts from which to choose: green *S. subulata* and its yellow-green selection 'Aurea'. Both lighten up a little when the tiny white flowers appear. Grow some pearlworts in a monopot and place them where they look their best, or match a few up with simpatico plants in a combopot. Other plants to paint with include *Dichondra argentea*, baby's tears (*Soleirolia*), and thyme

(*Thymus*). More will reveal themselves as you poke around gardens and nurseries, believe me, especially when you start looking at plants in terms of their design elements and not simply as plants. (The lecture on painting as part of container gardening is now concluded, class.)

Cultural tips: Pearlworts can grow in very shallow pots (barely 2 in. deep), but make sure they don't sit in water. Grow big pots of both colors and then cut them apart to create your abstract designs.

SALVIA
sage

Family: Lamiaceae
Cultural group: annuals, perennials, woody shrubs and trees
Height: 6 in. to 6 ft.
Width: 6 in. to 3 ft. or more
Light: sun to limited partial shade
Temperature: warm to hot
Overwintering: min. 55°F, water occasionally, bright light;

"Pearlwort" derives from the tiny white flowers that spangle the foliage (here on *Sagina subulata* 'Aurea'). The tiny brown balloons in the upper right are the capsules (spore-bearing structures) of a moss, which should give you an idea of the minuscule scale of the individual parts.

See me, feel me, touch me, heal you? While the gray-green, soft-fuzzy rosette of *Salvia argentea* compels sensory engagement, silver sage probably won't do much to help a medical condition, as others in the genus might (the generic name derives from the Latin *salvere*, "to save" or "to heal").

perennials variously hardy in Z5–10, shrubs (such as
  S. officinalis) in Z5–10

Moisture: moderate to ample

Drainage of medium: well drained (especially for
  S. argentea)

Fertility: low to average to high

Ease/speed of growth: easy to moderate/slow to moderate
  to fast

Propagation: division, seeds, cuttings

Problems: whitefly, aphids, mealybugs, spider mites,
  rots and spots

Principal interest: flowers (sometimes principally bracts),
  foliage, fragrance; attracts wildlife

Length of seasonal interest: brief to long (flowers); long
  (foliage and fragrance)

Design attributes

Color: flowers in all colors, yellow and orange being less
  common; foliage green, sometimes marked with white,
  yellow, or red-violet or entirely shaded with yellow,
  purple, or gray

Here's my case for a sensible approach to insects eating our garden plants: if the damage is slight (can you spot the damage here on the flowers of Salvia 'Hot Lips'?), let 'em live. Birds and other critters might like their own opportunity to decide those bugs' fates.

Line: from stems, elongated leaves, flower stems and
  clusters, and flowers

Form: shrubby (mostly), a few low-mounded to spreading,
  and one notable, informal rosette (S. argentea)

Space: from abundant (around flower stems and flowers)
  to nearly absent

Texture: medium to coarse

My early encounters with Salvia involved two senses: sight (S. splendens burned brightly in the patio garden at Grandma Rogers's apartment building) and taste (the strongly flavored wads of turkey stuffing served up at my grade school—there was no culinary sage at our house). "Colorful and tasty" could be used as a terse description of the genus, but that would oversimplify salvias, at best. Some of the tasty sages also please the eye, and others' leaves might also feel soothing when being rubbed to release their scent. Let's look at a small semi-alphabetical sample of species; I'll mention their most obvious or familiar sensory stimulator first, followed by any others.

S. argentea (silver sage) feels and looks like a nest of chinchillas. It's not small, spreading to 2 ft. or so when fully grown, but the touch and sight of it justify the space taken. I strongly suggest you remove the flower spike before it reaches 1 ft.; otherwise, it will become a gawky mess of white flowers. Also, a timely floralectomy often gives this biennial the chance to become a short-lived perennial. Z5–8.

The flowers of annual Texas sage, S. coccinea, come in a range of reds and pinks as well as white. Most grow about 2 ft. tall. 'Lady in Red' was everywhere some years ago, and 'Coral Nymph' (in white and pink) has been grabbing the spotlight lately. Annual, but they can reseed.

Many sages grow quite large (3–4 ft. and up, mostly) and bloom late, including ember-colored Ss. confertiflora, leucantha (in combinations of purple and white), and yellow madrensis (forsythia sage). For much of the season they will look like big green shrubs, but the late flowers add interest before frost knocks them down. For large containers only. Figure Z9–11.

S. discolor offers the extremely scarce color combination of gray-green leaves and near-black flowers, and its open, lax habit adds diversity to combopots. Figure a container-grown plant to reach 1–2 ft. high by 2–3 ft. wide in its first year unless cut back, but doing that will retard or eliminate those black flowers. Z9–10.

Deliciously scented and softly hairy S. dorisiana (fruit-scented sage) smells like fruit, of course, but which one(s) depends on your nose. Some smell peaches, while others detect fruit cocktail or no specific fruit at all. It easily grows to 3 ft. tall and wide if you let it. The red-violet flowers scream for attention. Z10–11.

Most people immediately pick up on the scent of S. elegans (pineapple sage). 'Golden Delicious' recalls the coloration of the apple by the same name as well as the scent of pineapple. Both produce small spikes of brilliant red flowers late in the season on plants easily reaching 3 ft. tall and almost as wide. Z8–10.

S. farinacea (mealycup sage) is usually seen in the open garden (often in big beds, in public gardens), where it produces its flower spikes in white and shades of blue for months. It does the same thing in containers, so try a few of them. 'Victoria' and 'Blue Bedder' are the old dark purple-blue reliables, and the newer 'Strata' looks cool in gray-white with dabs of blue. Most grow to about 2 ft. tall but not that wide. Annual, usually, but I've seen them overwinter in Z6.

You might want to try selections of the so-called hardy perennial sages (such as *Ss. nemorosa*, ×*sylvestris*, and ×*superba*) in containers. Most produce admittedly showy purple or blue flowers for a while but leave unimpressive lumps of foliage behind. They're not known for their fragrance, but you'll detect it when you remove the faded flowers. Grow them as

The foliage of culinary sage, *Salvia officinalis*, and its selections offers a palatable palette of color and form. 'Purpurea' is at the left, the large 'Berggarten' dominates the bottom, two narrow leaves of the species move from Northwest to Southeast, 'Tricolor' is at the right, and 'Icterina' floats at the top.

Apparently phosphorescent, *Salvia elegans* 'Golden Delicious' glows against a nearly black container (brighter colors would suppress the glow). Were you to grow this selection of pineapple sage, you'd be able to rub the foliage to release its fruity scent and later enjoy the vibrant red flower clusters.

A little plant of *Salvia officinalis* 'Aurea' holds its own among the moss and pansy foliage, but in a couple of years it should become an impressive, animated mound. Seen from a distance, the individually patterned leaves appear as a yellow-green mass.

'Red Hot Sally' and many other selections of *Salvia splendens* (scarlet sage) light fires wherever they go. Speaking of "go," — notice how the plants grow in separate pots, so they could be removed to another container if the spirit moved. That's one of the best features of container gardening: if you're not happy with a container planting (or it with you), relocate one, some, or all of the plants, or move the entire production to another spot.

Not all selections of *Salvia splendens* set fires solely with their flowers. However, if you picture the yellow-splashed foliage of 'Dancing Flame' with the typical inflorescences of scarlet sage, you'll have a conflagration on your (figurative) hands.

monopots for display while in bloom, but be prepared to hide them when not. Most reach 2–2.5 ft. tall in bloom. Z5–9.

Please do not confine uniquely scented (and tasty) *S. officinalis* (culinary sage) to the herb garden or herb-only container. Why deny yourself the opportunity of working with such beautifully colorful leaves? Every one of them is willing and able to combine with a wide range of companion plants, and they all can end up in stuffing and other tasty edibles. First-year plants won't reach 1 ft. tall and wide, but older ones can triple those dimensions. Frequent trimming (or chopping) back will keep them dense. Z5–8.

Finally we come to the familiar and too-often-maligned scarlet sage, *S. splendens*. Yes, the flowers on some of them might offend certain retinas and sensibilities, and you won't grow them for their scent, taste, or tactile interest, but if you're looking for a mass of long-lasting, easily grown, fiery color in a container, these will meet your needs. Over the years, many selections have come and gone, with chromatically obvious names such as 'Blaze of Fire', 'Bonfire', 'Flare', 'Lighthouse', 'Red Hot Sally', 'Sahara Red', 'Scarlet King', and 'St. John's Fire'. However, if you like the look of a scarlet sage plant but wish for less strident flower colors, your wish has come true. Look for the Firecracker, Hotline, and Sizzler series in near-white, red, pink, orange, blue, and purple. All grow 1–2.5 ft. tall and about as wide. Just for fun try 'Dancing Flame', a larger (to 3 ft. tall and wide), more open grower with less abundant red flowers and yellow-splashed leaves. Annual.

Virtually all salvias attract butterflies and hummingbirds that, with their humming and chirping, bring the fifth sense—sound—to your garden. So with a little careful selection, the genus *Salvia* can delight all five of your senses. Big time.

Cultural tips: Most salvias detest poor drainage but wilt quickly, too, so pay attention to their demands for water. Many blacken with the first frost; protect the late bloomers if you want to have a chance to enjoy the flowers. Sparingly fertilize culinary sage for denser plants.

SANSEVIERIA
devil's tongue, snake plant

Family: Dracaenaceae/Liliaceae
Cultural group: succulents
Height: 6 in. to 3 ft.
Width: 6 in. to 2 ft.
Light: sun to partial shade
Temperature: warm to hot
Overwintering: min. 50°F, water occasionally and sparingly, bright light
Moisture: on dry side to moderate
Drainage of medium: well drained

Fertility: low to average
Ease/speed of growth: easy to moderate/slow to moderate
Propagation: division, leaf cuttings
Problems: mealybugs, spider mites
Principal interest: form, foliage
Length of seasonal interest: all year

Design attributes

Color: foliage green, often marked with white, yellow,
  or silver
Line: immediately obvious to less so (in rosette forms),
  markings add to linear effect
Form: rosettes, paddles, fans, straps, flames, swords
Space: limited to abundant
Texture: medium to coarse

We've all seen plenty of sansevierias, most likely the mostly green *S. trifasciata* (mother-in-law's tongue) or its elaborately variegated selection 'Laurentii', in barbershop (and other) windows, as well as in various indoor settings. They show remarkable tolerance for less than optimal conditions, keeping many a plant body and soul together in low light (as well as intense sun), Saharan water levels, and comically undersized pots. This begs the question: why are plants that withstand so much adversity so infrequently seen in outdoor container plantings? Even a good-sized snake plant won't set you back much these days; I've seen big sheaves of them offered for about ten dollars at box stores. On a suburban patio, as part of an urban rooftop garden—whatever the setting, their elongated form creates an irresistible focal point. Grow them by themselves or contrast them with other like-minded but differently colored and shaped succulents in combopots. "They're too common," you say. Hmm. Are there any geraniums or impatiens or coleus in your pots? I rest my case.

Sansevieria contains dozens of species and many selections, but most are rarely encountered, except in the collections of succulent enthusiasts. Try these:

S. cylindrica will take the abuse just described, but it looks

The active striping of a big clump of *Sansevieria trifasciata* 'Laurentii' grabs and holds attention for a while before the eye moves on to other (less compelling) elements of the composition.

What a difference a setting makes: this might be a quiet spot at the Taj Mahal, but it's actually an elegant marble niche at Longwood Gardens. The lines of *Sansevieria trifasciata* 'Laurentii' (present in two different expressions of variegation) echo the sides of the niche and the vertical peek of a clump of bamboo.

far from mundane. Some see fans or coral in its form; I see the long brass "fingers" of Thai dancers or maybe the sparse but confident courtship display of a little green peacock. Plants take a while to reach 2 ft. high and wide and much longer to reach double that.

S. trifasciata contains the familiar mother-in-law's tongues in various heights and color combinations, including (besides 'Laurentii') 'Black Coral' (dark green with pale green horizontal banding) and 'Moonglow' (mostly light green). Other selections of *S. trifasciata* look more like birds' nests than tongues or snakes; these include 'Hahnii' (shades of green), 'Golden Hahnii' (green with yellow edges), and 'Silver Hahnii' (dark green with silver-white crossbandings).

Cultural tips: Taller snake plants become top-heavy with age, so avoid shallow pots (and stakes, which look ridiculous with sansevierias) and consider placing the pot inside another one (or within a marble niche) for more stability. If you do find a small plant of an unusual one, grab it, and be patient: many are slow growing, to say the least.

SCAEVOLA
fan flower (*S. aemula*)

Family: Goodeniaceae
Cultural group: annuals
Height: 1–2 ft.
Width: depends on training
Light: sun to partial shade
Temperature: warm to hot
Overwintering: not usually, but try min. 55°F, water occasionally, bright light
Moisture: moderate to ample
Drainage of medium: well drained
Fertility: average (although a little extra effort really pays dividends)
Ease/speed of growth: easy/moderate
Propagation: seeds, cuttings
Problems: aphids, root rot

The terete (cylindrical, hence the specific epithet) foliage of *Sansevieria cylindrica* fans out gracefully against the dark backround. How would this peacock look against a green backdrop?

Do you see the long, curving lines at the bottom of the mass of this blue *Scaevola aemula* selection? They are elongated flower stems that have borne many flowers, and they show no signs of stopping.

Principal interest: flowers, form

Length of seasonal interest: long (among the longest of all annuals)

Design attributes

Color: flowers white and blue; foliage medium to dark green

Line: from stems and pointy flowers in fans

Form: spreading-carpeting to cascading; flowers insect- or bird-like

Space: depends on training (also suggested by flowers)

Texture: medium

Many guests at Atlock Farm arrive asking for plants that bloom all season. A few genera would seem to answer the call—*Calibrachoa, Lantana, Petunia, Verbena*—but these often require deadheading or pruning to keep them blooming and looking well kempt. But not *Scaevola*, the champion bloomer of them all: here, in central New Jersey, fan flowers bloom from May until October's frosts shut them down, and the plants don't need any tidying up in the meantime. Even yours truly, who likes to see flowers and other things come and go at their appointed times, keeps going back to ever-blooming fan flower to create dazzling monopots and very satisfying combopots.

I should point out that not all fan flowers are created equal. Some of the selections with medium to dark blue-purple flowers ('Blue Wonder', 'Fancy') are super, but the same cannot be said of all the lighter selections or the mostly white ones, which can fall somewhat short in bloom production compared to the others, the exception being Whirlwind White (= 'Scawihatis'). The Aussies have been working with fan flower (it's native Down Under), so more excellent selections will soon make their way above the equator.

Cultural tips: Making all those flowers requires some extra fertilizer, but not as much as you might think, and fan flowers tolerate drought quite well. So is there anything that can bring Superplant down (besides frost)? Yes: poor drainage and not enough sun would be Superplant's kryptonite. Don't expect individual fan flower plants to bloom (or live) forever in frost-free climates. Even Superman met his end, sort of. Take cuttings or start over with new plants.

Scaevola aemula Whirlwind White (= 'Scawihatis') offers both icy and warm white (from the elongated flower lobes and the yellow spots, respectively) instead of the usual blue-violet shades of fan flower. Mixing white selections with the usual blues makes a refreshing color combination.

The flowers of *Scaevola aemula* 'Fancy' and the foliage of 'Freckles' coleus make an arresting combination: yellow-green, yellow-orange, and blue-violet compose an almost perfect split-complementary triad (something closer to pure purple would make it perfect).

Daggers of tiger grass (*Thysanolaena latifolia*) slice into a bustling crowd of *Scaevola aemula* 'Fancy'. Can you imagine the flower clusters fleeing in a panic as the phalanx of grass approaches?

A closeup of a couple of *Scaevola aemula* flower clusters reveals the inspiration for its generic and common names. The genus name derives from the Latin *scaevus* ("left-handed"), referring to the one-sided appearance of the individual flowers, and clearly the five segments of each resemble a fan. Cool(ing)

SEDUM
stonecrop

Family: Crassulaceae
Cultural group: succulents, perennials
Height: 1 in. to 2 ft. (*S. morganianum* more with time)
Width: 4 in. to 2 ft. or more
Light: sun to limited partial shade
Temperature: warm to hot
Overwintering: min. 45°F, water occasionally, bright light; variously hardy in Z3–10
Moisture: on dry side to moderate
Drainage of medium: well drained
Fertility: low to average
Ease/speed of growth: easy/moderate
Propagation: division, leaf cuttings, stem cuttings, seeds
Problems: slugs and snails, mealybugs, scale insects
Principal interest: foliage, form, flowers
Length of seasonal interest: long to all year (foliage and form); brief to moderate (flowers)

Design attributes

Color: foliage green, variously tinted with, marked with, or in solid shades of white, red, pink, yellow, orange, and purple; flowers white, red, yellow, and red-violet
Line: varies widely from nearly absent to readily apparent from leaves, stems, and flower stems
Form: carpeting to cascading to clumping-mounded to shrubby
Space: varies widely from nearly absent to visible throughout plant
Texture: fine to medium to coarse

The first sedum I knew was *S. sarmentosum*, which grew abundantly in the stone walls that flanked our driveway. The bright green foliage appeared and grew quickly in early spring, followed by clusters of golden yellow, starry flowers in late spring. However, by June, the plants looked like they had hit the wall, collapsing into stringy messes of pale green, deflated leaves and shriveled flowers. It was my job to rip out the sad remains. I'd carry a few buckets of the stuff down over the hill into the woods, where the stems tried to revive and root but always perished in the shade. The walls never lacked their spring displays of *S. sarmentosum*, though: bits of it always remained in the soil between the stones, lying dormant until the following spring, when the cycle began again.

While few of the stonecrops I've encountered since collapse so spectacularly, quite a few appreciate container conditions that approximate those sarmentosum-clad stone walls: very sunny, well drained, rarely any supplemental water or fertilizer, and tight quarters. Shallow pots filled with a very

Sedum morganianum (burro's tail) rushes from a charming container as a ring of echeveria rosettes and a crowd of crassulas watch from above and below. Who says succulents are dumpy? Who needs flowers all the time? Who wants to copy this masterpiece of container design?

Right: The bright yellow-green of *Sedum rupestre* 'Angelina' sets it apart from its companions in the containers as well as in the open ground. The gray trough prevents the stonecrop and the magenta delosperma from waging a color skirmish (which you might like).

open, almost rocky mix suit most of them to a T. Let's not forget that sedums are succulents!

S. acre makes a dense, dark green carpet no more than 2 in. high. In summer the abundant yellow flowers explain the common names of golden carpet and golden moss. 'Aureum' takes the gold idea one step further with bright yellow leaves, while inch-high 'Minus' reinforces the resemblance to moss. *S. dasyphyllum* looks like 'Minus' with gray-blue foliage. Z4–9.

Ss. cauticola, pluricaule, sieboldii, and hybrids 'Bertram Anderson' and 'Vera Jameson' all make neat little mounds about 1 ft. tall that spill over pot rims if given the chance. I like to showcase their gray-blue leaves and bright pink flowers in low gray or dark blue pots, and they don't fight too much with terracotta. *S. sieboldii* blooms quite late (October in central New Jersey and apparently elsewhere), which partially explains its common name of October daphne. Z5–9.

'Herbstfreude' ('Autumn Joy') and other larger stonecrops

Sedums do bloom, sometimes in vivid shades of red-violet, as evidenced by this flower cluster of *Sedum* 'Vera Jameson'. As if this genus needed to offer any more sumptuous coloration . . .

Who knew what orange and blue can do when toned down more than a notch or two? Yes, we're looking at a classic complementary pair, but the grayness of the blue *Sedum pluricaule* and the brown cast of the orange softens them both. Also, neither color is highly saturated.

Boom! A supernova releases massive amounts of energy as it meets its cosmic doom. This *Sedum sieboldii* 'Mediovariegatum' still hasn't put on its final show of the season, when bright pink flower clusters will flash at the ends of the stems.

Another example of *Sedum sieboldii* 'Mediovariegatum', this time with the flower buds just beginning to show. Their bright pink coloration will make an exciting combination with the rest of the plant (picking up on the color of the stems and leaf edges), and everything will show off beautifully against the muted gray of the pot.

under the blanket name of *S. spectabile* (as well as some of the smaller ones) are now sometimes considered members of the genus *Hylotelephium*. Whatever. They make almost burly, 2 by 2 ft. masses of thick leaves and very showy, flat clusters of flowers in white and shades of pink in late summer. 'Herbstfreude' has been deservedly popular for decades. Its flower buds turn from pale green to dark green and then open pink, gradually turning copper-pink-red and persisting on the plant until heavy snow knocks them over. Butterflies and bees cannot leave the flowers alone. Z4–9.

The trailing and powerfully linear *S. morganianum* (burro's tail, donkey's tail) readily sheds its pudgy little green leaves if not grown in a protected site, if knocked by a ball or dog's tail, if otherwise handled roughly, or (it seems) if looked at sideways. No matter: it keeps lengthening (easily to 2 ft. and often at least double that) and sending up new shoots from the base (and the leaves will probably root if placed back into the pot). I've never seen the pink to purple flowers, but online images indicate I'm not missing much. It's not one of the hardy boys: keep it above 40°F.

When growing actively, *Sedum rupestre* 'Angelina' adds bright yellow-green to the stonecrop repertoire, but cooler temperatures bring strong orange tones to the dormant foliage. Would you like the fire of 'Angelina' in this pot in colder weather?

Sedum morganianum almost demands to be used cleverly, as here at Chanticleer, where a conveyor chain lifts its blue-green ropes to new heights of appeal. This should get your creative juices flowing.

Sedum spathulifolium 'Cape Blanco' sometimes looks very subtle in pale pink and light more-blue-than-gray, but at other times it will be clad in a much darker gray or will sharply contrast with the bright yellow of its starry flowers. Aren't you glad plants don't look the same all the time?

S. rupestre 'Angelina' could easily have been called "Chameleon." The ropes of thin, almost needlelike leaves are yellow (almost gold) in full sun in summer, but both spring and fall (and increasing shade) bring out their inner chartreuse. The approach of winter tinges the foliage orange, which deepens with winter, and then spring brings all-new shoots and another round of color changes. Fantastic. Let its foot-long stems trail over the edge of a container or cover the surface of a large pot. Keep an eye out for 'Lemon Coral', a new selection that forms neat mounds of variably yellow-green foliage, 4–6 in. tall and about 1 ft. wide. 'Angelina' is listed as hardy in Z3–11, 'Lemon Coral' Z7–11. Time will tell.

S. spathulifolium 'Cape Blanco' brings gray to the *Sedum* color palette. Rosettes of stubby, thick leaves on pinkish stems slowly spread into clumps about 6 in. wide. I find the yellow flowers distracting, but you might not. Z6–9, 5 if grown in a very well-drained medium.

Cultural tips: Don't kill them with kindness; too much water and fertilizer make sedums flabby and weak. If in doubt, don't. Many sedums will grow in less than full sun, but the foliage coloration and bloom production will suffer.

SEMPERVIVUM
hen and chicks, houseleek

Family: Crassulaceae
Cultural group: succulents
Height: 2–6 in. (to 1 ft. or so in flower)
Width: individually 1–6 in., potentially to 1 ft. or more
Light: sun
Temperature: cool to warm to hot
Overwintering: min. 50°F, water occasionally, bright light; variously hardy in Z4–10
Moisture: on dry side to moderate
Drainage of medium: well drained
Fertility: low to average
Ease/speed of growth: easy/moderate
Propagation: division, seeds
Problems: slugs and snails, rots and spots, root rot
Principal interest: form, flowers (mostly as curiosities)
Length of seasonal interest: long

Design attributes
Color: foliage green, often marked with or solidly colored in shades of red, purple, or gray-blue and/or heavily white- or gray-hairy; flowers white, red, pink, yellow, and red-violet
Line: from leaves radiating out from center of rosette (or from "cobwebs" on *S. arachnoideum*); erect or curving flower stems

Form: rosettes, sometimes with odd-looking flowers rising up; like a bunch of little cabbages
Space: very little (except at edges of individual rosettes or of clump)
Texture: medium to coarse

To misquote Will Rogers, "I never met a sempervivum I didn't like," from the very small, densely clumping, intricately white-threaded, attractively pink-flowered *S. arachnoideum* (cobweb houseleek, as the spidery specific epithet hints) to the big, football-mum-like selections of *S. tectorum*. Your non-attention to all houseleeks (anything that can live on a roof—*tectorum* means "of roofs"—doesn't need to be pampered) will be repaid with satisfyingly plump, precisely sculpted, flower-like rosettes in rich, mineral shades, some with hair and others with eyelashes, and curiously eye-catching, gawky flower spikes. I've watched many sempervivums come and go, but two hybrids have managed to stick in my memory: the big (6-in.), gorgeous blue-gray 'Silverine' (it's stingy with the chicks, though), and the smaller, freely offsetting (chicking?)

Please pay attention to the composition in front of us, class. Do you see all five design elements? As always, the most abstract attribute is space; there's very little literal space, but the placement of the sempervivum rosettes against the yellow-green background creates the illusion of space.

Opposite: A pink and green lava flow of sempervivum (probably a selection or relative of *Sempervivum arachnoideum*) surges from a stone trough. Maybe you see it as a crocheted afghan or something else. In any case, the massive form of all the rosettes taken together makes the strongest design statement . . . or does it?

A closeup of the same mass of hen and chicks gives an idea of the staggering number of individual rosettes contained within the "coop." It also gives a better appreciation for the fine cobwebby texture that completely disappears at a not-too-great distance.

The angled placement of this monopot of *Sempervivum* 'Purple Beauty' adds visual appeal to the arrangement: picture how this would look if the sides of the pot were aligned with the sides of the railroad tie.

'Oddity', whose almost cylindrical green leaves bear sunken, black-painted areas at the tips instead of the usual points.

I like to combine the precise forms of sempervivums with the less buttoned-down shapes of sedums or let them fill a pot all by themselves. You might also want to grow them on a roof to catch a thief (they'll slip and slide on the moosh that houseleeks turn into under big barbarian feet) or to prevent sparks and embers from neighboring house fires from igniting your own home (again employing their succulent, water-filled leaves). By the way, avian hens and chicks (and other fowl) might destroy floral ones if given the chance. I don't know if the birds hope they contain juicy bugs or perhaps the fowl are interested in the juicy leaves, but whatever their intent, they might as well be cannibals.

Cultural tips: Don't fuss with hens and chicks. Give them a little very well-drained potting mix (it could be half poultry grit) in full sun, water them only if they look shriveled (which will probably be never, except in very dry areas), forget the fertilizer, and remove the dying rosettes after their flower spikes begin to fade.

SOLANUM

nightshade; potato vine (*S. laxum*); porcupine tomato (*S. pyracanthum*); naranjilla, bed of nails (*S. quitoense*); blue potato bush (*S. rantonnetii*)

Family: Solanaceae
Cultural group: annuals, climbers and trailers, tropicals
Height: 1–5 ft. or more
Width: 1–3 ft. or more; depends on training for climbers
Light: sun (to partial shade for *Ss. laxum* and *quitoense*)

Temperature: warm to hot
Overwintering: min. 55°F, water occasionally, bright light;
    hardy in Z8–10 (*S. laxum*)
Moisture: moderate to ample
Drainage of medium: well drained
Fertility: average to high (phosphorus if pushing flowers)
Ease/speed of growth: easy/moderate to fast
Propagation: seeds, cuttings, suckers
Problems: spider mites, aphids, whitefly, rots and spots
Principal interest: flowers, foliage, form
Length of seasonal interest: long

Design attributes
Color: flowers white, blue, and purple; foliage green,
    sometimes marked with yellow
Line: from not much to obvious long lines; elongated
    leaves, midribs, lobes, spines
Form: shrubby, depends on training
Space: from abundant to not obvious, depends on training
Texture: medium to coarse

Do you remember when Jerusalem cherry (*S. pseudocapsicum*) was a popular Christmas plant? I wanted to try to grow some from seeds, so one year, at a full-family gathering, I asked if I could pick a few fruits. "Don't eat those things! They're poisonous!" came the panicky reply. I assured Aunt Panic that I wasn't going to eat the "cherries," and Mom and Dad spoke up for me, so it was all systems go for harvesting a few little red mothballs—whose seeds, I found, looked just like tomato seeds. Yes, Jerusalem cherry is in the same family as tomatoes, as well as a heap of ornamental plants featured in this book. The point of this reminiscence? Plants are grouped into families based on shared characteristics that go beyond the obvious floral similarities. Many members of the Solanaceae have very similar-looking seeds, and a fair number of them contain poisonous alkaloids. Many also share cultural preferences, so if you know how to grow a tomato or a petunia, you can generally follow those guidelines for ornamental peppers or flowering tobacco or eggplant. Ditto for other plant families, but don't assume every member of a plant family wants the same cultural conditions. Do your research first!

Here's a sampling of solanums suitable for pots:

Both the foliage and five-parted flowers of *S. laxum* (aka *S. jasminoides*) look a whole lot like some climbing jasmines (*Jasminum*), hence another common name, jasmine nightshade. The species produces pale blue flowers and dark green leaves, and the weakly climbing stems can reach 4–6 ft. in one season. I've never grown it or the white-flowered 'Album', but I have enjoyed the irregularly yellow-edged 'Variegatum'. Let it cascade out of a pot or hanging basket, or train it onto a sim-

The overall color impression of the foliage of *Solanum laxum* 'Variegatum' emerges when looking at a mass of the leaves, while the individual details become less noticeable. Which effect do the white flowers exert?

Every little detail of a shoot of *Solanum laxum* 'Variegatum' stands out against its subtly toned container. The individual details can be lost against a more colorful container and will merge when seen en masse, as in the other photograph of this taxon.

Here's what you'll miss if you keep *Solanum pyracanthum* cut back severely. Pretty, yes (the medium purple and soft gray-green contrast pleasantly with the yellow stamens and orange spines), but the potentially painful plant will take up a good deal of space if you let it grow as it will. It's your choice.

ple teepee of stakes or more elaborate form. The white flowers don't do anything for me, but they're not offensive, either.

I grow *S. pyracanthum* for its orange spines, which arm the stems and major veins of the dandelion-like leaves (on both surfaces, just for added insurance). That's all. It needs to be kept cut back to 1–2 ft., or it will turn into a floppy, rangy, spiny, homely mess. Pursuing that program will prevent it from blooming, but that's OK. This definitely makes a conversation piece (as a monopot) or spiny surprise in waiting (when partially disguised among other plants in a combopot).

S. quitoense bears lots of little yellow-orange spines on the stems and larger, purple-tinged ones on the major leaf veins (on both sides, just like *S. pyracanthum*). While the spines are fun, it's the startlingly bold, coarse foliage that offers the most interest and potential for eye-catching textural contrasts. Obscured white flowers develop into clusters of golfball-sized orange fruits; the green juice of each *naranjilla* ("little orange") has a citrusy flavor. This species is grown in warm areas, and its fruits are used in beverages. You can do the same, turning *S. quitoense* into a double-duty, thorny and drinkable conver-

A young plant of *Solanum pyracanthum* (porcupine tomato) flaunts its toothed leaves and orange spines. In time, little Spiky will become big Tangly unless pruned aggressively and often.

The big, bold leaves of *Solanum quitoense* (naranjilla, bed of nails) hold their own against the more colorful, yellow-striped *Canna* 'Pretoria' behind them. Note how the "nails" subtly echo the dark foliage of *Ipomoea batatas* 'Blackie' trailing under them.

Keep the phosphorus fertilizer coming (and trim the rangy shoots back every now and then) to encourage *Solanum rantonnetii* to produce hundreds, if not thousands, of its yellow-centered purple discs. Can you tell their size (and abundance) from this photograph? Nope: closeups such as this one, appealing as they are, leave out some essential information.

A more distant view of a standard topiary of *Solanum rantonnetii* gives a better idea of the plant's habit and flower power, but you still can't tell how tall it is. Here's a clue: the grass below the head of leaves and flowers is about 5 ft. tall. The point: don't rely solely on photos to assess the dimensions of a plant. Read, too.

sation piece. A happy plant will easily fill a 3 × 3 ft. space. Rein it in at your peril. Occasionally a spineless (pointless?) plant will arise from seed.

S. rantonnetii won't hurt you if you get too close to it; instead, a well-fed plant in plenty of sun will produce literally hundreds of royal purple flowers in a single season, overshadowing the unremarkable foliage and plant form. I think the most effective way to grow blue potato bush is as a standard, which can easily be trained 6 ft. tall and allowed to spread about 3 ft. Chop it back hard after putting it outside again (you've overwintered it at least once by the time it's a good-sized topiary), and let it grow out into a purple-studded green cloud. You can also try keeping a smallish plant (1–2 ft. each way) in a largish pot with other plants, especially those with strongly colored flowers: yellow or orange *Lantana camara* or red *Salvia splendens*, for example.

Cultural tips: The ones grown for their foliage will benefit from plenty of nitrogen. Push bloom on *S. rantonnetii* with lots of phosphorus. Keep *S. quitoense* out of strong winds, which will (not "can") shred the big leaves. Propagate *Ss. laxum* and *rantonnetii* from cuttings, *S. pyracanthum* from suckers (or seeds, if you can get your hands on some), and *S. quitoense* from seed.

SOLEIROLIA
baby's tears, mind-your-own-business (*S. soleirolii*)

Family: Urticaceae
Cultural group: tropicals, annuals, climbers and trailers
Height: 1–2 in.
Width: depends on training
Light: partial shade
Temperature: cool to warm to hot
Overwintering: min. 40°F, water occasionally, bright light; hardy in Z10–11
Moisture: moderate to ample
Drainage of medium: well drained but tolerates shallow standing water
Fertility: low to average
Ease/speed of growth: easy/moderate to fast
Propagation: division, "cuttings" (ripped-up bits of stem)
Problems: none I've seen
Principal interest: foliage, form
Length of seasonal interest: all year

Design attributes
Color: medium green; chartreuse to yellow-gold in 'Aurea' or marked with white in 'Variegata' (appears blue-grayish); stems almost clear
Line: none unless trailing and divided into sections

A mass of baby's tears (*Soleirolia soleirolii*) makes a lush green collar for the topiary's stem and (more significantly) a wig or toupee for the pot. Even a little wad of baby's tears adds a bit of fine-textured, irresistibly touchable fun to a container planting.

Soleirolia soleirolii 'Aurea' brings the same fine texture and touchability as the more familiar green species, but not its color, of course. It glows in low light and turns almost gold in more light, but try to keep it out of too much sun: brown baby's tears are just sad.

Form: spreading-engulfing, impossibly delicate, fragile carpet made from little beads
Space: none unless cascading openly
Texture: fine, but only up close

A little misty ball of green on my aunt's kitchen windowsill caught my eye as a kid. It was a pot of baby's tears, and I soon learned how to keep one happy: make sure it always has moist soil by frequently refilling the saucer under the pot, and when the cloud of crystalline threads and minuscule, shiny green beads reach the saucer, trim it back to near the pot rim and let it fill back out again. My adult eye still appreciates the feeling created by a solid rush of green in a container. Baby's tears gives an impression of subtle *abbondanza* both as a monopot or in combopots, perhaps as a rambunctious groundcover for a much taller topiary. It also lends itself beautifully to being used as "paint" (see *Sagina*), especially if your palette holds the lively green of the species, the light-responsive yellows of 'Aurea', and the mysterious blue-gray-green of the white-edged 'Variegata'. Tear up pots of them, press the pieces into the canvas (a new, preferably shallow pot, that is), wait a little while for the plants to reroot and knit together, and voilà—your artwork will be ready for unveiling at an exhibition.

Don't be misled by the gentle appearance of baby's tears. Given the opportunity, it will carpet greenhouse floors, as it does at Atlock, where it slowly but determinedly engulfs pots and other inanimate objects, much to the amazement and delight of customers, kittens, and a self-contained mini-ecology of worms, sowbugs, centipedes, and other life, all sustained by water and fertilizer falling from the plants above, decomposing threads and beads, and each other. It might become a pest where it is cold-hardy outdoors, but it is capable of threatening the well-being of only a tiny rock garden plant or similar precious thing.

Cultural tips: Even black-thumbers should be able to grow some baby's tears, but don't handle it roughly or walk on it: plants bruise and tear easily. They will recover quickly if you don't fuss over them as you try to repair the damage. 'Aurea' is almost green in low light and chartreuse in bright light, glows gold in even brighter light, and turns brown in too much sun. Pick the color you like.

SOLENOSTEMON
coleus, flame nettle, painted nettle
(*S. scutellarioides*)

Family: Lamiaceae
Cultural group: annuals, tropicals
Height: 4 in. to 3 ft. or more
Width: 6 in. to 3 ft.
Light: sun to partial shade to shade

Temperature: warm to hot

Overwintering: min. 55°F, water occasionally, bright light

Moisture: moderate to ample but recovers remarkably from drought

Drainage of medium: well drained but tolerates shallow standing water

Fertility: average to high

Ease/speed of growth: easy/moderate to fast

Propagation: cuttings, seeds

Problems: mealybugs, spider mites, whitefly, downy mildew, root rot, rots and spots

Principal interest: foliage, form, sometimes flowers

Length of seasonal interest: long to all year

Design attributes

Color: foliage in just about every color except blue, usually marked with at least one other color; flowers blue

Line: obvious in the trailers, not much in others

Form: shrubby or trailing-cascading, depends on training

Space: often absent, depends on training

Texture: fine to medium (mostly) to coarse

Opposite: Can you find the flowers in this photo? Who needs them when you have coleus (and other foliage plants) on hand? Assertive yellow-green and orange coleus selections mingle with dark purple tradescantia and a cool variegated ivy selection, all under the benevolent watch of the tree fern. I want them to cover the pot completely . . .

There's so much to say about coleus, I should write a book . . . no, wait; I did. Check out *Coleus: Rainbow Foliage for Containers and Gardens* (Timber Press). In the meantime, I invite you to look at the photos presented here; they (and their captions) say far more than I could write in a reasonable space here about the merits of coleus as container plants. Here's a distillation of the glories of "cole'-eeze" (as my mother called them), presented as responses to a few widely held misconceptions about them:

"Every one is ridiculously gaudy and could not possibly be combined with more refined plants in containers." Well, if you consider solid shades of red, orange, yellow, green, and near-black "gaudy," then there's no converting you. Yes, quite a few flame nettles are unapologetic extroverts, but many of them offer subtle to rich mixtures of a bewildering array of colors.

This photo was *not* photoshopped! 'Henna', one of the most exciting and useful coleus to come along recently, sometimes looks like this. At other times it displays shades of warm brown (hence its name) along with one or both of the colors seen here. Those choppers (the teeth on the leaf margins) grab attention, too.

Some of the color from the edges of this 'Meandering Linda' coleus dripped off and turned into a fuchsia . . . or so it might appear. I really like how its dark-chocolate and raspberry colors are prevented from becoming too rich by the fresh lime sherbet of the hosta and the lemon ice of the pot. Are you hungry now?

Little-leaved coleus make cute little topiaries, provided you train and trim them following an informed routine. 'Tiny Toes' (in front) looks like a globular dog shaking itself after a bath (or maybe a startled puffer fish), and both 'India Frills' (on the left) and a larger-leaved sport of 'India Frills' (on the right) should conjure up images of your own.

A bird's-eye view reveals the intricate color pattern, frenzied linearity, and fine texture of the 'Tiny Toes' topiary, now seen against the blue-green tabletop. This raises a question: how often do you think about the design attributes of the settings you provide for your container plantings?

"They all need next to no care." This one isn't too far off the mark, actually; you could grow most coleus exactly the same way and without much effort. And that's a problem because …? Those of you who like a bit more of a challenge should try your hand at creating a coleus topiary 4 ft. high or a coleus hanging basket 4 ft. wide.

"I don't need any boring blobs in my container plantings." Hmm, people who hold that opinion haven't begun to explore the range of design potential among coleus. Color? You name it, except for bright purple and most shades of blue (although the flowers are blue, and some of them are surprisingly attractive if allowed to bloom). Line? Trailing coleus offer plenty of it. Form? OK, most can be unremarkable little bushes, but the trailers break that mold, and a well-grown standard coleus topiary can rival or surpass the appeal of more conventional choices. Space? Admittedly, it's often absent, but coleus topiaries and hanging baskets command (not simply suggest) the space around them. Texture? Choose from tiny, fingered leaves to some that exceed 1 ft. long and almost as wide, with fingers and lace and slashed edges in between.

"Coleus look good for a while and then make dirty-looking flowers before they fall apart and die." Some do, including a few of the much too widely circulated seed-grown strains, but most of the hundreds of available coleus selections will remain attractive all season if their basic cultural needs are met and they are provided some attentive pinching (to nip the flowers in the bud, quite literally, and to encourage denser, more compact growth).

And now [drumroll, please] for the biggest misconception of all: "Coleus need to be kept in the shade." Nononononononono! Very few require protection from the sun, and every new year brings more coleus that require all-day sunshine to develop their splendid coloration. Many thrive in the "happy medium," the gentler rays of morning sun. Here's how to figure out how much sun different coleus require to look their best: place your individually potted coleus in a spot that re-

'Inky Fingers', a trailing coleus, looks sinister to some (they might not like any dark-leaved plant) and happy to others (the amusing cut leaves and evocative name help there). Use it en masse (as here) or let just a few stems trail their fingers over a simpatico pot.

A flock of dark red birds emerges from a cloud of green mist above a tree-lined black pond at sunrise. Or, the bold textures of 'Atlas' coleus and a strap-leaved bromeliad contrast sharply with the needle-fine foliage of *Muhlenbergia dumosa* in a dark blue pot. Poetry and prose both have their roles in container gardening, and I recommend you pursue both.

ceives a few hours of morning sun. Any that begin to develop brown spots (probably ones with plenty of white or pale pink in the foliage) need shade. The rest of them can be placed in increasingly sunnier spots until they too begin to burn. Some never will, so give those all the sun you can throw at them.

Cultural tips: Container-grown coleus need more water and fertilizer than their in-ground buddies. Extremely hot weather may cause the colors to fade, but cooler temperatures will restore them. Don't panic if you see shoots that differ from your original plant. Many coleus are genetically unstable, frequently reverting or sporting into new color patterns. Remove sports and reversions to preserve the uniform look of a coleus, or let them go their crazy way. That's part of the fun, and since sports and reversions usually root very easily from cuttings, you might end up introducing your very own new coleus to gardening some day.

STROBILANTHES
Persian shield (*S. dyerianus*)

Family: Acanthaceae
Cultural group: annuals
Height: 2–3 ft.
Width: 2–4 ft.
Light: sun to partial shade
Temperature: warm to hot
Overwintering: min. 55°F, water occasionally, bright light
Moisture: moderate to ample
Drainage of medium: well drained
Fertility: average
Ease/speed of growth: moderate (can be erratic from year to year)/moderate
Propagation: cuttings, seeds
Problems: whitefly, spider mites

Principal interest: foliage
Length of seasonal interest: long

Design attributes

Color: foliage green and metallic purple, sometimes
   with silver
Line: stems, elongated leaves, and veining
Form: open shrubby to spreading
Space: within plant
Texture: medium

Persian shield (*S. dyerianus*) makes me crazy. In most seasons it reminds me of the beads and other trappings of Mardi Gras (especially when planted next to something gold, completing the classic Carnival combination of purple, green, and gold), and minerals brilliantly fluorescing under ultraviolet light. Fantastic. But every few years—and for no apparent good reason—the beads lose their shine and the ultra-

violet light goes off. The foliage is still colorful, but the verve, the zip, the *joie de vivre* is missing. Bummer. No matter; plenty of other plants (and people) have their off-times but return to their glorious selves in due time. So I can forgive *S. dyerianus* for an occasional down year and hope for splendor the next time around.

I think I've discovered a few tricks (in every other entry these would be "cultural tips," but "tricks" seems more appropriate here) for helping *S. dyerianus* look its iridescent best: keep it warm, pinch it at least once when young, regularly move small plants to larger pots, give it plenty of bright light (morning sun is nice, but hot afternoon sun is deadly), keep the nitrogenous fertilizer coming, and remove flower buds before they get large and threaten to bloom. Since plants might still fall a little short, I advise against growing them as a monopot, but by all means include them in combopots (at least 12 in. in diameter), where even a less-than-stellar specimen will still look impressive when seen against its compan-

When in top form, some plants clobber me over the head with their "It" factor. *Strobilanthes dyerianus* is one of them. With leaves that look like they were created by a jeweler working with a metalsmith and a fabric designer, how could Persian shield not impress? When it's off its game, that's when.

The silvery-white cast to the foliage of *Strobilanthes gossypinus* is reinforced by the splash of *Dichondra argentea* trailing from the container. The dark red sedge *Uncinia rubra* separates the two and offers a contrast in wiry form and fine grassy texture. Do you like the pot? It associates even more cordially with the strobilanthes in the golden glow of late-day sun.

ions. Purple and green are logical choices for creating color echoes, but don't overlook Mardi Gras gold (the closer you can get to suggesting metallic gold the better, such as from many coleus or golden durantas), light yellow, medium blue (think sapphires), and maybe even magenta.

For a completely different look and approach, turn to *S. gossypinus*. It's a new kid on the block and deserves wider appreciation (as well as a common name). From what I can tell from limited experience and some online research (there's not much there), this pale gold and gray-silver species colors up best in full sun and can withstand drought when established. It's shrubby (the stems quickly become woody), so occasional pinching should make it denser and more compact as well as encourage the production of more gold. I'm guessing it looks its best in its second year, so prepare to overwinter it. The increased maturity might also bring with it clusters of light blue-purple flowers, assuming you don't keep pinching the shoots.

The fun with *S. gossypinus* (or any other plant, whether new to you or comfortably familiar) comes with looking for color companions. When I want to come up with that "perfect" combination, I carry a cutting of a plant (or an entire potted plant, if manageable) around Atlock Farm. It turns out that *S. gossypinus* makes some gorgeous matchups (anything in near-black, dark red-purple, or rich, velvety red), is almost as stunning with apricot, coral, light blue, light green, and silver-gray, gets along nicely enough with some others (pink, yellow, gold, strong orange, medium to dark blue, medium to dark magenta, purple, and white in moderation), and doesn't get along at all with bright red, light magenta (big surprise there!), and too much white. I can't wait to plant a dark green pot with *S. gossypinus*, *Ipomoea batatas* 'Blackie', and *Pennisetum setaceum* 'Rubrum'.

Cultural tips: In addition to the aforementioned tricks? Don't worry if the pairs of leaves on Persian shields consist of one bigger and one noticeably smaller leaf; that's normal.

Strobilanthes gossypinus quietly impresses almost anyone who gives it more than a passing glance. This photo shows how the gold tinge of the new foliage gradually diminishes as the silvery leaves enlarge. How can fuzz be metallic?

SYNGONIUM
arrowhead vine, nephthytis (*S. podophyllum*)

Family: Araceae
Cultural group: tropicals, climbers and trailers
Height: 1–2 ft., maybe more
Width: 1–2 ft.
Light: partial shade to shade
Temperature: warm to hot
Overwintering: min. 50°F, water occasionally, bright light
Moisture: moderate to ample
Drainage of medium: well drained but tolerates standing water
Fertility: average
Ease/speed of growth: easy/moderate to fast
Propagation: cuttings, already rooted stems
Problems: spider mites, mealybugs, rots and spots
Principal interest: foliage
Length of seasonal interest: long to all year

Design attributes
Color: foliage green, often marked with or almost entirely in white or pink
Line: from petioles (more visible with age), elongated leaves, and markings
Form: dense mound to elongated to climbing-trailing, lotsa shields or arrowheads
Space: nearly absent to abundant (in time)
Texture: medium (as a result of markings) to coarse

A far cry from plain old green syngoniums, 'Neon' lights up shady spots with its foliage, which progresses from pink to eerie pale green, usually with at least a suggestion of silver. It looks best when trailing, climbing, or gently thinned (and when seen against simple, uncomplicated backgrounds), which allows the spearhead shapes of the leaves to stand out.

An established pot of *Syngonium podophyllum* 'White Butterfly' shows the one-of-a-kind mentality embraced by its leaves. No copycats here! Note how the green and white foliage combines pleasantly with the gaudier leaves of the rex begonias at the bottom. They'd make a nice pairing in a pot.

My Great Aunt Hazel had a green thumb and a sideboard decorated with syngoniums, which spent their lives in water, producing arrowhead-shaped leaves on ever-lengthening stems. I didn't like them, and that feeling persisted for many years, I confess. Too blah; no "It" factor there. But my opinion of them has changed, now that I see more of them parading their comeliness in nurseries. Like their relatives in *Caladium*, the leaves display mostly subtle patterns of white and pink on green, and in the manner of another bunch of cousins in *Philodendron*, the stems elongate, some quickly, others very reluctantly. They're still marketed mostly as houseplants, but in this age of houseplant liberation, syngoniums are showing up outdoors in container plantings. Bravo! Let them add their arrowheads and covert coloration to shady plantings; strong sun will damage them unless kept constantly wet, and even then they might still show some damage. The only selection I've ever seen that made a superb monopot is the almost shrubby, barely trailing 'White Butter-fly'; the stringier ones look their best in combopots and hanging baskets and when lashed to fiber or moss poles, I think.

In addition to the coolly fetching 'White Butterfly', you should be able to find several other white and green selections. Do make a point of looking for 'Neon' and the other pink ones showing up these days, which can send a pleasant jolt to an otherwise all-green container in shade. I think 'Neon' looks like a freezer-case full of Italian ices.

Cultural tips: Syngoniums can take a fair amount of neglect, except regarding their water needs, so keep them moist to wet. They root extremely easily from cuttings in water (placement on a sideboard is optional).

TALINUM
jewels of Opar (*T. paniculatum*)

Family: Portulacaceae
Cultural group: annuals
Height: 12–18 in. (to 3 ft. in flower)
Width: 12–24 in.
Light: sun to partial shade (especially colored forms)
Temperature: warm to hot
Overwintering: min. 50°F, water occasionally, bright light;
    hardy in Z9–11
Moisture: on dry side to moderate
Drainage of medium: well drained
Fertility: low to average
Ease/speed of growth: easy/moderate to fast
Propagation: seeds, cuttings
Problems: aphids, weediness (although many find it
    charming and appreciate the extra volunteer or two
    in a container)

All that yellow-green foliage and vaguely pinkish mist to the left is in fact growing in the tall pot. The lopsidedness of the *Talinum paniculatum* 'Kingwood Gold', the tense off-centered placement of the pot on the plinth, and the eruption of phormium at the top make for one exciting display.

Principal interest: flowers, fruit, foliage
Length of seasonal interest: long

Design attributes

Color: foliage medium green (sometimes marked with
    white) or chartreuse; flowers medium red-violet (yes,
    darn close to magenta); fruit dark red to red-violet
Line: from flower stems—though they're barely there
Form: bunch of leaves with little pink or red-violet insects;
    can cascade very attractively
Space: not much in foliage; almost nothing but space
    around flowers and fruit
Texture: foliage medium, flowers fine, fruit beyond fine

Familiar things and actions are pleasant parts of life, but they can become addictive and counterproductive. So I'm always open to trying new stuff, including plants. Who will be next to breed contempt? The jury's still out on *T. paniculatum*, or jewels of Opar (if that's not an evocative common name, what is?), but it has a very good chance of being awarded a spot on my short list of comfort plants. First, the mundane reason: it grows like a weed (and can become one, if you let its seeds come up and grow wherever they will), so it holds the potential for becoming very familiar, not to say contemptible, very quickly. Any unwanted seedlings pull up (or transplant) easily, though, so it won't take over unless you let it. But its pertinacity is not the only attribute I could offer by way of argument. Its design elements make their own case:

1. While the species itself catches my eye with its medium green leaves and red-violet flowers and fruit, the selections beguile me even more. The yellow-green (chartreuse) shades of the foliage on 'Aureum', 'Dart's Gold', 'Kingwood Gold', and 'Limon' create a subtle, arty tertiary color contrast with the red-violet stars and specks. The white-splashed, slightly blue-gray foliage of 'Variegatum' reminds me of privet (*Ligustrum*) or *Pittosporum* until the flowers appear, and then another tertiary color contrast emerges between blue-green and red-violet.
2. The flower/fruit spikes are almost pure line, and they extend the less obvious but still linear quality of the stems well beyond the foliage.
3. If allowed to cascade over the edge of a pot, the plant takes on the form of a slow but inexorable lava flow. Cool.
4. While very little space can be detected among the leaves, the flowers and fruit appear to be suspended in a vast space, especially if set against a uniform background.
5. The textural contrast between the mass of plain, relatively large leaves and the mist of tiny flowers and fruit couldn't be any more obvious and fascinating.

Who let the pods out? The fruits of *Talinum paniculatum* 'King-wood Gold' look like they're escaping from their leafy confines. Their jewel-like colors were, I suspect, the inspiration for the common name, jewels of Opar. Could there be a starker, more engaging contrast in texture anywhere?

Informal and formal coexist in front of a remarkably color-matched door. The round head of the myrtle echoes a hoop of a *Thunbergia alata* selection, its sunny flowers adding spots of color to what might otherwise be a subdued little tableau.

Time will tell whether *T. paniculatum* persuades my own personal jury to give it a spot on the comfort list. With Exhibits A and B (the two photos) as further evidence, it has certainly made a good case for itself so far.

Cultural tips: Treat it like a weed (short of pulling it out). It takes care of itself very well without extra water or fertilizer, and the chartreuse selections often become increasingly comely as the temperature goes up and the moisture and fertility levels of the potting mix go down.

THUNBERGIA
black-eyed Susan vine (*T. alata*); Bengal trumpet, sky vine (*T. grandiflora*)

Family: Acanthaceae
Cultural group: annuals, climbers and trailers
Height: 3–5 ft. (*T. alata*), 3–10 ft. (*T. grandiflora*)
Width: depends on training
Light: sun to partial shade
Temperature: warm to hot

Overwintering: min. 55°F, water occasionally, bright light (*T. grandiflora*)
Moisture: moderate to ample
Drainage of medium: well drained
Fertility: average to high (phosphorus to push bloom)
Ease/speed of growth: easy/moderate to fast (*T. alata*), easy to moderate/moderate to fast (*T. grandiflora*)
Propagation: seeds (*Tt. alata* and *grandiflora*), cuttings (*T. grandiflora*)
Problems: spider mites, mealybugs
Principal interest: flowers, form (particularly if trained)
Length of seasonal interest: long (*T. alata*); moderate to long (*T. grandiflora*)

Design attributes
Color: flowers orange (a few verge on red), yellow, and white, with or without black "eyes" (*T. alata*); shades of blue, rarely white (*T. grandiflora*)
Line: from stems, elongated leaves, flower stems
Form: long strands of leaves with flowers
Space: depends on training
Texture: medium

The starry, tropical-fruit-colored flowers and beaklike, lime-green calyces of a *Thunbergia alata* selection create a fascinating contrast of color and form. I want to connect the dots to see how many other forms I could produce.

The light yellow flowers of one example of *Thunbergia alata* 'Susie Mix' sure do light up the place. Just for fun, cover up the center of a flower or two to see how blind they look without the black eye.

Whether borne singly or in clusters, the violet-blue flowers of *Thunbergia grandiflora* stand out from the foliage. Don't be misled by the photo: sky vine can reach for the sky (well, it can get 10 ft. closer to the sky, anyway).

I've grown and admired black-eyed Susan vine (*T. alata*) for years, waiting and watching as the twisting little vines open their distinctive five-lobed flowers with black throats, or eyes. Plant some seeds in spring; by the end of summer, you'll have a pot full of black-eyed orange and yellow flowers. Usually the seedlings are trained onto teepees or hoops, which is a fine way to show off the surprisingly cheerful flowers, bird-beak calyces (which also resemble fish, and in time you'll see an entire school of them), and triangular leaves. But recently I've seen them cascading from hanging baskets—curtains of them—transforming the flowers from bruised eyes to constellations of stars. Being vines, some stems will climb up the wires that suspend the baskets, bringing more density and visual excitement to the show. Expect even the older flowers join in when their time comes, noticeably, almost noisily falling from the plants and strewing bits of color below the baskets.

I like to see either individual colors or mixes of *T. alata* spilling out of or clambering above monopots, but a few strings of black eyes add some punch (I had to use that word eventually, right?) to combopots, too. The familiar yellow, orange, and white selections (such as the Eyes, Susie, and Sunny series, and 'Superstar Orange') remain appealing, but the artier salmon-, flame-, and almost red-toned ones (including Blushing Susie and Salmon Shades) have been catching my eye recently.

For a change of pace, give *T. grandiflora* a try, but remember that it can easily grow three times as large as *T. alata*. The big blue flowers appear as lone blooms or in several-flowered clusters over a long season (one catalog promises a nine-month floral display) but not as freely as on *T. alata*. Grow one all by itself in a good-sized pot, overwintering it and building it up into an impressive specimen. It desperately needs a hoop, trellis, or other support to keep it looking reasonably neat, and you'll need to direct the stems and cut back the wayward ones.

Cultural tips: Be gentle with them; the stems can be brittle. Give them some high-phosphorous fertilizer every now and then to keep the flowers coming, especially on *T. alata*.

THYMUS
thyme

Family: Lamiaceae
Cultural group: perennials
Height: 6–12 in. or more
Width: 6–12 in.
Light: sun
Temperature: cool to warm to hot
Overwintering: keep totally dormant at just above freezing, no water, light not necessary; can be kept potted in their growing medium; variously hardy in Z4–9
Moisture: on dry side to moderate
Drainage of medium: well drained

Fertility: low to average
Ease/speed of growth: easy to moderate/slow to moderate
Propagation: division, cuttings, rooted stems, seeds
Problems: root rot
Principal interest: fragrance, foliage, flowers, form
Length of seasonal interest: long (all but flowers, which are
 usually brief)

Design attributes

Color: foliage green, sometimes marked with or entirely
 yellow, or marked with white; flowers white, pink,
 red-violet, and purple
Line: basically none unless allowed to trail thinly or
 cascade
Form: carpeting to low-shrubby to cascading
Space: very limited except when trailing thinly or cascading;
 might be implied between flowers
Texture: fine

I won't pretend to be an authority on thymes; in fact, my eyes tend to glaze over when I look at more than a few of them and try to sort them out. But I do know that many of them smell good, taste great (with meat, shellfish, and eggs, and in hearty soups, casseroles, and tomato sauces), and look like mounds of foam, wall-to-wall carpets, or sheer curtains in container plantings. Bees don't care about sorting them out, either, but they obviously appreciate their flowers, whatever their identity. Sensible bees. Start with these (the ones I do know) and branch out:

T. ×citriodorus, the distinctively lemon-scented lemon thyme, grows taller (to about 1 ft.) and more open than some and comes in a pleasant mix of selections with all-green, white-marked, or yellow-toned and marked foliage. You might detect another citrus scent in the amusingly rhyming 'Lime Thyme', but I haven't. Their light purple flowers add some interest.

T. serpyllum (mother of thyme) bears fuzzy leaves that often

A thyme pours from a shallow container balanced on a much taller, upside-down pot—a very simple, very satisfying illustration of the visual impact of a bunch of lines. This example also says a lot about the "busy" impression often expressed by fine texture.

First let's think about color, pondering how bits and flecks of it can be as eye-catching as big patches. Where's the line? Now let's think about form—or lumps and globs, in this case, but not negatively as the words might imply. Is space literal or implied here? Finally, consider texture, as in fine, finer, and finest. (By the way, the thyme is the bluish green crust in the front.)

Some thymes bloom, such as the vividly red-violet *Thymus serpyllum* 'Coccineus', much to the satisfaction of bees. Others look nice to us humans, especially variegated ones, such as *T. ×citriodorus* (lemon thyme), seen here. I don't know if the bees can smell or taste thymes, but we sure can. At least we should, and often.

temporarily disappear under the mostly purple flowers. The flowers of 'Coccineus' dazzle in rich red-violet, especially when seen next to lighter colors. Some selections barely reach 4 in. tall, and 'Minimus' usually reaches a lofty 2 in., although many of them soon spread 1–2 ft.

T. vulgaris is the common thyme of cooking and most likely the one that comes up if you plant a package of seeds labeled "thyme." It makes delicate little shrubs 6–12 in. tall and about as wide.

Traditionalists grow thymes to perfection in a strawberry jar, but I invite you to let them encrust a trough or trickle from a tall container. A collection of them in small, shallow monopots would make an interactive decoration for a dining table (who could resist, while waiting for the soup course, reaching over to release the scent from the nearest leaves?), as would several of them mixing it up in a larger pot or as carpeting for a combopot. Whichever method you choose, frequently take time to give them a little brushing or rub and then inhale their saliva-stimulating fragrances.

Cultural tips: Prune (or harvest, if you will) the shrubby ones to encourage denser, more compact growth. All tolerate

drought and don't need very much fertilizer to do well, but don't think you can get away with growing them in shade. They'll become thin, spindly, and sad-looking, and flowering will be drastically reduced or eliminated. You and the bees won't like that.

TRADESCANTIA
spiderwort; white velvet (*T. sillamontana*)

Family: Commelinaceae
Cultural group: tropicals, climbers and trailers
Height: 6–12 in.
Width: 6–12 in. or more; depends on training for trailers
Light: limited sun to shade
Temperature: warm to hot
Overwintering: min. 55°F, water occasionally, bright light
Moisture: moderate to ample
Drainage of medium: well drained; the vigorous trailers tolerate shallow standing water, and rooted cuttings can remain in water for a long time

Fertility: average to high (nitrogen to push growth)
Ease/speed of growth: easy/moderate (*T. sillamontana*)
    to fast (others)
Propagation: cuttings, rooted stems
Problems: spider mites
Principal interest: foliage, form, maybe flowers
Length of seasonal interest: long to all year

Design attributes

Color: foliage green, often marked with or entirely in white
    and/or red-violet or purple (can look shiny or metallic),
    blue-green (*T. sillamontana*); flowers white or red-violet
Line: abundant from stems, elongated leaves, and linear
    markings
Form: spreading-trailing (*T. sillamontana* upright to spread-
    ing); strings of knife blades or pointed spoons; fuzzy
    ladders or little critters
Space: at edges of plant, depends on training
Texture: medium to coarse

Gotta love those tertiary colors! The blue-green of the *Trades-cantia sillamontana* foliage and their red-violet flowers combine beautifully with the yellow-green of the *Lysimachia nummularia* 'Aurea'. Note that the younger growth of this tradescantia often appears much grayer: living color combinations (unlike diamonds) aren't forever.

My Great Aunt Hazel (she of syngonium-on-the-sideboard fame) kept a big patch of hardy perennial spiderwort going outside her kitchen door. All I remember of it were the floppy slashes of stems and leaves and the Trinity-esque three-parted flowers (which reminded me of the design carved into the end of each pew at our church). It didn't impress me, and to this day I'm not a fan of the herbaceous-perennial Andersoniana Group of *Tradescantia*, except for the potently colored 'Sweet Kate', which adds pizzazz to a combopot (a monopot could easily end up looking like those floppy slashes of my childhood), where sturdy, supportive companions might coordinate, contrast, or compete with its strong coloration (from the blue-purple flowers and chartreuse foliage) as you see fit.

Other members of *Tradescantia* take the flop-and-slash motif in other design directions, and I wouldn't want to garden in containers without them:

Both *Tt. fluminensis* and *zebrina* (wandering Jew, inch plant) are variations on the basic theme of masses of pointed-oval leaves on cascading stems; the former bears white flowers, and the latter blooms in shades of purple. *T. fluminensis* 'Albovittata' looks as refreshing as lemonade (minus any yellow or pink food-color fakery) with plenty of chipped ice and some mint in it, and 'Aurea', with golden wings of bright chartreuse, brings a suggestion of light wherever it goes. Even a stem or two dangling against a container will do the job.

The most familiar selection of *T. zebrina* bears dark green leaves with two crystalline-silver bands, but you might also be inspired by 'Quadricolor', which produces foliage striped with variable amounts of light and dark green plus light and dark red-violet. (That's how I get four colors; others see white, cream, and silver in it.)

A lone shoot of *Tradescantia fluminensis* 'Aurea' swoops down from its elegant container in search of a place to root. In the meantime, it reminds us not to be afraid to thin vigorously growing trailers so that their design attributes (other than color) can be better observed and appreciated.

When it's color you want, by all means let a tradescantia burgeon as it will. Compare this photo of *Tradescantia fluminensis* 'Aurea' to the other, and you'll appreciate the dramatic design difference between a single shoot of a plant and a mass of it.

This secondary triad of purple, green, and orange is a rather sedate expression of *Tradescantia pallida* 'Purpurea'. Its dark purple-green dramatically sets off just about every color (except maybe black and gray, which would result in a gloom worthy of Edgar Allan Poe).

Somebody could knit a sweater with wool gathered from the foliage of *Tradescantia sillamontana*. It appears even more abundant on the newly emerged shoots, making them look like they're made from silvery gray felt. Of course the colors that combine with this foliage are legion.

Purple spiderwort, *T. pallida* 'Purpurea' (aka 'Purple Heart', *Setcreasea purpurea*) might suggest the flop and slash of the herbaceous perennials, but I see chains of purple knife blades instead. Every pale color I can think of looks luminous when combined with it, and bright colors almost scream against the rich purple-green blades.

T. sillamontana goes against the *Tradescantia* grain in notable and very appealing ways: it's fuzzy, it grows distinctly upright before succumbing to its generic tendency to spread and hang, and the red-violet flowers are worth looking at. Cut back rangy specimens to renew the upright growth. Use it as you would other gray-leaved plants (liberally, I hope). While a stem or two adds spice to a combopot, an established (as in overwintered) monopot specimen will make you forget all about those slashy, floppy spiderworts.

Cultural tips: Pinch young plants to encourage branching. None require very much fertilizer to grow, but plenty of nitrogen will make them flourish. Don't be afraid to thin them out if they grow too well. The stems are brittle, so handle them carefully; any that do break off can be easily rooted, however.

TROPAEOLUM
nasturtium (*T. majus*)

Family: Tropaeolaceae
Cultural group: annuals, climbers and trailers, perennials
Height: mounded forms 1 ft., climbers and trailers to 3 ft., maybe more
Width: 1–2 ft. or more; depends on training for climbers
Light: sun
Temperature: warm to hot
Overwintering: min. 55°F, water regularly but not

excessively, bright light (for cutting-propagated selections only; the rest are annuals)

Moisture: moderate to ample

Drainage of medium: well drained

Fertility: low to average

Ease/speed of growth: easy/moderate to fast

Propagation: seeds, cuttings

Problems: aphids, cabbage butterfly caterpillars, whitefly, slugs and snails

Principal interest: flowers, foliage, form, fragrance

Length of seasonal interest: long

Design attributes

Color: flowers red, yellow, and orange (a few approach white); foliage light to medium green, sometimes entirely purple-green or marked with white

Line: from petioles, leaf veining, and flower spurs; stems on trailing sorts. Also, there are plenty of circular lines here, so plants can appear as a mass of motion.

Form: mounding to climbing-trailing; green chips or cookies with exotic birds

Space: little, usually (climbers and trailers can have more throughout)

Texture: medium to coarse

Nasturtiums have always fascinated me. Their edible flowers suggest stocky, colorful tropical birds with long tails, scratching and flying among lively, (mostly) green foliage umbrellas. Brush the plants, and up rises a strong, sharp, spicy-cabbagey fragrance, and that same combination hits your tongue if you nibble a flower or bud. They laugh at poor soil; in fact, they bloom far more abundantly in potting mixes with low nutrient levels. Heat and strong sun bring out their can-do attitude as well (but don't think that they treat drought with the same insouciance; these are plants, after all, not plastic, and they do have some needs). Most fascinating of all, they seem to pull black aphids out of thin air: even if you've never

Strong backlighting reveals the unusual vein pattern of the peltate foliage of *Tropaeolum majus* (nasturtium). The petioles are inserted in the middle of the round leaves, conjuring images of umbrellas, spider webs, and Van de Graaff generators—in action. The flowers are interesting, too.

Nasturtium foliage receives plenty of attention, but the flowers deserve a closer look, too. Their structure truly sets them apart: (usually) five "bearded" petals with skinny handles are attached in the center, and a long spur sticks out the back. After you finish pulling one apart, eat it.

seen black aphids on other plants in your garden, chances are very good that you'll see them on your nasturtiums. Lots of them. Moving in unison like a school of fish if you move your finger closely along the colonies living on the petioles.

"FFFFFuuuuuuuuyyyyuuuuuuwwwww," you think. "What's so fascinating about a bunch of bugs on my plants?" Two things: one, they don't cause any damage that I've ever noticed, and two, they serve as food for the larvae of lacewings, syrphids (flower flies), and ladybugs (as well as the adults), and no doubt other insects. Some of those insects end up as food for bees and wasps, birds, toads, and other organisms. All that life happens because nasturtiums can support a population of black bugs that don't damage their hosts. That's green. These days, that's a sensible thing to do for our world.

How many different variegated plants can you find in this photograph? Equal amounts of each would be dizzying, but the much larger mass of a nasturtium from the Alaska series offers a place for the eye to rest for a bit before venturing on to other foliage patterns. Of course I want you to cover the orange flowers to see what both their absence and presence add to the mix.

Below: A lively mass of nasturiums almost seems to leap out from the very mellow gray background. The orange flowers of this selection contrast attractively with the foliage, and see what happens when you cover the pot.

Whether you agree with me or not about the aphids, I think we should all enjoy a few nasturtiums in pots. The climbers and trailers can be trained onto teepees, hoops, or trellises, or they can suggest bits of fire falling from hanging baskets. A monopot of one of the bushy selections would make a perfect addition to a dining table—you could pick the buds and flowers and nibble on them as the meal progresses—or add a plant or two to a combopot.

If you favor the climbers and trailers, go for the Double Gleam series in a mix of colors, or 'Moonlight' in light yellow. Both easily grow at least 3 ft. long. Most selections offered these days make bushy, 1-ft. mounds, including those in the Alaska series, in a range of colors among white-splashed foliage; the Jewel mix; the double red 'Hermine Grashoff', which can be propagated only from cuttings; the sumptuous 'Empress of India', with purple-green foliage and orange-red, semidouble flowers (it becomes more of a trailer than a bush in time); and 'Peach Melba' in peach-yellow with red spots, one per petal. All should support a healthy colony of black aphids; you probably won't even see them unless you look for them and the other life they support.

Cultural tips: If you do choose to grow the climbers, put the frame in the container when you sow the seeds or plant the seedlings, and then be prepared to help them wrap around their supports.

TULIPA
tulip

Family: Liliaceae
Cultural group: bulbs
Height: 6–24 in.
Width: individually 6–12 in.
Light: sun
Temperature: cool to warm
Overwintering: many hardy in Z4–6, progressively less satisfactory in Z7 and warmer; most require a long cold period to bloom; treat as a forced hardy bulb (see *Narcissus*)
Moisture: moderate (to ample when in flower)
Drainage of medium: well drained
Fertility: not an issue when forcing; otherwise, average
Ease/speed of growth: easy to challenging/fast
Propagation: offsets, seeds (for the very patient and dedicated)
Problems: insufficient cold period, drought, aphids, bulb mold (although most molds are harmless)
Principal interest: flowers, form
Length of seasonal interest: brief

Design attributes
Color: flowers range widely—white, red, pink, orange, yellow, red-violet, purple, and green, often marked with at least one other color; foliage usually light to medium grayish blue-green, sometimes marked with white or red-purple
Line: from flower stems, leaves, sometimes flowers (starry, lily-like)
Form: upright, like some kind of leafy vegetable with spectacular flowers as a garnish; flowers in a surprising range of forms
Space: at edge of plants and around flowers
Texture: medium to coarse

I hope to grow tulips in pots—and generally be bowled over by their dazzling and colorful diversity—until I too am planted. Like other hardy bulbs, tulips can be grown in containers, whether forced into bloom earlier than their normal

Tulipa 'Mickey Mouse' emerges from a gorgeous, rustic pot like flames (red, yellow, and even green) flickering from a witch's cauldron. I probably wouldn't have come up with that image if all the flowers appeared in a straight line above the foliage. What do you see?

outdoor flowering time or allowed to do their thing at the same time as their in-ground relatives. As with daffodils, I like to force tulips as monopots, but maybe some day I'll try combining them with other hardy bulbs and other plants in combopots. Beware: Some tulips force much more easily and successfully than others. I suggest you start with these, listed by their type:

Single Early: 'Christmas Marvel' (bright pink), 'Couleur Cardinal' (intense red), 'Mickey Mouse' (yellow with red flames), 'Prinses Irene' (orange with purple flames).

Double Early: 'Monsella' (yellow with red marks), 'Monte Carlo' (yellow).

Triumph: 'Apricot Beauty' (more orangey pink than apricot), 'Calgary' (short, to about 1 ft., white), 'Inzell' (pure white, and taller, to 18 in.), 'Leen van der Mark' (red, edged cream turning white).

Double Late: The only one I've seen do well is 'Angélique' (light to medium pink).

Single Late, lily-flowered, fringed, viridiflora ("green"), and multi-flowering tulips present more of a challenge, often blooming erratically or poorly. I've seen some of the Darwin hybrids ('Banja Luka', 'Ollioules', and some in the Impression series) forced successfully by experienced growers in a big greenhouse; likewise, some of the species (*Tt. fosteriana*, *greigii*, *humilis*, *linifolia*) have made impressive pots, but they too were grown by those in the know. However, if you're growing them in pots that remain outdoors all winter for bloom during their normal flowering time, anything goes.

Cultural tips: The entry on *Narcissus* presents my take on how to succeed with daffodils in pots, and much of that information applies to tulips, with a few modifications: 1) Place tulips in single layers, not multiples. 2) Position bulbs so that the flat side (you'll find it easily on most of them) faces away from the center of the pot, which will allow the first and largest leaves to appear in a neat conformation instead of every which way. 3) Expect many of them to take longer to bloom

Forced pots of tulips brighten a February day (or any day from December through May, depending on your forcing schedule). Note how the purity of *Tulipa* 'Inzell' peaceably separates the other two selections, whose colors might not make an appealing combination if placed smack up against each other.

(when forced) than most daffodils. 4) They don't appreciate being kept as wet as daffodils. 5) Keep an eye out for aphids, whose populations can explode seemingly overnight and make a sticky mess out of your tulips.

VERBENA
vervain

Family: Verbenaceae
Cultural group: climbers and trailers, perennials
Height: mostly 6–12 in.; *V. bonariensis* to 6 ft.
Width: 1–2 ft. or more; *V. bonariensis* 1 ft.
Light: sun to limited partial shade
Temperature: warm to hot
Overwintering: min. 55°F, water occasionally, bright light; hardy in Z6–10 (*V. canadensis*), Z7–11 (*V. bonariensis*)
Moisture: moderate to ample
Drainage of medium: well drained
Fertility: average to high (phosphorus to push flowers)
Ease/speed of growth: easy/moderate
Propagation: seeds, cuttings
Problems: whitefly (members of the Verbenaceae are magnets for them), aphids, powdery mildew, rots and spots
Principal interest: flowers, form (if trained); *V. bonariensis* needs no training to show its form
Length of seasonal interest: long

Design attributes
Color: flowers white, red, pink, orange, red-violet, blue, and purple (often with white eyes); foliage medium to dark green
Line: from stems and flower stems in most; finely cut foliage in some; *V. bonariensis* extremely linear except for flower clusters
Form: spreading to cascading, like a bunch of brooches tossed on a plant; *V. bonariensis* an upright and skinny, peek-a-boo scrim
Space: limited on most (although it can be strongly implied); *V. bonariensis* could take the prize for most spacious plant
Texture: medium (*V. bonariensis* fine)

A spreading-cascading, stridently magenta selection of *V. canadensis* came up and bloomed every year without fail in our garden outside of Pittsburgh. As The Weeder, I learned to recognize its dark green, cutleaf seedlings, transplanting some of them into safe spots in the stone walls and elsewhere around the garden. Another pleasant routine involved deadheading the spent flower clusters to promote further bloom, but a few were always spared the shears to produce seeds for the next crop of volunteers. I've enjoyed many verbenas since

those days, including the eye-popping red *V. ×hybrida* 'Blaze' (c. 1968). It and others came and went—they never volunteered—but they all (save for *V. bonariensis*) offered variations on the theme of a spreading green mat studded with colorful brooches that make people happy just to see them. Grow most verbenas as jaw-droppingly colorful hanging baskets, or mix

Haze upon haze. The linear, very spacious *Verbena bonariensis* allows your eye to see through the purple and take in the extreme linearity and fine texture of the *Miscanthus sinensis* 'Morning Light' behind it. There's no pot under these mists, but there could be.

The fuzzed-out background illustrates a point about color: be careful when using pale and bright shades of the same or related colors. While the pale pink and bright red-violet of *Verbena* Escapade Bright Eye (= 'Esca Bright Eye') go together beautifully, note how the out-of-focus flowerheads seem to be in pain against the bright red haze. Also, there's just enough yellow in that red to have a spat with the blue cast of the pink.

them up with other plants in combopots, letting them cascade out of and over their containers.

V. bonariensis is a notable exception, sending its little clusters of short-lived, rich lilac flowers up to 6 ft. into the air. "Air" is the operative word here, because any planting of *V. bonariensis* consists of more space than plant, creating a delicate screen of upright and crossing green line and spots of lilac. A few in a large combopot will lift the planting and the area around it into the stratosphere. While butterflies visit most verbenas, they assault *V. bonariensis*, knocking the flowers off with their vigorous legs and proboscises in their excitement.

While I no longer grow (or often see) good old *V. canadensis*, one of its selections, the deservedly popular 'Homestead Purple', always catches my eye with its abundant, rich purple brooches. Although it is touted as hardy, I advise treating it as an annual in areas colder than Z6, certainly when growing in a pot. It looks positively regal when combined with strong yellow, a color that *Lantana camara* and its selections offer in abundance.

V. ×hybrida encompasses a stupefying and ever-increasing number of plants. The 2009 catalog of a major commercial seed producer listed five mixes and series and one selection— and one of those series offered fifteen colors and three "sub-

A massive ball of *Verbena* 'Babylon Blue Carpet' is the 800-pound gorilla in this room. It's a pleasant, colorful gorilla, but still the thing receiving all the attention. That's another way to describe a focal point.

A super closeup reveals the tiny, delicate flowers of *Verbena bonariensis*. It also makes we want to include some of them in a container with a bright yellow-green foliage plant. Of course I'll need to be a very tall person so that I can look down on it and see the colors together. . . or put the pot in front of a tall yellow-green background. It could happen.

The lovely green and peach of *Verbena* 'Peaches 'n' Cream' contrast strongly with the rich, dark color of *Alternanthera* 'Gail's Choice', the blue-gray of the container, and the almost hairlike leaves of *Carex testacea*. How do you feel about the colors of the brick wall and bluestone ledge?

mixes" ("eyed mix," "mix," and "pastel mix") from which to choose. An embarrassment of riches, indeed, and one worth exploiting. I'll recommend only two specific selections: the luscious 'Peaches 'n' Cream', and 'Lanai Blush White', which reminds me of a pure white, puffy summer cloud barely fogged with palest pink at the earliest hint of sunset.

Also look for and grow the icy, silvery, misty, pale purplish blue *V. rigida* 'Polaris' and the perfectly named moss verbena, *V. tenuisecta*, in white and shades of blue and purple. Like other verbenas (except for oddball *V. bonariensis*, which might overwinter or reseed), these root easily from cuttings taken from overwintered plants, so you might want to try to propagate a particularly attractive specimen that catches your eye.

Cultural tips: Plenty of sun helps keep powdery mildew at bay. Poor drainage spells death for verbenas. They will bounce back from severe drought.

VINCA
periwinkle, greater periwinkle, vinca vine (*V. major*)

Family: Apocynaceae
Cultural group: annuals, perennials
Height: 3–6 ft. or more
Width: depends on training
Light: sun to partial shade
Temperature: cool to warm to hot
Overwintering: min. 50°F, water occasionally, bright light;
    hardy in Z7–11
Moisture: moderate to ample
Drainage of medium: well drained
Fertility: average
Ease/speed of growth: easy/moderate to fast
Propagation: cuttings, division
Problems: aphids, spider mites, rots and spots, ubiquity
Principal interest: foliage, form, flowers
Length of seasonal interest: long (flowers, if they appear
    at all, come and go)

Design attributes
Color: foliage dark green, often marked with white or
    yellow and contrasting greens; flowers blue and purple
Line: extremely obvious, especially when more than
    2 ft. long
Form: lines with some leaves attached
Space: abundant
Texture: fine to medium

Name confusion alert: if you're looking for the shrubby, white- and pink-flowered annuals commonly called "vinca," please see *Catharanthus*. Here we're considering vining members of the genus *Vinca*. You know what I mean:

vinca vine, the plant that looks like a rope ladder that severely height-challenged elves might use to escape from window-boxes. Most often seen as the cream-splashed 'Variegata' (which can reach 8 ft. in length) or the newer 'Expoflora', other selections are worth searching out, including the variably gold-centered 'Maculata', gold-netted 'Reticulata', and the variably cream-variegated, less far-reaching 'Wojo's Jem' (which displays all-green and all-cream foliage extremes, in time). All present a golden opportunity for you to express your gardening creativity, provided you do something other than plant them and let them grow a spindly 3 ft. or more. Pinch them a few times early on to stimulate more, less straggly-looking shoots, train them onto a globular or spiral wire form (using string, raffia, or some other sort of tie), or weave them through their companions in a combopot for some unexpected interest. Even mundane vinca vine can be transformed with a little imagination.

A familiar relative, *V. minor*, also and often simply called vinca, myrtle, or periwinkle, can be grown in containers (and

Don't be an automaton by relegating *Vinca major* 'Wojo's Jem' to a second-story windowbox and nowhere else. Its variably cream-variegated leaves bear close inspection and admiration.

should withstand Z5 winters), but I think that once its starry flowers have faded, there's not much there there. Maybe I'm as jaded by *V. minor* as others are by *V. major* and should try being a little more adventuresome with it. Six-inch mounds of shiny leaves with longer stems trailing from them might provide a handsome background for other, flashier companions.

Cultural tips: Vinca vine will root where it touches open ground, and it can quickly become a pest in warmer areas of its hardiness range. Beware.

VIOLA
pansy

Family: Violaceae
Cultural group: annuals
Height: 6–9 in.
Width: 6–12 in.
Light: sun to partial shade
Temperature: cool to warm (heat tolerance is improving)
Overwintering: min. 45°F, water occasionally, bright light; some are hardy in Z7–9
Moisture: moderate
Drainage of medium: well drained
Fertility: average
Ease/speed of growth: easy (if you understand their temperature needs)/moderate
Propagation: seeds, cuttings
Problems: hot weather, aphids, slugs and snails, root rot, rots and spots
Principal interest: flowers
Length of seasonal interest: moderate to long

A ball of little purple-haired monkeys hangs from a cross beam . . . or maybe you see little purple-haired guys with big handle-bar mustaches. In any case, I'll bet you didn't immediately recognize these as pansies—who puts pansies in hanging baskets? Well, some people do, and the pansies can put on a big show.

Where's the windowbox? Usually seen diving out of one, *Vinca major* makes an attractive specimen all by itself in a gray pot (and on a gray bench, which lets us look at every bit of the vinca without any distraction). This is 'Expoflora', but any selection would look good as a monopot.

A very familiar groundcover, *Vinca minor* blooms in periwinkle blue, blue, red-violet, purple, and white, as shown here, and some selections offer variegated foliage. That's nice, but this is definitely a group of plants I consider to be bit players in a container.

Design attributes

Color: flowers white, red, yellow, orange, blue, and purple, many marked with black and/or another color; foliage medium to dark green

Line: from flower stems

Form: mounded to almost shrubby

Space: limited, although it can be implied around the flowers

Texture: medium

I'm going to cut to the chase with this entry: think of pansies and violas almost exclusively as color. No, make that paint, which you can pour or spread or splash around in almost any container that holds potting mix and provides drainage. Don't even think about their line, form, space, or texture, which should be easy, because those four design elements pale in comparison to their palette of seemingly endless colors. You can find literally *hundreds* of different pansies and violas in catalogs and online. That's a whole lot of color!

We're not talking about a fussy medium here. Pansies and violas are workhorses, easily transplanted and otherwise re-arranged if you don't like how they look with other plants. Their one limitation—which is becoming less of a problem as the hybridizers continue to work with them—is their tendency to slow down and die as the temperature rises. But don't let that make you shy away from using them: many bloom for at least a couple of months, beginning in late winter and continuing bravely into late spring in colder-winter areas, and often starting in fall and flowering throughout winter and into spring in areas with warmer winters.

Broadly speaking (or painting with a broad brush, if you will), pansies have larger but fewer flowers than violas, and violas usually grow taller and look more like plants than a plate of flower-strewn salad. Also, violas often tolerate more heat and cold than pansies and therefore bloom longer. Panolas, the new kid in town, essentially provide pansy-sized flowers on viola-sized plants and tolerate heat well. They seem to be catching on down South. Whichever your preferences, choose your paints and canvases, and let the creativity begin.

So which from among the hundreds of choices do I enjoy and recommend? Long-time favorite *V. tricolor* (Johnny-jump-up, heartsease) bears cute (I use that word very sparingly, but it fits here) barely inch-wide flowers in seemingly endless combinations of white, yellow, and purple patches, lines, and spots. Each plant might reach 6 in. wide and tall, but no one grows Johnny-jump-ups as individual plants (do they?). Mass them in monopots or scatter them around in combopots and then watch as the abundant self-sown seedlings pop up in all sorts of unexpectedly perfect places. Other favorites include the ones that appear in front of me in a nursery or garden and catch my eye.

Trust your local nursery or garden center to stock the se-

This pot of pansies fills a more traditional role, but kudos to the person who thought to put this *Viola ×wittrockiana* selection in a dark mustard-colored pot placed in front of impossibly purple salvia. Hello, Sunshine!

A clowder, a clutter, a glaring, a pounce of feline faces looks out from their container. Smaller-flowered violas and pansies, such as this *Viola ×wittrockiana* 'Plentifall Lavender Blue', often have whiskered (instead of black-eyed and -mustachioed) faces.

lections that should do well in your area. Write down the names of the ones that please you, and then hope that they'll be offered again. In the meantime, I bet the hybridizers will come up with even more selections that push the cold- or heat-tolerance range and/or bloom in yet another paint color.

Cultural tips: Don't let them wilt, but don't allow them to sit in sodden potting mix, either. Providing high-phosphorus fertilizer will promote more blooms, as will deadheading them (if you have the time and inclination).

XANTHOSOMA
elephant ear

Family: Araceae
Cultural group: tropicals
Height: 3–6 ft.
Width: 3–5 ft.
Light: partial shade
Temperature: warm to hot

Overwintering: min. 50–55°F, water occasionally but sparingly, bright light (you might try a darker site to force dry, leafless dormancy); hardy to Z7b, according to some sources
Moisture: moderate to ample
Drainage of medium: well drained but tolerates shallow standing water
Fertility: average to high
Ease/speed of growth: easy/moderate to fast
Propagation: division (of tubers)
Problems: rots and spots
Principal interest: foliage, form
Length of seasonal interest: long

Design attributes

Color: green foliage, sometimes chartreuse or almost yellow
Line: from petioles, elongated leaves, and midribs
Form: a nicely gathered bunch of shields and spears
Space: usually abundant around and within the entire plant
Texture: flat-out coarse

'Chartreuse Giant' xanthosoma is just getting up a head of steam in this photo, taken in June. By the end of the season, it probably towered over its companions (and the people who might have sat in the chairs). It totally lives up to both parts of its cultivar name. Which color(s) would you remove from this grouping, if any?

Finally, we meet the last in the series of genera commonly and confusingly known as elephant ear (others are *Alocasia*, *Bergenia*, *Caladium*, and *Colocasia*). At least they all seem to merit the common name, once you get over the small matter that not a single one displays a pachyderm's gray coloration. Artistic license triumphs again.

Here's how I sort out the four elephant ears in the Araceae (*Bergenia* has a very different habit and totally different flowers, so that genus stands out). Caladiums are the little guys and grow from tubers. Alocasias are much bigger, and most of them produce long rhizomes instead of tubers. The remaining two, both tuberous, resemble each other a great deal; basically, *Xanthosoma* is the New World's version of the Old World's *Colocasia*. When grown in containers, all four genera like to think that they're back in the moist, organic soils and partially shaded spots of their hot-tropical homelands, so try your best to duplicate those conditions. In return, they'll quickly become traffic stoppers.

If you've read this book alphabetically, you already know I'm partial toward chartreuse. If you haven't, let me glow over the desirability of yellow-green foliage and flowers. They seem to emit light instead of being illuminated by or reflecting it, and a lengthy list of colors combines beautifully or at least satisfyingly with chartreuse. I can't think of any color other than gray that looks terrible next to it. Some of my favorite color combinations include purple-black with chartreuse, rusty orange with chartreuse, medium blue-violet with chartreuse, cream with chartreuse, bright pink with chartreuse … you get the idea.

So it should come as no surprise that I recommend growing chartreuse selections of *Xanthosoma*. However, I'll confess to a bit of confusion regarding two allegedly different members of the genus, 'Chartreuse Giant' and 'Lime Zinger'. They look the same to me, but various authorities and references can't agree on their heritage. Whatever, expect plants to easily reach 3 ft. tall by 4–5 ft. wide in their first year from a decent-sized tuber, and more if overwintered. Dig around in the potting mix, and you'll probably find some little starter tubers to separate and plant into their own pots.

Once you stop marveling at the ethereal color of a well-grown plant (if you can), take a little time to appreciate its other design attributes: clearly drawn, precise lines; severe and immediately obvious form; big spaces defined by the equally large leaves and stems; and in-your-face bold, coarse texture. This is the sort of plant that pushes others into supporting roles.

Cultural tips: Morning sun (before it gets hot and really bright) suits them best and brings out the glowing coloration. More light brings out the yellow; less light, the green.

ZANTEDESCHIA
calla lily, arum lily

Family: Araceae
Cultural group: bulbs, tropicals
Height: 1–3 ft.
Width: 1–3 ft. or more
Light: sun to limited partial shade
Temperature: warm to hot, although some are quite tolerant of cool temps
Overwintering: min. 50°F, water regularly but not excessively, bright light; or keep totally dormant at 50–60°F, very little to no water, light not necessary; can be kept potted in their growing medium; some are hardy in Z8–10
Moisture: moderate to ample
Drainage of medium: well drained but tolerates some standing water (*Z. aethiopica* can take 1 ft. of standing water)

Of all the images in this book, this could well be the most abstract, but it speaks volumes about color, line, form, space, and texture. Like any calla lily, *Zantedeschia* 'Captain Sonora' can bring oodles of design presence to a container planting. Meditate upon this photo for a little while, and you'll see what I mean.

Fertility: average to high

Ease/speed of growth: easy to moderate/moderate to fast

Propagation: division, seeds

Problems: spider mites, rots and spots

Principal interest: flowers, foliage

Length of seasonal interest: brief to intermittent (flowers); long (foliage)

Design attributes

Color: flowers white and solidly colored in or marked with green, red, pink, orange, yellow, and purple; foliage green, sometimes marked with white, yellow, or dark purple

Line: from petioles, elongated leaves, flower stems, flowers

Form: masses of broad-headed arrows with goblets/cups/ vases/soft ice-cream creations

Space: variable; can be ample around flowers

Texture: medium to coarse

Calla lilies have a stigma attached to them. No, not the yellow structure that rises out of the center of the swirly part; that's the spadix (which holds quite a few tiny individual female pistils, each ending in a stigma, as well as little male stamens) surrounded by the leaf-like spathe. The stigma I'm referring to is an ethnobotanical one. Calla lilies, in more than a few minds and for more than a few years, have been associated with flower arrangements at funerals and with death in general. But the times they are a-changin'. The magnificent, energetic, sensual paintings and photographs by Georgia O'Keeffe and Robert Mapplethorpe don't bring the Grim Reaper to my mind, and these days callas are likely to turn up in stunning bridal bouquets and other wedding paraphernalia.

Once seen only in white (or maybe occasionally in yellow), calla lilies are now found in a distinctly non-funereal range of colors and an equally broad range of plant sizes, all of which look splendid and grow beautifully in containers. Fortunately, the plants have been reduced to more manageable, even com-

Which did you see first, the plants or the pots? Admit it, it was the in-your-face oversized chartreuse pots, but then I hope your eye traveled to the fluttering bird wings and champagne flutes of the masses of a *Zantedeschia elliottiana* selection. This is garden theater at its very best, worthy of a conductor and a choreographer.

A full moon shines among the stars on a clear night. The pristine whiteness and simple form of a white calla lily (here, *Zantedeschia aethiopica* 'Spotted Giant') grabs attention, even from people who think callas are funereal. At least they should.

pact sizes, although the three-footers can still command attention if you wish. Note: some bloom for a few weeks and then that's it for the season (much like many hardy and non-hardy bulbs, perennials, and woody plants), but they leave behind impressive, often white- or silver-spotted foliage.

I think the big ones look and do their best as specimens in monopots (especially when seen in multiples), but by all means use the smaller ones in combopots.

Z. aethiopica is a big boy, with most selections reaching 3 ft.; a clump easily spreads 4–5 ft. wide. It can bloom for months in cooler areas. Called the "hardy calla" (Z8–10), its selection 'Crowborough' allegedly pushes the hardiness limit a bit more. The ethereally beautiful 'Green Goddess' features variable, air-brushed green markings on otherwise white spathes. 'Spotted Giant' has dark green leaves blotched (if that's not too negative a word) with white.

Z. elliottiana (golden calla) bears all-yellow inflorescences above delicately white-spotted foliage. Actually, the spots let light shine through them, providing the opportunity for sen-

sational light effects around sunrise and sunset as the spots turn into a little light show. *Z. elliottiana* gave rise to several cream and yellow selections (and, surprisingly, the sultry 'Majestic Red' and nearly black 'Black Star'). This group reaches 1–3 ft. tall.

Cultural tips: Providing plenty of moisture and fertilizer will encourage strong growth and flowering and also results in quickly multiplying clumps.

ZINNIA
youth-in-old-age

Family: Asteraceae
Cultural group: annuals
Height: 6 in. to 3 ft.
Width: 6 in. to 2 ft.
Light: sun
Temperature: warm to hot
Overwintering: nope, ain't gonna happen
Moisture: moderate to ample
Drainage of medium: well drained
Fertility: average
Ease/speed of growth: easy/moderate to fast
Propagation: seeds
Problems: powdery mildew, rots and spots, spider mites, Japanese beetles, caterpillars
Principal interest: flowers (and, for me, fragrance—seriously)
Length of seasonal interest: long

Design attributes

Color: flowers white, green, red, pink, orange, yellow, red-violet, and purple, sometimes in combinations of two colors; foliage green
Line: from stems, leaves, flower stems, elongated "petals"
Form: variations on the theme of shrubs with stars or pompoms
Space: variable; can be abundant in the skinny-leaved forms
Texture: medium to coarse

Ah, zinnias. As a kid, I loved the almost shrubby, scratchy-leaved, uniquely scented (rub the foliage sometime), large-flowered selections (such as the State Fair and Zenith series, or simply unnamed mixes from beguiling seed packets). It seemed to take forever for the "zee-knees" (Mom's pronunciation) to bloom, but then the little beadlike flower buds would begin to appear in the center of the paired leaves, swelling into pinecone-like balls. Finally, individual "petals" (technically ray flowers) poked their way out of the pinecones to

The red-violet starbursts of *Zinnia* 'Profusion Cherry' compete for attention with the chartreuse geese on the wing (I mean *Ipomoea* 'Sweet Caroline Light Green'). Almost any zinnia will grow in pots, but you'll improve your chances of success and satisfaction by growing the shorter selections.

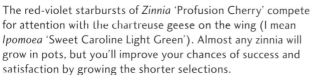

Hmm, here's the last photo in this book, and what can I say? *Zinnia* 'Profusion Fire' has more than taken care of color. Now there's the linear interest provided by the . . .

form a tiny, Stonehenge-like ring, and soon after, full-blown, golden-centered, party-colored flowers studded the plants. We overlooked the mildew-clouded foliage and persecuted the Japanese beetles that could ruin the flowers in a few hours, and we even looked the other way as the lower leaves turned brown and made a mess. But those flowers were treasures.

I would never grow the zee-knees of my childhood in containers today, though. Too many handicaps. But other container-worthy zinnias have come along, and they definitely earn their keep in pots.

'Orange Star' and 'Star White', selections of *Z. haageana* (Mexican zinnia), have been around for a while now. Abundant little, single (few-"petaled") flowers (about 1 in. wide) bloom from summer to frost on foot-tall mounds of elongated leaves that resist mildew far better than their big relatives. Their diminutive stature suits them perfectly for containers.

The Profusion series deserves every superlative heaped upon them; they're bushy, compact (about 1 ft. tall), long blooming, and mildew resistant. They combine the smaller flowers and low stature of *Z. haageana* with the broader color range and foliage of *Z. elegans* (the parent to the big ones of my childhood). At least ten different selections are available in white and shades of red, orange, and yellow, as single and double, 2-in. flowers. See the photographs! They're super!

You might not be able to resist growing the eerily green hybrid 'Envy' in containers, especially if you find chartreuse as irresistible and combinable as I do. Unlike most zinnias, 'Envy' needs protection from strong sun to fully express one of the seven deadly sins. The flowers range from single to double on plants that usually remain shy of 3 ft. tall. Watch out for mildew and ugly foliage below their knees. Or their zee-knees, if you will.

Cultural tips: Zinnias are annuals—there's no getting around it (as far as I know). Full sun, please (except for 'Envy'), and make sure the potting mix drains very well. Keep the hose or watering can handy, though.

Index